EVERYMAN, I will go with thee,

and be thy guide,

In thy most need to go by thy side

WILLIAM HAZLITT

Born in 1778 and intended for the Unitarian
ministry. Studied painting, wrote dramatic
criticism. Continental tour, 1824–5. Died
in 1830.

WILLIAM HAZLITT

The Round Table

Characters
of Shakespear's Plays

INTRODUCTION BY
CATHERINE MACDONALD MACLEAN
M.A., D.LITT., F.R.S.L.

DENT: LONDON
EVERYMAN'S LIBRARY
DUTTON: NEW YORK

NO. 65

SBN: 460 00065 9

INTRODUCTION

WHEN Hazlitt came to London in January 1812 to deliver a course of lectures on English Philosophy at the Russell Institution, he was struggling and obscure. For over fourteen years he had been trying to earn a living by literature and painting. He had just given up portrait-painting, because he had lost the hope of ever becoming a great painter, and he disdained a second best. His work as a writer, although steady and continuous, had not proved very rewarding. Much of it was little more than a kind of literary navvying. In 1812 he was glad to turn his hand to anything a publisher would take, from a grammar to a biography hastily strapped together, from a compilation to an abridgment of other men's work. Although he was earning a living, it was a bare and precarious one. As he put it himself, his 'little bark' was still '"hulling on the flood" in a kind of dubious twilight.'

Within the next two years all this was changed. In October 1812, in consequence of a strong recommendation from Charles Lamb, he was engaged as a parliamentary reporter on the *Morning Chronicle*, the leading Whig daily. He found his work in the House dull, for he hated commonplace, and it seemed to him that the House of Commons hated 'anything *but* a commonplace,' but he quickly made an entry for himself into other departments of the newspaper. In September 1813 his first essay appeared in its columns. In September 1813, too, he became its dramatic critic. From the moment his first work as dramatic critic appeared, he never looked back. His article on *The Beggar's Opera*, which appeared in the *Chronicle* on 23rd October 1813, struck a new note in criticism. Its sparkle, its challenge, its reference to principle delighted some of the best critics of the day. His article on *Antony and Cleopatra*, when the play was brought out at Covent Garden in November with additions from Dryden's *All for Love*, contained a spirited protest against the mingling of the 'gold of Shakespear . . . with the heavy tinsel of Dryden,' which showed that not only a dramatic critic but a literary critic of rare discrimination and penetration had arrived. On 26th January 1814 Edmund Kean appeared at Drury Lane Theatre as Shylock. This was all that was needed to set Hazlitt's genius ablaze. He was fond of quoting:

> the fire i' the flint
> Shows not till it be struck.

'The fire i' the flint' showed itself clearly enough now. Hazlitt was charmed by Kean's courage, which he saluted in the words: 'In one who *dares* so much, there is indeed little indeed to blame.'

INTRODUCTION

When Kean played Richard III in February, Hamlet in March, and in May Othello, his masterpiece, Hazlitt's articles were no less electrifying than Kean's performances.

Within a short space of time he was entrusted by James Perry, the editor of the *Chronicle*, not only with dramatic criticism, but with literary criticism, criticism of art, and political commentary. He was, he said, 'in a kind of honey-moon of authorship.' 'Something I did, *took*,' he told his friend Northcote afterwards, when explaining the manner of his release from the heavy and obscure labours of his earlier years, 'and I was called upon to do a number of things all at once. I was in the middle of the stream, and must sink or swim.'

Swim he did, despite difficulties made for him by his own 'cursed temperament' and the passion for Napoleon which sometimes estranged him not only from his editors but from his friends. A coolness which developed between him and Perry, shortly after the abdication of Napoleon, led to the loss of his work for the *Chronicle*, but this was no misfortune for it sent him on to editors who being themselves fine men of letters were better qualified than Perry to realize the distinction of his writing, Leigh Hunt of the *Examiner* and John Scott of the *Champion*. He became the art critic of the *Champion*. His connection with the *Examiner* tended to develop him as an essayist. In March 1815 he became its regular dramatic critic.

Early in 1815 also he was invited to contribute to the *Edinburgh Review*. This meant that he was regarded by Jeffrey as having won his spurs.

Of the two characteristic works which he published in 1817, *The Round Table* contains what he wished to preserve from his writing for newspapers and periodicals from 1813[1] onwards, barring the 'gunpowder stuff,' the blistering political commentary, which was reserved for a later volume; *Characters of Shakespear's Plays* contains a set of sensitive and penetrating studies, few of which had previously appeared in print, the fruit of his own lifelong passion for Shakespeare, stimulated by Kean's acting, much of which seemed to him 'the finest commentary that ever was made on Shakespear,' and by the conversation of Charles Lamb, to whom the book was dedicated 'as a mark of Old Friendship and lasting esteem.'

In the 'Advertisement' which prefaced *The Round Table* Hazlitt explained that the title had been borrowed from one of the sections of the *Examiner* in which Leigh Hunt and he had proposed 'to publish a series of papers in ... the manner of the early periodical essayists, Addison and Steele.' This in no way suggests the character and quality of his own work, nor defines it. Indeed it is misleading, for it is the characteristic of Hazlitt as an essayist, that being a great and original writer he drew his material straight

---

[1] The only earlier work contained in it is 'Character of the late Mr Pitt.'

rom nature, and therefore had to create a form of essay which was
is and his alone. What had served his predecessors, Montaigne,
Bacon, Addison, Swift, Goldsmith, Johnson, and his favourite,
Steele, would not serve him. It was his task to fashion a new
instrument, one which would convey his own very distinctive
approach to life, literature, art, and human nature. He came far
nearer defining the nature of his work when he claimed, in later
years, that his writings were 'the thoughts of a metaphysician
expressed by a painter.'

The first essay in *The Round Table*, 'On the Love of Life,' which
was also the first essay he published in the *Morning Chronicle*,
shows that he was already master of a new form. The essay, as
evolved by Hazlitt, had no predecessors. It has had no successors.
n approach, in method, in manner, it attempted something new.
Hazlitt's approach to the essay was through an occasional thought
r opinion thrown out for discussion; his method was to seek out
a principle in relation to which this opinion might be discussed;
his manner, to follow the quest for truth in all its ramifications and
occasional surprises, as it might be pursued among a group of
friends, much as he had heard it pursued on many an evening at
Charles Lamb's fireside, when an opinion lightly ventured might
lead in the end to 'a flight of high and earnest talk that took one
half-way to the stars.' In 'On the Love of Life,' which is slight,
we can see—as it were—the bone-work of this new form. In later
essays, such as 'Whether Genius is Conscious of its Powers,' in
which the opinion is thrown out for discussion: 'Those who are
conscious of their powers never do anything'; or 'Guy Faux,'
the theme of which is: 'The better part of valour is indiscretion'; or
'On the Feeling of Immortality in Youth,' in which he develops the
most poignant of all these occasional thoughts: 'No young man
believes he shall ever die'—although the characteristic framework,
or bone-work, is there, it is less easily distinguishable, because of
the richness of the illustrative material superimposed on it. In
'On the Love of Life' it is almost bare. The opinion thrown out
for analysis in this delicate yet powerful essay is the paradox:
'We may be said to nurse our existence with the greatest tenderness according to the pain it has cost us.' In discussing it,
Hazlitt—as he says—seeks out the principle which will justify it.
His conclusion is that it is not happiness which makes us seek to
prolong our lives. The most passionate tenacity is often shown,
not by the happy, but by those who cling to life only by the most
fine agonizing threads. The reason we cling to life is that, never
having been satisfied by it, we go on hoping that the future may
make us 'amends for all.' In other words, the mainspring of life
is not joy, but hope.

Such an essay is the fruit of long-continued and patient soliciting
of the mind. Its appeal is to the mind, the feeling, and the
experience of the reader. In the most characteristic of the essays
in *The Round Table* the appeal is similar.

INTRODUCTION

The theme of Hazlitt's essays throughout, no matter what the immediate subject-matter may be—and it is extraordinarily varied—is 'the Science of Man.'[1] The special aspect of the 'Science' he sought to illuminate was the mixed nature of man, the self-conflict by which human nature is rent, conditioning the entire movement of human affairs. It is his consistent interpretation of this theme which gives his essays, desultory in their commentary on life though they may at first sight appear, an organic character throughout.

It might be thought that with such a method as Hazlitt's, inveterately analytical, and with such a theme, his work would have been too sombre to please. John Scott, although he himself relished Hazlitt's work intensely, said of it that it would be 'caviare to the million,' and that in the nature of things it could never be otherwise. But Hazlitt quickly created the taste by which he was enjoyed. It is his distinction that he succeeded in turning metaphysical discussion into exquisite entertainment. Miss Mitford wrote of him: 'So poignant is he, and so rich, everything seems insipid after him.' These words describe well the effect of Hazlitt's writing. He wrote under strong excitement, and he communicates this excitement to the reader. His phrases sting. His conclusions startle. He meant them to startle. Indeed it might be said of him that he quickly became a master of the art of attracting by startling, or even by repelling. When he wrote in his essay 'On Good-Nature': 'The most disagreeable people are the most amiable,' and 'Good-nature is humanity that costs nothing,' he threw out a deliberate challenge to the complacent. When he opened his essay 'On the Causes of Methodism' with the words: 'The first Methodist on record was David. He was the first eminent person we read of who made a regular compromise between religion and morality, between faith and good works'—he meant to shock the readers most likely to be attracted by such a title. But if deliberately provocative, he was never boring. He sent none to sleep. Few would lay down the essay which opened with this biting character-sketch until they had finished it.

Yet Hazlitt's hold over the better mind of his generation is to be explained neither by the challenge of his work, nor by his strong antipathies, nor by the vivid force of his expression of them. His sympathies, arising from his extreme sensibility, were even more passionate than his antipathies. This extreme sensibility was the source of his appeal. It was also the source of his genius, even as it was of Rousseau's. Perhaps he was conscious of this, for the sole claim he made for himself was: 'The only faculty I do possess is that of a certain morbid interest in things.' Like Rousseau, 'he seems to gather up the past moments of his being like drops of honey-dew to distil a precious liquor from them.' This sensibility,

[1] This is the phrase Hazlitt used in his essay 'On the Spirit of Philosophy.'

INTRODUCTION

or awareness, was sensual no less than spiritual. It makes his criticism startlingly alive. A fine example of this is given in the tender voluptuousness of his treatment of Imogen, his favourite among Shakespeare's women. While he wrote of her as if he had fallen in love with her for the grace of her spirit he wrote too as if both his senses and his imagination had been enchanted by the description of the

> mole, cinque-spotted, like the crimson drops
> I' th' bottom of a cowslip

on her left breast. He seldom mentions Imogen without dwelling on 'the proud beauty' of this image, the 'rich surfeit of the fancy.' It was the sensibility shown in criticism of this kind that Keats—who owed much to him—saluted when he said that Hazlitt's 'depth of taste' was one of the three things that reconciled him to the age and civilization in which he lived. Hazlitt's extreme sensibility awakened the men of his generation to feeling with which hitherto they had been unacquainted, and so gave them an extension of experience. This extension of experience is still the best thing he has to offer to his readers.

Hazlitt's first essay, 'On the Love of Life,' is so finished that it might seem as if there were no room for development in the type of essay he had fashioned for himself; but this is not so. There was little room for development in craft, but as Hazlitt's experience deepened, there came to him a great extension of power. This may be seen if 'On the Love of Life' be compared with its exquisite complement, 'On the Fear of Death,' which concludes *Table Talk*, or if the essay, 'On Mr Kean's Iago,' in which Hazlitt finds the solution of Iago's character in the love of power, be compared with the impassioned descant in *The Plain Speaker* on the original sin which has robbed the world of its peace from the beginning of time.

It is in *The Plain Speaker* that the great arterial essays are to be found. But the earlier, more light-hearted essays, the fruit of the years when he was 'in a kind of honey-moon of authorship,' have their own special appeal, and give their own special pleasure. '"The first sprightly runnings" are there.'

CATHERINE MACDONALD MACLEAN.

1957.

SELECT BIBLIOGRAPHY

SEPARATE WORKS. *Essay on the Principles of Human Action . . . with Remarks on the System of Hartley and Helvetius*, 1805; *Free Thoughts on Public Affairs* 1806; *Abridgment of Abraham Tucker's 'Light of Nature'*, 1807; *Eloquence of the British Senate* (Parliamentary Speeches and Notes), 1807; *Reply to Malthus* 1807; *A New and Improved Grammar of the English Tongue*, etc., 1810; *Memoir of Thomas Holcroft*, written by himself, etc., continued by Hazlitt, 1816; *The Round Table* (from *The Examiner*), 1817; *Characters of Shakespear's Plays* 1817, 1818; *A View of the English Stage; or, a Series of Dramatic Criticisms* 1818, 1821; *Lectures on the English Poets*, 1818, 1819; *Lectures on the English Comic Writers*, 1819; *Letter to William Gifford*, 1819; *Political Essays, with Sketches of Public Characters*, 1819, 1822; *Lectures on the Dramatic Literature of the Reign of Queen Elizabeth*, 1820; *Table Talk; or, Original Essays on Men and Manners*, 1821–2, 1824; *Liber Amoris; or, The New Pygmalion*, 1823; *Characteristics, in the manner of Rochefoucauld's Maxims*, 1823, 1837; *Sketches of the Principal Picture Galleries in England*, with a criticism on *Marriage à la Mode* (in part from *London Magazine*), 1824; *The Spirit of the Age; or, Contemporary Portraits*, 1825; *The Plain Speaker; or, Opinions on Books, Men, and Things*, 1826; *Notes of a Journey through France and Italy* (from *Morning Chronicle*), 1826; *Boswell Redivivus*, 1827; *The Life of Napoleon Buonaparte*, vols. i and ii, 1828; iii and iv, 1830; *Conversations of James Northcote, Esq., R.A.*, 1830.

COLLECTED WORKS. Edited by P. P. Howe, after the edition of Waller and Glover, in 21 vols., 1930–4, and including much hitherto unpublished material.

BIOGRAPHY AND CRITICISM. Augustine Birrell, *William Hazlitt* (English Men of Letters series), 1902; P. P. Howe, *The Life of William Hazlitt*, 1922; E. Schneider, *The Aesthetics of William Hazlitt*, Philadelphia, 1933; Hesketh Pearson, *The Fool of Love*, 1934; Catherine Maclean, *Born Under Saturn*, 1943; S. C. Wilcox, *Hazlitt in the Workshop: the Manuscript of 'The Fight'*, Baltimore, 1943; C. W. and L. H. Houtchens, *The English Romantic Poets and Essayists: A review of Research and Criticism*, New York, 1957; H. Baker, *William Hazlitt*, 1962.

CONTENTS

THE ROUND TABLE

BIBLIOGRAPHICAL NOTE

Published in 1817 in two small 8vo volumes with the following title-page: 'The Round Table: A Collection of Essays on Literature, Men, and Manners, By William Hazlitt. Edinburgh: Printed for Archibald Constable and Co. And Longman, Hurst, Rees, Orme, and Brown, London, 1817.' The volumes were printed by George Ramsay & Co., Edinburgh, and do not appear to have been reprinted or reissued. Twelve of the fifty-two essays were by Leigh Hunt, as Hazlitt's 'Advertisement' explains.

A so-called 'third edition,' edited by the author's son, was published in one 12mo volume in 1841. In this edition many essays were omitted; three unreprinted essays were added; and Leigh Hunt's essays were retained. In the Bohn edition (8vo, 1871), edited by the author's grandson, Mr W. C. Hazlitt, Hazlitt's essays as published in the two volumes of 1817 were restored, and Leigh Hunt's essays were for the first time omitted.

The present text is an exact reproduction of Hazlitt's essays from the edition of 1817, except that the numbering of the essays is omitted; that a few obvious printer's errors have been corrected; and that for the essay, 'On the Midsummer Night's Dream,' which was in substance reprinted in *Characters of Shakespear's Plays*, Hazlitt's notice for the *Examiner* of a performance of the play at Covent Garden in January 1816 has been substituted, together with the notice, 'Theatrical Debuts,' which appeared in the *Examiner* in the same year.

ADVERTISEMENT TO THE EDITION
OF 1817

THE following work falls somewhat short of its title and original intention. It was proposed by my friend, Mr. Hunt, to publish a series of papers in the Examiner, in the manner of the early periodical Essayists, the Spectator and Tatler. These papers were to be contributed by various persons on a variety of subjects; and Mr. Hunt, as the Editor, was to take the characteristic or dramatic part of the work upon himself. I undertook to furnish occasional Essays and Criticisms; one or two other friends promised their assistance; but the essence of the work was to be miscellaneous. The next thing was to fix upon a title for it. After much doubtful consultation, that of THE ROUND TABLE was agreed upon as most descriptive of its nature and design. But our plan had been no sooner arranged and entered upon, than Buonaparte landed at Frejus, *et voila la Table Ronde dissoûte*. Our little congress was broken up as well as the great one; Politics called off the attention of the Editor from the *Belles Lettres*; and the task of continuing the work fell chiefly upon the person who was least able to give life and spirit to the original design. A want of variety in the subjects and mode of treating them, is, perhaps, the least disadvantage resulting from this circumstance. All the papers, in the two volumes here offered to the public, were written by myself and Mr. Hunt, except a letter communicated by a friend in the seventeenth number. Out of the fifty-two numbers, twelve are Mr. Hunt's, with the signatures L. H. or H. T. For all the rest I am answerable.

W. HAZLITT

January 5, 1817.

CONTENTS

[1] These two pieces have been chosen to replace the essay on *A Midsummer Night's Dream* which appeared in the 1817 edition and was reprinted with very slight alterations in *Characters of Shakespear's Plays*, where it will be found on p. 244 of this volume. The two substituted pieces were written for the *Examiner* in 1816 and reprinted in *A View of the English Stage*, 1818.

THE ROUND TABLE

ON THE LOVE OF LIFE

It is our intention, in the course of these papers, occasionally to expose certain vulgar errors, which have crept into our reasonings on men and manners. Perhaps one of the most interesting of these, is that which relates to the source of our general attachment to life. We are not going to enter into the question, whether life is, on the whole, to be regarded as a blessing, though we are by no means inclined to adopt the opinion of that sage, who thought 'that the best thing that could have happened to a man was never to have been born, and the next best to have died the moment after he came into existence.' The common argument, however, which is made use of to prove the value of life, from the strong desire which almost every one feels for its continuance, appears to be altogether inconclusive. The wise and the foolish, the weak and the strong, the lame and the blind, the prisoner and the free, the prosperous and the wretched, the beggar and the king, the rich and the poor, the young and the old, from the little child who tries to leap over his own shadow, to the old man who stumbles blindfold on his grave, all feel this desire in common. Our notions with respect to the importance of life, and our attachment to it, depend on a principle, which has very little to do with its happiness or its misery.

The love of life is, in general, the effect not of our enjoyments, but of our passions. We are not attached to it so much for its own sake, or as it is connected with happiness, as because it is necessary to action. Without life there can be no action—no objects of pursuit—no restless desires—no tormenting passions. Hence it is that we fondly cling to it—that we dread its termination as the close, not of enjoyment, but of hope. The proof that our attachment to life is not absolutely owing to the immediate satisfaction we find in it, is, that those persons are commonly found most loth to part with it who have the least enjoyment of it, and who have the greatest difficulties to struggle with, as losing gamesters are the most desperate. And farther, there are not many persons who, with all their pretended love of life, would not, if it had been in their power, have melted down the longest life to a few hours. 'The school-boy,' says Addison, 'counts the time till the return of the holidays; the minor longs to be of age; the lover is impatient till he is married.'—'Hope and fantastic expectations spend much of our lives; and while with passion we look for a coronation, or the death of an enemy, or a day of joy, passing from fancy to possession without any intermediate notices, we throw away a precious year' (Jeremy Taylor). We would willingly, and without remorse, sacrifice not only the present moment, but all the interval (no matter how long) that separates us from any favourite object. We chiefly look upon life, then, as the means to an end. Its common enjoyments and its daily evils are alike disregarded for any idle purpose we have in view. It should seem as if there were a few green sunny spots in the desert of life, to which we are always hastening forward: we eye them wistfully in the distance, and care not what perils or suffering we endure, so that we arrive at them at last. However weary we may be of the same stale round—however sick of the past—however hopeless of the future—the mind still revolts at the thought of death, because the fancied possibility of good, which always remains with life, gathers strength as it is about to be torn from us for ever, and the dullest scene looks bright compared with the darkness of the grave. Our reluctance to part with existence evidently does not depend on the calm and even current of our lives, but on the force and impulse of the passions. Hence that indifference to death which has been sometimes remarked in people who lead a solitary and peaceful life in remote and barren districts. The pulse of life in them does not beat strong enough to occasion any violent revulsion of the frame when it ceases. He who treads the green mountain turf, or he who sleeps beneath it, enjoys an almost equal quiet. The death of those persons has always been accounted happy, who had attained their utmost wishes, who had nothing left to regret or to desire. Our repugnance to death increases in proportion to our consciousness of having lived in vain—to the violence of our efforts, and the keenness of our disappointments—and to our earnest desire to find in the future, if possible, a rich amends for the past. We may be said to nurse our existence with the greatest tenderness, according to the pain it has cost us; and feel at every step of our varying progress the truth of that line of the poet—

'An ounce of sweet is worth a pound of sour.'

The love of life is in fact the sum of all our passions and of all our enjoyments; but these are by no means the same thing, for the vehemence of our passions is irritated, not less by disappointment than by the prospect of success. Nothing seems to be a match for this general tenaciousness of existence, but such an extremity either of bodily or mental suffering as destroys at once the power both of habit and imagination. In short, the question, whether life is accompanied with a greater quantity of pleasure or pain, may be fairly set aside as frivolous, and of no practical utility; for our attachment to life depends on our interest in it; and it cannot be denied that we have more interest in this moving, busy scene, agitated with a thousand hopes and fears, and checkered with every diversity of joy and sorrow, than in a dreary blank. To be something is better than to be nothing, because we can feel no interest in *nothing*. Passion, imagination, selfwill, the sense of power, the very consciousness of our existence, bind us to life, and hold us fast in its chains, as by a magic spell, in spite of every other consideration. Nothing can be more philosophical than the reasoning which Milton puts into the mouth of the fallen angel:—

> ' And that must end us, that must be our cure,
> To be no more; Sad cure: For who would lose,
> Though full of pain, this intellectual being,
> Those thoughts that wander through eternity,
> To perish rather, swallow'd up and lost
> In the wide womb of uncreated night,
> Devoid of sense and motion?'

Nearly the same account may be given in answer to the question which has been asked, *Why so few tyrants kill themselves?* In the first place, they are never satisfied with the mischief they have done, and cannot quit their hold of power, after all sense of pleasure is fled. Besides, they absurdly argue from the means of happiness placed within their reach to the end itself; and, dazzled by the pomp and pageantry of a throne, cannot relinquish the persuasion that they *ought* to be happier than other men. The prejudice of opinion, which attaches us to life, is in them stronger than in others, and incorrigible to experience. The Great are life's fools—dupes of the splendid shadows that surround them, and wedded to the very mockeries of opinion.

Whatever is our situation or pursuit in life, the result will be much the same. The strength of the passion seldom corresponds to the pleasure we find in its indulgence. The miser ' robs himself to increase his store '; the ambitious man toils up a slippery precipice only to be tumbled headlong from its height: the lover is infatuated with the charms of his mistress, exactly in proportion to the mortifications he has received from her. Even those who succeed in nothing, who, as it has been emphatically expressed—

> 'Are made desperate by too quick a sense
> Of constant infelicity; cut off
> From peace like exiles, on some barren rock,
> Their life's sad prison, with no more of ease,
> Than sentinels between two armies set';

are yet as unwilling as others to give over the unprofitable strife: their harassed feverish existence refuses rest, and frets the languor of exhausted hope into the torture of unavailing regret. The exile, who has been unexpectedly restored to his country and to liberty, often finds his courage fail with the accomplishment of all his wishes, and the struggle of life and hope ceases at the same instant.

We once more repeat, that we do not, in the foregoing remarks, mean to enter into a comparative estimate of the value of human life, but merely to shew that the strength of our attachment to it is a very fallacious test of its happiness.   W. H.

ON CLASSICAL EDUCATION

THE study of the Classics is less to be regarded as an exercise of the intellect, than as 'a discipline of humanity.' The peculiar advantage of this mode of education consists not so much in strengthening the understanding, as in softening and refining the taste. It gives men liberal views; it accustoms the mind to take an interest in things foreign to itself; to love virtue for its own sake; to prefer fame to life, and glory to riches; and to fix our thoughts on the remote and permanent, instead of narrow and fleeting objects. It teaches us to believe that there is something really great and excellent in the world, surviving all the shocks of accident and fluctuations of opinion, and raises us above that low and servile fear, which bows only to present power and upstart authority. Rome and Athens filled a place in the history of mankind, which can never be occupied again. They were two cities set on a hill, which could not be hid; all eyes have seen them, and their light shines like a mighty sea-mark into the abyss of time.

> 'Still green with bays each ancient altar stands,
> Above the reach of sacrilegious hands;
> Secure from flames, from envy's fiercer rage,
> Destructive war, and all-involving age.

ON CLASSICAL EDUCATION

Hail, bards triumphant, born in happier days,
Immortal heirs of universal praise !
Whose honours with increase of ages grow,
As streams roll down, enlarging as they flow !'

It is this feeling, more than anything else, which produces a
marked difference between the study of the ancient and modern
languages, and which, from the weight and importance of the consequences attached to the former, stamps every word with a monumental firmness. By conversing with the *mighty dead*, we imbibe
sentiment with knowledge ; we become strongly attached to those
who can no longer either hurt or serve us, except through the influence
which they exert over the mind. We feel the presence of that power
which gives immortality to human thoughts and actions, and catch
the flame of enthusiasm from all nations and ages.

It is hard to find in minds otherwise formed, either a real love of
excellence, or a belief that any excellence exists superior to their own.
Everything is brought down to the vulgar level of their own ideas
and pursuits. Persons without education certainly do not want either
acuteness or strength of mind in what concerns themselves, or in
things immediately within their observation ; but they have no power
of abstraction, no general standard of taste, or scale of opinion. They
see their objects always near, and never in the horizon. Hence arises
that egotism which has been remarked as the characteristic of self-
taught men, and which degenerates into obstinate prejudice or petulant
fickleness of opinion, according to the natural sluggishness or activity
of their minds. For they either become blindly bigoted to the first
opinions they have struck out for themselves, and inaccessible to conviction ; or else (the dupes of their own vanity and shrewdness) are
everlasting converts to every crude suggestion that presents itself, and
the last opinion is always the true one. Each successive discovery
flashes upon them with equal light and evidence, and every new fact
overturns their whole system. It is among this class of persons,
whose ideas never extend beyond the feeling of the moment, that we
find partizans, who are very honest men, with a total want of principle,
and who unite the most hardened effrontery, and intolerance of opinion,
to endless inconsistency and self-contradiction.

A celebrated political writer of the present day, who is a great
enemy to classical education, is a remarkable instance both of what
can and what cannot be done without it.

It has been attempted of late to set up a distinction between the
education *of words*, and the education *of things*, and to give the
preference in all cases to the latter. But, in the first place, the knowledge of things, or of the realities of life, is not easily to be taught

5

except by things themselves, and, even if it were, is not so absolutely indispensable as it has been supposed. 'The world is too much with us, early and late'; and the fine dream of our youth is best prolonged among the visionary objects of antiquity. We owe many of our most amiable delusions, and some of our superiority, to the grossness of mere physical existence, to the strength of our associations with words. Language, if it throws a veil over our ideas, adds a softness and refinement to them, like that which the atmosphere gives to naked objects. There can be no true elegance without taste in style. In the next place, we mean absolutely to deny the application of the principle of utility to the present question. By an obvious transposition of ideas, some persons have confounded a knowledge of useful things with useful knowledge. Knowledge is only useful in itself, as it exercises or gives pleasure to the mind : the only knowledge that is of use in a practical sense, is professional knowledge. But knowledge, considered as a branch of general education, can be of use only to the mind of the person acquiring it. If the knowledge of language produces pedants, the other kind of knowledge (which is proposed to be substituted for it) can only produce quacks. There is no question, but that the knowledge of astronomy, of chemistry, and of agriculture, is highly useful to the world, and absolutely necessary to be acquired by persons carrying on certain professions : but the practical utility of a knowledge of these subjects ends there. For example, it is of the utmost importance to the navigator to know exactly in what degree of longitude and latitude such a rock lies : but to us, sitting here about our Round Table, it is not of the smallest consequence whatever, whether the map-maker has placed it an inch to the right or to the left; we are in no danger of running against it. So the art of making shoes is a highly useful art, and very proper to be known and practised by some body : that is, by the shoemaker. But to pretend that every one else should be thoroughly acquainted with the whole process of this ingenious handicraft, as one branch of useful knowledge, would be preposterous. It is sometimes asked, What is the use of poetry ? and we have heard the argument carried on almost like a parody on *Falstaff's* reasoning about Honour. 'Can it set a leg ? No. Or an arm ? No. Or take away the grief of a wound ? No. Poetry hath no skill in surgery then ? No.' It is likely that the most enthusiastic lover of poetry would so far agree to the truth of this statement, that if he had just broken a leg, he would send for a surgeon, instead of a volume of poems from a library. But, 'they that are whole need not a physician.' The reasoning would be well founded, if we lived in an hospital, and not in the world.

W. H.

ON THE TATLER

Of all the periodical Essayists, (our ingenious predecessors), the *Tatler* has always appeared to us the most accomplished and agreeable. Montaigne, who was the father of this kind of personal authorship among the moderns, in which the reader is admitted behind the curtain, and sits down with the writer in his gown and slippers, was a most magnanimous and undisguised egotist; but Isaac Bickerstaff, Esq. was the more disinterested gossip of the two. The French author is contented to describe the peculiarities of his own mind and person, which he does with a most copious and unsparing hand. The English journalist, goodnaturedly, lets you into the secret both of his own affairs and those of his neighbours. A young lady, on the other side of Temple Bar, cannot be seen at her glass for half a day together, but Mr. Bickerstaff takes due notice of it; and he has the first intelligence of the symptoms of the *belle* passion appearing in any young gentleman at the west end of the town. The departures and arrivals of widows with handsome jointures, either to bury their grief in the country, or to procure a second husband in town, are regularly recorded in his pages. He is well acquainted with the celebrated beauties of the last age at the Court of Charles ii. and the old gentleman often grows romantic in recounting the disastrous strokes which his youth suffered from the glances of their bright eyes and their unaccountable caprices. In particular, he dwells with a secret satisfaction on one of his mistresses who left him for a rival, and whose constant reproach to her husband, on occasion of any quarrel between them, was,—'I, that might have married the famous Mr. Bickerstaff, to be treated in this manner!' The club at the *Trumpet* consists of a set of persons as entertaining as himself. The cavalcade of the justice of the peace, the knight of the shire, the country squire, and the young gentleman, his nephew, who waited on him at his chambers, in such form and ceremony, seem not to have settled the order of their precedence to this hour; and we should hope the Upholsterer and his companions in the Green Park stand as fair a chance for immortality as some modern politicians. Mr. Bickerstaff himself is a gentleman and a scholar, a humourist and a man of the world; with a great deal of nice easy *naïveté* about him. If he walks out and is caught in a shower of rain, he makes us amends for this unlucky accident, by a criticism on the shower in Virgil, and concludes with a burlesque copy of verses on a city-shower. He entertains us, when he dates from his own apartment, with a quotation from Plutarch or a moral reflection; from the Grecian

7

coffeehouse with politics; and from Will's or the Temple with the poets and players, the beaux and men of wit and pleasure about town In reading the pages of the *Tatler*, we seem as if suddenly transported to the age of Queen Anne, of toupees and full-bottomed periwigs. The whole appearance of our dress and manners undergoes a delightful metamorphosis. We are surprised with the rustling of hoops and the glittering of paste buckles. The beaux and the belles are of a quite different species; we distinguish the dappers, the smarts, and the pretty fellows, as they pass; we are introduced to Betterton and Mrs. Oldfield behind the scenes; are made familiar with the persons of Mr. Penkethman and Mr. Bullock; we listen to a dispute at a tavern on the merits of the Duke of Marlborough or Marshal Turenne; or are present at the first rehearsal of a play by Vanbrugh, or the reading of a new poem by Mr. Pope.—The privilege of thus virtually transporting ourselves to past times, is even greater than that of visiting distant places. London, a hundred years ago, would be better worth seeing than Paris at the present moment.

It may be said that all this is to be found, in the same or a greater degree, in the *Spectator*. We do not think so; or, at least, there is in the last work a much greater proportion of common-place matter. We have always preferred the *Tatler* to the *Spectator*. Whether it is owing to our having been earlier or better acquainted with the one than the other, our pleasure in reading the two works is not at all in proportion to their comparative reputation. The *Tatler* contains only half the number of volumes, and we will venture to say, at least an equal quantity of sterling wit and sense. 'The first sprightly runnings' are there: it has more of the original spirit, more of the freshness and stamp of nature. The indications of character and strokes of humour are more true and frequent, the reflections that suggest themselves arise more from the occasion, and are less spun out into regular dissertations. They are more like the remarks which occur in sensible conversation, and less like a lecture. Something is left to the understanding of the reader. Steele seems to have gone into his closet only to set down what he observed out-of-doors; Addison seems to have spun out and wire-drawn the hints, which he borrowed from Steele, or took from nature, to the utmost. We do not mean to depreciate Addison's talents, but we wish to do justice to Steele, who was, upon the whole, a less artificial and more original writer. The descriptions of Steele resemble loose sketches or fragments of a comedy; those of Addison are ingenious paraphrases on the genuine text. The characters of the club, not only in the *Tatler*, but in the *Spectator*, were drawn by Steele. That of Sir Roger de Coverley is among them. Addison has gained himself eternal honour by his manner of filling up this last character. Those of Will Wimble and Will Honeycomb are not a whit behind it in delicacy and felicity. Many of the most exquisite pieces in the *Tatler* are also Addison's, as the Court of Honour, and the Personification of Musical Instruments. We do not know whether the picture of the family of an old acquaintance, in which the children run to let Mr. Bickerstaff in at the door, and the one that loses the race that way turns back to tell the father that he is come,—with the nice gradation of incredulity in the little boy, who is got into *Guy of Warwick* and *The Seven Champions*, and who shakes his head at the veracity of *Æsop's Fables*,— is Steele's or Addison's.[1] The account of the two sisters, one of whom held her head up higher than ordinary, from having on a pair of flowered garters, and of the married lady who complained to the *Tatler* of the neglect of her husband, are unquestionably Steele's. If the *Tatler* is not inferior to the *Spectator* in manners and character, it is very superior to it in the interest of many of the stories. Several of the incidents related by Steele have never been surpassed in the heart-rending pathos of private distress. We might refer to those of the lover and his mistress when the theatre caught fire, of the bridegroom who, by accident, kills his bride on the day of their marriage, the story of Mr. Eustace and his wife, and the fine dream about his own mistress when a youth. What has given its superior popularity to the *Spectator*, is the greater gravity of its pretensions, its moral dissertations and critical reasonings, by which we confess we are less edified than by other things. Systems and opinions change, but nature is always true. It is the extremely moral and didactic tone of the *Spectator* which makes us apt to think of Addison (according to Mandeville's sarcasm) as 'a parson in a tie-wig.' Some of the moral essays are, however, exquisitely beautiful and happy. Such are the reflections in Westminster Abbey, on the Royal Exchange, and some very affecting ones on the death of a young lady. These, it must be allowed, are the perfection of elegant sermonising. His critical essays we do not think quite so good. We prefer Steele's occasional selection of beautiful poetical passages, without any affectation of analysing their beauties, to Addison's fine-spun theories. The best criticism in the *Spectator*, that on the *Cartoons* of Raphael, is by Steele. We owed

---

[1] It is Steele's; and the whole paper (No. 95) is in his most delightful manner. The dream about the mistress, however, is given to Addison by the Editors, and the general style of that number is his; though, from the story being related personally of Bickerstaff, who is also represented as having been at that time in the army, we conclude it to have originally come from Steele, perhaps in the course of conversation. The particular incident is much more like a story of his than of Addison's.—H. T.

this acknowledgment to a writer who has so often put us in good humour with ourselves and every thing about us, when few things else could.[1]   W. H.

ON MODERN COMEDY

THE question which has often been asked, *Why there are so few good modern Comedies?* appears in a great measure to answer itself. It is because so many excellent Comedies have been written, that there are none written at present.   Comedy naturally wears itself out— destroys the very food on which it lives; and by constantly and successfully exposing the follies and weaknesses of mankind to ridicule, in the end leaves itself nothing worth laughing at.   It holds the mirror up to nature; and men, seeing their most striking peculiarities and defects pass in gay review before them, learn either to avoid or conceal them.   It is not the criticism which the public taste exercises upon the stage, but the criticism which the stage exercises upon public manners, that is fatal to comedy, by rendering the subject-matter of it tame, correct, and spiritless.   We are drilled into a sort or stupid decorum, and forced to wear the same dull uniform of outward appearance; and yet it is asked, why the Comic Muse does not point, as she was wont, at the peculiarities of our gait and gesture, and exhibit the picturesque contrast of our dress and costume, in all that graceful variety in which she delights.   The genuine source of comic writing,

> 'Where it must live, or have no life at all,'

is undoubtedly to be found in the distinguishing peculiarities of men and manners.   Now, this distinction can subsist, so as to be strong pointed, and general, only while the manners of different classes are formed immediately by their particular circumstances, and the characters of individuals by their natural temperament and situation, without being everlastingly modified and neutralised by intercourse with the world—by knowledge and education.   In a certain stage of society, men may be said to vegetate like trees, and to become rooted to the soil in which they grow.   They have no idea of anything beyond themselves and their immediate sphere of action; they are, a

---

[1] We had in our hands the other day an original copy of the *Tatler*, and a list of the subscribers.   It is curious to see some names there which we should hardly think of, (that of Sir Isaac Newton is among them), and also to observe the degree of interest excited by those of the different persons, which is not adjusted according to the rules of the Heralds' College.

t were, circumscribed, and defined by their particular circumstances; they are what their situation makes them, and nothing more. Each is absorbed in his own profession or pursuit, and each in his turn contracts that habitual peculiarity of manners and opinions, which makes him the subject of ridicule to others, and the sport of the Comic Muse. Thus the physician is nothing but a physician, the lawyer is a mere lawyer, the scholar degenerates into a pedant, the country squire is a different species of being from the fine gentleman, the citizen and the courtier inhabit a different world, and even the affectation of certain characters, in aping the follies or vices of their betters, only serves to show the immeasurable distance which custom or fortune has placed between them. Hence the early comic writers, taking advantage of this mixed and solid mass of ignorance, folly, pride, and prejudice, made those deep and lasting incisions into it,—have given those sharp and nice touches, that bold relief to their characters,—have opposed them in every variety of contrast and collision, of conscious self-satisfaction and mutual antipathy, with a power which can only find full scope in the same rich and inexhaustible materials. But in proportion as comic genius succeeds in taking off the mask from ignorance and conceit, as it teaches us to

'See ourselves as others see us,'—

in proportion as we are brought out on the stage together, and our prejudices clash one against the other, our sharp angular points wear off; we are no longer rigid in absurdity, passionate in folly, and we prevent the ridicule directed at our habitual foibles, by laughing at them ourselves.

If it be said, that there is the same fund of absurdity and prejudice in the world as ever—that there are the same unaccountable perversities lurking at the bottom of every breast,—I should answer, be it so : but at least we keep our follies to ourselves as much as possible—we palliate, shuffle, and equivocate with them—they sneak into by-corners, and do not, like *Chaucer's Canterbury Pilgrims*, march along the highroad, and form a procession—they do not entrench themselves strongly behind custom and precedent—they are not embodied in professions and ranks in life—they are not organised into a system—they do not openly resort to a standard, but are a sort of straggling nondescripts, that, like *Wart*, 'present no mark to the foeman.' As to the gross and palpable absurdities of modern manners, they are too shallow and barefaced, and those who affect, are too little *serious* in them, to make them worth the detection of the Comic Muse. They proceed from an idle, impudent affectation of folly in general, in the dashing *bravura* style, not from an infatuation with any of its characteristic modes. In short, the proper object of ridicule is *egotism*; and a man cannot be a very great egotist who every day sees himself represented on the stage. We are deficient in Comedy, because we are without characters in real life—as we have no historical pictures, because we have no faces proper for them.

It is, indeed, the evident tendency of all literature to generalise and *dissipate* character, by giving men the same artificial education, and the same common stock of ideas; so that we see all objects from the same point of view, and through the same reflected medium;—we learn to exist, not in ourselves, but in books;—all men become alike mere readers—spectators, not actors in the scene, and lose all proper personal identity. The templar, the wit, the man of pleasure, and the man of fashion, the courtier and the citizen, the knight and the squire, the lover and the miser—*Lovelace*, *Lothario*, *Will Honeycomb*, and *Sir Roger de Coverley*, *Sparkish* and *Lord Foppington*, *Western* and *Tom Jones*, *My Father*, and *My Uncle Toby*, *Millamant* and *Sir Sampson Legend*, *Don Quixote* and *Sancho*, *Gil Blas* and *Guzman d'Alfarache*, *Count Fathom* and *Joseph Surface*,—have all met, and exchanged common-places on the barren plains of the *haute littérature* —toil slowly on to the Temple of Science, seen a long way off upon a level, and end in one dull compound of politics, criticism, chemistry, and metaphysics!

We cannot expect to reconcile opposite things. If, for example, any of us were to put ourselves into the stage-coach from Salisbury to London, it is more than probable we should not meet with the same number of odd accidents, or ludicrous distresses on the road, that befell *Parson Adams*; but why, if we get into a common vehicle, and submit to the conveniences of modern travelling, should we complain of the want of adventures? Modern manners may be compared to a modern stage-coach: our limbs may be a little cramped with the confinement, and we may grow drowsy; but we arrive safe, without any very amusing or very sad accident, at our journey's end.

Again, the alterations which have taken place in conversation and dress in the same period, have been by no means favourable to Comedy. The present prevailing style of conversation is not *personal*, but critical and analytical. It consists almost entirely in the discussion of general topics, in dissertations on philosophy or taste: and Congreve would be able to derive no better hints from the conversations of our toilettes or drawing-rooms, for the exquisite raillery or poignant repartee of his dialogues, than from a deliberation of the Royal Society. In the same manner, the extreme simplicity and graceful uniformity of modern dress, however favourable to the arts, has certainly stript Comedy of one of its richest ornaments and most expressive symbols.

ON MODERN COMEDY

The sweeping pall and buskin, and nodding plume, were never more serviceable to Tragedy, than the enormous hoops and stiff stays worn by the belles of former days were to the intrigues of Comedy. They assisted wonderfully in heightening the mysteries of the passion, and adding to the intricacy of the plot. Wycherley and Vanbrugh could not have spared the dresses of Vandyke. These strange fancy-dresses, perverse disguises, and counterfeit shapes, gave an agreeable scope to the imagination. 'That sevenfold fence' was a sort of foil to the lusciousness of the dialogue, and a barrier against the sly encroachments of *double entendre*. The greedy eye and bold hand of indiscretion were repressed, which gave a greater licence to the tongue. The senses were not to be gratified in an instant. Love was entangled in the folds of the swelling handkerchief, and the desires might wander for ever round the circumference of a quilted petticoat, or find a rich lodging in the flowers of a damask stomacher. There was room for years of patient contrivance, for a thousand thoughts, schemes, conjectures, hopes, fears, and wishes. There seemed no end of difficulties and delays; to overcome so many obstacles was the work of ages. A mistress was an angel concealed behind whalebone, flounces, and brocade. What an undertaking to penetrate through the disguise! What an impulse must it give to the blood, what a keenness to the invention, what a volubility to the tongue! 'Mr. Smirk, you are a brisk man,' was then the most significant commendation. But now-a-days—a woman can be *but undressed*!

The same account might be extended to Tragedy. Aristotle has ong since said, that Tragedy purifies the mind by terror and pity; hat is, substitutes an artificial and intellectual interest for real passion. Tragedy, like Comedy, must therefore defeat itself; for its patterns must be drawn from the living models within the breast, from feeling or from observation; and the materials of Tragedy cannot be found among a people, who are the habitual spectators of Tragedy, whose interests and passions are not their own, but ideal, remote, sentimental, and abstracted. It is for this reason chiefly, we conceive, that the highest efforts of the Tragic Muse are in general the earliest; where the strong impulses of nature are not lost in the refinements and glosses of art; where the writers themselves, and those whom they saw about them, had 'warm hearts of flesh and blood beating in their bosoms, and were not embowelled of their natural entrails, and stuffed with paltry blurred sheets of paper.' Shakspeare, with all his genius, could not have written as he did, if he had lived in the present times. Nature would not have presented itself to him in the same freshness and vigour; he must have seen it through all the refractions of successive dullness, and his powers would have languished in the dense atmosphere of logic and criticism. 'Men's minds,' he somewhere says, 'are parcel of their fortunes'; and his age was necessary to him. It was this which enabled him to grapple at once with Nature, and which stamped his characters with her image and superscription. W. H.

ON MR. KEAN'S IAGO

WE certainly think Mr. Kean's performance of the part of Iago one of the most extraordinary exhibitions on the stage. There is no one within our remembrance who has so completely foiled the critics as this celebrated actor: one sagacious person imagines that he must perform a part in a certain manner,—another virtuoso chalks out a different path for him; and when the time comes, he does the whole off in a way that neither of them had the least conception of, and which both of them are therefore very ready to condemn as entirely wrong. It was ever the trick of genius to be thus. We confess that Mr. Kean has thrown us out more than once. For instance, we are very much inclined to adopt the opinion of a contemporary critic, that his *Richard* is not gay enough, and that his *Iago* is not grave enough. This he may perhaps conceive to be the mere caprice of idle criticism; but we will try to give our reasons, and shall leave them to Mr. Kean's better judgment. It is to be remembered, then, that *Richard* was a princely villain, borne along in a sort of triumphal car of royal state, buoyed up with the hopes and privileges of his birth, reposing even on the sanctity of religion, trampling on his devoted victims without remorse, and who looked out and laughed from the high watch-tower of his confidence and his expectations on the desolation and misery he had caused around him. He held on his way, unquestioned, 'hedged in with the divinity of kings,' amenable to no tribunal, and abusing his power *in contempt of mankind.* But as for *Iago*, we conceive differently of him. He had not the same natural advantages. He was a mere adventurer in mischief, a pains-taking plodding knave, without patent or pedigree, who was obliged to work his up-hill way by wit, not by will, and to be the founder of his own fortune. He was, if we may be allowed a vulgar allusion, a sort of prototype of modern Jacobinism, who thought that talents ought to decide the place,—a man of 'morbid sensibility,' (in the fashionable phrase), full of distrust, of hatred, of anxious and corroding thoughts, and who, though he might assume a temporary superiority over others by superior adroitness, and pride himself in his skill, could not be supposed to assume it as a matter of course, as if he had been entitled to it from his birth. We do not here mean to enter into the characters of the two men, but something must be allowed to the difference of their situations. There might be the same insensibility in both as to the end in view, but there could not well be the same security as to the success of the means. *Iago* had to pass through a different ordeal: he had no appliances and means to boot; no royal road to the completion of his tragedy. His pretensions were not backed by authority; they were not baptized at the font; they were not holy-waterproof. He had the whole to answer for in his own person, and could not shift the responsibility to the heads of others. Mr. Kean's *Richard* was, therefore, we think, deficient in something of that regal jollity and reeling triumph of success which the part would bear; but this we can easily account for, because it is the traditional commonplace idea of the character, that he is to 'play the dog—to bite and snarl.'—The extreme unconcern and laboured levity of his *Iago*, on the contrary, is a refinement and original device of the actor's own mind, and therefore deserves consideration. /The character of *Iago*, in fact, belongs to a class of characters common to Shakspeare, and at the same time peculiar to him—namely, that of great intellectual activity, accompanied with a total want of moral principle, and therefore displaying itself at the constant expence of others, making use of reason as a pander to will—employing its ingenuity and its resources to palliate its own crimes and aggravate the faults of others, and seeking to confound the practical distinctions of right and wrong, by referring them to some overstrained standard of speculative refinement.—Some persons, more nice than wise, have thought the whole of the character of *Iago* unnatural. Shakspeare, who was quite as good a philosopher as he was a poet, thought otherwise. He knew that the love of power, which is another name for the love of mischief, was natural to man. He would know this as well or better than if it had been demonstrated to him by a logical diagram, merely from seeing children paddle in the dirt, or kill flies for sport. We might ask those who think the character of *Iago* not natural, why they go to see it performed, but from the interest it excites, the sharper edge which it sets on their curiosity and imagination? Why do we go to see tragedies in general? Why do we always read the accounts in the newspapers of dreadful fires and shocking murders, but for the same reason? Why do so many persons frequent executions and trials, or why do the lower classes almost universally take delight in barbarous sports and cruelty to animals, but because there is a natural tendency in the mind to strong excitement, a desire to have its

B 65 15

faculties roused and stimulated to the utmost? Whenever this principle is not under the restraint of humanity, or the sense of moral obligation, there are no excesses to which it will not of itself give rise, without the assistance of any other motive, either of passion or self-interest. *Iago* is only an extreme instance of the kind; that is, of diseased intellectual activity, with an almost perfect indifference to moral good or evil, or rather with a preference of the latter, because it falls more in with his favourite propensity, gives greater zest to his thoughts, and scope to his actions.—Be it observed, too, (for the sake of those who are for squaring all human actions by the maxims of Rochefoucault), that he is quite or nearly as indifferent to his own fate as to that of others; that he runs all risks for a trifling and doubtful advantage; and is himself the dupe and victim of his ruling passion—an incorrigible love of mischief—an insatiable craving after action of the most difficult and dangerous kind. Our 'Ancient' is a philosopher, who fancies that a lie that kills has more point in it than an alliteration or an antithesis; who thinks a fatal experiment on the peace of a family a better thing than watching the palpitations in the heart of a flea in an air-pump; who plots the ruin of his friends as an exercise for his understanding, and stabs men in the dark to prevent *ennui*. Now this, though it be sport, yet it is dreadful sport. There is no room for trifling and indifference, nor scarcely for the appearance of it; the very object of his whole plot is to keep his faculties stretched on the rack, in a state of watch and ward, in a sort of breathless suspense, without a moment's interval of repose. He has a desperate stake to play for, like a man who fences with poisoned weapons, and has business enough on his hands to call for the whole stock of his sober circumspection, his dark duplicity, and insidious gravity. He resembles a man who sits down to play at chess, for the sake of the difficulty and complication of the game, and who immediately becomes absorbed in it. His amusements, if they are amusements, are severe and saturnine—even his wit blisters. His gaiety arises from the success of his treachery; his ease from the sense of the torture he has inflicted on others. Even, if other circumstances permitted it, the part he has to play with *Othello* requires that he should assume the most serious concern, and something of the plausibility of a confessor. 'His cue is villainous melancholy, with a sigh like Tom o' Bedlam.' He is repeatedly called 'honest *Iago*,' which looks as if there were something suspicious in his appearance, which admitted a different construction. The tone which he adopts in the scenes with *Roderigo*, *Desdemona*, and *Cassio*, is only a relaxation from the more arduous business of the play. Yet there is in all his conversation an inveterate misanthropy, a licentious keenness of perception, which is always sagacious of evil, and snuffs up the tainted scent of its quarry with rancorous delight. An exuberance of spleen is the essence of the character. The view which we have here taken of the subject (if at all correct) will not therefore justify the extreme alteration which Mr. Kean has introduced into the part. Actors in general have been struck only with the wickedness of the character, and have exhibited an assassin going to the place of execution. Mr. Kean has abstracted the wit of the character, and makes *Iago* appear throughout an excellent good fellow, and lively bottle-companion. But though we do not wish him to be represented as a monster, or fiend, we see no reason why he should instantly be converted into a pattern of comic gaiety and good-humour. The light which illumines the character should rather resemble the flashes of lightning in the mirky sky, which make the darkness more terrible. Mr. Kean's *Iago* is, we suspect, too much in the sun. His manner of acting the part would have suited better with the character of *Edmund* in *King Lear*, who, though in other respects much the same, has a spice of gallantry in his constitution, and has the favour and countenance of the ladies, which always gives a man the smug appearance of a bridegroom!

W. H.

ON THE LOVE OF THE COUNTRY

TO THE EDITOR OF THE ROUND TABLE.

Sir,—I do not know that any one has ever explained satisfactorily the true source of our attachment to natural objects, or of that soothing emotion which the sight of the country hardly ever fails to infuse into the mind. Some persons have ascribed this feeling to the natural beauty of the objects themselves, others to the freedom from care, the silence and tranquillity which scenes of retirement afford—others to the healthy and innocent employments of a country life—others to the simplicity of country manners—and others to different causes; but none to the right one. All these causes may, I believe, have a share in producing this feeling; but there is another more general principle, which has been left untouched, and which I shall here explain, endeavouring to be as little sentimental as the subject will admit.

Rousseau, in his Confessions, (the most valuable of all his works), relates, that when he took possession of his room at Annecy, at the house of his beloved mistress and friend, he found that he could see 'a

little spot of green' from his window, which endeared his situation
the more to him, because, he says, it was the first time he had had
this object constantly before him since he left Boissy, the place where
he was at school when a child.[1] Some such feeling as that here
described will be found lurking at the bottom of all our attachments of
this sort. Were it not for the recollections habitually associated with
them, natural objects could not interest the mind in the manner they
do. No doubt, the sky is beautiful; the clouds sail majestically along
its bosom; the sun is cheering; there is something exquisitely graceful in the manner in which a plant or tree puts forth its branches; the
motion with which they bend and tremble in the evening breeze is
soft and lovely; there is music in the babbling of a brook; the view
from the top of a mountain is full of grandeur; nor can we behold
the ocean with indifference. Or, as the Minstrel sweetly sings—

> 'Oh how can'st thou renounce the boundless store
> Of charms which Nature to her votary yields!
> The warbling woodland, the resounding shore,
> The pomp of groves, and garniture of fields;
> All that the genial ray of morning gilds,
> And all that echoes to the song of even,
> All that the mountain's sheltering bosom shields,
> And all the dread magnificence of heaven,
> Oh how can'st thou renounce, and hope to be forgiven!'

It is not, however, the beautiful and magnificent alone that
we admire in Nature; the most insignificant and rudest objects are
often found connected with the strongest emotions; we become
attached to the most common and familiar images as to the face of a
friend whom we have long known, and from whom we have received
many benefits. It is because natural objects have been associated
with the sports of our childhood, with air and exercise, with our
feelings in solitude, when the mind takes the strongest hold of things,
and clings with the fondest interest to whatever strikes its attention;
with change of place, the pursuit of new scenes, and thoughts of
distant friends: it is because they have surrounded us in almost all
situations, in joy and in sorrow, in pleasure and in pain; because they
have been one chief source and nourishment of our feelings, and a
part of our being, that we love them as we do ourselves.

There is, generally speaking, the same foundation for our love of
Nature as for all our habitual attachments, namely, association of
ideas. But this is not all. That which distinguishes this attachment

---

[1] Pope also declares that he had a particular regard for an old post which stood
in the court-yard before the house where he was brought up.

ON THE LOVE OF THE COUNTRY

from others is the transferable nature of our feelings with respect to physical objects; the associations connected with any one object extending to the whole class. My having been attached to any particular person does not make me feel the same attachment to the next person I may chance to meet; but, if I have once associated strong feelings of delight with the objects of natural scenery, the tie becomes indissoluble, and I shall ever after feel the same attachment to other objects of the same sort. I remember when I was abroad, the trees, and grass, and wet leaves, rustling in the walks of the Thuilleries, seemed to be as much English, to be as much the same trees and grass, that I had always been used to, as the sun shining over my head was the same sun which I saw in England; the faces only were foreign to me. Whence comes this difference? It arises from our always imperceptibly connecting the idea of the individual with man, and only the idea of the class with natural objects. In the one case, the external appearance or physical structure is the least thing to be attended to; in the other, it is every thing. The springs that move the human form, and make it friendly or adverse to me, lie hid within it. There is an infinity of motives, passions, and ideas contained in that narrow compass, of which I know nothing, and in which I have no share. Each individual is a world to himself, governed by a thousand contradictory and wayward impulses. I can, therefore, make no inference from one individual to another; nor can my habitual sentiments, with respect to any individual, extend beyond himself to others. But it is otherwise with respect to Nature. There is neither hypocrisy, caprice, nor mental reservation in her favours. Our intercourse with her is not liable to accident or change, interruption or disappointment. She smiles on us still the same. Thus, to give an obvious instance, if I have once enjoyed the cool shade of a tree, and been lulled into a deep repose by the sound of a brook running at its feet, I am sure that wherever I can find a tree and a brook, I can enjoy the same pleasure again. Hence, when I imagine these objects, I can easily form a mystic personification of the friendly power that inhabits them, Dryad or Naiad, offering its cool fountain or its tempting shade. Hence the origin of the Grecian mythology. All objects of the same kind being the same, not only in their appearance, but in their practical uses, we habitually confound them together under the same general idea; and, whatever fondness we may have conceived for one, is immediately placed to the common account. The most opposite kinds and remote trains of feeling gradually go to enrich the same sentiment; and in our love of Nature, there is all the force of individual attachment, combined with the most airy abstraction. It is this circumstance which gives that refinement, expansion, and wild

19

interest to feelings of this sort, when strongly excited, which every one must have experienced who is a true lover of Nature. The sight of the setting sun does not affect me so much from the beauty of the object itself, from the glory kindled through the glowing skies, the rich broken columns of light, or the dying streaks of day, as that it indistinctly recals to me numberless thoughts and feelings with which, through many a year and season, I have watched his bright descent in the warm summer evenings, or beheld him struggling to cast a 'farewel sweet' through the thick clouds of winter. I love to see the trees first covered with leaves in the spring, the primroses peeping out from some sheltered bank, and the innocent lambs running races on the soft green turf; because, at that birth-time of Nature, I have always felt sweet hopes and happy wishes—which have not been fulfilled! The dry reeds rustling on the side of a stream,—the woods swept by the loud blast,—the dark massy foliage of autumn,—the grey trunks and naked branches of the trees in winter,—the sequestered copse and wide extended heath,—the warm sunny showers, and December snows,—have all charms for me; there is no object, however trifling or rude, that has not, in some mood or other, found the way to my heart; and I might say, in the words of the poet,

> ' To me the meanest flower that blows can give
> Thoughts that do often lie too deep for tears.'

Thus Nature is a kind of universal home, and every object it presents to us an old acquaintance with unaltered looks.

> ——' Nature did ne'er betray
> The heart that lov'd her, but through all the years
> Of this our life, it is her privilege
> To lead from joy to joy.'

For there is that consent and mutual harmony among all her works, one undivided spirit pervading them throughout, that, if we have once knit ourselves in hearty fellowship to any of them, they will never afterwards appear as strangers to us, but, which ever way we turn, we shall find a secret power to have gone out before us, moulding them into such shapes as fancy loves, informing them with life and sympathy, bidding them put on their festive looks and gayest attire at our approach, and to pour all their sweets and choicest treasures at our feet. For him, then, who has well acquainted himself with Nature's works, she wears always one face, and speaks the same well known language, striking on the heart, amidst unquiet thoughts and the tumult of the world, like the music of one's native tongue heard in some far-off country.

ON POSTHUMOUS FAME

We do not connect the same feelings with the works of art as with those of nature, because we refer them to man, and associate with them the separate interests and passions which we know belong to those who are the authors or possessors of them. Nevertheless, there are some such objects, as a cottage, or a village church, which excite in us the same sensations as the sight of nature, and which are, indeed, almost always included in descriptions of natural scenery.

> ' Or from the mountain's sides
> View wilds and swelling floods,
> And hamlets brown, and dim-discover'd spires,
> And hear their simple bell.'

Which is in part, no doubt, because they are surrounded with natural objects, and, in a populous country, inseparable from them ; and also because the human interest they excite relates to manners and feelings which are simple, common, such as all can enter into, and which, therefore, always produce a pleasing effect upon the mind.   A.

ON POSTHUMOUS FAME,—WHETHER SHAKSPEARE WAS INFLUENCED BY A LOVE OF IT ?

It has been much disputed whether Shakspeare was actuated by the love of fame, though the question has been thought by others not to admit of any doubt, on the ground that it was impossible for any man of great genius to be without this feeling. It was supposed, that that immortality, which was the natural inheritance of men of powerful genius, must be ever present to their minds, as the reward, the object, and the animating spring, of all their efforts. This conclusion does not appear to be well founded, and that for the following reasons :

First, The love of fame is the offspring of taste, rather than of genius. The love of fame implies a knowledge of its existence. The men of the greatest genius, whether poets or philosophers, who lived in the first ages of society, only just emerging from the gloom of ignorance and barbarism, could not be supposed to have much idea of those long trails of lasting glory which they were to leave behind them, and of which there were as yet no examples. But, after such men, inspired by the love of truth and nature, have struck out those lights which become the gaze and admiration of after times,— when those who succeed in distant generations read with wondering rapture the works which the bards and sages of antiquity have bequeathed to them,—when they contemplate the imperishable power of intellect which survives the stroke of death and the revolutions of empire,—it is then that the passion for fame becomes an habitual feeling in the mind, and that men naturally wish to excite the same sentiments of admiration in others which they themselves have felt, and to transmit their names with the same honours to posterity. It is from the fond enthusiastic veneration with which we recal the names of the celebrated men of past times, and the idolatrous worship we pay to their memories, that we learn what a delicious thing fame is, and would willingly make any efforts or sacrifices to be thought of in the same way. It is in the true spirit of this feeling that a modern writer exclaims—

> 'Blessings be with them, and eternal praise,
> The poets—who on earth have made us heirs
> Of truth and pure delight in deathless lays!
> Oh! might my name be number'd among theirs,
> Then gladly would I end my mortal days!'

The love of fame is a species of emulation; or, in other words, the love of admiration is in proportion to the admiration with which the works of the highest genius have inspired us, to the delight we have received from their habitual contemplation, and to our participation in the general enthusiasm with which they have been regarded by mankind. Thus there is little of this feeling discoverable in the Greek writers, whose ideas of posthumous fame seem to have been confined to the glory of heroic actions; whereas the Roman poets and orators, stimulated by the reputation which their predecessors had acquired, and having those exquisite models constantly before their eyes, are full of it. So Milton, whose capacious mind was imbued with the rich stores of sacred and of classic lore, to whom learning opened her inmost page, and whose eye seemed to be ever bent back to the great models of antiquity, was, it is evident, deeply impressed with a feeling of lofty emulation, and a strong desire to produce some work of lasting and equal reputation :—

> ——'Nor sometimes forget
> Those other two, equall'd with me in fate,
> So were I equall'd with them in renown,
> Blind Thamyris and blind Mæonides,
> And Tiresias and Phineus, prophets old.'[1]

[1] See also the passage in his prose works relating to the first design of *Paradise Lost*.

ON POSTHUMOUS FAME

Spenser, who was a man of learning, had a high opinion of the regard due to 'famous poets' wit'; and Lord Bacon, whose vanity is as well known as his excessive adulation of that of others, asks, in a tone of proud exultation, 'Have not the poems of Homer lasted five-and-twenty hundred years, and not a syllable of them is lost?' Chaucer seems to have derived his notions of fame more immediately from the reputation acquired by the Italian poets, his contemporaries, which had at that time spread itself over Europe; while the latter, who were the first to unlock the springs of ancient learning, and who slaked their thirst of knowledge at that pure fountain-head, would naturally imbibe the same feeling from its highest source. Thus, Dante has conveyed the finest image that can perhaps be conceived of the power of this principle over the human mind, when he describes the heroes and celebrated men of antiquity as 'serene and smiling,' though in the shades of death,

> —— 'Because on earth their names
> In Fame's eternal volume shine for aye.'

But it is not so in Shakspeare. There is scarcely the slightest trace of any such feeling in his writings, nor any appearance of anxiety for their fate, or of a desire to perfect them or make them worthy of that immortality to which they were destined. And this indifference may be accounted for from the very circumstance, that he was almost entirely a man of genius, or that in him this faculty bore sway over every other: he was either not intimately conversant with the productions of the great writers who had gone before him, or at least was not much indebted to them: he revelled in the world of observation and of fancy; and perhaps his mind was of too prolific and active a kind to dwell with intense and continued interest on the images of beauty or of grandeur presented to it by the genius of others. He seemed scarcely to have an individual existence of his own, but to borrow that of others at will, and to pass successively through 'every variety of untried being,'—to be now *Hamlet*, now *Othello*, now *Lear*, now *Falstaff*, now *Ariel*. In the mingled interests and feelings belonging to this wide range of imaginary reality, in the tumult and rapid transitions of this waking dream, the author could not easily find time to think of himself, nor wish to embody that personal identity in idle reputation after death, of which he was so little tenacious while living. To feel a strong desire that others should think highly of us, it is, in general, necessary that we should think highly of ourselves. There is something of egotism, and even pedantry, in this sentiment; and there is no author who was so little tinctured with these as Shakspeare. The passion for fame, like other passions, requires an exclusive and exaggerated admiration of its object, and attaches more consequence to literary attainments and pursuits than they really possess. Shakspeare had looked too much abroad into the world, and his views of things were of too universal and comprehensive a cast, not to have taught him to estimate the importance of posthumous fame according to its true value and relative proportions. Though he might have some conception of his future fame, he could not but feel the contrast between that and his actual situation; and, indeed, he complains bitterly of the latter in one of his sonnets.[1] He would perhaps think, that, to be the idol of posterity, when we are no more, was hardly a full compensation for being the object of the glance and scorn of fools while we are living; and that, in truth, this universal fame so much vaunted, was a vague phantom of blind enthusiasm; for what is the amount even of Shakspeare's fame? That, in that very country which boasts his genius and his birth, perhaps not one person in ten has ever heard of his name, or read a syllable of his writings!

We will add another observation in connection with this subject, which is, that men of the greatest genius produce their works with too much facility (and, as it were, spontaneously) to require the love of fame as a stimulus to their exertions, or to make them seem deserving of the admiration of mankind as their reward. It is, indeed, one characteristic mark of the highest class of excellence to appear to come naturally from the mind of the author, without consciousness or effort. The work seems like inspiration—to be the gift of some God or of the Muse. But it is the sense of difficulty which enhances the admiration of power, both in ourselves and in others. Hence it is that there is nothing so remote from vanity as true genius. It is almost as natural for those who are endowed with the highest powers of the human mind to produce the miracles of art, as for other men to breathe or move. Correggio, who is said to have produced some of his divinest works almost without having seen a picture, probably did not know that he had done anything extraordinary. **Z.**

<hr />

[1] 'Oh! for my sake do you with fortune chide,
   The guilty goddess of my harmless deeds,
   That did not better for my life provide,
   Than public means which public manners breeds.
   Thence comes it that my name receives a brand,
   And almost thence my nature is subdued
   To what it works in, like the dyer's hand.'

At another time, we find him 'desiring this man's art, and that man's scope': so little was Shakspeare, as far as we can learn, enamoured of himself!

ON HOGARTH'S MARRIAGE A-LA-MODE

THE superiority of the pictures of Hogarth, which we have seen in the late collection at the British Institution, to the common prints, is confined chiefly to the *Marriage a-la-Mode*. We shall attempt to illustrate a few of their most striking excellencies, more particularly with reference to the expression of character. Their merits are indeed so prominent, and have been so often discussed, that it may be thought difficult to point out any new beauties; but they contain so much truth of nature, they present the objects to the eye under so many aspects and bearings, admit of so many constructions, and are so pregnant with meaning, that the subject is in a manner inexhaustible.

Boccacio, the most refined and sentimental of all the novel-writers, has been stigmatised as a mere inventor of licentious tales, because readers in general have only seized on those things in his works which were suited to their own taste, and have reflected their own grossness back upon the writer. So it has happened that the majority of critics having been most struck with the strong and decided expression in Hogarth, the extreme delicacy and subtle gradations of character in his pictures have almost entirely escaped them. In the first picture of the *Marriage a-la-Mode*, the three figures of the young Nobleman, his intended Bride, and her inamorato, the Lawyer, shew how much Hogarth excelled in the power of giving soft and effeminate expression. They have, however, been less noticed than the other figures, which tell a plainer story and convey a more palpable moral. Nothing can be more finely managed than the differences of character in these delicate personages. The Beau sits smiling at the looking-glass, with a reflected simper of self-admiration, and a languishing inclination of the head, while the rest of his body is perked up on his high heels with a certain air of tip-toe elevation. He is the Narcissus of the reign of George II., whose powdered peruke, ruffles, gold lace, and patches, divide his self-love unequally with his own person,—the true Sir Plume of his day;

> 'Of amber-lidded snuff-box justly vain,
> And the nice conduct of a clouded cane.'

There is the same felicity in the figure and attitude of the Bride, courted by the Lawyer. There is the utmost flexibility, and yielding softness in her whole person, a listless languor and tremulous suspense in the expression of her face. It is the precise look and air which

Pope has given to his favourite Belinda, just at the moment of the *Rape of the Lock*. The heightened glow, the forward intelligence, and loosened soul of love in the same face, in the assignation scene before the masquerade, form a fine and instructive contrast to the delicacy, timidity, and coy reluctance expressed in the first. The Lawyer in both pictures is much the same—perhaps too much so—though even this unmoved, unaltered appearance may be designed as characteristic. In both cases he has 'a person, and a smooth dispose, framed to make woman false.' He is full of that easy good-humour and easy good opinion of himself, with which the sex are delighted. There is not a sharp angle in his face to obstruct his success, or give a hint of doubt or difficulty. His whole aspect is round and rosy, lively and unmeaning, happy without the least expense of thought, careless and inviting; and conveys a perfect idea of the uninterrupted glide and pleasing murmur of the soft periods that flow from his tongue.

The expression of the Bride in the Morning Scene is the most highly seasoned, and at the same time the most vulgar in the series. The figure, face, and attitude of the Husband are inimitable. Hogarth has with great skill contrasted the pale countenance of the husband with the yellow whitish colour of the marble chimney-piece behind him, in such a manner as to preserve the fleshy tone of the former. The airy splendour of the view of the inner room in this picture is probably not exceeded by any of the productions of the Flemish School.

The Young Girl in the third picture, who is represented as the victim of fashionable profligacy, is unquestionably one of the artist's *chef-d'œuvres*. The exquisite delicacy of the painting is only surpassed by the felicity and subtlety of the conception. Nothing can be more striking than the contrast between the extreme softness of her person, and the hardened indifference of her character. The vacant stillness, the docility to vice, the premature suppression of youthful sensibility, the doll-like mechanism of the whole figure, which seems to have no other feeling but a sickly sense of pain,—shew the deepest insight into human nature, and into the effects of those refinements in depravity by which it has been good-naturedly asserted, that 'vice loses half its evil in losing all its grossness.' The story of this picture is in some parts very obscure and enigmatical. It is certain that the Nobleman is not looking straightforward to the Quack, whom he seems to have been threatening with his cane, but that his eyes are turned up with an ironical leer of triumph to the Procuress. The commanding attitude and size of this woman, the swelling circumference of her dress, spread out like a turkey-cock's feathers,—the fierce, ungovernable, inveterate malignity of her counte nance, which hardly needs the comment of the clasp-knife to explain her purpose, are all admirable in themselves, and still more so, as they are opposed to the mute insensibility, the elegant negligence of the dress, and the childish figure of the girl, who is supposed to be her *protégée*. As for the Quack, there can be no doubt entertained about him. His face seems as if it were composed of salve, and his features exhibit all the chaos and confusion of the most gross, ignorant, and impudent empiricism.

The gradations of ridiculous affectation in the Music Scene are finely imagined and preserved. The preposterous, overstrained admiration of the Lady of Quality, the sentimental, insipid, patient delight of the Man with his hair in papers and sipping his tea,—the pert, smirking, conceited, half-distorted approbation of the figure next to him, the transition to the total insensibility of the round face in profile, and then to the wonder of the Negro-boy at the rapture of his Mistress, form a perfect whole. The sanguine complexion and flame-coloured hair of the female Virtuoso throw an additional light on the character. This is lost in the print. The continuing the red colour of the hair into the back of the chair has been pointed out as one of those instances of alliteration in colouring, of which these pictures are everywhere full. The gross bloated appearance of the Italian Singer is well relieved by the hard features of the instrumental performer behind him, which might be carved of wood. The Negro-boy, holding the chocolate, both in expression, colour, and execution, is a masterpiece. The gay, lively derision of the other Negro boy, playing with the Actæon, is an ingenious contrast to the profound amazement of the first. Some account has already been given of the two lovers in this picture. It is curious to observe the infinite activity of mind which the artist displays on every occasion. An instance occurs in the present picture. He has so contrived the papers in the hair of the Bride, as to make them look almost like a wreath of half-blown flowers, while those which he has placed on the head of the musical Amateur very much resemble a *cheveux-de-frise* of horns, which adorn and fortify the lack-lustre expression and mild resignation of the face beneath.

The Night Scene is inferior to the rest of the series. The attitude of the Husband, who is just killed, is one in which it would be impossible for him to stand or even to fall. It resembles the loose pasteboard figures they make for children. The characters in the last picture, in which the Wife dies, are all masterly. We would particularly refer to the captious, petulant self-sufficiency of the Apothecary, whose face and figure are constructed on exact physiognomical principles, and to the fine example of passive obedience and non-resistance in the Servant, whom he is taking to task, and whose coat of green and yellow livery is as long and melancholy as his face. The disconsolate look, the haggard eyes, the open mouth, the comb sticking in the hair, the broken, gapped teeth, which, as it were, hitch in an answer—every thing about him denotes the utmost perplexity and dismay. The harmony and gradations of colour in this picture are uniformly preserved with the greatest nicety, and are well worthy the attention of the artist.

THE SUBJECT CONTINUED

IT has been observed, that Hogarth's pictures are exceedingly unlike any other representations of the same kind of subjects—that they form a class, and have a character, peculiar to themselves. It may be worth while to consider in what this general distinction consists.

In the first place, they are, in the strictest sense, *Historical* pictures ; and if what Fielding says be true, that his novel of *Tom Jones* ought to be regarded as an epic prose-poem, because it contained a regular developement of fable, manners, character, and passion, the compositions of Hogarth will, in like manner, be found to have a higher claim to the title of Epic Pictures than many which have of late arrogated that denomination to themselves. When we say that Hogarth treated his subjects historically, we mean that his works represent the manners and humours of mankind in action, and their characters by varied expression. Every thing in his pictures has life and motion in it. Not only does the business of the scene never stand still, but every feature and muscle is put into full play ; the exact feeling of the moment is brought out, and carried to its utmost height, and then instantly seized and stamped on the canvass for ever. The expression is always taken *en passant*, in a state of progress or change, and, as it were, at the salient point. Besides the excellence of each individual face, the reflection of the expression from face to face, the contrast and struggle of particular motives and feelings in the different actors in the scene, as of anger, contempt, laughter, compassion, are conveyed in the happiest and most lively manner. His figures are not like the back-ground on which they are painted : even the pictures on the wall have a peculiar look of their own Again, with the rapidity, variety, and scope of history, Hogarth's heads have all the reality and correctness of portraits. He gives the extremes of character and expression, but he gives them with perfect truth and accuracy. This is, in fact, what distinguishes his compositions from all others of the same kind, that they are equally remote from caricature, and from mere still life. It of course happens in subjects from common life, that the painter can procure real models, and he can get them to sit as long as he pleases. Hence, in general, those attitudes and expressions have been chosen which could be assumed the longest; and in imitating which, the artist, by taking pains and time, might produce almost as complete fac-similes as he could of a flower or a flower-pot, of a damask curtain, or a china vase. The copy was as perfect and as uninteresting in the one case as in the other. On the contrary, subjects of drollery and ridicule affording frequent examples of strange deformity and peculiarity of features, these have been eagerly seized by another class of artists, who, without subjecting themselves to the laborious drudgery of the Dutch School and their imitators, have produced our popular caricatures, by rudely copying or exaggerating the casual irregularities of the human countenance. Hogarth has equally avoided the faults of both these styles, the insipid tameness of the one, and the gross vulgarity of the other, so as to give to the productions of his pencil equal solidity and effect. For his faces go to the very verge of caricature, and yet never (we believe in any single instance) go beyond it: they take the very widest latitude, and yet we always see the links which bind them to nature: they bear all the marks and carry all the conviction of reality with them, as if we had seen the actual faces for the first time, from the precision, consistency, and good sense, with which the whole and every part is made out. They exhibit the most uncommon features with the most uncommon expressions, but which are yet as familiar and intelligible as possible, because with all the boldness they have all the truth of nature. Hogarth has left behind him as many of these memorable faces, in their memorable moments, as perhaps most of us remember in the course of our lives, and has thus doubled the quantity of our observation.

We have, in a former paper, attempted to point out the fund of observation, physical and moral, contained in one set of these pictures, the *Marriage a-la-Mode*. The rest would furnish as many topics to descant upon, were the patience of the reader as inexhaustible as the painter's invention. But as this is not the case, we shall content ourselves with barely referring to some of those figures in the other pictures, which appear the most striking, and which we see not only while we are looking at them, but which we have before us at all other times. For instance, who having seen can easily forget that exquisite frost-piece of religion and morality, the antiquated Prude in the Morning Scene; or that striking commentary on the *good old times*, the little wretched appendage of a Foot-boy, who crawls half famished and half frozen behind her? The French Man and Woman in the Noon are the perfection of flighty affectation and studied grimace; the amiable *fraternisation* of the two old Women saluting each other is not enough to be admired; and in the little Master, in the same national group, we see the early promise and personification of that eternal principle of wondrous self-complacency, proof against all circumstances, and which makes the French the only people who are vain even of being cuckolded and being conquered! Or shall we prefer to this the outrageous distress and unmitigated terrors of the Boy, who has dropped his dish of meat, and who seems red all over with shame and vexation, and bursting with the noise he makes? Or what can be better than the good housewifery of the Girl underneath, who is devouring the lucky fragments, or than the plump, ripe, florid, luscious look of the Servant-wench, embraced by a greasy rascal of an Othello, with her pye-dish tottering like her virtue, and with the most precious part of its contents running over? Just—no, not quite—as good is the joke of the Woman overhead, who, having quarrelled with her husband, is throwing their Sunday's dinner out of the window, to complete this chapter of accidents of baked-dishes. The Husband in the Evening Scene is certainly as meek as any recorded in history; but we cannot say that we admire this picture, or the Night Scene after it. But then, in the Taste in High Life, there is that inimitable pair, differing only in sex, congratulating and delighting one another by ' all the mutually reflected charities' of folly and affectation, with the young Lady coloured like a rose, dandling her little, black, pug-faced, white-teethed, chuckling favourite, and with the portrait of Mons. Des Noyers in the back-ground, dancing in a grand ballet, surrounded by butterflies. And again, in the Election Dinner, is the immortal Cobler, surrounded by his Peers, who, ' frequent and full,'—

' In *loud* recess and *brawling* conclave sit':—

the Jew in the second picture, a very Jew in grain—innumerable fine sketches of heads in the Polling for Votes, of which the Nobleman overlooking the caricaturist is the best; and then the irresistible tumultuous display of broad humour in the Chairing the Member, which is, perhaps, of all Hogarth's pictures, the most full of laughable incidents and situations—the yellow, rusty-faced thresher, with his swinging flail, breaking the head of one of the Chairmen, and his redoubted antagonist, the Sailor, with his oak-stick, and stumping wooden leg, a supplemental cudgel—the persevering ecstasy of the hobbling Blind Fiddler, who, in the fray, appears to have been trod upon by the artificial excrescence of the honest Tar—Monsieur, the Monkey, with piteous aspect, speculating the impending disaster of the triumphant candidate, and his brother Bruin, appropriating the paunch—the precipitous flight of the Pigs, souse over head into the water, the fine Lady fainting, with vermilion lips, and the two Chimney-sweepers, satirical young rogues! We had almost forgot the Politician who is burning a hole through his hat with a candle in reading the newspaper; and the Chickens, in the *March to Finchley*, wandering in search of their lost dam, who is found in the pocket of the Serjeant. Of the pictures in the *Rake's Progress* in this collection, we shall not here say any thing, because we think them, on the whole, inferior to the prints, and because they have already been criticised by a writer, to whom we could add nothing, in a paper which ought to be read by every lover of Hogarth and of English genius.[1]

W. H

ON MILTON'S LYCIDAS

> ' At last he rose, and twitch'd his mantle blue:
> To-morrow to fresh woods, and pastures new.'

Of all Milton's smaller poems, *Lycidas* is the greatest favourite with us. We cannot agree to the charge which Dr. Johnson has brought against it, of pedantry and want of feeling. It is the fine emanation of classical sentiment in a youthful scholar—'most musical, most melancholy.' A certain tender gloom overspreads it, a wayward abstraction, a forgetfulness of his subject in the serious reflections that arise out of it. The gusts of passion come and go like the sounds of music borne on the wind. The loss of the friend whose death he laments seems to have recalled, with double force, the reality of those speculations which they had indulged together; we are transported to classic ground, and a mysterious strain steals responsive on the ear while we listen to the poet,

> ' With eager thought warbling his Doric lay.

We shall proceed to give a few passages at length in support of our opinion. The first we shall quote is as remarkable for the truth and

---

[1] See an Essay on the genius of Hogarth, by C. Lamb, published in a periodical work, called the *Reflector*.

sweetness of the natural descriptions as for the characteristic elegance
of the allusions :

> 'Together both, ere the high lawns appear'd
> Under the opening eye-lids of the morn,
> We drove a-field; and both together heard
> What time the gray-fly winds her sultry horn,
> Battening our flocks with the fresh dews of night,
> Oft till the star that rose at evening bright
> Towards Heaven's descent had sloped his westering wheel.
> Meanwhile the rural ditties were not mute,
> Temper'd to the oaten flute :
> Rough satyrs danced, and fauns with cloven heel
> From the glad sound would not be absent long,
> And old Dametas loved to hear our song.
> But oh the heavy change, now thou art gone,
> Now thou art gone, and never must return !
> Thee, shepherd, thee the woods and desert caves
> With wild thyme and the gadding vine o'ergrown,
> And all their echoes mourn.
> The willows and the hazel copses green
> Shall now no more be seen
> Fanning their joyous leaves to thy soft lays.
> As killing as the canker to the rose,
> Or taint-worm to the weanling herds that graze,
> Or frost to flowers that their gay wardrobe wear,
> When first the white-thorn blows ;
> Such, Lycidas, thy loss to shepherd's ear ! '

After the fine apostrophe on Fame which Phœbus is invoked to
utter, the poet proceeds :

> 'Oh fountain Arethuse, and thou honour'd flood,
> Smooth-sliding Mincius, crown'd with vocal reeds,
> That strain I heard was of a higher mood ;
> But now my oat proceeds,
> And listens to the herald of the sea
> That came in Neptune's plea.
> He ask'd the waves, and ask'd the felon winds,
> What hard mishap hath doom'd this gentle swain ?
> And question'd every gust of rugged winds
> That blows from off each beaked promontory.
> They knew not of his story :
> And sage Hippotades their answer brings,
> That not a blast was from his dungeon stray'd,
> The air was calm, and on the level brine
> Sleek Panope with all her sisters play'd.'

If this is art, it is perfect art ; nor do we wish for anything better.
The measure of the verse, the very sound of the names, would almost

produce the effect here described. To ask the poet not to make use of such allusions as these, is to ask the painter not to dip in the colours of the rainbow, if he could. In fact, it is the common cant of criticism to consider every allusion to the classics, and particularly in a mind like Milton's, as pedantry and affectation. Habit is a second nature; and, in this sense, the pedantry (if it is to be called so) of the scholastic enthusiast, who is constantly referring to images of which his mind is full, is as graceful as it is natural. It is not affectation in him to recur to ideas and modes of expression, with which he has the strongest associations, and in which he takes the greatest delight. Milton was as conversant with the world of genius before him as with the world of nature about him; the fables of the ancient mythology were as familiar to him as his dreams. To be a pedant, is to see neither the beauties of nature nor of art. Milton saw both; and he made use of the one only to adorn and give new interest to the other. He was a passionate admirer of nature; and, in a single couplet of his, describing the moon,—

> 'Like one that had been led astray
> Through the heaven's wide pathless way,'—

there is more intense observation, and intense feeling of nature (as if he had gazed himself blind in looking at her), than in twenty volumes of descriptive poetry. But he added to his own observation of nature the splendid fictions of ancient genius, enshrined her in the mysteries of ancient religion, and celebrated her with the pomp of ancient names.

> 'Next Camus, reverend sire, went footing slow,
> His mantle hairy and his bonnet sedge,
> Inwrought with figures dim, and on the edge
> Like to that sanguine flower inscrib'd with woe.
> Oh! who hath reft (quoth he) my dearest pledge?
> Last came, and last did go,
> The pilot of the Galilean lake.'

There is a wonderful correspondence in the rhythm of these lines to the idea which they convey. This passage, which alludes to the clerical character of *Lycidas*, has been found fault with, as combining the truths of the Christian religion with the fictions of the heathen mythology. We conceive there is very little foundation for this objection, either in reason or good taste. We will not go so far as to defend Camoens, who, in his *Lusiad*, makes Jupiter send Mercury with a dream to propagate the Catholic religion; nor do we know that it is generally proper to introduce the two things in the same poem, though we see no objection to it here; but of this we are quite sure, that there is no inconsistency or natural repugnance between this poetical and religious faith in the same mind. To the understanding, the belief of the one is incompatible with that of the other; but in the imagination, they not only may, but do constantly co-exist. We will venture to go farther, and maintain, that every classical scholar, however orthodox a Christian he may be, is an honest Heathen at heart. This requires explanation. Whoever, then, attaches a reality to any idea beyond the mere name, has, to a certain extent, (though not an abstract), an habitual and practical belief in it. Now, to any one familiar with the names of the personages of the Heathen mythology, they convey a positive identity beyond the mere name. We refer them to something out of ourselves. It is only by an effort of abstraction that we divest ourselves of the idea of their reality; all our involuntary prejudices are on their side. This is enough for the poet. They impose on the imagination by all the attractions of beauty and grandeur. They come down to us in sculpture and in song. We have the same associations with them, as if they had really been; for the belief of the fiction in ancient times has produced all the same effects as the reality could have done. It was a reality to the minds of the ancient Greeks and Romans, and through them it is reflected to us. And, as we shape towers, and men, and armed steeds, out of the broken clouds that glitter in the distant horizon, so, throned above the ruins of the ancient world, Jupiter still nods sublime on the top of blue Olympus, Hercules leans upon his club, Apollo has not laid aside his bow, nor Neptune his trident; the sea-gods ride upon the sounding waves, the long procession of heroes and demi-gods passes in endless review before us, and still we hear

> ——'The Muses in a ring
> Aye round about Jove's altar sing:
>
> . . . .
>
> Have sight of Proteus coming from the sea,
> And hear old Triton blow his wreathed horn.'

If all these mighty fictions had really existed, they could have done no more for us! We shall only give one other passage from *Lycidas*; but we flatter ourselves that it will be a treat to our readers, if they are not already familiar with it. It is the passage which contains that exquisite description of the flowers:

> 'Return, Alpheus; the dread voice is past
> That shrunk thy streams; return, Sicilian Muse,
> And call the vales, and bid them hither cast
> Their bells, and flow'rets of a thousand hues.

ON MILTON'S LYCIDAS

Ye valleys low, where the mild whispers use
Of shades and wanton winds and gushing brooks,
On whose fresh lap the swart star sparely looks,
Throw hither all your quaint enamell'd eyes,
That on the green turf suck the honied showers,
And purple all the ground with vernal flowers;
Bring the rathe primrose that forsaken dies,
The tufted crow-toe, and pale jessamine,
The white pink, and the pansy freak'd with jet,
The glowing violet,
The musk-rose, and the well-attired woodbine,
With cowslips wan, that hang the pensive head,
And every flower that sad embroidery wears;
Bid amaranthus all his beauty shed,
And daffadillies fill their cups with tears,
To strew the laureat hearse where Lycid lies.
For so to interpose a little ease
Let our frail thoughts dally with false surmise.
Ay me! Whilst thee the shores and sounding seas
Waft far away, where'er thy bones are hurl'd,
Whether beyond the stormy Hebrides,
Where thou perhaps under the whelming tide
Visit'st the bottom of the monstrous world;
Or whether thou, to our moist vows denied,
Sleep'st by the fable of Bellerus old,
Where the great vision of the guarded mount
Looks towards Namancos and Bayona's hold,
Look homeward, Angel, now, and melt with ruth,
And, O ye Dolphins, waft the hapless youth.'

Dr. Johnson is very much offended at the introduction of these Dolphins; and indeed, if he had had to guide them through the waves, he would have made much the same figure as his old friend Dr. Burney does, swimming in the *Thames* with his wig on, with the water-nymphs, in the picture by Barry at the Adelphi.

There is a description of flowers in the *Winter's Tale*, which we shall give as a parallel to Milton's. We shall leave it to the reader to decide which is the finest; for we dare not give the preference. *Perdita* says,

——'Here 's flowers for you,
Hot lavender, mints, savoury, marjoram,
The marygold, that goes to bed with the sun,
And with him rises weeping; these are flowers
Of middle summer, and I think, they 're given
To men of middle age. Y'are welcome.
'*Camillo.* I should leave grazing, were I of your flock,
And only live by gazing.

> ' *Perdita.*   Out, alas!
> You 'd be so lean, that blasts of January
> Would blow you through and through. Now, my fairest friend,
> I would I had some flowers o' th' spring, that might
> Become your time of day : O Proserpina,
> For the flowers now, that, frighted, you let fall
> From Dis's waggon ! Daffodils,
> That come before the swallow dares, and take
> The winds of March with beauty ; violets dim,
> But sweeter than the lids of Juno's eyes,
> Or Cytherea's breath ; pale primroses,
> That die unmarried, ere they can behold
> Bright Phœbus in his strength, a malady
> Most incident to maids ; bold oxlips, and
> The crown imperial ; lilies of all kinds,
> The flower de lis being one. O, these I lack
> To make you garlands of, and my sweet friend,
> To strew him o'er and o'er.'

Dr. Johnson's general remark, that Milton's genius had not room to show itself in his smaller pieces, is not well-founded. Not to mention *Lycidas*, the *Allegro*, and *Penseroso*, it proceeds on a false estimate of the merits of his great work, which is not more distinguished by strength and sublimity than by tenderness and beauty. The last were as essential qualities of Milton's mind as the first. The battle of the angels, which has been commonly considered as the best part of the *Paradise Lost*, is the worst.   W. H.

ON MILTON'S VERSIFICATION

MILTON's works are a perpetual invocation to the Muses ; a hymn to Fame. His religious zeal infused its character into his imagination ; and he devotes himself with the same sense of duty to the cultivation of his genius, as he did to the exercise of virtue, or the good of his country. He does not write from casual impulse, but after a severe examination of his own strength, and with a determination to leave nothing undone which it is in his power to do. He always labours, and he almost always succeeds. He strives to say the finest things in the world, and he does say them. He adorns and dignifies his subject to the utmost. He surrounds it with all the possible associations of beauty or grandeur, whether moral, or physical, or intellectual. He refines on his descriptions of beauty, till the sense almost aches at them, and raises his images of terror to a gigantic elevation, that ' makes Ossa like a wart.' He has a high standard, with which he is constantly comparing himself, and nothing short of which can satisfy him :

> ——' Sad task, yet argument
> Not less but more heroic than the wrath
> Of stern Achilles on his foe pursued,
> If answerable stile I can obtain.
> —— Unless an age too late, or cold
> Climate, or years, damp my intended wing.'

Milton has borrowed more than any other writer; yet he is perfectly distinct from every other writer. The power of his mind is stamped on every line. He is a writer of centos, and yet in originality only inferior to Homer. The quantity of art shews the strength of his genius; so much art would have overloaded any other writer. Milton's learning has all the effect of intuition. He describes objects of which he had only read in books, with the vividness of actual observation. His imagination has the force of nature. He makes words tell as pictures :

> ' Him followed Rimmon, whose delightful seat
> Was fair Damascus, on the fertile banks
> Of Abbana and Pharphar, *lucid* streams.'

And again :

> ' As when a vulture on Imaus bred,
> Whose snowy ridge the roving Tartar bounds,
> Dislodging from a region scarce of prey
> To gorge the flesh of lambs or yeanling kids
> On hills where flocks are fed, *flies towards the springs*
> *Of Ganges or Hydaspes, Indian streams ;*
> *But in his way lights on the barren plains*
> *Of Sericana, where Chineses drive*
> *With sails and wind their cany waggons light.*'

Such passages may be considered as demonstrations of history. Instances might be multiplied without end. There is also a decided tone in his descriptions, an eloquent dogmatism, as if the poet spoke from thorough conviction, which Milton probably derived from his spirit of partisanship, or else his spirit of partisanship from the natural firmness and vehemence of his mind. In this Milton resembles Dante, (the only one of the moderns with whom he has anything in common), and it is remarkable that Dante, as well as Milton, was a political partisan. That approximation to the severity of impassioned prose which has been made an objection to Milton's poetry, is one of its chief excellencies. It has been suggested, that the vividness with which he describes visible objects, might be owing to their having acquired a greater strength in his mind after the privation of sight; but we find the same palpableness and solidity in the descriptions which occur in his early poems. There is, indeed, the same depth of impression in his descriptions of the objects of the other senses. Milton had as much of what is meant by *gusto* as any poet. He forms the most intense conceptions of things, and then embodies them by a single stroke of his pen. Force of style is perhaps his first excellence. Hence he stimulates us most in the reading, and less afterwards.

It has been said that Milton's ideas were musical rather than picturesque, but this observation is not true, in the sense in which it was meant. The ear, indeed, predominates over the eye, because it is more immediately affected, and because the language of music blends more immediately with, and forms a more natural accompaniment to, the variable and indefinite associations of ideas conveyed by words. But where the associations of the imagination are not the principal thing, the individual object is given by Milton with equal force and beauty. The strongest and best proof of this, as a characteristic power of his mind, is, that the persons of Adam and Eve, of Satan, etc., are always accompanied, in our imagination, with the grandeur of the naked figure; they convey to us the ideas of sculpture. As an instance, take the following:

> —— 'He soon
> Saw within ken a glorious Angel stand,
> The same whom John saw also in the sun:
> His back was turned, but not his brightness hid;
> Of beaming sunny rays a golden tiar
> Circled his head, nor less his locks behind
> Illustrious on his shoulders fledged with wings
> Lay waving round; on some great charge employ'd
> He seem'd, or fix'd in cogitation deep.
> Glad was the spirit impure, as now in hope
> To find who might direct his wand'ring flight
> To Paradise, the happy seat of man,
> His journey's end, and our beginning woe.
> But first he casts to change his proper shape,
> Which else might work him danger or delay:
> And now a stripling cherub he appears,
> Not of the prime, yet such as in his face
> Youth smiled celestial, and to every limb
> Suitable grace diffus'd, so well he feign'd:
> Under a coronet his flowing hair

ON MILTON'S VERSIFICATION

> In curls on either cheek play'd; wings he wore
> Of many a colour'd plume sprinkled with gold,
> His habit fit for speed succinct, and held
> Before his decent steps a silver wand.'

The figures introduced here have all the elegance and precision of a Greek statue.

Milton's blank verse is the only blank verse in the language (except Shakspeare's) which is readable. Dr. Johnson, who had modelled his ideas of versification on the regular sing-song of Pope, condemns the *Paradise Lost* as harsh and unequal. We shall not pretend to say that this is not sometimes the case; for where a degree of excellence beyond the mechanical rules of art is attempted the poet must sometimes fail. But we imagine that there are more perfect examples in Milton of musical expression, or of an adaptation of the sound and movement of the verse to the meaning of the passage, than in all our other writers, whether of rhyme or blank verse, put together, (with the exception already mentioned). Spenser is the most harmonious of our poets, and Dryden is the most sounding and varied of our rhymists. But in neither is there anything like the same ear for music, the same power of approximating the varieties of poetical to those of musical rhythm, as there is in our great epic poet. The sound of his lines is moulded into the expression of the sentiment, almost of the very image. They rise or fall, pause or hurry rapidly on, with exquisite art, but without the least trick or affectation, as the occasion seems to require.

The following are some of the finest instances:

> —— 'His hand was known
> In Heaven by many a tower'd structure high;
> Nor was his name unheard or unador'd
> In ancient Greece: and in the Ausonian land
> Men called him Mulciber: and how he fell
> From Heav'n, they fabled, thrown by angry Jove
> Sheer o'er the crystal battlements; from morn
> To noon he fell, from noon to dewy eve,
> A summer's day; and with the setting sun
> Dropt from the zenith like a falling star
> On Lemnos, the Ægean isle: this they relate,
> Erring.'

> —— 'But chief the spacious hall
> Thick swarm'd, both on the ground and in the air,
> Brush'd with the hiss of rustling wings. As bees
> In spring time, when the sun with Taurus rides,
> Pour forth their populous youth about the hive
> In clusters; they among fresh dews and flow'rs

Fly to and fro: or on the smoothed plank,
The suburb of their straw-built citadel,
New rubb'd with balm, expatiate and confer
Their state affairs.   So thick the airy crowd
Swarm'd and were straiten'd; till the signal giv'n,
Behold a wonder !   They but now who seem'd
In bigness to surpass earth's giant sons,
Now less than smallest dwarfs, in narrow room
Throng numberless, like that Pygmean race
Beyond the Indian mount, or fairy elves,
Whose midnight revels by a forest side
Or fountain, some belated peasant sees,
Or dreams he sees, while over-head the moon
Sits arbitress, and nearer to the earth
Wheels her pale course: they on their mirth and dance
Intent, with jocund music charm his ear ;
At once with joy and fear his heart rebounds.'

We can only give another instance ; though we have some difficulty in leaving off. 'What a pity,' said an ingenious person of our acquaintance, 'that Milton had not the pleasure of reading *Paradise Lost* !'—

'Round he surveys (and well might, where he stood
So high above the circling canopy
Of night's extended shade) from eastern point
Of Libra to the fleecy star that bears
Andromeda far off Atlantic seas
Beyond th' horizon : then from pole to pole
He views in breadth, and without longer pause
Down right into the world's first region throws
His flight precipitant, and winds with ease
Through the pure marble air his oblique way
Amongst innumerable stars that shone
Stars distant, but nigh hand seem'd other worlds;
Or other worlds they seem'd or happy isles,' etc.

The verse, in this exquisitely modulated passage, floats up and down as if it had itself wings.   Milton has himself given us the theory of his versification.

'In many a winding bout
Of linked sweetness long drawn out.'

Dr. Johnson and Pope would have converted his vaulting Pegasus into a rocking-horse.   Read any other blank verse but Milton's,— Thomson's, Young's, Cowper's, Wordsworth's,—and it will be found,

om the want of the same insight into 'the hidden soul of harmony,'
be mere lumbering prose.   W. H.

To the President of The Round Table.

Sir,—It is somewhat remarkable, that in *Pope's Essay on Criticism* (not a very
ng poem) there are no less than half a score couplets rhyming to the word *sense*.

'But of the two, less dangerous is the offence,
To tire our patience than mislead our sense.'—*lines* **3, 4.**

'In search of wit these lose their common sense,
And then turn critics in their own defence.'—*l.* **28, 29.**

'Pride, where wit fails, steps in to our defence,
And fills up all the mighty void of sense.'—*l.* **209, 10.**

'Some by old words to fame have made pretence,
Ancients in phrase, mere moderns in their sense.'—*l.* **324, 5.**

''Tis not enough no harshness gives offence;
The sound must seem an echo to the sense.'—*l.* **364, 5.**

'At every trifle scorn to take offence;
That always shews great pride or little sense.'—*l.* **386, 7.**

'Be silent always, when you doubt your sense,
And speak, though sure, with seeming diffidence.'—*l.* **566, 7.**

'Be niggards of advice on no pretence,
For the worst avarice is that of sense.'—*l.* **578, 9.**

'Strain out the last dull dropping of their sense,
And rhyme with all the rage of impotence.'—*l.* **608, 9.**

'Horace still charms with graceful negligence,
And without method talks us into sense.'—*l.* **653, 4.**

I am, Sir, your humble servant,

A Small Critic.

ON MANNER

It was the opinion of Lord Chesterfield, that *manner* is of more
importance than *matter*. This opinion seems at least to be warranted
by the practice of the world; nor do we think it so entirely without
foundation as some persons of more solid than shewy pretensions
would make us believe. In the remarks which we are going to
make, we can scarcely hope to have any party very warmly on our
side; for the most superficial coxcomb would be thought to owe his
success to sterling merit.

What any person says or does is one thing; the mode in which

he says or does it is another. The last of these is what we under
stand by *manner*. In other words, manner is the involuntary or
incidental expression given to our thoughts and sentiments by looks,
tones, and gestures. Now, we are inclined in many cases to prefer
this latter mode of judging of what passes in the mind to more
positive and formal proof, were it for no other reason than that it is
involuntary. 'Look,' says Lord Chesterfield, 'in the face of the
person to whom you are speaking, if you wish to know his real
sentiments; for he can command his words more easily than his
countenance.' We may perform certain actions from design, or repeat
certain professions by rote: the manner of doing either will in general
be the best test of our sincerity. The mode of conferring a favour
is often thought of more value than the favour itself. The actual
obligation may spring from a variety of questionable motives, vanity,
affectation, or interest: the cordiality with which the person from
whom you have received it asks you how you do, or shakes you by
the hand, does not admit of misinterpretation. The manner of doing
any thing, is that which marks the degree and force of our internal
impressions; it emanates most directly from our immediate or habitual
feelings; it is that which stamps its life and character on any action;
the rest may be performed by an automaton. What is it that makes
the difference between the best and the worst actor, but the manner
of going through the same part? The one has a perfect idea of the
degree and force with which certain feelings operate in nature, and
the other has no idea at all of the workings of passion. There would
be no difference between the worst actor in the world and the best,
placed in real circumstances, and under the influence of real passion.
A writer may express the thoughts he has borrowed from another,
but not with the same force, unless he enters into the true spirit of
them. Otherwise he will resemble a person reading what he does
not understand, whom you immediately detect by his wrong emphasis.
His illustrations will be literally exact, but misplaced and awkward;
he will not gradually warm with his subject, nor feel the force of
what he says, nor produce the same effect on his readers. An
author's style is not less a criterion of his understanding than his
sentiments. The same story told by two different persons shall, from
the difference of the manner, either set the table in a roar, or not
relax a feature in the whole company. We sometimes complain
(perhaps rather unfairly) that particular persons possess more vivacity
than wit. But we ought to take into the account, that their very
vivacity arises from their enjoying the joke; and their humouring a
story by drollery of gesture or archness of look, shews only that they
are acquainted with the different ways in which the sense of the

udicrous expresses itself. It is not the mere dry jest, but the relish which the person himself has of it, with which we sympathise. For in all that tends to pleasure and excitement, the capacity for enjoyment is the principal point. One of the most pleasant and least iresome persons of our acquaintance is a humourist, who has three or four quaint witticisms and proverbial phrases, which he always repeats over and over; but he does this with just the same vivacity and freshness as ever, so that you feel the same amusement with less effort than if he had startled his hearers with a succession of original conceits. Another friend of ours, who never fails to give vent to one or two real *jeu-d'esprits* every time you meet him, from the pain with which he is delivered of them, and the uneasiness he seems to suffer all the rest of the time, makes a much more interesting than comfortable companion. If you see a person in pain for himself, it naturally puts you in pain for him. The art of pleasing consists in being pleased. To be amiable is to be satisfied with one's self and others. Good-humour is essential to pleasantry. It is this circumstance, among others, that renders the wit of Rabelais so much more delightful than that of Swift, who, with all his satire, is 'as dry as the remainder biscuit after a voyage.' In society, good-temper and animal spirits are nearly everything. They are of more importance than sallies of wit, or refinements of understanding. They give a general tone of cheerfulness and satisfaction to the company. The French have the advantage over us in external manners. They breathe a lighter air, and have a brisker circulation of the blood. They receive and communicate their impressions more freely. The interchange of ideas costs them less. Their constitutional gaiety is a kind of natural intoxication, which does not require any other stimulus; and *Falstaff's* commendation on sack was evidently intended for his countrymen,—whose 'learning is often a mere hoard of gold kept by a devil, till wine commences it, and sets it in act and use.'[1] More undertakings fail for want of spirit than for want of sense. Confidence gives a fool the advantage over a wise man. In general, a strong passion for any object will ensure success, for the desire of the end will point out the means. We apprehend that people usually complain, without reason, of not succeeding in various pursuits according to their deserts. Such persons, we

---

[1] 'A good sherris-sack hath a twofold operation in it; it ascends me into the brain, dries me there all the foolish, dull, and crudy vapours which environ it; and makes it apprehensive, quick, forgetive, full of nimble, fiery, and delectable shapes, which, delivered over to the tongue, becomes excellent wit,' etc.—*Second Part of Henry IV.*

will grant, may have great merit in all other respects; but in that
which they fail, it will almost invariably hold true, that they do n
deserve to succeed. For instance, a person who has spent his li
in thinking will acquire a habit of reflection; but he will neith
become a dancer nor a singer, rich nor beautiful. In like manne
if any one complains of not succeeding in affairs of gallantry, we wi
venture to say, it is because he is not gallant. He has mistaken h
talent—that's all. If any person of exquisite sensibility makes lov
awkwardly, it is because he does not feel it as he should. One o
these disappointed sentimentalists may very probably feel it upo
reflection, may brood over it till he has worked himself up to a pitc
of frenzy, and write his mistress the finest love-letters in the world
in her absence; but, be assured, he does not feel an atom of th
passion in her presence. If, in paying her a compliment, he frown
with more than usual severity, or, in presenting her with a bunch o
flowers, seems as if he was going to turn his back upon her, he ca
only expect to be laughed at for his pains; nor can he plead a
excess of feeling as an excuse for want of common sense. She ma
say, 'It is not with me you are in love, but with the ridiculou
chimeras of your own brain. You are thinking of *Sophia Wester*
or some other heroine, and not of me. Go and make love to you
romances.'

Lord Chesterfield's character of the Duke of Marlborough is a
good illustration of his general theory. He says, 'Of all the men
I ever knew in my life, (and I knew him extremely well), the lat
Duke of Marlborough possessed the graces in the highest degree
not to say engrossed them; for I will venture (contrary to the
custom of profound historians, who always assign deep causes fo
great events) to ascribe the better half of the Duke of Marlborough'
greatness and riches to those graces. He was eminently illiterate
wrote bad English, and spelt it worse. He had no share of wha
is commonly called parts; that is, no brightness, nothing shining in
his genius. He had most undoubtedly an excellent good plai
understanding with sound judgment. But these alone would pro
bably have raised him but something higher than they found him
which was page to King James II.'s Queen. There the Grace
protected and promoted him; for while he was Ensign of the Guards
the Duchess of Cleveland, then favourite mistress of Charles II.
struck by these very graces, gave him £5000, with which he imme
diately bought an annuity of £500 a year, which was the foundatio
of his subsequent fortune. His figure was beautiful, but his manne
was irresistible by either man or woman. It was by this engaging
graceful manner, that he was enabled, during all his wars, to connec

he various and jarring powers of the grand alliance, and to carry
hem on to the main object of the war, notwithstanding their private
nd separate views, jealousies, and wrongheadedness. Whatever
ourt he went to (and he was often obliged to go himself to some
esty and refractory ones), he as constantly prevailed, and brought
hem into his measures.' [1]

Grace in women has more effect than beauty. We sometimes
ee a certain fine self-possession, an habitual voluptuousness of char-
cter, which reposes on its own sensations, and derives pleasure from
ll around it, that is more irresistible than any other attraction.
There is an air of languid enjoyment in such persons, 'in their eyes,
n their arms, and their hands, and their faces,' which robs us of our-
elves, and draws us by a secret sympathy towards them. Their
ninds are a shrine where pleasure reposes. Their smile diffuses a
ensation like the breath of spring. Petrarch's description of Laura
nswers exactly to this character, which is indeed the Italian char-
cter. Titian's portraits are full of it: they seem sustained by
entiment, or as if the persons whom he painted sat to music. There
s one in the Louvre (or there was) which had the most of this
expression we ever remember. It did not look downward; 'it
ooked forward, beyond this world.' It was a look that never passed
way, but remained unalterable as the deep sentiment which gave
oirth to it. It is the same constitutional character (together with
nfinite activity of mind) which has enabled the greatest man in
nodern history to bear his reverses of fortune with gay magnanimity,
nd to submit to the loss of the empire of the world with as little
liscomposure as if he had been playing a game at chess.

Grace has been defined as the outward expression of the inward
narmony of the soul. Foreigners have more of this than the English,
—particularly the people of the southern and eastern countries.
Their motions appear (like the expression of their countenances) to
have a more immediate communication with their feelings. The
nhabitants of the northern climates, compared with these children
of the sun, are like hard inanimate machines, with difficulty set in
motion. A strolling gipsy will offer to tell your fortune with a grace
and an insinuation of address that would be admired in a court.[2] The

[1] We have an instance in our own times of a man, equally devoid of understanding and principle, but who manages the House of Commons by his *manner*
alone.

[2] Mr. Wordsworth, who has written a sonnet to the King on the good that he
has done in the last fifty years, has made an attack on a set of gipsies for having
done nothing in four and twenty hours. 'The stars had gone their rounds, but
they had not stirred from their place.' And why should they, if they were comfortable where they were? We did not expect this turn from Mr. Wordsworth,

Hindoos that we see about the streets are another example of this They are a different race of people from ourselves. They wander about in a luxurious dream. They are like part of a glittering procession,—like revellers in some gay carnival. Their life is a dance, a measure; they hardly seem to tread the earth, but are borne along in some more genial element, and bask in the radiance of brighter suns. We may understand this difference of climate by recollecting the difference of our own sensations at different times, in the fine glow of summer, or when we are pinched and dried up by a north-east wind. Even the foolish Chinese, who go about twirling their fans and their windmills, shew the same delight in them as the children they collect around them. The people of the East make it their business to sit and think and do nothing. They indulge in endless reverie; for the incapacity of enjoyment does not impose on them the necessity of action. There is a striking example of this passion for castle-building in the story of the glass-man in the Arabian Nights.

After all, we would not be understood to say that manner is every thing. Nor would we put Euclid or Sir Isaac Newton on a level with the first *petit-maître* we might happen to meet. We consider *Æsop's Fables* to have been a greater work of genius than Fontaine's translation of them; though we doubt whether we should not prefer Fontaine, for his style only, to Gay, who has shewn a great deal of original invention. The elegant manners of people of fashion have been objected to us to shew the frivolity of external accomplishments,

whom we had considered as the prince of poetical idlers, and patron of the philosophy of indolence, who formerly insisted on our spending our time 'in a wise passiveness.' Mr. W. will excuse us if we are not converts to his recantation of his original doctrine; for he who changes his opinion loses his authority. We did not look for this Sunday-school philosophy from him. What had he himself been doing in these four and twenty hours? Had he been admiring a flower, or writing a sonnet? We hate the doctrine of utility, even in a philosopher, and much more in a poet : for the only real utility is that which leads to enjoyment, and the end is, in all cases, better than the means. A friend of ours from the North of England proposed to make Stonehenge of some use, by building houses with it. Mr. W.'s quarrel with the gipsies is an improvement on this extravagance, for the gipsies are the only living monuments of the first ages of society. They are an everlasting source of thought and reflection on the advantages and disadvantages of the progress of civilisation : they are a better answer to the cotton manufactories than Mr. W. has given in the *Excursion*. 'They are a grotesque ornament to the civil order.' We should be sorry to part with Mr. Wordsworth's poetry, because it amuses and interests us : we should be still sorrier to part with the tents of our old friends, the Bohemian philosophers, because they amuse and interest us more. If any one goes a journey, the principal event in it is his meeting with a party of gipsies. The pleasantest trait in the character of Sir Roger de Coverley, is his interview with the gipsy fortune-teller. This is enough.

nd the facility with which they are acquired. As to the last point, ve demur. There is no class of people who lead so laborious a life, r who take more pains to cultivate their minds as well as persons, nan people of fashion. A young lady of quality, who has to devote o many hours a day to music, so many to dancing, so many to rawing, so many to French, Italian, etc., certainly does not pass her ime in idleness; and these accomplishments are afterwards called into ction by every kind of external or mental stimulus, by the excitements f pleasure, vanity, and interest. A Ministerial or Opposition lord goes hrough more drudgery than half a dozen literary hacks; nor does a eviewer by profession read half the same number of productions as a nodern fine lady is obliged to labour through. We confess, however, ve are not competent judges of the degree of elegance or refinement mplied in the general tone of fashionable manners. The successful xperiment made by *Peregrine Pickle*, in introducing his strolling nistress into genteel company, does not redound greatly to their redit. In point of elegance of external appearance, we see no lifference between women of fashion and women of a different char-cter, who dress in the same style. T T

ON THE TENDENCY OF SECTS

THERE is a natural tendency in sects to narrow the mind.

The extreme stress laid upon differences of minor importance, to he neglect of more general truths and broader views of things, gives n inverted bias to the understanding; and this bias is continually ncreased by the eagerness of controversy, and captious hostility to he prevailing system. A party-feeling of this kind once formed will nsensibly communicate itself to other topics; and will be too apt to ead its votaries to a contempt for the opinions of others, a jealousy of very difference of sentiment, and a disposition to arrogate all sound principle as well as understanding to themselves, and those who think with them. We can readily conceive how such persons, from fixing too high a value on the practical pledge which they have given of the independence and sincerity of their opinions, come at last to entertain a suspicion of every one else as acting under the shackles of prejudice or the mask of hypocrisy. All those who have not given in their unqualified protest against received doctrines and established authority, are supposed to labour under an acknowledged incapacity to form a rational determination on any subject whatever Any argument, not having the presumption of singularity in its favour, is immediately set aside as nugatory. There is, however, no prejudice so strong as that which arises from a fancied exemption from all prejudice. For this last implies not only the practical conviction that it is right, but the theoretical assumption that it cannot be wrong. From considering all objections as in this manner 'null and void,' the mind becomes so thoroughly satisfied with its own conclusions, as to render any further examination of them superfluous, and confounds its exclusive pretensions to reason with the absolute possession of it. Those who, from their professing to submit everything to the test of reason, have acquired the name of rational Dissenters, have their weak sides as well as other people : nor do we know of any class of disputants more disposed to take their opinions for granted, than those who call themselves Freethinkers. A long habit of objecting to every thing establishes a monopoly in the right of contradiction ; a prescriptive title to the privilege of starting doubts and difficulties in the common belief, without being liable to have our own called in question. There cannot be a more infallible way to prove that we must be in the right, than by maintaining roundly that every one else is in the wrong ! Not only the opposition of sects to one another, but their unanimity among themselves, strengthens their confidence in their peculiar notions. They feel themselves invulnerable behind the double fence of sympathy with themselves, and antipathy to the rest of the world. Backed by the zealous support of their followers, they become equally intolerant with respect to the opinions of others, and tenacious of their own. They fortify themselves within the narrow circle of their new-fangled prejudices ; the whole exercise of their right of private judgment is after a time reduced to the repetition of a set of watch-words, which have been adopted as the Shiboleth of the party ; and their extremest points of faith pass as current as the bead-roll and legends of the Catholics, or St. Athanasius's Creed, and the Thirty-nine Articles. We certainly are not going to recommend the establishment of articles of faith, or implicit assent to them, as favourable to the progress of philosophy ; but neither has the spirit of opposition to them this tendency, as far as relates to its immediate effects, however useful it may be in its remote consequences. The spirit of controversy substitutes the irritation of personal feeling for the independent exertion of the understanding ; and when this irritation ceases, the mind flags for want of a sufficient stimulus to urge it on. It discharges all its energy with its spleen. Besides, this perpetual cavilling with the opinions of others, detecting petty flaws in their arguments, calling them to a literal account for their absurdities, and squaring their doctrines by a pragmatical standard of our own, is necessarily dverse to any great enlargement of mind, or original freedom of thought.[1] The constant attention bestowed on a few contested points, by at once flattering our pride, our prejudices, and our indolence, supersedes more general inquiries; and the bigoted controversialist, by dint of repeating a certain formula of belief, shall not only convince himself that all those who differ from him are undoubtedly wrong on that point, but that their knowledge on all others must be comparatively slight and superficial. We have known some very worthy and well-informed biblical critics, who, by virtue of having discovered that one was not three, or that the same body could not be in two places at once, would be disposed to treat the whole Council of Trent, with Father Paul at their head, with very little deference, and to consider Leo x. with all his court, as no better than drivellers. Such persons will hint to you, as an additional proof of his genius, that Milton was a non-conformist, and will excuse the faults of Paradise Lost, as Dr. Johnson magnified them, because the author was a republican. By the all-sufficiency of their merits in believing certain truths which have been 'hid from ages,' they are elevated, in their own imagination, to a higher sphere of intellect, and are released from the necessity of pursuing the more ordinary tracks of inquiry. Their faculties are imprisoned in a few favourite dogmas, and they cannot break through the trammels of a sect. Hence we may remark a hardness and setness in the ideas of those who have been brought up in this way, an aversion to those finer and more delicate operations of the intellect, of taste and genius, which require greater flexibility and variety of thought, and do not afford the same opportunity for dogmatical assertion and controversial cabal. The distaste of the Puritans, Quakers, etc. to pictures, music, poetry, and the fine arts in general, may be traced to this source as much as to their affected disdain of them, as not sufficiently spiritual and remote from the gross impurity of sense.[2]

We learn from the interest we take in things, and according to

[1] The Dissenters in this country (if we except the founders of sects, who fall under a class by themselves) have produced only two remarkable men, Priestley and Jonathan Edwards. The work of the latter on the Will is written with as much power of logic, and more in the true spirit of philosophy, than any other metaphysical work in the language. His object throughout is not to perplex the question, but to satisfy his own mind and the reader's. In general, the principle of dissent arises more from want of sympathy and imagination, than from strength of reason. The spirit of contradiction is not the spirit of philosophy.

[2] The modern Quakers come as near the mark in these cases as they can. They do not go to plays, but they are great attenders of spouting-clubs and lectures. They do not frequent concerts, but run after pictures. We do not know exactly how they stand with respect to the circulating libraries. A Quaker poet would be a literary phenomenon.

the number of things in which we take an interest. Our ignorance of the real value of different objects and pursuits, will in general keep pace with our contempt for them. To set out with denying common sense to every one else, is not the way to be wise ourselves; nor shall we be likely to learn much, if we suppose that no one can teach us any thing worth knowing. Again, a contempt for the habits and manners of the world is as prejudicial as a contempt for their opinions. A puritanical abhorrence of every thing that does not fall in with our immediate prejudices and customs, must effectually cut us off, not only from a knowledge of the world and of human nature, but of good and evil, of vice and virtue; at least, if we can credit the assertion of Plato, (which, to some degree, we do), that the knowledge of every thing implies the knowledge of its opposite. 'There is some soul of goodness in things evil.' A most respectable sect among ourselves (we mean the Quakers) have carried this system of negative qualities nearly to perfection. They labour diligently, and with great success, to exclude all ideas from their minds which they might have in common with others. On the principle that evil communications corrupt good manners, they retain a virgin purity of understanding, and laudable ignorance of all liberal arts and sciences; they take every precaution, and keep up a perpetual quarantine against the infection of other people's vices—or virtues; they pass through the world like figures cut out of pasteboard or wood, turning neither to the right nor the left; and their minds are no more affected by the example of the follies, the pursuits, the pleasures, or the passions of mankind, than the clothes which they wear. Their ideas want *airing*; they are the worse for not being used: for fear of soiling them, they keep them folded up and laid by in a sort of mental clothes-press, through the whole of their lives. They take their notions on trust from one generation to another, (like the scanty cut of their coats), and are so wrapped up in these traditional maxims, and so pin their faith on them, that one of the most intelligent of this class of people, not long ago, assured us that 'war was a thing that was going quite out of fashion'! This abstract sort of existence may have its advantages, but it takes away all the ordinary sources of a moral imagination, as well as strength of intellect. Interest is the only link that connects them with the world. We can understand the high enthusiasm and religious devotion of monks and anchorites, who gave up the world and its pleasures to dedicate themselves to a sublime contemplation of a future state. But the sect of the Quakers, who have transplanted the maxims of the desert into manufacturing towns and populous cities, who have converted the solitary cells of the religious orders into counting-houses, their beads

nto ledgers, and keep a regular debtor and creditor account
etween this world and the next, puzzle us mightily! The Dis-
enter is not vain, but conceited: that is, he makes up by his own
ood opinion for the want of the cordial admiration of others. But
his often stands their self-love in so good stead that they need not
nvy their dignified opponents who repose on lawn sleeves and ermine.
The unmerited obloquy and dislike to which they are exposed has
made them cold and reserved in their intercourse with society. The
ame cause will account for the dryness and general homeliness of
heir style. They labour under a sense of the want of public sym-
athy. They pursue truth, for its own sake, into its private recesses
nd obscure corners. They have to dig their way along a narrow
nder-ground passage. It is not their object to shine; they have
one of the usual incentives of vanity, light, airy, and ostentatious.
Archiepiscopal Sees and mitres do not glitter in their distant horizon.
They are not wafted on the wings of fancy, fanned by the breath of
opular applause. The voice of the world, the tide of opinion, is
not with them. They do not therefore aim at *éclat*, at outward
pomp and shew. They have a plain ground to work upon, and they
do not attempt to embellish it with idle ornaments. It would be in
vain to strew the flowers of poetry round the borders of the Unitarian
controversy.

There is one quality common to all sectaries, and that is, a principle
of strong fidelity. They are the safest partisans, and the steadiest
friends. Indeed, they are almost the only people who have any idea
of an abstract attachment either to a cause or to individuals, from a
sense of duty, independently of prosperous or adverse circumstances,
and in spite of opposition.[1]   Z.

ON JOHN BUNCLE

John Buncle is the English *Rabelais*. This is an author with whom,
perhaps, many of our readers are not acquainted, and whom we therefore wish to introduce to their notice. As most of our countrymen
delight in English Generals and in English Admirals, in English
Courtiers and in English Kings, so our great delight is in English
authors.

---

[1] We have made the above observations, not as theological partisans, but as
natural historians. We shall some time or other give the reverse of the picture;
for there are vices inherent in establishments and their thorough-paced adherents,
which well deserve to be distinctly pointed out.

The soul of Francis Rabelais passed into John Amory, the author of *The Life and Adventures of John Buncle*. Both were physicians, and enemies of too much gravity. Their great business was to enjoy life. Rabelais indulges his spirit of sensuality in wine, in dried neats' tongues, in Bologna sausages, in botargos. John Buncle shews the same symptoms of inordinate satisfaction in tea and bread and butter. While Rabelais roared with Friar John and the Monks, John Buncle gossiped with the ladies; and with equal and uncontrolled gaiety. These two authors possessed all the insolence of health, so that their works give a fillip to the constitution; but they carried off the exuberance of their natural spirits in different ways. The title of one of Rabelais' chapters (and the contents answer to the title) is—'How they chirped over their cups.' The title of a corresponding chapter in John Buncle would run thus: 'The author is invited to spend the evening with the divine Miss Hawkins, and goes accordingly, with the delightful conversation that ensued.' Natural philosophers are said to extract sun-beams from ice: our author has performed the same feat upon the cold, quaint subtleties of theology. His constitutional alacrity overcomes every obstacle. He converts the thorns and briars of controversial divinity into a bed of roses. He leads the most refined and virtuous of their sex through the mazes of inextricable problems with the air of a man walking a minuet in a drawing-room; mixes up in the most natural and careless manner the academy of compliments with the rudiments of algebra; or passes with rapturous indifference from the First of St. John and a disquisition on the Logos, to the no less metaphysical doctrines of the principle of self-preservation, or the continuation of the species. *John Buncle* is certainly one of the most singular productions in the language; and herein lies its peculiarity. It is a Unitarian romance; and one in which the soul and body are equally attended to. The hero is a great philosopher, mathematician, anatomist, chemist, philologist, and divine, with a good appetite, the best spirits, and an amorous constitution, who sets out on a series of strange adventures to propagate his philosophy, his divinity, and his species, and meets with a constant succession of accomplished females, adorned with equal beauty, wit, and virtue, who are always ready to discuss all kinds of theoretical and practical points with him. His angels (and all his women are angels) have all taken their degrees in more than one science: love is natural to them. He is sure to find

'A mistress and a saint in every grove.'

Pleasure and business, wisdom and mirth, take their turns with the most agreeable regularity. *A jocis ad seria, in seriis vicissim ad jocos transire.* After a chapter of calculations in fluxions, or on the descent of tongues, the lady and gentleman fall from Platonics to hoydening, in a manner as truly edifying as anything in the scenes of Vanbrugh or Sir George Etherege. No writer ever understood so well the art of relief. The effect is like travelling in Scotland, and coming all of a sudden to a spot of habitable ground. His mode of making love is admirable. He takes it quite easily, and never thinks of a refusal. His success gives him confidence, and his confidence gives him success. For example: in the midst of one of his rambles in the mountains of Cumberland, he unexpectedly comes to an elegant country-seat, where, walking on the lawn with a book in her hand, he sees a most enchanting creature, the owner of the mansion: our hero is on fire, leaps the ha-ha which separates them, presents himself before the lady with an easy but respectful air, begs to know the subject of her meditation, they enter into conversation, mutual explanations take place, a declaration of love is made, and the wedding-day is fixed for the following Tuesday. Our author now leads a life of perfect happiness with his beautiful Miss Noel, in a charming solitude, for a few weeks; till, on his return from one of his rambles in the mountains, he finds her a corpse. He '*sits with his eyes shut for seven days,*' absorbed in silent grief; he then bids adieu to melancholy reflections, not being one of that sect of philosophers who think that 'man was made to mourn,'—takes horse and sets out for the nearest watering-place. As he alights at the first inn on the road, a lady dressed in a rich green riding-habit steps out of a coach, John Buncle hands her into the inn, they drink tea together, they converse, they find an exact harmony of sentiment, a declaration of love follows as a matter of course, and that day week they are married. Death, however, contrives to keep up the ball for him; he marries seven wives in succession, and buries them all. In short, John Buncle's gravity sat upon him with the happiest indifference possible. He danced the hays with religion and morality with the ease of a man of fashion and of pleasure. He was determined to see fair-play between grace and nature, between his immortal and his mortal part, and in case of any difficulty, upon the principle of 'first come, first served,' made sure of the present hour. We sometimes suspect him of a little hypocrisy, but upon a closer inspection, it appears to be only an affectation of hypocrisy. His fine constitution comes to his relief, and floats him over the shoals and quicksands that lie in his way, 'most dolphin-like.' You see him from mere happiness of nature chuckling with inward satisfaction in the midst of his periodical penances, his grave grimaces, his death's-heads, and *memento moris.*

> ——'And there the antic sits
> Mocking his state, and grinning at his pomp.'

As men make use of olives to give a relish to their wine, so John
Buncle made use of philosophy to give a relish to life. He stops in a
ball-room at Harrowgate to moralise on the small number of faces that
appeared there out of those he remembered some years before: all
were gone whom he saw at a still more distant period; but this casts
no damper on his spirits, and he only dances the longer and better for
it. He suffers nothing unpleasant to remain long upon his mind.
He gives, in one place, a miserable description of two emaciated
valetudinarians whom he met at an inn, supping a little mutton-broth
with difficulty, but he immediately contrasts himself with them in
fine relief. 'While I beheld things with astonishment, the servant,'
he says, 'brought in dinner—a pound of rump-steaks and a quart of
green peas, two cuts of bread, a tankard of strong beer, and a pint
of port-wine; *with a fine appetite, I soon despatched my mess, and
over my wine, to help digestion, began to sing the following lines!*'
The astonishment of the two strangers was now as great as his own
had been.

We wish to enable our readers to judge for themselves of the style
of our whimsical moralist, but are at a loss what to chuse—whether
his account of his man O'Fin; or of his friend Tom Fleming; or of
his being chased over the mountains by robbers, 'whisking before them
like the wind away,' as if it were high sport; or his address to the
Sun, which is an admirable piece of serious eloquence; or his character
of six Irish gentlemen, Mr. Gollogher, Mr. Gallaspy, Mr. Dunkley,
Mr. Makins, Mr. Monaghan, and Mr. O'Keefe, the last 'descended
from the Irish kings, and first cousin to the great O'Keefe, who was
buried not long ago in Westminster Abbey.' He professes to give
an account of these Irish gentlemen, 'for the honour of Ireland, and
as they were curiosities of the human kind.' Curiosities, indeed, but
not so great as their historian!

'Mr. Makins was the only one of the set who was not tall and
handsome. He was a very low, thin man, not four feet high,
and had but one eye, with which he squinted most shockingly. But
as he was matchless on the fiddle, sung well, and chatted agreeably,
he was a favourite with the ladies. They preferred ugly Makins
(as he was called) to many very handsome men. He was a
Unitarian.'

'Mr. Monaghan was an honest and charming fellow. This gentle-
man and Mr. Dunkley married ladies they fell in love with at
Harrowgate Wells; Dunkley had the fair Alcmena, Miss Cox of
Northumberland; and Monaghan, Antiope with haughty charms,
Miss Pearson of Cumberland. They lived very happy many years,
and their children, I hear, are settled in Ireland.'

ON JOHN BUNCLE

Gentle reader, here is the character of Mr. Gallaspy:

'Gallaspy was the tallest and strongest man I have ever seen, well made, and very handsome: had wit and abilities, sung well, and talked with great sweetness and fluency, but was so extremely wicked that it were better for him if he had been a natural fool. By his vast strength and activity, his riches and eloquence, few things could withstand him. He was the most profane swearer I have known: fought every thing, whored every thing, and drank seven in hand: that is, seven glasses so placed between the fingers of his right hand, that, in drinking, the liquor fell into the next glasses, and thereby he drank out of the first glass seven glasses at once. This was a common thing, I find from a book in my possession, in the reign of Charles II., in the madness that followed the restoration of that profligate and worthless prince.[1] But this gentleman was the only man I ever saw who could or would attempt to do it; and he made but one gulp of whatever he drank He did not swallow a fluid like other people, but if it was a quart, poured it in as from pitcher to pitcher. When he smoked tobacco, he always blew two pipes at once, one at each corner of his mouth, and threw the smoke out at both his nostrils. He had killed two men in duels before I left Ireland, and would have been hanged, but that it was his good fortune to be tried before a judge who never let any man suffer for killing another in this manner. (This was the late Sir John St. Leger.) He debauched all the women he could, and many whom he could not corrupt. . . .' The rest of this passage would, we fear, be too rich for the Round Table, as we cannot insert it, in the manner of Mr. Buncle, in a sandwich of theology. Suffice it to say, that the candour is greater than the candour of Voltaire's *Candide*, and the modesty equal to Colley Cibber's.

To his friend Mr. Gollogher, he consecrates the following irresistible *petit souvenir*:

'He might, if he had pleased, have married any one of the most illustrious and richest women in the kingdom; but he had an aversion to matrimony, and could not bear the thoughts of a wife. Love and a bottle were his taste: he was, however, the most honourable of men in his amours, and never abandoned any woman in distress, as too many men of fortune do, when they have gratified desire. All the distressed were ever sharers in Mr. Gollogher's fine estate, and especially the girls he had taken to his breast. He provided happily for them all, and left nineteen daughters he had by several women, a

---

[1] Is all this a rhodomontade, or literal matter of fact, not credible in these degenerate days?

*c 65

thousand pounds each. This was acting with a temper worthy of a man ; *and to the memory of the benevolent Tom Gollogher, I devote this memorandum.*'

Lest our readers should form rather a coarse idea of our author from the foregoing passages, we will conclude with another list of friends in a different style :

'The Conniving-house (as the gentlemen of Trinity called it in my time, and long after) was a little public-house, kept by Jack Macklean, about a quarter of a mile beyond Rings-end, on the top of the beach, within a few yards of the sea. Here we used to have the finest fish at all times ; and, in the season, green peas, and all the most excellent vegetables. The ale here was always extraordinary, and everything the best ; which, with its delightful situation, rendered it a delightful place of a summer's evening. Many a delightful evening have I passed in this pretty thatched house with the famous Larry Grogan, who played on the bagpipes extremely well ; dear Jack Lattin, matchless on the fiddle, and the most agreeable of companions ; that ever-charming young fellow, Jack Wall, the most worthy, the most ingenious, the most engaging of men, the son of Counsellor Maurice Wall ; and many other delightful fellows, who went in the days of their youth to the shades of eternity. When I think of them and their evening songs—' *We will go to Johnny Macklean's, to try if his ale be good or no,*' etc. and that years and infirmities begin to oppress me—What is life ! '

We have another English author, very different from the last mentioned one, but equal in *naïveté*, and in the perfect display of personal character ; we mean Isaac Walton, who wrote the *Complete Angler*. That well-known work has an extreme simplicity, and an extreme interest, arising out of its very simplicity. In the description of a fishing tackle you perceive the piety and humanity of the author's mind. This is the best pastoral in the language, not excepting Pope's or Philips's. We doubt whether Sannazarius's *Piscatory Eclogues* are equal to the scenes described by Walton on the banks of the River Lea. He gives the feeling of the open air. We walk with him along the dusty roadside, or repose on the banks of the river under a shady tree, and in watching for the finny prey, imbibe what he beautifully calls 'the patience and simplicity of poor, honest fishermen.' We accompany them to their inn at night, and partake of their simple but delicious fare, while Maud, the pretty milkmaid, at her mother's desire, sings the classical ditties of Sir Walter Raleigh. Good cheer is not neglected in this work, any more than in *John Buncle*, or any other history which sets a proper value on the good things of life. The prints in the *Complete Angler* give an additional reality and

interest to the scenes it describes. While Tottenham Cross shall
stand, and longer, thy work, amiable and happy old man. shall last ! [1]

W. H.

ON THE CAUSES OF METHODISM

THE first Methodist on record was David. He was the first eminent
person we read of, who made a regular compromise between religion
and morality, between faith and good works. After any trifling
peccadillo in point of conduct, as a murder, adultery, perjury, or the
like, he ascended with his harp into some high tower of his palace ;
and having chaunted, in a solemn strain of poetical inspiration, the
praises of piety and virtue, made his peace with heaven and his own
conscience. This extraordinary genius, in the midst of his personal
errors, retained the same lofty abstract enthusiasm for the favourite
objects of his contemplation ; the character of the poet and the
prophet remained unimpaired by the vices of the man—

> 'Pure in the last recesses of the mind' ;

and the best test of the soundness of his principles and the elevation of
his sentiments, is, that they were proof against his practice. The
Gnostics afterwards maintained, that it was no matter what a man's
actions were, so that his understanding was not debauched by them—
so that his opinions continued uncontaminated, and *his heart,* as the
phrase is, *right towards God.* Strictly speaking, this sect (whatever
name it might go by) is as old as human nature itself; for it has
existed ever since there was a contradiction between the passions
and the understanding—between what we are, and what we desire
to be. The principle of Methodism is nearly allied to hypocrisy,
and almost unavoidably slides into it : yet it is not the same thing ;
for we can hardly call any one a hypocrite, however much at variance
his professions and his actions, who really wishes to be what he would
be thought.

The Jewish bard, whom we have placed at the head of this class
of devotees, was of a sanguine and robust temperament. Whether

---

[1] One of the most interesting traits of the amiable simplicity of Walton, is the
circumstance of his friendship for Cotton, one of the 'swash-bucklers' of the age.
Dr. Johnson said there were only three works which the reader was sorry to come
to the end of, *Don Quixote, Robinson Crusoe,* and the *Pilgrim's Progress.* Perhaps
Walton's *Angler* might be added to the number.

he chose 'to sinner it or saint it,' he did both most royally, with a fulness of gusto, and carried off his penances and his *faux-pas* in a style of oriental grandeur. This is by no means the character of his followers among ourselves, who are a most pitiful set. They may rather be considered as a collection of religious invalids; as the refuse of all that is weak and unsound in body and mind. To speak of them as they deserve, they are not well in the flesh, and therefore they take refuge in the spirit; they are not comfortable here, and they seek for the life to come; they are deficient in steadiness of moral principle, and they trust to grace to make up the deficiency; they are dull and gross in apprehension, and therefore they are glad to substitute faith for reason, and to plunge in the dark, under the supposed sanction of superior wisdom, into every species of mystery and jargon. This is the history of Methodism, which may be defined to be religion with its slobbering-bib and go-cart. It is a bastard kind of Popery, stripped of its painted pomp and outward ornaments, and reduced to a state of pauperism. 'The whole need not a physician.' Popery owed its success to its constant appeal to the senses and to the weaknesses of mankind. The Church of England deprives the Methodists of the pride and pomp of the Romish Church; but it has left open to them the appeal to the indolence, the ignorance, and the vices of the people; and the secret of the success of the Catholic faith and evangelical preaching is the same—both are a religion by proxy. What the one did by auricular confession, absolution, penance, pictures, and crucifixes, the other does, even more compendiously, by grace, election, faith without works, and words without meaning.

In the first place, the same reason makes a man a religious enthusiast that makes a man an enthusiast in any other way, an uncomfortable mind in an uncomfortable body. Poets, authors, and artists in general, have been ridiculed for a pining, puritanical, poverty-struck appearance, which has been attributed to their real poverty. But it would perhaps be nearer the truth to say, that their being poets, artists, etc. has been owing to their original poverty of spirit and weakness of constitution. As a general rule, those who are dissatisfied with themselves, will seek to go out of themselves into an ideal world. Persons in strong health and spirits, who take plenty of air and exercise, who are 'in favour with their stars,' and have a thorough relish of the good things of this life, seldom devote themselves in despair to religion or the Muses. Sedentary, nervous, hypochondriacal people, on the contrary, are forced, for want of an appetite for the real and substantial, to look out for a more airy food and speculative comforts. 'Conceit in weakest bodies strongest works.'

ON THE CAUSES OF METHODISM

A journeyman sign-painter, whose lungs have imbibed too great a quantity of the effluvia of white-lead, will be seized with a fantastic passion for the stage; and *Mawworm*, tired of standing behind his counter, was eager to mount a tub, mistaking the suppression of his animal spirits for the communication of the Holy Ghost![1] If you live near a chapel or tabernacle in London, you may almost always tell, from physiognomical signs, which of the passengers will turn the corner to go there. We were once staying in a remote place in the country, where a chapel of this sort had been erected by the force of missionary zeal; and one morning, we perceived a long procession of people coming from the next town to the consecration of this same chapel. Never was there such a set of scarecrows. Melancholy tailors, consumptive hair-dressers, squinting coblers, women with child or in the ague, made up the forlorn hope of the pious cavalcade. The pastor of this half-starved flock, we confess, came riding after, with a more goodly aspect, as if he had 'with sound of bell been knolled to church, and sat at good men's feasts.' He had in truth lately married a thriving widow, and been pampered with hot suppers to strengthen the flesh and the spirit. We have seen several of these 'round fat oily men of God,

> "'That shone all glittering with ungodly dew.'"

They grow sleek and corpulent by getting into better pasture, but they do not appear healthy. They retain the original sin of their constitution, an atrabilious taint in their complexion, and do not put a right-down, hearty, honest, good-looking face upon the matter, like the regular clergy.

Again, Methodism, by its leading doctrines, has a peculiar charm for all those, who have an equal facility in sinning and repenting,—in whom the spirit is willing but the flesh is weak,—who have neither fortitude to withstand temptation, nor to silence the admonitions of conscience,—who like the theory of religion better than the practice, and who are willing to indulge in all the raptures of speculative devotion, without being tied down to the dull, literal performance of its duties. There is a general propensity in the human mind (even in the most vicious) to pay virtue a distant homage; and this desire is only checked by the fear of condemning ourselves by our own acknowledgments. What an admirable expedient then in 'that

[1] Oxberry's manner of acting this character is a very edifying comment on the text: he flings his arms about, like those of a figure pulled by strings, and seems actuated by a pure spirit of infatuation, as if one blast of folly had taken possession of his whole frame,

'And filled up all the mighty void of sense.'

burning and shining light,' Whitefield, and his associates, to make this very disposition to admire and extol the highest patterns of goodness, a substitute for, instead of an obligation to, the practice of virtue, to allow us to be quit for ''.he vice that most easily besets us,' by canting lamentations over the depravity of human nature, and loud hosannahs to the Son of David! How comfortably this doctrine must sit on all those who are loth to give up old habits of vice, or are just tasting the sweets of new ones; on the withered hag who looks back on a life of dissipation, or the young devotee who looks forward to a life of pleasure; the knavish tradesman retiring from business or entering on it; the battered rake; the sneaking politician, who trims between his place and his conscience, wriggling between heaven and earth, a miserable two-legged creature, with sanctified face and fawning gestures; the maudling sentimentalist, the religious prostitute, the disinterested poet-laureate, the humane war-contractor, or the Society for the Suppression of Vice! This scheme happily turns morality into a sinecure, takes all the practical drudgery and trouble off your hands, 'and sweet religion makes a rhapsody of words.' Its proselytes besiege the gates of heaven, like sturdy beggars about the doors of the great, lie and bask in the sunshine of divine grace, sigh and groan and bawl out for mercy, expose their sores and blotches to excite commiseration, and cover the deformities of their nature with a garb of borrowed righteousness!

The jargon and nonsense which are so studiously inculcated in the system, are another powerful recommendation of it to the vulgar. It does not impose any tax upon the understanding. Its essence is to be unintelligible. It is *carte blanche* for ignorance and folly! Those, 'numbers without number,' who are either unable or unwilling to think connectedly or rationally on any subject, are at once released from every obligation of the kind, by being told that faith and reason are opposed to one another, and the greater the impossibility, the greater the merit of the faith. A set of phrases which, without conveying any distinct idea, excite our wonder, our fear, our curiosity and desires, which let loose the imagination of the gaping multitude, and confound and baffle common sense, are the common stock-in-trade of the conventicle They never stop for the distinctions of the understanding, and have thus got the start of other sects, who are so hemmed in with the necessity of giving reasons for their opinions, that they cannot get on at all. 'Vital Christianity' is no other than an attempt to lower all religion to the level of the capacities of the lowest of the people. One of their favourite places of worship combines the noise and turbulence of a drunken brawl at an ale-house, with the indecencies of a bagnio. They strive to gain a vertigo by abandoning their reason, and give themselves up to the intoxications of a distempered zeal, that

> ' Dissolves them into ecstasies,
>   And brings all heaven before their eyes.'

Religion, without superstition, will not answer the purposes of fanaticism, and we may safely say, that almost every sect of Christianity is a perversion of its essence, to accommodate it to the prejudices of the world. The Methodists have greased the boots of the Presbyterians, and they have done well. While the latter are weighing their doubts and scruples to the division of a hair, and shivering on the narrow brink that divides philosophy from religion, the former plunge without remorse into hell-flames, soar on the wings of divine love, are carried away with the motions of the spirit, are lost in the abyss of unfathomable mysteries,—election, reprobation, predestination,—and revel in a sea of boundless nonsense. It is a gulf that swallows up every thing. The cold, the calculating, and the dry, are not to the taste of the many ; religion is an anticipation of the preternatural world, and it in general requires preternatural excitements to keep it alive. If it takes a definite consistent form, it loses its interest : to produce its effect it must come in the shape of an apparition. Our quacks treat grown people as the nurses do children ;— terrify them with what they have no idea of, or take them to a puppet-show.   W. H.

THE MIDSUMMER NIGHT'S DREAM

The Examiner.   *January 21, 1816.*

WE hope we have not been accessory to murder, in recommending a delightful poem to be converted into a dull pantomime; for such is the fate of the *Midsummer Night's Dream.* We have found to our cost, once for all, that the regions of fancy and the boards of Covent-Garden are not the same thing. All that is fine in the play, was lost in the representation. The spirit was evaporated, the genius was fled; but the spectacle was fine: it was that which saved the play. Oh, ye scene-shifters, ye scene-painters, ye machinists and dressmakers, ye manufacturers of moon and stars that give no light, ye musical composers, ye men in the orchestra, fiddlers and trumpeters and players on the double drum and loud bassoon, rejoice! This is your triumph; it is not ours: and ye full-grown, well-fed, substantial, real fairies,

Messieurs Treby, and Truman, and Atkins, and Misses Matthews, Carew, Burrell, and Mac Alpine, we shall remember you: we shall believe no more in the existence of your fantastic tribe. Flute the bellows-mender, Snug the joiner, Starveling the tailor, farewell! you have lost the charm of your names; but thou, Nic Bottom, thou valiant Bottom, what shall we say to thee? Thou didst console us much; thou didst perform a good part well; thou didst top the part of Bottom the weaver! He comes out of thy hands as clean and clever a fellow as ever. Thou art a person of exquisite whim and humour; and thou didst hector over thy companions well, and fall down flat before the Duke, like other bullies, well; and thou didst sing the song of the Black Ousel well; but chief, thou didst noddle thy ass's head, which had been put upon thee, well; and didst seem to say, significantly, to thy new attendants, Peaseblossom, Cobweb, Moth, and Mustard-seed, 'Gentlemen, I can present you equally to my friends, and to my enemies!' [1]

All that was good in this piece (except the scenery) was Mr. Liston's Bottom, which was an admirable and judicious piece of acting. Mr. Conway was Theseus. Who would ever have taken this gentleman for the friend and companion of Hercules? Miss Stephens played the part of Hermia, and sang several songs very delightfully, which however by no means assisted the progress or interest of the story. Miss Foote played Helena. She is a very sweet girl, and not at all a bad actress; yet did any one feel or even hear her address to Hermia? To shew how far asunder the closet and the stage are, we give it here once more entire:

> 'Injurious Hermia, most ungrateful maid,
> Have you conspired, have you with these contriv'd
> To bait me with this foul derision?
> Is all the counsel that we two have shar'd,
> The sisters' vows, the hours that we have spent,
> When we have chid the hasty-footed time
> For parting us—Oh! and is all forgot?
> All school days' friendship, childhood innocence?
> We, Hermia, like two artificial Gods,
> Created with our needles both one flower,
> Both on one sampler, sitting on one cushion;
> Both warbling of one song, both in one key;
> As if our hands, our sides, voices and minds,
> Had been incorporate. So we grew together,
> Like to a double cherry, seeming parted,
> But yet an union in partition.

---

[1] What Louis XVIII. said to his new National Guards.

> And will you rend our ancient love asunder,
> And join with men in scorning your poor friend?
> It is not friendly, 'tis not maidenly:
> Our sex as well as I may chide you for it,
> Though I alone do feel the injury.'

In turning to Shakespear to look for this passage, the book opened at the Midsummer Night's Dream, the title of which half gave us back our old feeling; and in reading this one speech twice over, we have completely forgot all the noise we have heard and the sights we have seen. Poetry and the stage do not agree together. The attempt to reconcile them fails not only of effect, but of decorum. The *ideal* has no place upon the stage, which is a picture without perspective; every thing there is in the foreground. That which is merely an airy shape, a dream, a passing thought, immediately becomes an unmanageable reality. Where all is left to the imagination, every circumstance has an equal chance of being kept in mind, and tells according to the mixed impression of all that has been suggested. But the imagination cannot sufficiently qualify the impressions of the senses. Any offence given to the eye is not to be got rid of by explanation. Thus Bottom's head in the play is a fantastic illusion, produced by magic spells: on the stage it is an ass's head, and nothing more; certainly a very strange costume for a gentleman to appear in. Fancy cannot be represented any more than a simile can be painted; and it is as idle to attempt it as to personate Wall or Moonshine. Fairies are not incredible, but fairies six feet high are so. Monsters are not shocking, if they are seen at a proper distance. When ghosts appear in mid-day, when apparitions stalk along Cheapside, then may the Midsummer Night's Dream be represented at Covent-Garden or at Drury-Lane; for we hear, that it is to be brought out there also, and that we have to undergo another crucifixion.

Mrs. Faucit played the part of Titania very well, but for one circumstance—that she is a woman. The only glimpse which we caught of the possibility of acting the imaginary scenes properly, was from the little girl who dances before the fairies (we do not know her name), which seemed to shew that the whole might be carried off in the same manner—by a miracle.

THE ROUND TABLE

THEATRICAL DEBUTS

The Examiner.   *October 20, 1816.*

THERE have been two theatrical or operatic debuts, to which we are in arrears, and of which we must say a word—Miss Mori's Rosetta in *Love in a Village*, at Covent-Garden, and Miss Keppel's Polly in the *Beggar's Opera*, at Drury-Lane. Both of them appeared to us to be indifferent. Miss Mori is by much the best singer of the two, but there is something exceedingly unprepossessing and hard both in her voice and manner. She sings without the least feeling, or lurking consciousness that such a thing is required in a singer. The notes proceed from her mouth as mechanically, as *unmitigated* by the sentiment, as if they came from the sharp hautboy or grating bassoon. We do not mean that her voice is disagreeable in itself, but it wants softness and sweetness of modulation. The words of the songs neither seem to tremble on her lips, nor play around her heart. Miss Mori did not look the character. Rosetta is to be sure a waiting-maid, but then she is also a young lady in disguise. There was no appearance of the *incognita* in Miss Mori. She seemed in downright earnest, like one of the country girls who come to be hired at the statute-fair. She was quite insensible of her situation, and came forward to prove herself a fine singer, as one of her fellow-servants might have done to answer to a charge of having stolen something. We never saw a *debutante* more at ease with the audience: we suppose she has played in the country. Miss Matthews, who is a good-natured girl, and wished to *patronize* her on so delicate an emergency, presently found there was no occasion for her services, and withdrew from the attempt with some trepidation.

If Miss Mori did not enchant us by her incomprehensible want of sensibility, neither did Miss Keppel by the affectation of it. Sensibility is a very pretty thing, but it will not do to make a plaything of, at least in public. It is not enough that an actress tries to atone for defects by throwing herself on the indulgence of the audience:—their eyes and ears must be satisfied, as well as their self-love. Miss Keppel acts with very little grace, and sings very much out of tune. There were some attempts made to prejudice the audience against this young lady before she appeared: but they only had the effect which they deserved, of procuring a more flattering reception than she would otherwise have met with: but we do not think she will ever become a favourite with the town.

ON THE BEGGAR'S OPERA

ON THE BEGGAR'S OPERA

WE have begun this Essay on a very coarse sheet of damaged foolscap, and we find that we are going to write it, whether for the sake of contrast, or from having a very fine pen, in a remarkably nice hand. Something of a similar process seems to have taken place in Gay's mind, when he composed his *Beggar's Opera*. He chose a very unpromising ground to work upon, and he has prided himself in adorning it with all the graces, the precision and brilliancy of style. It is a vulgar error to call this a vulgar play. So far from it, that we do not scruple to declare our opinion that it is one of the most refined productions in the language. The elegance of the composition is in exact proportion to the coarseness of the materials: by 'happy alchemy of mind,' the author has extracted an essence of refinement from the dregs of human life, and turns its very dross into gold. The scenes, characters, and incidents are, in themselves, of the lowest and most disgusting kind: but, by the sentiments and reflections which are put into the mouths of highwaymen, turnkeys, their mistresses, wives, or daughters, he has converted this motley group into a set of fine gentlemen and ladies, satirists and philosophers. He has also effected this transformation without once violating probability, or 'o'erstepping the modesty of nature.' In fact Gay has turned the tables on the critics ; and by the assumed licence of the mock-heroic style, has enabled himself to *do justice to nature*, that is, to give all the force, truth, and locality of real feeling to the thoughts and expressions, without being called to the bar of false taste and affected delicacy. The extreme beauty and feeling of the song, 'Woman is like the fair flower in its lustre,' is only equalled by its characteristic propriety and *naïveté*. It may be said that this is taken from Tibullus ; but there is nothing about Covent Garden in Tibullus. *Polly* describes her lover going to the gallows with the same touching simplicity, and with all the natural fondness of a young girl in her circumstances, who sees in his approaching catastrophe nothing but the misfortunes and the personal accomplishments of the object of her affections. 'I see him sweeter than the nosegay in his hand : the admiring crowd lament that so lovely a youth should come to an untimely end :—even butchers weep, and Jack Ketch refuses his fee rather than consent to tie the fatal knot.' The preservation of the character and costume is complete. It has been said by a great authority, 'There is some soul of goodness in things evil': and the *Beggar's Opera* is a goodnatured but instructive comment on this text. The poet has thrown all the gaiety and sunshine of the imagination, all the intoxication of pleasure, and the vanity of despair, round th short-lived existence of his heroes; while *Peachum* and *Lockitt* ar seen in the back-ground, parcelling out their months and weeks betwee them. The general view exhibited of human life, is of the mos masterly and abstracted kind. The author has, with great felicity brought out the good qualities and interesting emotions almost insepar able from the lowest conditions; and with the same penetrating glanc has detected the disguises which rank and circumstances lend t exalted vice. Every line in this sterling comedy sparkles with wit and is fraught with the keenest sarcasm. The very wit, however takes off from the offensiveness of the satire; and we have seen grea statesmen, very great statesmen, heartily enjoying the joke, laughin most immoderately at the compliments paid to them as not much worse than pickpockets and cut-throats in a different line of life, and pleased, as it were, to see themselves humanised by some sort o fellowship with their kind. Indeed, it may be said that the moral of the piece is to show the *vulgarity* of vice; and that the same violations of integrity and decorum, the same habitual sophistry in palliating their want of principle, are common to the great and powerful, with the lowest and most contemptible of the species. What can be more convincing than the arguments used by these would-be politicians, to shew that in hypocrisy, selfishness, and treachery, they do not come up to many of their betters? The exclamation of *Mrs. Peachum*, when her daughter marries *Macheath*, 'Hussey, hussey, you will be as ill used, and as much neglected, as if you had married a lord,' is worth all Miss Hannah More's laboured invectives on the laxity of the manners of high life! [1]   W. H.

[1] The late ingenious Baron Grimm, of acute critical memory, was up to the merit of the *Beggar's Opera*. In his Correspondence, he says, 'If it be true that the nearer a writer is to Nature, the more certain he is of pleasing, it must be allowed that the English, in their dramatic pieces, have greatly the advantage over us. There reigns in them an inestimable tone of nature, which the timidity of our taste has banished from French pieces. M. Patu has just published, in two volumes, *A selection of smaller dramatic pieces, translated from the English,* which will eminently support what I have advanced. The principal one among this selection is the celebrated *Beggar's Opera* of Gay, which has had such an amazing run in England. We are here in the very worst company imaginable; the *Dramatis Personæ* are robbers, pickpockets, gaolers, prostitutes, and the like; yet we are highly amused, and in no haste to quit them; and why? Because there is nothing in the world more original or more natural. There is no occasion to compare our most celebrated comic operas with this, to see how far we are removed from truth and nature, and this is the reason that, notwithstanding our wit, we are almost always flat and insipid. Two faults are generally committed by our writers, which they seem incapable of avoiding. They think they have done wonders if they have only faithfully copied the dictionaries of the personages they bring upon the stage, forgetting that the great art is to chuse the moments of character and passion in

ON PATRIOTISM

ON PATRIOTISM.—A FRAGMENT

PATRIOTISM, in modern times, and in great states, is and must be the creature of reason and reflection, rather than the offspring of physical or local attachment. Our country is a complex, abstract existence, recognised only by the understanding. It is an immense riddle, containing numberless modifications of reason and prejudice, of thought and passion. Patriotism is not, in a strict or exclusive sense, a natural or personal affection, but a law of our rational and moral nature, strengthened and determined by particular circumstances and associations, but not born of them, nor wholly nourished by them. It is not possible that we should have an individual attachment to sixteen millions of men, any more than to sixty millions. We cannot be *habitually* attached to places we never saw, and people we never heard of. Is not the name of Englishman a general term, as well as that of man? How many varieties does it not combine within it? Are the opposite extremities of the globe our native place, because they are a part of that geographical and political denomination, our country? Does natural affection expand in circles of latitude and longitude? What personal or instinctive sympathy has the English peasant with the African slave-driver, or East Indian Nabob? Some of our wretched bunglers in metaphysics would fain persuade us to discard all general humanity, and all sense of abstract justice, as a violation of natural affection, and yet do not see that the love of our country itself is in the list of our general affections. The common notions of patriotism are transmitted down to us from the savage tribes, where the fate and condition of all was the same, or from the states of Greece and Rome, where the country of the citizen was the town in which he was born. Where this is no longer the case,— where our country is no longer contained within the narrow circle of the same walls,—where we can no longer behold its glimmering horizon from the top of our native mountains—beyond these limits, it is not a natural but an artificial idea, and our love of it either a deliberate dictate of reason, or a cant term. It was said by an acute observer, and eloquent writer (Rousseau) that the love of mankind

those who are to speak, since it is those moments alone that render them interesting. For want of this discrimination, the piece necessarily sinks into insipidity and monotony. Why do almost all M. Vade's pieces fatigue the audience to death? Because all his characters speak the same language; because each is a perfect resemblance of the other. Instead of this, in the *Beggar's Opera*, among eight or ten girls of the town, each has her separate character, her peculiar traits, her peculiar modes of expression, which give her a marked distinction from her companions.'—Vol. i p. 185.

was nothing but the love of justice: the same might be said, with considerable truth, of the love of our country. It is little more than another name for the love of liberty, of independence, of peace, and social happiness. We do not say that other indirect and collateral circumstances do not go to the superstructure of this sentiment (as language,[1] literature, manners, national customs), but this is the broad and firm basis.

ON BEAUTY

IT is about sixty years ago that Sir Joshua Reynolds, in three papers which he wrote in the *Idler*, advanced the notion, which has prevailed very much ever since, that Beauty was entirely dependent on custom, or on the conformity of objects to a given standard. Now, we could never persuade ourselves that custom, or the association of ideas, though a very powerful, was the only principle of the preference which the mind gives to certain objects over others. Novelty is surely one source of pleasure; otherwise we cannot account for the well-known epigram, beginning—

'Two happy things in marriage are allowed,' etc.

Nor can we help thinking, that, besides custom, or the conformity of certain objects to others of the same general class, there is also a certain conformity of objects to themselves, a symmetry of parts, a principle of proportion, gradation, harmony (call it what you will), which makes certain things naturally pleasing or beautiful, and the want of it the contrary.

We will not pretend to define what Beauty is, after so many learned authors have failed; but we shall attempt to give some examples of what constitutes it, to shew that it is in some way inherent in the object, and that if custom is a second nature, there is another nature which ranks before it. Indeed, the idea that all pleasure and pain depend on the association of ideas is manifestly absurd: there must be something in itself pleasurable or painful, before it could become possible for the feelings of pleasure or pain to be transferred by association from one object to another.

Regular features are generally accounted handsome; but regular features are those, the outlines of which answer most nearly to each other, or undergo the fewest abrupt changes. We shall attempt to explain this idea by a reference to the Greek and African face; the

[1] He who speaks two languages has no country. The French, when they made their language the common language of the Courts of Europe, gained more than by all their subsequent conquests.

first of which is beautiful, because it is made up of lines corresponding with or melting into each other: the last is not so, because it is made up almost entirely of contradictory lines and sharp angular projections.

The general principle of the difference between the two heads is this: the forehead of the Greek is square and upright, and, as it were, overhangs the rest of the face, except the nose, which is a continuation of it almost in an even line. In the Negro or African, the tip of the nose is the most projecting part of the face; and from that point the features retreat back, both upwards towards the forehead, and downwards to the chin. This last form is an approximation to the shape of the head of the animal, as the former bears the strongest stamp of humanity.

The Grecian nose is regular, the African irregular. In other words, the Grecian nose seen in profile forms nearly a straight line with the forehead, and falls into the upper lip by two curves, which balance one another: seen in front, the two sides are nearly parallel to each other, and the nostrils and lower part form regular curves, answering to one another, and to the contours of the mouth. On the contrary, the African pug-nose is more 'like an ace of clubs.' Whichever way you look at it, it presents the appearance of a triangle. It is narrow, and drawn to a point at top, broad and flat at bottom. The point is peaked, and recedes abruptly to the level of the forehead or the mouth, and the nostrils are as if they were drawn up with hooks towards each other. All the lines cross each other at sharp angles. The forehead of the Greeks is flat and square, till it is rounded at the temples; the African forehead, like the ape's, falls back towards the top, and spreads out at the sides, so as to form an angle with the cheek-bones. The eyebrows of the Greeks are either straight, so as to sustain the lower part of the tablet of the forehead, or gently arched, so as to form the outer circle of the curves of the eyelids. The form of the eyes gives all the appearance of orbs, full, swelling, and involved within each other; the African eyes are flat, narrow at the corners, in the shape of a tortoise, and the eyebrows fly off slantwise to the sides of the forehead. The idea of the superiority of the Greek face in this respect is admirably expressed in Spenser's description of Belphœbe:

> ' Her ivory forehead, full of bounty brave,
>   Like a broad table did itself dispread,
>   For love therein his triumphs to engrave,
>   And write the battles of his great Godhead.
>
>   .   .   .
>
>   Upon her eyelids many Graces sat
>   Under the shadow of her even brows.'

The head of the girl in the *Transfiguration* (which Raphael took from the *Niobe*) has the same correspondence and exquisite involution of the outline of the forehead, the eyebrows, and the eyes (circle within circle) which we here speak of. Every part of that delightful head is blended together, and every sharp projection moulded and softened down, with the feeling of a sculptor, or as if nothing should be left to offend the *touch* as well as eye. Again, the Greek mouth is small, and little wider than the lower part of the nose: the lips form waving lines, nearly answering to each other; the African mouth is twice as wide as the nose, projects in front, and falls back towards the ears—is sharp and triangular, and consists of one protruding and one distended lip. The chin of the Greek face is round and indented, curled in, forming a fine oval with the outline of the cheeks, which resemble the two halves of a plane parallel with the forehead, and rounded off like it. The Negro chin falls inwards like a dewlap, is nearly bisected in the middle, flat at bottom, and joined abruptly to the rest of the face, the whole contour of which is made up of jagged cross-grained lines. The African physiognomy appears, indeed, splitting in pieces, starting out in every oblique direction, and marked by the most sudden and violent changes throughout: the whole of the Grecian face blends with itself in a state of the utmost harmony and repose.[1] There is a harmony of expression as well as a symmetry of form. We sometimes see a face melting into beauty by the force of sentiment—an eye that, in its liquid mazes, for ever expanding and for ever retiring within itself, draws the soul after it, and tempts the rash beholder to his fate. This is, perhaps, what Werter meant, when he says of Charlotte, 'Her full dark eyes are ever before me, like a sea, like a precipice.' The historical in expression is the consistent and harmonious,—whatever in thought or feeling communicates the same movement, whether voluptuous or impassioned, to all the parts of the face, the mouth, the eyes, the forehead, and shews that they are all actuated by the same spirit. For this reason it has been observed, that all intellectual and impassioned faces are historical,—the heads of philosophers, poets, lovers, and madmen.

Motion is beautiful as it implies either continuity or gradual change.

---

[1] There is, however, in the African physiognomy a grandeur and a force, arising from this uniform character of violence and abruptness. It is consistent with itself throughout. Entire deformity can only be found where the features have not only no symmetry or softness in themselves, but have no connection with one another, presenting every variety of wretchedness, and a jumble of all sorts of defects, such as we see in Hogarth or in the streets of London; for instance, a large bottle-nose, with a small mouth twisted awry.

ON BEAUTY

The motion of a hawk is beautiful, either returning in endless circles with suspended wings, or darting right forward in one level line upon its prey. We have, when boys, often watched the glittering down of the thistle, at first scarcely rising above the ground, and then, mingling with the gale, borne into the upper sky with varying fantastic motion. How delightful, how beautiful! All motion is beautiful that is not contradictory to itself,—that is free from sudden jerks and shocks,—that is either sustained by the same impulse, or gradually reconciles different impulses together. Swans resting on the calm bosom of a lake, in which their image is reflected, or moved up and down with the heaving of the waves, though by this the double image is disturbed, are equally beautiful. Homer describes Mercury as flinging himself from the top of Olympus, and skimming the surface of the ocean. This is lost in Pope's translation, who suspends him in the incumbent air. The beauty of the original image consists in the idea which it conveys of smooth, uninterrupted speed, of the evasion of every let or obstacle to the progress of the God.[1] Awkwardness is occasioned by a difficulty in moving, or by disjointed

[1] The following version, communicated by a classical friend, is exact and elegant :

> ' He said ; and strait the herald Argicide
> Beneath his feet his winged sandals tied,
> Immortal, golden, that his flight could bear
> O'er seas and lands, like waftage of the air.
> His rod too, that can close the eyes of men
> In balmy sleep, and open them again,
> He took, and holding it in hand, went flying :
> Till, from Pieria's top the sea descrying,
> Down to it sheer he dropp'd ; and scour'd away
> Like the wild gull, that, fishing o'er the bay,
> Flaps on, with pinions dipping in the brine ;—
> So went on the far sea the shape divine.'
>
> *Odyssey*, book v.

> ——' That was Arion crown'd :—
> So went he playing on the wat'ry plain.'
>
> *Faerie Queen.*

There is a striking description in Mr. Burke's Reflections of the late Queen of France, whose charms had left their poison in the heart of this Irish orator and patriot, and set the world in a ferment sixteen years afterwards. ' And surely never lighted on this orb, which she hardly seemed to touch, a more delightful vision.' The idea is in Don Quixote, where the Duenna speaks of the air with which the Duchess ' treads, or rather seems to disdain the ground she walks on.' We have heard the same account of the gracefulness of Marie Antoinette from an artist, who saw her at Versailles much about the same time that Mr. Burke did. He stood in one corner of a little antechamber, and as the doors were narrow, she was obliged to pass sideways with her hoop. She glided by him in an instant, as if borne on a cloud.

movements, that distract the attention and defeat each other. Grace is the absence of every thing that indicates pain or difficulty, or hesitation or incongruity. The only graceful dancer we ever saw was Deshayes, the Frenchman. He came on bounding like a stag. It was not necessary to have seen good dancing before to know that this was really fine. Whoever has seen the sea in motion, the branches of a tree waving in the air, would instantly perceive the resemblance. Flexibility and grace are to be found in nature as well as at the opera. Mr. Burke, in his Essay on the Sublime and Beautiful, has very admirably described the bosom of a beautiful woman, almost entirely with reference to the ideas of motion. Those outlines are beautiful which describe pleasant motions. A fine use is made of this principle by one of the apocryphal writers, in describing the form of the rainbow. 'He hath set his bow in the heavens, and his hands have bended it.' Harmony in colour has not been denied to be a natural property of objects, consisting in the gradations of intermediate colours. The principle appears to be here the same as in some of the former instances. The effect of colour in Titian's Bath of Diana, at the Marquis of Stafford's, is perhaps the finest in the world, made up of the richest contrasts, blended together by the most masterly gradations. Harmony of sound depends apparently on the same principle as harmony of colour. Rhyme depends on the pleasure derived from a recurrence of similar sounds, as symmetry of features does on the correspondence of the different outlines. The prose style of Dr Johnson originated in the same principle. The secret consisted in rhyming on the sense, and balancing one half of the sentence uniformly and systematically against the other. The Hebrew poetry was constructed in the same manner.

W.

ON IMITATION

OBJECTS in themselves disagreeable or indifferent, often please in the imitation. A brick-floor, a pewter-plate, an ugly cur barking, a Dutch boor smoking or playing at skittles, the inside of a shamble, a fishmonger's or a greengrocer's stall, have been made very interesting as pictures by the fidelity, skill, and spirit, with which they have been copied. One source of the pleasure thus received is undoubtedly the surprise or feeling of admiration, occasioned by the unexpected coincidence between the imitation and the object. The deception however, not only pleases at first sight, or from mere novelty; but

ON IMITATION

t continues to please upon farther acquaintance, and in proportion to he insight we acquire into the distinctions of nature and of art. By ar the most numerous class of connoisseurs are the admirers of pictures f *still life*, which have nothing but the elaborateness of the execution o recommend them. One chief reason, it should seem then, why mitation pleases, is, because, by exciting curiosity, and inviting a com-arison between the object and the representation, it opens a new field f inquiry, and leads the attention to a variety of details and distinc-ions not perceived before. This latter source of the pleasure derived rom imitation has never been properly insisted on.

The anatomist is delighted with a coloured plate, conveying the xact appearance of the progress of certain diseases, or of the internal arts and dissections of the human body. We have known a ennerian Professor as much enraptured with a delineation of the ifferent stages of vaccination, as a florist with a bed of tulips, or an uctioneer with a collection of Indian shells. But in this case, we nd that not only the imitation pleases,—the objects themselves give as nuch pleasure to the professional inquirer, as they would pain to the ninitiated. The learned amateur is struck with the beauty of the oats of the stomach laid bare, or contemplates with eager curiosity he transverse section of the brain, divided on the new Spurzheim rinciples. It is here, then, the number of the parts, their dis-inctions, connections, structure, uses; in short, an entire new set of leas, which occupies the mind of the student, and overcomes the ense of pain and repugnance, which is the only feeling that the sight f a dead and mangled body presents to ordinary men. It is the ame in art as in science. The painter of still life, as it is called, akes the same pleasure in the object as the spectator does in the mitation; because by habit he is led to perceive all those distinctions n nature, to which other persons never pay any attention till they are ointed out to them in the picture. The vulgar only see nature as it reflected to them from art; the painter sees the picture in nature, efore he transfers it to the canvass. He refines, he analyses, he emarks fifty things, which escape common eyes; and this affords a istinct source of reflection and amusement to him, independently of ie beauty or grandeur of the objects themselves, or of their con-ection with other impressions besides those of sight. The charm of ie Fine Arts, then, does not consist in any thing peculiar to imitation, ven where only imitation is concerned, since *there*, where art exists a the highest perfection, namely, in the mind of the artist, the bject excites the same or greater pleasure, before the imitation exists. mitation renders an object, displeasing in itself, a source of pleasure, ot by repetition of the same idea, but by suggesting new ideas, by

73

detecting new properties, and endless shades of difference, just as a close and continued contemplation of the object itself would do. Art shows us nature, divested of the medium of our prejudices. It divides and decompounds objects into a thousand curious parts, which may be full of variety, beauty, and delicacy in themselves, though the object to which they belong may be disagreeable in its general appearance, or by association with other ideas. A painted marigold is inferior to a painted rose only in form and colour: it loses nothing in point of smell. Yellow hair is perfectly beautiful in a picture. To a person lying with his face close to the ground in a summer's day the blades of spear-grass will appear like tall forest trees, shooting up into the sky; as an insect seen through a microscope is magnified into an elephant. Art is the microscope of the mind, which sharpens the wit as the other does the sight; and converts every object into a little universe in itself.[1] Art may be said to draw aside the veil from nature. To those who are perfectly unskilled in the practice, unimbued with the principles of art, most objects present only a confused mass. The pursuit of art is liable to be carried to a contrary excess, as where it produces a rage for the *picturesque*. You cannot go a step with a person of this class, but he stops you to point out some choice bit of landscape, or fancied improvement, and teazes you almost to death with the frequency and insignificance of his discoveries!

It is a common opinion, (which may be worth noticing here), that the study of physiognomy has a tendency to make people satirical, and the knowledge of art to make them fastidious in their taste. Knowledge may, indeed, afford a handle to ill-nature; but it takes away the principal temptation to its exercise, by supplying the mind with better resources against *ennui*. Idiots are always mischievous, and the most superficial persons are the most disposed to find fault, because they understand the fewest things. The English are more apt than any other nation to treat foreigners with contempt, because they seldom see anything but their own dress and manners; and it is only in petty provincial towns that you meet with persons who pride themselves on being satirical. In every country place in England there are one or two persons of this description who keep the whole neigh-

---

[1] In a fruit or flower-piece by Vanhuysum, the minutest details acquire a certain grace and beauty from the delicacy with which they are finished. The eye dwells with a giddy delight on the liquid drops of dew, on the gauze wings of an insect, on the hair and feathers of a bird's nest, the streaked and speckled egg-shells, the fine legs of the little travelling caterpillar. Who will suppose that the painter had not the same pleasure in detecting these nice distinctions in nature, that the critic has in tracing them in the picture?

ON IMITATION

bourhood in terror. It is not to be denied that the study of the *ideal* in art, if separated from the study of nature, may have the effect above stated, of producing dissatisfaction and contempt for everything but itself, as all affectation must; but to the genuine artist, truth, nature, beauty, are almost different names for the same thing.

Imitation interests, then, by exciting a more intense perception of truth, and calling out the powers of observation and comparison: wherever this effect takes place the interest follows of course, with or without the imitation, whether the object is real or artificial. The gardener delights in the streaks of a tulip, or 'pansy freak'd with jet'; the mineralogist in the varieties of certain strata, because he understands them. Knowledge is pleasure as well as power. A work of art has in this respect no advantage over a work of nature, except inasmuch as it furnishes an additional stimulus to curiosity. Again, natural objects please in proportion as they are uncommon, by fixing the attention more steadily on their beauties or differences. The same principle of the effect of novelty in exciting the attention, may account, perhaps, for the extraordinary discoveries and lies told by travellers, who, opening their eyes for the first time in foreign parts, are startled at every object they meet.

Why the excitement of intellectual activity pleases, is not here the question; but that it does so, is a general and acknowledged law of the human mind. We grow attached to the mathematics only from finding out their truth; and their utility chiefly consists (at present) in the contemplative pleasure they afford to the student. Lines, points, angles, squares, and circles are not interesting in themselves; they become so by the power of mind exerted in comprehending their properties and relations. People dispute for ever about Hogarth. The question has not in one respect been fairly stated. The merit of his pictures does not so much depend on the nature of the subject, as on the knowledge displayed of it, on the number of ideas they excite, on the fund of thought and observation contained in them. They are to be looked on as works of science; they gratify our love of truth; they fill up the void of the mind: they are a series of plates of natural history, and also of that most interesting part of natural history, the history of man. The superiority of high art over the common or mechanical consists in combining truth of imitation with beauty and grandeur of subject. The historical painter is superior to the flower-painter, because he combines or ought to combine human interests and passions with the same power of imitating external nature; or, indeed, with greater, for the greatest difficulty of imitation is the power of imitating expression. The difficulty of copying increases with our knowledge of the object; and that again with the interest we take in it. The same argument might be applied to shew that the poet and painter of imagination are superior to the mere philosopher or man of science, because they exercise the powers of reason and intellect combined with nature and passion. They treat of the highest categories of the human soul, pleasure and pain.

From the foregoing train of reasoning, we may easily account for the too great tendency of art to run into pedantry and affectation. There is 'a pleasure in art which none but artists feel.' They see beauty where others see nothing of the sort, in wrinkles, deformity, and old age. They see it in Titian's Schoolmaster as well as in Raphael's Galatea; in the dark shadows of Rembrandt as well as in the splendid colours of Rubens; in an angel's or in a butterfly's wings. They see with different eyes from the multitude. But true genius, though it has new sources of pleasure opened to it, does not lose its sympathy with humanity. It combines truth of imitation with effect, the parts with the whole, the means with the end. The mechanic artist sees only that which nobody else sees, and is conversant only with the technical language and difficulties of his art. A painter, if shewn a picture, will generally dwell upon the academic skill displayed in it, and the knowledge of the received rules of composition. A musician, if asked to play a tune, will select that which is the most difficult and the least intelligible. The poet will be struck with the harmony of versification, or the elaborateness of the arrangement in a composition. The conceits in Shakspeare were his greatest delight; and improving upon this perverse method of judging, the German writers, Goethe and Schiller, look upon Werter and The Robbers as the worst of all their works, because they are the most popular. Some artists among ourselves have carried the same principle to a singular excess.[1] If professors themselves are liable to this kind of pedantry, connoisseurs and dilettanti, who have less sensibility and more affectation, are almost wholly swayed by it. They see nothing in a picture but the execution. They are proud of their

---

[1] We here allude particularly to Turner, the ablest landscape painter now living, whose pictures are, however, too much abstractions of aerial perspective and representations not so properly of the objects of nature as of the medium through which they are seen. They are the triumph of the knowledge of the artist, and of the power of the pencil over the barrenness of the subject. They are pictures of the elements of air, earth, and water. The artist delights to go back to the first chaos of the world, or to that state of things when the waters were separated from the dry land, and light from darkness, but as yet no living thing nor tree bearing fruit was seen upon the face of the earth. All is 'without form and void.' Some one said of his landscapes that they were *pictures of nothing, and very like.*

nowledge in proportion as it is a secret. The worst judges of pictures
n the United Kingdom are, first, picture-dealers; next, perhaps, the
Directors of the British Institution; and after them, in all probability,
he Members of the Royal Academy.   T. T.

ON *GUSTO*

Gusto in art is power or passion defining any object. It is not so
ifficult to explain this term in what relates to expression (of which
t may be said to be the highest degree) as in what relates to things
vithout expression, to the natural appearances of objects, as mere
olour or form. In one sense, however, there is hardly any object
ntirely devoid of expression, without some character of power belong-
ng to it, some precise association with pleasure or pain: and it is in
iving this truth of character from the truth of feeling, whether in the
ighest or the lowest degree, but always in the highest degree of which
he subject is capable, that gusto consists.

There is a gusto in the colouring of Titian. Not only do his heads
eem to think—his bodies seem to feel. This is what the Italians
nean by the *morbidezza* of his flesh-colour. It seems sensitive and
live all over; not merely to have the look and texture of flesh, but
ne feeling in itself. For example, the limbs of his female figures
ave a luxurious softness and delicacy, which appears conscious of the
leasure of the beholder. As the objects themselves in nature would
roduce an impression on the sense, distinct from every other object,
nd having something divine in it, which the heart owns and the
nagination consecrates, the objects in the picture preserve the same
npression, absolute, unimpaired, stamped with all the truth of passion,
ne pride of the eye, and the charm of beauty. Rubens makes his
esh-colour like flowers; Albano's is like ivory; Titian's is like flesh,
nd like nothing else. It is as different from that of other painters,
s the skin is from a piece of white or red drapery thrown over it.
'he blood circulates here and there, the blue veins just appear, the
est is distinguished throughout only by that sort of tingling sensation
) the eye, which the body feels within itself. This is gusto.
'andyke's flesh-colour, though it has great truth and purity, wants
usto. It has not the internal character, the living principle in it.
t is a smooth surface, not a warm, moving mass. It is painted with-
ut passion, with indifference. The hand only has been concerned.
'he impression slides off from the eye, and does not, like the tones
f Titian's pencil, leave a sting behind it in the mind of the spectator.

The eye does not acquire a taste or appetite for what it sees. In a word, gusto in painting is where the impression made on one sense excites by affinity those of another.

Michael Angelo's forms are full of gusto. They everywhere obtrude the sense of power upon the eye. His limbs convey an idea of muscular strength, of moral grandeur, and even of intellectual dignity: they are firm, commanding, broad, and massy, capable of executing with ease the determined purposes of the will. His faces have no other expression than his figures, conscious power and capacity. They appear only to think what they shall do, and to know that they can do it. This is what is meant by saying that his style is hard and masculine. It is the reverse of Correggio's, which is effeminate. That is, the gusto of Michael Angelo consists in expressing energy of will without proportionable sensibility, Correggio's in expressing exquisite sensibility without energy of will. In Correggio's faces as well as figures we see neither bones nor muscles, but then what a soul is there, full of sweetness and of grace—pure, playful, soft, angelical! There is sentiment enough in a hand painted by Correggio to set up a school of history painters. Whenever we look at the hands of Correggio's women or of Raphael's, we always wish to touch them.

Again, Titian's landscapes have a prodigious gusto, both in the colouring and forms. We shall never forget one that we saw many years ago in the Orleans Gallery of Acteon hunting. It had a brown, mellow, autumnal look. The sky was of the colour of stone. The winds seemed to sing through the rustling branches of the trees, and already you might hear the twanging of bows resound through the tangled mazes of the wood. Mr. West, we understand, has this landscape. He will know if this description of it is just. The landscape back-ground of the St. Peter Martyr is another well known instance of the power of this great painter to give a romantic interest and an appropriate character to the objects of his pencil, where every circumstance adds to the effect of the scene,—the bold trunks of the tall forest trees, the trailing ground plants, with that tall convent spire rising in the distance, amidst the blue sapphire mountains and the golden sky.

Rubens has a great deal of gusto in his Fauns and Satyrs, and in all that expresses motion, but in nothing else. Rembrandt has it in everything; everything in his pictures has a tangible character. If he puts a diamond in the ear of a burgomaster's wife, it is of the first water; and his furs and stuffs are proof against a Russian winter. Raphael's gusto was only in expression; he had no idea of the character of anything but the human form. The dryness and poverty of his style in other respects is a phenomenon in the art. His trees are like sprigs of grass stuck in a book of botanical specimens. Was it that Raphael never had time to go beyond the walls of Rome? That he was always in the streets, at church, or in the bath? He was not one of the Society of Arcadians.[1]

Claude's landscapes, perfect as they are, want gusto. This is not easy to explain. They are perfect abstractions of the visible images of things; they speak the visible language of nature truly. They resemble a mirror or a microscope. To the eye only they are more perfect than any other landscapes that ever were or will be painted; they give more of nature, as cognisable by one sense alone; but they lay an equal stress on all visible impressions. They do not interpret one sense by another; they do not distinguish the character of different objects as we are taught, and can only be taught, to distinguish them by their effect on the different senses. That is, his eye wanted imagination: it did not strongly sympathise with his other faculties. He saw the atmosphere, but he did not feel it. He painted the trunk of a tree or a rock in the foreground as smooth—with as complete an abstraction of the gross, tangible impression, as any other part of the picture. His trees are perfectly beautiful, but quite immovable; they have a look of enchantment. In short, his landscapes are unequalled imitations of nature, released from its subjection to the elements, as if all objects were become a delightful fairy vision, and the eye had rarefied and refined away the other senses.

The gusto in the Greek statues is of a very singular kind. The sense of perfect form nearly occupies the whole mind, and hardly suffers it to dwell on any other feeling. It seems enough for them *to be*, without acting or suffering. Their forms are ideal, spiritual. Their beauty is power. By their beauty they are raised above the frailties of pain or passion; by their beauty they are deified.

The infinite quantity of dramatic invention in Shakspeare takes from his gusto. The power he delights to show is not intense, but discursive. He never insists on anything as much as he might, except a quibble. Milton has great gusto. He repeats his blows twice; grapples with and exhausts his subject. His imagination has a double

---

[1] Raphael not only could not paint a landscape; he could not paint people in a landscape. He could not have painted the heads or the figures, or even the dresses, of the St. Peter Martyr. His figures have always an *in-door* look, that is, a set, determined, voluntary, dramatic character, arising from their own passions, or a watchfulness of those of others, and want that wild uncertainty of expression, which is connected with the accidents of nature and the changes of the elements. He has nothing *romantic* about him.

relish of its objects, an inveterate attachment to the things he describes
and to the words describing them.

> ———' Or where Chineses drive
> With sails and wind their *cany* waggons *light*.'

. . .

'Wild above rule or art, *enormous* bliss.'

There is a gusto in Pope's compliments, in Dryden's satires, and
Prior's tales; and among prose writers Boccacio and Rabelais had
the most of it. We will only mention one other work which appears
to us to be full of gusto, and that is the *Beggar's Opera*. If it is
not, we are altogether mistaken in our notions on this delicate subject.

W. H.

ON PEDANTRY

THE power of attaching an interest to the most trifling or painful
pursuits, in which our whole attention and faculties are engaged, is
one of the greatest happinesses of our nature. The common soldier
mounts the breach with joy; the miser deliberately starves himself
to death; the mathematician sets about extracting the cube-root with
a feeling of enthusiasm; and the lawyer sheds tears of admiration
over Coke upon Littleton. It is the same through human life.
He who is not in some measure a pedant, though he may be a wise,
cannot be a very happy man.

The chief charm of reading the old novels is from the picture they
give of the egotism of the characters, the importance of each individual
to himself, and his fancied superiority over every one else. We like,
for instance, the pedantry of Parson Adams, who thought a school-
master the greatest character in the world, and that he was the greatest
schoolmaster in it. We do not see any equivalent for the satisfaction
which this conviction must have afforded him in the most nicely
graduated scale of talents and accomplishments to which he was an
utter stranger. When the old-fashioned Scotch pedagogue turns
Roderick Random round and round, and surveys him from head to
foot with such infinite surprise and laughter, at the same time breaking out himself into gestures and exclamations still more uncouth and
ridiculous, who would wish to have deprived him of this burst of
extravagant self-complacency? When our follies afford equal delight
to ourselves and those about us, what is there to be desired more?
We cannot discover the vast advantage of ' seeing ourselves as others

e us.' It is better to have a contempt for any one than for
rselves !

One of the most constant butts of ridicule, both in the old comedies
d novels, is the professional jargon of the medical tribe. Yet it
nnot be denied that this jargon, however affected it may seem, is
e natural language of apothecaries and physicians, the mother-
ngue of pharmacy ! It is that by which their knowledge first comes
them, that with which they have the most obstinate associations,
at in which they can express themselves the most readily and with
e best effect upon their hearers ; and though there may be some
sumption of superiority in all this, yet it is only by an effort of
rcumlocution that they could condescend to explain themselves in
dinary language. Besides, there is a delicacy at bottom ; as it is
e only language in which a nauseous medicine can be decorously
lministered, or a limb taken off with the proper degree of secrecy.
the most blundering coxcombs affect this language most, what does
signify, while they retain the same dignified notions of themselves
d their art, and are equally happy in their knowledge or their
norance ? The ignorant and pretending physician is a capital
aracter in Moliere : and, indeed, throughout his whole plays the
eat source of the comic interest is in the fantastic exaggeration of
ind self-love, in letting loose the habitual peculiarities of each indi-
dual from all restraint of conscious observation or self-knowledge,
giving way to that specific levity of impulse which mounts at once
the height of absurdity, in spite of the obstacles that surround it,
a fluid in a barometer rises according to the pressure of the external
r ! His characters are almost always pedantic, and yet the most
nconscious of all others. Take, for example, those two worthy
ntlemen, Monsieur Jourdain and Monsieur Pourceaugnac.[1]

Learning and pedantry were formerly synonymous ; and it was
ell when they were so. Can there be a higher satisfaction than
r a man to understand Greek, and to believe that there is nothing
se worth understanding ? Learning is the knowledge of that which

---

[1] A good-natured man will always have a smack of pedantry about him. A
wyer, who talks about law, *certioraris*, *noli prosequis*, and silk gowns, though he
ay be a blockhead, is by no means dangerous. It is a very bad sign (unless
here it arises from singular modesty) when you cannot tell a man's profession
om his conversation. Such persons either feel no interest in what concerns
em most, or do not express what they feel. ' Not to admire any thing ' is a very
nsafe rule. A London apprentice, who did not admire the Lord Mayor's coach,
ould stand a good chance of being hanged. We know but one person absurd
ough to have formed his whole character on the above maxim of Horace, and
ho affects a superiority over others from an uncommon degree of natural and
tificial stupidity.

is not generally known. What an ease and a dignity in pretension
founded on the ignorance of others! What a pleasure in wondering
what a pride in being wondered at! In the library of the fami
where we were brought up, stood the *Fratres Poloni*; and we ca
never forget or describe the feeling with which not only their appea
ance, but the names of the authors on the outside inspired u
Pripscovius, we remember, was one of the easiest to pronounce. T
gravity of the contents seemed in proportion to the weight of t
volumes; the importance of the subjects increased with our igno
ance of them. The trivialness of the remarks, if ever we looke
into them,—the repetitions, the monotony, only gave a greater soler
nity to the whole, as the slowness and minuteness of the eviden
adds to the impressiveness of a judicial proceeding. We knew th
the authors had devoted their whole lives to the production of the
works, carefully abstaining from the introduction of any thing amusi
or lively or interesting. In ten folio volumes there was not one sal
of wit, one striking reflection. What, then, must have been the
sense of the importance of the subject, the profound stores of kno
ledge which they had to communicate! 'From all this world
encumbrance they did themselves assoil.' Such was the notion w
then had of this learned lumber; yet we would rather have th
feeling again for one half-hour than be possessed of all the acutene
of Bayle or the wit of Voltaire!

It may be considered as a sign of the decay of piety and learnin
in modern times, that our divines no longer introduce texts of t
original Scriptures into their sermons. The very sound of t
original Greek or Hebrew would impress the hearer with a mo
lively faith in the sacred writers than any translation, however liter
or correct. It may be even doubted whether the translation of t
Scriptures into the vulgar tongue was any advantage to the peopl
The mystery in which particular points of faith were left involve
gave an awe and sacredness to religious opinions: the general purpo
of the truths and promises of revelation was made known by oth
means; and nothing beyond this general and implicit conviction ca
be obtained, where all is undefined and infinite.

Again, it may be questioned whether, in matters of mere huma
reasoning, much has been gained by the disuse of the learned la
guages. Sir Isaac Newton wrote in Latin; and it is perhaps one
Bacon's fopperies that he translated his works into English.
certain follies have been exposed by being stripped of their form
disguise, others have had a greater chance of succeeding, by bei
presented in a more pleasing and popular shape. This has be
remarkably the case in France, (the least pedantic country in t

orld), where the women mingle with everything, even with metayysics, and where all philosophy is reduced to a set of phrases for e toilette. When books are written in the prevailing language of the untry, every one becomes a critic who can read. An author is no nger tried by his peers. A species of universal suffrage is introiced in letters, which is only applicable to politics. The good old atin style of our forefathers, if it concealed the dullness of the riter, at least was a barrier against the impertinence, flippancy, and norance of the reader. However, the immediate transition from e pedantic to the popular style in literature was a change that must ive been very delightful at the time. Our illustrious predecessors, e *Tatler* and *Spectator*, were very happily off in this respect. They ore the public favour in its newest gloss, before it had become rnished and common—before familiarity had bred contempt. It as the honey-moon of authorship. Their Essays were among the ·st instances in this country of learning sacrificing to the graces, and ‑ a mutual understanding and good-humoured equality between the riter and the reader. This new style of composition, to use the araseology of Mr. Burke, 'mitigated authors into companions, and mpelled wisdom to submit to the soft collar of social esteem.' The riginal papers of the *Tatler*, printed on a half sheet of common olscap, were regularly served up at breakfast-time with the silver a-kettle and thin slices of bread and butter; and what the ingenious Ir. Bickerstaff wrote overnight in his easy chair, he might flatter imself would be read the next morning with elegant applause by the air, the witty, the learned, and the great, in all parts of this kingdom, which civilisation had made any considerable advances. The perection of letters is when the highest ambition of the writer is to lease his readers, and the greatest pride of the reader is to undercand his author. The satisfaction on both sides ceases when the wn becomes a club of authors, when each man stands with his anuscript in his hand waiting for his turn of applause, and when the laims on our admiration are so many, that, like those of common eggars, to prevent imposition they can only be answered with general eglect. Our self-love would be quite bankrupt, if critics by proession did not come forward as beadles to keep off the crowd, and relieve us from the importunity of these innumerable candidates or fame, by pointing out their faults and passing over their beauties. n the more auspicious period just alluded to an author was regarded y the better sort as a man of genius, and by the vulgar, as a kind of rodigy; insomuch that the Spectator was obliged to shorten his esidence at his friend Sir Roger de Coverley's, from his being taken or a conjuror. Every state of society has its advantages and dis-

advantages. An author is at present in no danger of being taken f
a conjuror!

THE SAME SUBJECT CONTINUED

LIFE is the art of being well deceived; and in order that the dece
tion may succeed, it must be habitual and uninterrupted. A consta
examination of the value of our opinions and enjoyments, compare
with those of others, may lessen our prejudices, but will leave nothir
for our affections to rest upon. A multiplicity of objects unsettle
the mind, and destroys not only all enthusiasm, but all sincerity
attachment, all constancy of pursuit; as persons accustomed to a
itinerant mode of life never feel themselves at home in any place.
is by means of habit that our intellectual employments mix like ow
food with the circulation of the blood, and go on like any other pa
of the animal functions. To take away the force of habit and pr
judice entirely, is to strike at the root of our personal existence. Th
book-worm, buried in the depth of his researches, may well say t
the obtrusive shifting realities of the world, ' Leave me to my repose !
We have seen an instance of a poetical enthusiast, who would hav
passed his life very comfortably in the contemplation of *his own ide*
if he had not been disturbed in his reverie by the Reviewers; and fo
our own parts, we think we could pass our lives very learnedly an
classically in one of the quadrangles at Oxford, without any idea a
all, vegetating merely on the air of the place. Chaucer has drawn
beautiful picture of a true scholar in his Clerk of Oxenford :

> ' A Clerk ther was of Oxenforde also,
> That unto logik, hadde longe ygo.
> As lene was his hors as is a rake,
> And he was not right fat, I undertake;
> But loked holwe, and thereto soberly,
> Ful thredbare was his overest courtepy,
> For he hadde geten him yit no benefice,
> Ne was nought worldly to have an office.
> For him was lever have at his beddes hed
> A twenty bokes, clothed in blak or red,
> Of Aristotle and his philosophie,
> Then robes riche, or fidel, or sautrie.
> But all be that he was a philosophre,
> Yet hadde he but litel gold in cofre,
> But al that he might of his frendes hente,
> On bokes and on lerning he it spente,
> And besily gan for the soules praie
> Of hem, that gave him wherwith to scolaie.'

ON PEDANTRY

> Of studie toke he moste care and hede.
> Not a word spake he more than was nede;
> And that was said in forme and reverence,
> And short, and quike, and full of high sentence.
> Sowning in moral vertue was his speche,
> And gladly wolde he lerne, and gladly teche.'

If letters have profited little by throwing down the barrier between learned prejudice and ignorant presumption, the arts have profited still less by the universal diffusion of accomplishment and pretension An artist is no longer looked upon as any thing, who is not at the same time 'chemist, statesman, fiddler, and buffoon.' It is expected of him that he should be well-dressed, and he is poor; that he should move gracefully, and he has never learned to dance; that he should converse on all subjects, and he understands but one; that he should be read in different languages, and he only knows his own. Yet there is one language, the language of Nature, in which it is enough for him to be able to read, to find everlasting employment and solace to his thoughts—

> 'Tongues in the trees, books in the running brooks,
> Sermons in stones, and good in every thing.'

He will find no end of his labours or of his triumphs there; yet still feel all his strength not more than equal to the task he has begun— his whole life too short for art. Rubens complained, that just as he was beginning to understand his profession, he was forced to quit it. It was a saying of Michael Angelo, that 'painting was jealous, and required the whole man to herself.' Is it to be supposed that Rembrandt did not find sufficient resources against the spleen in the little cell, where mystery and silence hung upon his pencil, or the noontide ray penetrated the solemn gloom around him, without the aid of modern newspapers, novels, and reviews? Was he not more wisely employed, while devoted solely to his art—married to that immortal bride! We do not imagine Sir Joshua Reynolds was much happier for having written his lectures, nor for the learned society he kept, friendship apart; and learned society is not necessary to friendship. He was evidently, as far as conversation was concerned, little at his ease in it; and he was always glad, as he himself said, after he had been entertained at the houses of the great, to get back to his painting-room again. Any one settled pursuit, together with the ordinary alternations of leisure, exercise, and amusement, and the natural feelings and relations of society, is quite enough to take up the whole of our thoughts, time, and affections; and any thing

85

beyond this will, generally speaking, only tend to dissipate and dis tract the mind. There is no end of accomplishments, of the prospec of new acquisitions of taste or skill, or of the uneasiness arising from the want of them, if we once indulge in this idle habit of vanity and affectation. The mind is never satisfied with what it is, but is always looking out for fanciful perfections, which it can neither attain nor practise. Our failure in any one object is fatal to our enjoyment of all the rest; and the chances of disappointment multiply with the number of our pursuits. In catching at the shadow, we lose the substance. No man can thoroughly master more than one art or science. The world has never seen a perfect painter. What would it have availed for Raphael to have aimed at Titian's colouring, or for Titian to have imitated Raphael's drawing, but to have diverted each from the true bent of his natural genius, and to have made each sensible of his own deficiencies, without any probability of supplying them? Pedantry in art, in learning, in every thing, is the setting an extraordinary value on that which we can do, and that which we understand best, and which it is our business to do and under- stand. Where is the harm of this? To possess or even understand all kinds of excellence equally, is impossible; and to pretend to admire that to which we are indifferent, as much as that which is of the greatest use, and which gives the greatest pleasure to us, is not liberality, but affectation. Is an artist, for instance, to be required to feel the same admiration for the works of Handel as for those of Raphael? If he is sincere, he cannot: and a man, to be free from pedantry, must be either a coxcomb or a hypocrite. Vestris was so far in the right, in saying that Voltaire and he were the two greatest men in Europe. Voltaire was so in the public opinion, and he was so in his own. Authors and literary people have been unjustly accused for arrogating an exclusive preference to letters over other arts. They are justified in doing this, because words are the most natural and universal language, and because they have the sympathy of the world with them. Poets, for the same reason, have a right to be the vainest of authors. The prejudice attached to established reputation is, in like manner, perfectly well founded, because that which has longest excited our admiration and the admiration of mankind, is most entitled to admiration, on the score of habit, sympathy, and deference to public opinion. There is a sentiment attached to classical reputa- tion, which cannot belong to new works of genius, till they become old in their turn.

There appears to be a natural division of labour in the ornamental as well as the mechanical arts of human life. We do not see why a nobleman should wish to shine as a poet, any more than to be dubbed a knight, or to be created Lord Mayor of London. If he succeeds, he gains nothing; and then if he is damned, what a ridiculous figure he makes! The great, instead of rivalling them, should keep authors, as they formerly kept fools,—a practice in itself highly laudable, and the disuse of which might be referred to as the first symptom of the degeneracy of modern times, and dissolution of the principles of social order! But of all the instances of a profession now unjustly obsolete, commend us to the alchemist. We see him sitting fortified in his prejudices, with his furnace, his diagrams, and his alembics; smiling at disappointments as proofs of the sublimity of his art, and the earnest of his future success: wondering at his own knowledge and the incredulity of others; fed with hope to the last gasp, and having all the pleasures without the pain of madness. What is there in the discoveries of modern chemistry equal to the very names of the ELIXIR VITÆ and the AURUM POTABILE!

In *Froissard's Chronicles* there is an account of a reverend Monk who had been a robber in the early part of his life, and who, when he grew old, used feelingly to lament that he had ever changed his profession. He said, ' It was a goodly sight to sally out from his castle, and to see a troop of jolly friars coming riding that way, with their mules well laden with viands and rich stores, to advance towards them, to attack and overthrow them, returning to the castle with a noble booty.' He preferred this mode of life to counting his beads and chaunting his vespers, and repented that he had ever been prevailed on to relinquish so laudable a calling. In this confession of remorse, we may be sure that there was no hypocrisy.

The difference in the character of the gentlemen of the present age and those of the old school, has been often insisted on. The character of a gentleman is a *relative term*, which can hardly subsist where there is no marked distinction of persons. The diffusion of knowledge, of artificial and intellectual equality, tends to level this distinction, and to confound that nice perception and high sense of honour, which arises from conspicuousness of situation, and a perpetual attention to personal propriety and the claims of personal respect. The age of chivalry is gone with the improvements in the art of war, which superseded the exercise of personal courage; and the character of a gentleman must disappear with those general refinements in manners, which render the advantages of rank and situation accessible almost to every one. The bag-wig and sword naturally followed the fate of the helmet and the spear, when these outward insignia no longer implied acknowledged superiority, and were a distinction without a difference.

The spirit of chivalrous and romantic love proceeded on the same exclusive principle. It was an enthusiastic adoration, an idolatrous worship paid to sex and beauty. This, even in its blindest excess, was better than the cold indifference and prostituted gallantry of this philosophic age. The extreme tendency of civilisation is to dissipate all intellectual energy, and dissolve all moral principle. We are sometimes inclined to regret the innovations on the Catholic religion. It was a noble charter for ignorance, dullness, and prejudice of all kinds, (perhaps, after all, 'the sovereign'st things on earth'), and put an effectual stop to the vanity and restlessness of opinion. 'It wrapped the human understanding all round like a blanket.' Since the Reformation, altars, unsprinkled by holy oil, are no longer sacred; and thrones, unsupported by the divine right, have become uneasy and insecure.   W. H.

ON THE CHARACTER OF ROUSSEAU

MADAME DE STAEL, in her Letters on the Writings and Character of Rousseau, gives it as her opinion, 'that the imagination was the first faculty of his mind, and that this faculty even absorbed all the others.'[1] And she farther adds, 'Rousseau had great strength of reason on abstract questions, or with respect to objects, which have no reality but in the mind.'[2] Both these opinions are radically wrong. Neither imagination nor reason can properly be said to have been the original predominant faculties of his mind. The strength both of imagination and reason, which he possessed, was borrowed from the excess of another faculty; and the weakness and poverty of reason and imagination, which are to be found in his works, may be traced to the same source, namely, that these faculties in him were artificial, secondary, and dependant, operating by a power not theirs, but lent to them. The only quality which he possessed in an eminent degree, which alone raised him above ordinary men, and which gave to his writings and opinions an influence greater, perhaps, than has been exerted by any individual in modern times, was extreme sensibility, or an acute and even morbid feeling of all that related to his own impressions, to the objects and events of his life He had the most intense consciousness of his own existence. No object that had once made an impression on him was ever after effaced. Every feeling in his mind became a passion. His craving after

[1] 'Je crois que l'imagination étoit la première de ses facultés, et qu'elle absorboit même toutes les autres.'—P. 80.

[2] 'Il avoit une grande puissance de raison sur les matieres abstraites, sur les objets qui n'ont de réalité que dans la pensée,' etc.—P. 81.

excitement was an appetite and a disease. His interest in his own thoughts and feelings was always wound up to the highest pitch ; and hence the enthusiasm which he excited in others. He owed the power which he exercised over the opinions of all Europe, by which he created numberless disciples, and overturned established systems, to the tyranny which his feelings, in the first instance, exercised over himself. The dazzling blaze of his reputation was kindled by the same fire that fed upon his vitals.[1] His ideas differed from those of other men only in their force and intensity. His genius was the effect of his temperament. He created nothing, he demonstrated nothing, by a pure effort of the understanding. His fictitious characters are modifications of his own being, reflections and shadows of himself. His speculations are the obvious exaggerations of a mind, giving a loose to its habitual impulses, and moulding all nature to its own purposes. Hence his enthusiasm and his eloquence, bearing down all opposition. Hence the warmth and the luxuriance, as well as the sameness of his descriptions. Hence the frequent verboseness of his style ; for passion lends force and reality to language, and makes words supply the place of imagination. Hence the tenaciousness of his logic, the acuteness of his observations, the refinement and the inconsistency of his reasoning. Hence his keen penetration, and his strange want of comprehension of mind : for the same intense feeling which enabled him to discern the first principles of things, and seize some one view of a subject in all its ramifications, prevented him from admitting the operation of other causes which interfered with his favourite purpose, and involved him in endless wilful contradictions. Hence his excessive egotism, which filled all objects with himself, and would have occupied the universe with his smallest interest. Hence his jealousy and suspicion of others ; for no attention, no respect or sympathy, could come up to the extravagant claims of his self-love. Hence his dissatisfaction with himself and with all around him ; for nothing could satisfy his ardent longings after good, his restless appetite of being. Hence his feelings, overstrained and exhausted, recoiled upon themselves, and produced his love of silence and repose, his feverish aspirations after the quiet and solitude of nature. Hence in part also his quarrel with the artificial institutions and distinctions of society, which opposed so many barriers to the unrestrained indulgence of his will, and allured his imagination to scenes of

---

[1] He did more towards the French Revolution than any other man. Voltaire, by his wit and penetration, had rendered superstition contemptible, and tyranny odious : but it was Rousseau who brought the feeling of irreconcilable enmity to rank and privileges, *above humanity*, home to the bosom of every man,—identified it with all the pride of intellect, and with the deepest yearnings of the human heart.

pastoral simplicity or of savage life, where the passions were either no
excited or left to follow their own impulse,—where the petty vexation
and irritating disappointments of common life had no place,—and
where the tormenting pursuits of arts and sciences were lost in pur
animal enjoyment, or indolent repose. Thus he describes the firs
savage wandering for ever under the shade of magnificent forests, or
by the side of mighty rivers, smit with the unquenchable love of
nature!

The best of all his works is the *Confessions*, though it is that which
has been least read, because it contains the fewest set paradoxes or
general opinions. It relates entirely to himself; and no one was eve
so much at home on this subject as he was. From the strong hold
which they had taken of his mind, he makes us enter into his feeling
as if they had been our own, and we seem to remember every inciden
and circumstance of his life as if it had happened to ourselves. W
are never tired of this work, for it everywhere presents us with
pictures which we can fancy to be counterparts of our own existence
The passages of this sort are innumerable. There is the interesting
account of his childhood, the constraints and thoughtless liberty of
which are so well described; of his sitting up all night readin
romances with his father, till they were forced to desist by hearin
the swallows twittering in their nests; his crossing the Alps, describe
with all the feelings belonging to it, his pleasure in setting out, hi
satisfaction in coming to his journey's end, the delight of 'coming
and going he knew not where'; his arriving at Turin; the figure of
Madame Basile, drawn with such inimitable precision and elegance
the delightful adventure of the Chateau de Toune, where he passe
the day with Mademoiselle G**** and Mademoiselle Galley; the
story of his Zulietta, the proud, the charming Zulietta, whose las
words, '*Va Zanetto, e studia la Matematica*,' were never to be for
gotten; his sleeping near Lyons in a niche of the wall, after a fin
summer's day, with a nightingale perched above his head; hi
first meeting with Madame Warens, the pomp of sound with
which he has celebrated her name, beginning '*Louise Eleonor
de Warens etoit une demoiselle de la Tour de Pil, noble et ancienn
famille de Vevai, ville du pays de Vaud*' (sounds which we stil
tremble to repeat); his description of her person, her angelic smile
her mouth of the size of his own; his walking out one day while the
bells were chiming to vespers, and anticipating in a sort of wakin
dream the life he afterwards led with her, in which months and years
and life itself passed away in undisturbed felicity; the sudden dis
appointment of his hopes; his transport thirty years after at seeing the
same flower which they had brought home together from one of their

ambles near Chambery; his thoughts in that long interval of time; his suppers with Grimm and Diderot after he came to Paris; the first idea of his prize dissertation on the savage state; his account of writing the *New Eloise*, and his attachment to Madame d'Houdetot; his literary projects, his fame, his misfortunes, his unhappy temper; his last solitary retirement in the lake and island of Bienne, with his dog and his boat; his reveries and delicious musings there; all these crowd into our minds with recollections which we do not chuse to express. There are no passages in the *New Eloise* of equal force and beauty with the best descriptions in the *Confessions*, if we except the excursion on the water, Julia's last letter to St. Preux, and his letter to her, recalling the days of their first loves. We spent two whole years in reading these two works; and (gentle reader, it was when we were young) in shedding tears over them

——' As fast as the Arabian trees
Their medicinal gums.'

They were the happiest years of our life. We may well say of them, sweet is the dew of their memory, and pleasant the balm of their recollection! There are, indeed, impressions which neither time nor circumstances can efface.[1]

[1] We shall here give one passage as an example, which has always appeared to us the very perfection of this kind of personal and local description. It is that where he gives an account of his being one of the choristers at the Cathedral at Chambery: 'On jugera bien que la vie de la maîtrise toujours chantante et gaie, avec les Musiciens et les Enfans de chœur, me plaisoit plus que celle du Séminaire avec les Peres de S. Lazare. Cependant, cette vie, pour être plus libre, n'en étoit pas moins égale et réglée. J'étois fait pour aimer l'indépendance et pour n'en abuser jamais. Durant six mois entiers, je ne sortis pas une seule fois, que pour aller chez Maman ou à l'Église, et je n'en fus pas même tenté. Cette intervalle est un de ceux où j'ai vécu dans le plus grand calme, et que je me suis rappelé avec le plus de plaisir. Dans les situations diverses où je me suis trouvé, quelques uns ont été marqués par un tel sentiment de bien-être, qu'en les remémorant j'en suis affecté comme si j'y étois encore. Non seulement je me rappelle les tems, les lieux, les personnes, mais tous les objets environnans, la température de l'air, son odeur, sa couleur, une certaine impression locale qui ne s'est fait sentir que là, et dont le souvenir vif m'y transporte de nouveau. Par exemple, tout ce qu'on répétait à la maîtrise, tout ce qu'on chantoit au chœur, tout ce qu'on y faisoit, le bel et noble habit des Chanoines, les hasubles des Prêtres, les mitres des Chantres, la figure des Musiciens, un vieux Charpentier boiteux qui jouoit de la contrebasse, un petit Abbé blondin qui jouoit du violon, le lambeau de soutane qu'après avoir posé son épée, M. le Maître endossoit par-dessus son habit laïque, et le beau surplis fin dont il en couvrait les loques pour aller au chœur; l'orgueil avec lequel j'allois, tenant ma petite flûte à bec, m'établir dans l'orchestre, à la tribune, pour un petit bout de récit que M. le Maître avoit fait exprès pour moi : le bon diner qui nous attendoit ensuite, le bon appétit qu'on y portoit :—ce concours d'objets vivement retracé m'a cent fois charmé dans ma mémoire, autant et plus que dans la realité. J'ai gardé toujours une affection tendre pour un certain air du *Conditor alme syderum* qui

Rousseau, in all his writings, never once lost sight of himself. H
was the same individual from first to last. The spring that move
his passions never went down, the pulse that agitated his heart neve
ceased to beat. It was this strong feeling of interest, accumulating i
nis mind, which overpowers and absorbs the feelings of his readers
He owed all his power to sentiment. The writer who most nearl
resembles him in our own times is the author of the *Lyrical Ballads*
We see no other difference between them, than that the one wrote i
prose and the other in poetry; and that prose is perhaps better adapte
to express those local and personal feelings, which are inveterat
nabits in the mind, than poetry, which embodies its imaginary
creations. We conceive that Rousseau's exclamation, ' *Ah, voila d
la pervenche,*' comes more home to the mind than Mr. Wordsworth'
discovery of the linnet's nest ' with five blue eggs,' or than his addres
to the cuckoo, beautiful as we think it is; and we will confidently
match the Citizen of Geneva's adventures on the Lake of Bienne
against the Cumberland Poet's floating dreams on the Lake o
Grasmere. Both create an interest out of nothing, or rather out o
their own feelings; both weave numberless recollections into one
sentiment; both wind their own being round whatever object occurs
to them. But Rousseau, as a prose-writer, gives only the habitual
and personal impression. Mr. Wordsworth, as a poet, is forced to
lend the colours of imagination to impressions which owe all their
force to their identity with themselves, and tries to paint what is only
to be felt. Rousseau, in a word, interests you in certain objects by
interesting you in himself: Mr. Wordsworth would persuade you that
the most insignificant objects are interesting in themselves, because
he is interested in them. If he had met with Rousseau's favourite
periwinkle, he would have *translated* it into the most beautiful of
flowers. This is not imagination, but want of sense. If his jealousy
of the sympathy of others makes him avoid what is beautiful and grand
in nature, why does he undertake elaborately to describe other objects?
His nature is a mere Dulcinea del Toboso, and he would make a
Vashti of her. Rubens appears to have been as extravagantly attached
to his three wives, as Raphael was to his Fornarina; but their faces
were not so classical. The three greatest egotists that we know

marche par iambes ; parce qu'un Dimanche de l'Avent j'entendis de mon lit chanter
cette hymne, avant le jour, sur le perron de la Cathédrale, selon un rite de cette
eglise là. Mlle. *Merceret,* femme de chambre de Maman, savoit un peu de
musique ; je n'oublierai jamais un petit motet *afferte,* que M. le Maître me fit
chanter avec elle, et que sa maîtresse écoutait avec tant de plaisir. Enfin tout,
jusqu'a la bonne servante *Perrine,* qui étoit si bonne fille, et que les enfans de chœur
faisoient tant endêver—tout dans les souvenirs de ces tems de bonheur et d'innocence revient souvent me ravir et m'attrister.'—*Confessions,* LIV. iii. p. 283.

of, that is, the three writers who felt their own being most powerfully and exclusively, are Rousseau, Wordsworth, and Benvenuto
Cellini. As Swift somewhere says, we defy the world to furnish out
a fourth.   W. H.

ON DIFFERENT SORTS OF FAME

THERE is a half serious, half ironical argument in Melmoth's
Fitz-Osborn's Letters, to shew the futility of posthumous fame,
which runs thus : 'The object of any one who is inspired with this
passion is to be remembered by posterity with admiration and delight,
as having been possessed of certain powers and excellences which
distinguished him above his contemporaries. But posterity, it is said,
can know nothing of the individual but from the memory of these
qualities which he has left behind him. All that we know of Julius
Cæsar, for instance, is that he was the person who performed certain
actions, and wrote a book called his *Commentaries*. When, therefore,
we extol Julius Cæsar for his actions or his writings, what do we say
but that the person who performed certain things did perform them ;
that the author of such a work was the person who wrote it ; or, in
short, that Julius Cæsar was Julius Cæsar ? Now this is a mere
truism, and the desire to be the subject of such an identical proposition must, therefore, be an evident absurdity.' The sophism is a
tolerably ingenious one, but it is a sophism, nevertheless. It would
go equally to prove the nullity, not only of posthumous fame, but of
living reputation ; for the good or the bad opinion which my next-
door neighbour may entertain of me is nothing more than his conviction that such and such a person having certain good or bad
qualities is possessed of them ; nor is the figure, which a Lord-Mayor
elect, a prating demagogue, or popular preacher, makes in the eyes
of the admiring multitude—*himself*, but an image of him reflected in
the minds of others, in connection with certain feelings of respect and
wonder. In fact, whether the admiration we seek is to last for a day
or for eternity, whether we are to have it while living or after we are
dead, whether it is to be expressed by our contemporaries or by
future generations, the principle of it is the same—*sympathy with the
feelings of others*, and the necessary tendency which the idea or consciousness of the approbation of others has to strengthen the suggestions
of our self-love.[1] We are all inclined to think well of ourselves, of

---

[1] Burns, when about to sail for America after the first publication of his poems,
consoled himself with 'the delicious thought of being regarded as a clever fellow,
though on the other side of the Atlantic.'

our sense and capacity in whatever we undertake; but from this very desire to think well of ourselves, we are (as *Mrs. Peachum* says) '*bitter* bad judges' of our own pretensions; and when our vanity flatters us most, we ought in general to suspect it most. We are, therefore, glad to get the good opinion of a friend, but that may be partial; the good word of a stranger is likely to be more sincere, but he may be a blockhead; the multitude will agree with us, if we agree with them; accident, the caprice of fashion, the prejudice of the moment, may give a fleeting reputation; our only certain appeal, therefore, is to posterity; the voice of fame is alone the voice of truth. In proportion, however, as this award is final and secure, it is remote and uncertain. Voltaire said to some one, who had addressed an Epistle to Posterity, 'I am afraid, my friend, this letter will never be delivered according to its direction.' It can exist only in imagination; and we can only presume upon our claim to it, as we prefer the hope of lasting fame to every thing else. The love of fame is almost another name for the love of excellence; or it is the ambition to attain the highest excellence, sanctioned by the highest authority, that of time. Vanity, and the love of fame, are quite distinct from each other; for the one is voracious of the most obvious and doubtful applause, whereas the other rejects or overlooks every kind of applause but that which is purified from every mixture of flattery, and identified with truth and nature itself. There is, therefore, something disinterested in this passion, inasmuch as it is abstracted and ideal, and only appeals to opinion as a standard of truth; it is this which 'makes ambition virtue.' Milton had as fine an idea as any one of true fame; and Dr. Johnson has very beautifully described his patient and confident anticipations of the success of his great poem in the account of *Paradise Lost*. He has, indeed, done the same thing himself in *Lycidas*:

'Fame is the spur that the clear spirit doth raise
(That last infirmity of noble mind)
To scorn delights, and live laborious days;
But the fair Guerdon when we hope to find,
And think to burst out into sudden blaze,
Comes the blind Fury with th' abhorred shears,
And slits the thin-spun life. But not the praise,
Phœbus replied, and touch'd my trembling ears.'

None but those who have sterling pretensions can afford to refer them to time; as persons who live upon their means cannot well go into Chancery. No feeling can be more at variance with the true love of fame than that impatience which we have sometimes witnessed to 'pluck its fruits, unripe and crude,' before the time, to make a little echo of popularity mimic the voice of fame, and to convert a prize-medal or a newspaper-puff into a passport to immortality.

When we hear any one complaining that he has not the same fame as some poet or painter who lived two hundred years ago, he seems to us to complain that he has not been dead these two hundred years. When his fame has undergone the same ordeal, that is, has lasted as long, it will be as good, if he really deserves it. We think it equally absurd, when we sometimes find people objecting, that such an acquaintance of theirs, who has not an idea in his head, should be so much better off in the world than they are. But it is for this very reason; they have preferred the indulgence of their ideas to the pursuit of realities. It is but fair that he who has no ideas should have something in their stead. If he who has devoted his time to the study of beauty, to the pursuit of truth, whose object has been to govern opinion, to form the taste of others, to instruct or to amuse the public, succeeds in this respect, he has no more right to complain that he has not a title or a fortune, than he who has not purchased a ticket, that is, who has taken no means to the end, has a right to complain that he has not a prize in the lottery.

In proportion as men can command the immediate and vulgar applause of others, they become indifferent to that which is remote and difficult of attainment. We take pains only when we are compelled to do it. Little men are remarked to have courage; little women to have wit; and it is seldom that a man of genius is a coxcomb in his dress. Rich men are contented not to be thought wise; and the Great often think themselves well off, if they can escape being the jest of their acquaintance. Authors were actuated by the desire of the applause of posterity, only so long as they were debarred of that of their contemporaries, just as we see the map of the gold-mines of Peru hanging in the room of Hogarth's *Distressed Poet.* In the midst of the ignorance and prejudices with which they were surrounded, they had a sort of *forlorn hope* in the prospect of immortality. The spirit of universal criticism has superseded the anticipation of posthumous fame, and instead of waiting for the award of distant ages, the poet or prose-writer receives his final doom from the next number of the *Edinburgh* or *Quarterly Review.* According as the nearness of the applause increases, our impatience increases with it. A writer in a weekly journal engages with reluctance in a monthly publication: and again, a contributor to a daily paper sets about his task with greater spirit than either of them. It is like prompt payment. The effort and the applause go together. We, indeed, have known a man of genius and eloquence, to whom, from a habit of excessive talking, the certainty of seeing what he wrote in print the next day was too remote a stimulus for his imagination, and who constantly laid aside his pen in the middle of an article, if a friend dropped in, to finish the subject more effectually aloud, so that the approbation of his hearer, and the sound of his own voice might be co-instantaneous. Members of Parliament seldom turn authors, except to print their speeches when they have not been distinctly heard or understood; and great orators are generally very indifferent writers, from want of sufficient inducement to exert themselves, when the immediate effect on others is not perceived, and the irritation of applause or opposition ceases.

There have been in the last century two singular examples of literary reputation, the one of an author without a name, and the other of a name without an author. We mean the author of *Junius's Letters*, and the translator of the mottos to the *Rambler*, whose name was Elphinstone. The *Rambler* was published in the year 1750, and the name of Elphinstone prefixed to each paper is familiar to every literary reader, since that time, though we know nothing more of him. We saw this gentleman, since the commencement of the present century, looking over a clipped hedge in the country, with a broad-flapped hat, a venerable countenance, and his dress cut out with the same formality as his ever-greens. His name had not only survived half a century in conjunction with that of Johnson, but he had survived with it, enjoying all the dignity of a classical reputation, and the ease of a literary sinecure, on the strength of his mottos. The author of *Junius's Letters* is, on the contrary, as remarkable an instance of a writer who has arrived at all the public honours of literature, without being known by name to a single individual, and who may be said to have realised all the pleasure of posthumous fame, while living, without the smallest gratification of personal vanity. An anonymous writer may feel an acute interest in what is said of his productions, and a secret satisfaction in their success, because it is not the effect of personal considerations, as the overhearing any one speak well of us is more agreeable than a direct compliment. But this very satisfaction will tempt him to communicate his secret. This temptation, however, does not extend beyond the circle of his acquaintance. With respect to the public, who know an author only by his writings, it is of little consequence whether he has a real or a fictitious name, or a signature, so that they have some clue by which to associate the works with the author. In the case of *Junius*, therefore, where other personal considerations of interest or connections might immediately counteract and set aside this temptation, the triumph over the mere vanity of authorship might not have cost him so dear as we are at first inclined to imagine. Suppose it to have been the old Marquis of ———? It is quite out of the question that he should keep his places and not keep his secret. If ever the King should die, we think it not impossible that the secret may out. Certainly the *accouchement* of any princess in Europe would not excite an equal interest. 'And you, then, Sir, are the author of *Junius*!' What a recognition for the public and the author! That between Yorick and the Frenchman was a trifle to it.

We have said that we think the desire to be known by name as an author chiefly has a reference to those to whom we are known personally, and is strongest with regard to those who know most of our persons and least of our capacities. We wish to *subpœna* the public to our characters. Those who, by great services or great meannesses, have attained titles, always take them from the place with which they have the earliest associations, and thus strive to throw a veil of importance over the insignificance of their original pretensions, or the injustice of fortune. When Lord Nelson was passing over the quay at Yarmouth, to take possession of the ship to which he had been appointed, the people exclaimed, 'Why make that little fellow a captain?' He thought of this when he fought the battles of the Nile and Trafalgar. The same sense of personal insignificance which made him great in action made him a fool in love. If Bonaparte had been six inches higher, he never would have gone on that disastrous Russian expedition, nor 'with that addition' would he ever have been Emperor and King. For our own parts, one object which we have in writing these Essays, is to send them in a volume to a person who took some notice of us when children, and who augured, perhaps, better of us than we deserved. In fact, the opinion of those who know us most, who are a kind of second self in our recollections, is a sort of second conscience; and the approbation of one or two friends is all the immortality *we* pretend to.　　　　　　　　　　**A.**

CHARACTER OF JOHN BULL

In a late number of a respectable publication, there is the following description of the French character :—

'Extremes meet. This is the only way of accounting for that enigma, the French character. It has often been remarked, that this ingenious nation exhibits more striking contradictions than any other that ever existed. They are the gayest of the gay, and the gravest of the grave. Their very faces pass at once from an expression of the most lively animation, when they are in conversation or in action, to a melancholy blank. They are the lightest and most volatile, and at the same time the most plodding, mechanical, and laborious people in Europe. They are one moment the slaves of the most contemptible prejudices, and the next launch out into all the extravagance of the most abstract speculations. In matters of taste they are as inexorable as they are lax in questions of morality; they judge of the one by rules, of the other by their inclinations. It seems at times as if nothing could shock them, and yet they are offended at the merest trifles. The smallest things make the greatest impression on them. From the facility with which they can accommodate themselves to circumstances, they have no fixed principles or real character. They are always that which gives them least pain, or costs them least trouble. They easily disentangle their thoughts from whatever causes the slightest uneasiness, and direct their sensibility to flow in any channels they think proper. Their whole existence is more theatrical than real—their sentiments put on or off like the dress of an actor. Words are with them equivalent to things. They say what is agreeable, and believe what they say. Virtue and vice, good and evil, liberty and slavery, are matters almost of indifference. Their natural self-complacency stands them in stead of all other advantages.'

The foregoing account is pretty near the truth; we have nothing to say against it; but we shall here endeavour to do a like piece of justice to our countrymen, who are too apt to mistake the vices of others for so many virtues in themselves.

If a Frenchman is pleased with every thing, John Bull is pleased with nothing, and that is a fault. He is, to be sure, fond of having his own way, till you let him have it. He is a very headstrong animal, who mistakes the spirit of contradiction for the love of independence, and proves himself to be in the right by the obstinacy with which he stickles for the wrong. You cannot put him so much out of his way as by agreeing with him. He is never in such good-humour as with what gives him the spleen, and is most satisfied when he is sulky. If you find fault with him, he is in a rage; and if you praise him, suspects you have a design upon him. He recommends himself to another by affronting him, and if that will not do, knocks him down to convince him of his sincerity. He gives himself such airs as no mortal ever did, and wonders at the rest of the world for not thinking him the most amiable person breathing. John means well too, but he has an odd way of showing it, by a total disregard of other people's feelings and opinions. He is sincere, for he tells you at the first word he does not like you; and never deceives, for he never offers to serve you. A civil answer is too much to expect from him. A word costs him more than a blow. He is silent because he has nothing to say, and he looks stupid because he is so.

He has the strangest notions of beauty. The expression he values most in the human countenance is an appearance of roast beef and plum-pudding; and if he has a red face and round belly, thinks himself a great man. He is a little purse-proud, and has a better opinion of himself for having made a full meal. But his greatest delight is in a bugbear. This he must have, be the consequence what it may. Whoever will give him that, may lead him by the nose, and pick his pocket at the same time. An idiot in a country town, a Presbyterian parson, a dog with a cannister tied to his tail, a bull-bait, or a fox-hunt, are irresistible attractions to him. The Pope was formerly his great aversion, and latterly, a cap of liberty is a thing he cannot abide. He discarded the Pope, and defied the Inquisition, called the French a nation of slaves and beggars, and abused their *Grand Monarque* for a tyrant, cut off one king's head, and exiled another, set up a Dutch Stadtholder, and elected a Hanoverian Elector to be king over him, to shew he would have his own way, and to teach the rest of the world what they should do: but since other people took to imitating his example, John has taken it into his head to hinder them, will have a monopoly of rebellion and regicide to himself, has become sworn brother to the Pope, and stands by the Inquisition, restores his old enemies, the Bourbons, and reads *a great moral lesson* to their subjects, persuades himself that the Dutch Stadtholder and the Hanoverian Elector came to reign over him by divine right, and does all he can to prove himself a beast to make other people slaves. The truth is, John was always a surly, meddlesome, obstinate fellow, and of late years his *head* has not been quite right! In short, John is a great blockhead and a great bully, and requires (what he has been long labouring for) a hundred years of slavery to bring him to his senses. He will have it that he is a great patriot, for he hates all other countries; that he is wise, for he thinks all other people fools; that he is honest, for he calls all other people whores and rogues. If being in an ill-humour all one's life is the perfection of human nature, then John is very near it. He beats his wife, quarrels with his neighbours, damns his servants, and gets drunk to kill the time and keep up his spirits, and firmly believes himself the only unexceptionable, accomplished, moral, and religious character in Christendom. He boasts of the excellence of the laws, and the goodness of his own disposition; and yet there are more people hanged in England than in all Europe besides: he boasts of the modesty of his countrywomen, and yet there are more prostitutes in the streets of London than in all the capitals of Europe put together. He piques himself on his comforts, because he is the most uncomfortable of mortals; and because he has no enjoyment in society, seeks it, as he says, at his fireside, where he may be stupid as a matter of course, sullen as a matter of right, and as ridiculous as he chuses without being laughed at. His liberty is the effect of his self-will; his religion owing to the spleen; his temper to the climate. He is an industrious animal, because he has no taste for amusement, and had rather work six days in the week than be idle one. His awkward attempts at gaiety are the jest of other nations 'They,' (the English), says Froissard, speaking of the meeting of the Black Prince and the French King, 'amused themselves sadly, according to the custom of their country,'—*se rejouissoient tristement, selon la coutume de leur pays.* Their patience of labour is confined to what is repugnant and disagreeable in itself, to the drudgery of the mechanic arts, and does not extend to the fine arts; that is, they are indifferent to pain, but insensible to pleasure. They will stand in a trench, or march up to a breach, but they cannot bear to dwell long on an agreeable object. They can no more submit to regularity in art than to decency in behaviour. Their pictures are as coarse and slovenly as their address. John boasts of his great men, without much right to do so; not that he has not had them, but because he neither knows nor cares anything about them but to swagger over other nations. That which chiefly hits John's fancy in Shakspeare is that he was a deer-stealer in his youth; and, as for Newton's discoveries, he hardly knows to this day that the earth is round. John's oaths, which are quite characteristic, have got him the nickname of *Monsieur God-damn-me.* They are profane, a Frenchman's indecent. One swears by his vices, the other by their punishment. After all John's blustering, he is but a dolt. His habitual jealousy of others makes him the inevitable dupe of quacks and impostors of all sorts; he goes all lengths with one party out of spite to another; his zeal is as furious as his antipathies are unfounded; and there is nothing half so absurd or ignorant of its own intentions as an English mob.   Z.

ON GOOD-NATURE

Lord Shaftesbury somewhere remarks, that a great many people pass for very good-natured persons, for no other reason than because they care about nobody but themselves; and, consequently, as nothing annoys them but what touches their own interest, they never irritate themselves unnecessarily about what does not concern them, and seem to be made of the very milk of human kindness.

Good-nature, or what is often considered as such, is the most selfish of all the virtues: it is nine times out of ten mere indolence of disposition. A good-natured man is, generally speaking, one who does not like to be put out of his way; and as long as he can help it, that is, till the provocation comes home to himself, he will not. He does not create fictitious uneasiness out of the distresses of others; he does not fret and fume, and make himself uncomfortable about things he cannot mend, and that no way concern him, even if he could: but then there is no one who is more apt to be disconcerted by what puts him to any personal inconvenience, however trifling; who is more tenacious of his selfish indulgences, however unreasonable; or who resents more violently any interruption of his ease and comforts, the very trouble he is put to in resenting it being felt as an aggravation of the injury. A person of this character feels no emotions of anger or detestation, if you tell him of the devastation of a province, or the massacre of the inhabitants of a town, or the enslaving of a people; but if his dinner is spoiled by a lump of soot falling down the chimney, he is thrown into the utmost confusion, and can hardly recover a decent command of his temper for the whole day. He thinks nothing can go amiss, so long as he is at his ease, though a pain in his little finger makes him so peevish and quarrelsome, that nobody can come near him. Knavery and injustice in the abstract are things that by no means ruffle his temper, or alter the serenity of his countenance, unless he is to be the sufferer by them; nor is he ever betrayed into a passion in answering a sophism, if he does not think it immediately directed against his own interest.

On the contrary, we sometimes meet with persons who regularly heat themselves in an argument, and get out of humour on every occasion, and make themselves obnoxious to a whole company about nothing. This is not because they are ill-tempered, but because they are in earnest. Good-nature is a hypocrite: it tries to pass off its love of its own ease and indifference to everything else for a particular softness and mildness of disposition. All people get in a passion, and lose their temper, if you offer to strike them, or cheat them of their money, that is, if you interfere with that which they are really interested in. Tread on the heel of one of these good-natured persons, who do not care if the whole world is in flames, and see how he will bear it. If the truth were known, the most disagreeable people are the most amiable. They are the only persons who feel an interest in what does not concern them. They have as much regard for others as they have for themselves. They have as many vexations and causes of complaint as there are in the world. They are general righters of wrongs, and redressers of grievances. They not only are annoyed by what they can help, by an act of inhumanity done in the next street, or in a neighbouring country by their own countrymen, they not only do not claim any share in the glory, and hate it the more, the more brilliant the success,—but a piece of injustice done three thousand years ago touches them to the quick. They have an unfortunate attachment to a set of abstract phrases, such as *liberty, truth, justice, humanity, honour*, which are continually abused by knaves, and misunderstood by fools, and they can hardly contain themselves for spleen. They have something to keep them in perpetual hot water. No sooner is one question set at rest than another rises up to perplex them. They wear themselves to the bone in the affairs of other people, to whom they can do no manner of service, to the neglect of their own business and pleasure. They tease themselves to death about the morality of the Turks, or the politics of the French. There are certain words that afflict their ears, and things that lacerate their souls, and remain a plague-spot there forever after. They have a fellow-feeling with all that has been done, said, or thought in the world. They have an interest in all science and in all art. They hate a lie as much as a wrong, for truth is the foundation of all justice. Truth is the first thing in their thoughts, then mankind, then their country, last themselves. They love excellence, and bow to fame, which is the shadow of it. Above all, they are anxious to see justice done to the dead, as the best encouragement to the living, and the lasting inheritance of future generations. They do not like to see a great principle undermined, or the fall of a great man. They would sooner forgive a blow in the face than a wanton attack on acknowledged reputation. The contempt in which the French hold Shakspeare is a serious evil to them; nor do they think the matter mended, when they hear an Englishman, who would be thought a profound one, say that Voltaire was a man without wit. They are vexed to see genius playing at Tom Fool, and honesty turned bawd. It gives them a cutting sensation to see a number of things which, as they are unpleasant to see, we shall not here repeat. In short, they have a passion for truth; they feel the same attachment to the idea of what is right, that a knave does to his interest, or that a good-natured man does to his ease; and they have as many sources of uneasiness as there are actual or supposed deviations from this standard in the sum of things, or as there is a possibility of folly and mischief in the world.

Principle is a passion for truth; an incorrigible attachment to a general proposition. Good-nature is humanity that costs nothing. No good-natured man was ever a martyr to a cause, in religion or politics. He has no idea of striving against the stream. He may become a good courtier and a loyal subject; and it is hard if he does not, for he has nothing to do in that case but to consult his ease, nterest, and outward appearances. The Vicar of Bray was a good-natured man. What a pity he was but a vicar! A good-natured man is utterly unfit for any situation or office in life that requires integrity, fortitude, or generosity,—any sacrifice, except of opinion, or any exertion, but to please. A good-natured man will debauch his friend's mistress, if he has an opportunity ; and betray his friend, sooner than share disgrace or danger with him. He will not forego the smallest gratification to save the whole world. He makes his own convenience the standard of right and wrong. He avoids the feeling of pain in himself, and shuts his eyes to the sufferings of others. He will put a malefactor or an innocent person (no matter which) to the rack, and only laugh at the uncouthness of the gestures, or wonder that he is so unmannerly as to cry out. There is no villainy to which he will not lend a helping hand with great coolness and cordiality, for he sees only the pleasant and profitable side of things. He will assent to a falsehood with a leer of complacency, and applaud any atrocity that comes recommended in the garb of authority. He will betray his country to please a Minister, and sign the death-warrant of thousands of wretches, rather than forfeit the congenial smile, the well-known squeeze of the hand. The shrieks of death, the torture of mangled limbs, the last groans of despair, are things that shock his smooth humanity too much ever to make an impression on it : his good-nature sympathizes only with the smile, the bow, the gracious salutation, the fawning answer : vice loses its sting, and corruption its poison, in the oily gentleness of his disposition. He will not hear of any thing wrong in Church or State. He will defend every abuse by which any thing is to be got, every dirty job, every act of every Minister In an extreme case, a very good-natured man indeed may try to hang twelve honester men than himself to rise at the Bar, and forge the seal of the realm to continue his colleagues a week longer in office. He is a slave to the will of others, a coward to their prejudices, a tool of their vices. A good-natured man is no more fit to be trusted in public affairs, than a coward or a woman is to lead an army. Spleen is the soul of patriotism and of public good. Lord Castlereagh is a good-natured man, Lord Eldon is a good-natured man, Charles Fox was a good-natured man. The last instance is the most decisive. The definition of a true patriot is *a good hater*.

A king, who is a good-natured man, is in a fair way of being a great tyrant. A king ought to feel concern for all to whom his power extends ; but a good-natured man cares only about himself. If he has a good appetite, eats and sleeps well, nothing in the universe besides can disturb him. The destruction of the lives or liberties of his subjects will not stop him in the least of his caprices, but will concoct well with his bile, and 'good digestion wait on appetite, and health on both.' He will send out his mandate to kill and destroy with the same indifference or satisfaction that he performs any natural function of his body. The consequences are placed beyond the reach of his imagination, or would not affect him if they were not, for he is a fool, and good-natured. A good-natured man hates more than any one else whatever thwarts his will, or contradicts his prejudices; and if he has the power to prevent it, depend upon it, he will use it without remorse and without control.

There is a lower species of this character which is what is usually understood by a *well-meaning man*. A well-meaning man is one who often does a great deal of mischief without any kind of malice. He means no one any harm, if it is not for his interest. He is not a knave, nor perfectly honest. He does not easily resign a good place Mr. Vansittart is a well-meaning man.

The Irish are a good-natured people; they have many virtues, but their virtues are those of the heart, not of the head. In their passions and affections they are sincere, but they are hypocrites in understanding. If they once begin to calculate the consequences, self-interest prevails. An Irishman who trusts to his principles, and a Scotchman who yields to his impulses, are equally dangerous. The Irish have wit, genius, eloquence, imagination, affections: but they want coherence of understanding, and consequently have no standard of thought or action. Their strength of mind does not keep pace with the warmth of their feelings, or the quickness of their concep- tions. Their animal spirits run away with them: their reason is a jade. There is something crude, indigested, rash, and discordant, in almost all that they do or say. They have no system, no abstract ideas. They are 'everything by starts, and nothing long.' They are a wild people. They hate whatever imposes a law on their understandings, or a yoke on their wills. To betray the principles they are most bound by their own professions and the expectations of others to maintain, is with them a reclamation of their original rights, and to fly in the face of their benefactors and friends, an assertion of their natural freedom of will. They want consistency and good faith. They unite fierceness with levity. In the midst of their headlong impulses, they have an under-current of selfishness and cunning, which in the end gets the better of them. Their feelings, when no longer excited by novelty or opposition, grow cold and stagnant. Their blood, if not heated by passion, turns to poison. They have a rancour in their hatred of any object they have abandoned, proportioned to the attachment they have professed to it. Their zeal, converted against itself, is furious. The late Mr. Burke was an ınstance of an Irish patriot and philosopher. He abused metaphysics, because he could make nothing out of them, and turned his back upon liberty, when he found he could get nothing more by her.[1]—See to the same purpose the winding up of the character of *Judy* in Miss Edgeworth's *Castle Rackrent*.   T. T.

ON THE CHARACTER OF MILTON'S EVE

THE difference between the character of *Eve* in Milton and Shakspeare's female characters is very striking, and it appears to us to be this: Milton describes *Eve* not only as full of love and tenderness for *Adam*, but as the constant object of admiration in herself. She is the idol of the poet's imagination, and he paints her whole person with a studied profusion of charms. She is the wife, but she is still as much as ever the mistress, of *Adam*. She is represented, indeed, as devoted to her husband, as twining round him for support 'as the vine curls her tendrils,' but her own grace and beauty are never lost sight of in the picture of conjugal felicity. *Adam's* attention and regard are as much turned to her as hers to him; for 'in that first garden of their innocence,' he had no other objects or pursuits to distract his attention; she was both his business and his pleasure. Shakspeare's females, on the contrary, seem to exist only in their attachment to others. They are pure abstractions of the affections. Their features are not painted, nor the colour of their hair. Their hearts only are laid open. We are acquainted with *Imogen*, *Miranda*, *Ophelia*, or *Desdemona*, by what they thought and felt, but we cannot tell whether they were black, brown, or fair. But Milton's *Eve* is all of ivory and gold. Shakspeare seldom tantalises the

---

[1] This man (Burke) who was a half poet and a half philosopher, has done more mischief than perhaps any other person in the world. His understanding was not competent to the discovery of any truth, but it was sufficient to palliate a falsehood; his reasons, of little weight in themselves, thrown into the scale of power, were dreadful. Without genius to adorn the beautiful, he had the art to throw a dazzling veil over the deformed and disgusting; and to strew the flowers of imagination over the rotten carcass of corruption, not to prevent, but to communicate the infection. His jealousy of Rousseau was one chief cause of his opposition to the French Revolution. The writings of the one had changed the institutions of a kingdom; while the speeches of the other, with the intrigues of his whole party, had changed nothing but the *turnspit of the King's kitchen*. He would have blotted out the broad pure light of Heaven, because it did not first shine in at the little Gothic windows of St. Stephen's Chapel. The genius of Rousseau had levelled the towers of the Bastile with the dust; our zealous reformist, who would rather be doing mischief than nothing, tried, therefore, to patch them up again, by calling that loathsome dungeon the King's castle, and by fulsome adulation of the virtues of a Court strumpet. This man,—but enough of him here.

reader with a luxurious display of the personal charms of his heroines, with a curious inventory of particular beauties, except indirectly, and for some other purpose, as where *Jachimo* describes *Imogen* asleep, or the old men in the *Winter's Tale* vie with each other in invidious praise of *Perdita*. Even in *Juliet*, the most voluptuous and glowing of the class of characters here spoken of, we are reminded chiefly of circumstances connected with the physiognomy of passion, as in her leaning with her cheek upon her arm, or which only convey the general impression of enthusiasm made on her lover's brain. One thing may be said, that Shakspeare had not the same opportunities as Milton : for his women were clothed, and it cannot be denied that Milton took *Eve* at a considerable disadvantage in this respect. He has accordingly described her in all the loveliness of nature, tempting to sight as the fruit of the Hesperides guarded by that Dragon old, herself the fairest among the flowers of Paradise !

The figures both of *Adam* and *Eve* are very prominent in this poem. As there is little action in it, the interest is constantly kept up by the beauty and grandeur of the images. They are thus introduced :

'Two of far nobler shape, erect and tall,
Godlike erect, with native honour clad,
In naked majesty seemed lords of all,
And worthy seemed ; for in their looks divine
The image of their glorious Maker shone :

.   .   .   .   .

———— Though both
Not equal, as their sex not equal seem'd ;
For contemplation he and valour form'd,
For softness she and sweet attractive grace ;
He for God only, she for God in him.
His fair large front and eye sublime declar'd
Absolute rule ; and hyacinthine locks
Round from his parted forelock manly hung
Clust'ring, but not beneath his shoulders broad ;
She as a veil down to the slender waist
Her unadorned golden tresses wore
Dishevell'd, but in wanton ringlets wav'd
As the vine curls her tendrils, which implied
Subjection, but required with gentle sway,
And by her yielded, by him best receiv'd,
Yielded with coy submission, modest pride,
And sweet reluctant amorous delay.'

Eve is not only represented as beautiful, but with conscious beauty. Shakspeare's heroines are almost insensible of their charms, and wound without knowing it. They are not coquets. If the salvation

of mankind had depended upon one of them, we don't know—but the
Devil might have been baulked.   This is but a conjecture!   *Eve* has
a great idea of herself, and there is some difficulty in prevailing on her
to quit her own image, the first time she discovers its reflection in
the water.   She gives the following account of herself to *Adam*:

> ' That day I oft remember, when from sleep
> I first awak'd, and found myself repos'd
> Under a shade on flow'rs, much wond'ring where
> And what I was, whence thither brought and how.
> Not distant far from thence a murmuring sound
> Of waters issued from a cave, and spread
> Into a liquid plain, then stood unmov'd
> Pure as the expanse of Heav'n ; I thither went
> With unexperienc'd thought, and laid me down
> On the green bank, to look into the clear
> Smooth lake, that to me seem'd another sky.
> As I bent down to look, just opposite
> A shape within the watery gleam appear'd,
> Bending to look on me ; I started back,
> It started back ; but pleas'd I soon return'd,
> Pleas'd it return'd as soon with answ'ring looks
> Of sympathy and love.' .

The poet afterwards adds :

> ' So spake our general mother, and with eyes
> Of conjugal attraction unreprov'd,
> And meek surrender, half-embracing lean'd
> On our first father ; half her swelling breast
> Naked met his under the flowing gold
> Of her loose tresses hid : he in delight
> Both of her beauty and submissive charms ;
> Smil'd with superior love, as Jupiter
> On Juno smiles, when he impregns the clouds
> That shed May flowers.'

The same thought is repeated with greater simplicity, and perhaps
even beauty, in the beginning of the Fifth Book :

> ——' So much the more
> His wonder was to find unawaken'd Eve
> With tresses discompos'd and glowing cheek,
> As through unquiet rest : he on his side
> Leaning half-rais'd, with looks of cordial love
> Hung over her enamour'd, and beheld
> Beauty, which whether waking or asleep
> Shot forth peculiar graces ; then, with voice
> Mild, as when Zephyrus on Flora breathes,

THE ROUND TABLE

> Her hand soft touching, whisper'd thus.   Awake
> My fairest, my espous'd, my latest found,
> Heav'n's last best gift, my ever new delight,
> Awake' . . .

The general style, indeed, in which *Eve* is addressed by *Adam*, or described by the poet, is in the highest strain of compliment :

> 'When Adam thus to Eve.   Fair consort, the hour
> Of night approaches.' . . .

> 'To whom thus Eve, with perfect beauty adorn'd.'

> 'To whom our general ancestor replied,
> Daughter of God and Man, accomplish'd Eve.'

Eve is herself so well convinced that these epithets are her due, that the idea follows her in her sleep, and she dreams of herself as the paragon of nature, the wonder of the universe :

> ———' Methought
> Close at mine ear one call'd me forth to walk,
> With gentle voice, I thought it thine ; it said,
> Why sleep'st thou, Eve ?   Now is the pleasant time,
> The cool, the silent, save where silence yields
> To the night-warbling bird, that now awake
> Tunes sweetest his love-labour'd song ; now reigns
> Full-orb'd the moon, and with more pleasing light
> Shadowy sets off the face of things ; in vain,
> If none regard ; Heav'n wakes with all his eyes,
> Whom to behold but thee, Nature's desire ?
> In whose sight all things joy, with ravishment
> Attracted by thy beauty still to gaze.'

This is the very topic, too, on which the Serpent afterwards enlarges with so much artful insinuation and fatal confidence of success.   ' So talked the spirited sly snake.'   The conclusion of the foregoing scene, in which *Eve* relates her dream and *Adam* comforts her, is such an exquisite piece of description, that, though not to our immediate purpose, we cannot refrain from quoting it :

> ' So cheer'd he his fair spouse, and she was cheer'd ;
> But silently a gentle tear let fall
> From either eye, and wip'd them with her hair ;
> Two other precious drops that ready stood,
> Each in their crystal sluice, he ere they fell
> Kiss'd, as the gracious signs of sweet remorse
> And pious awe, that fear'd to have offended.'

ON THE CHARACTER OF MILTON'S EVE

The formal eulogy on *Eve* which *Adam* addresses to the Angel, in giving an account of his own creation and hers, is full of elaborate grace:

> ' Under his forming hands a creature grew,
> .   .   .   .   so lovely fair,
> That what seem'd fair in all the world, seem'd now
> Mean, or in her summ'd up, in her contained
> And in her looks, which from that time infus'd
> Sweetness into my heart, unfelt before,
> And into all things from her air inspir'd
> The spirit of love and amorous delight.'

That which distinguishes Milton from the other poets, who have pampered the eye and fed the imagination with exuberant descriptions of female beauty, is the moral severity with which he has tempered them. There is not a line in his works which tends to licentiousness, or the impression of which, if it has such a tendency, is not effectually checked by thought and sentiment. The following are two remarkable instances:

> ——' In shadier bower
> More secret and sequester'd, though but feign'd,
> Pan or Sylvanus never slept, nor Nymph,
> Nor Faunus haunted. Here in close recess,
> With flowers, garlands, and sweet-smelling herbs,
> Espoused Eve deck'd first her nuptial bed,
> And heavenly quires the hymenœan sung,
> What day the genial Angel to our sire
> Brought her in naked beauty more adorn'd,
> More lovely than Pandora, whom the Gods
> Endow'd with all their gifts, and O too like
> In sad event, when to th' unwiser son
> Of Japhet brought by Hermes, she ensnar'd
> Mankind by her fair looks, to be aveng'd
> On him who had stole Jove's authentic fire.'

The other is a passage of extreme beauty and pathos blended. It is the one in which the Angel is described as the guest of our first ancestors:

> ——' Meanwhile at table Eve
> Minister'd naked, and their flowing cups
> With pleasant liquors crown'd: O innocence
> Deserving Paradise ! if ever, then,
> Then had the sons of God excuse to have been
> Enamour'd at that sight ; but in those hearts
> Love unlibidinous reigned, nor jealousy
> Was understood, the injur'd lover's Hell.'

The character which a living poet has given of Spenser, would b
much more true of Milton:

> ———'Yet not more sweet
> Than pure was he, and not more pure than wise;
> High Priest of all the Muses' mysteries.'

Spenser, on the contrary, is very apt to pry into mysteries whic
do not belong to the Muses. Milton's voluptuousness is not lasciv
ous or sensual. He describes beautiful objects for their own sake
Spenser has an eye to the consequences, and steeps everything i
pleasure, often not of the purest kind. The want of passion has bee
brought as an objection against Milton, and his *Adam* and *Eve* hav
been considered as rather insipid personages, wrapped up in on
another, and who excite but little sympathy in any one else. We d
not feel this objection ourselves: we are content to be spectators i
such scenes, without any other excitement. In general, the interest i
Milton is essentially epic, and not dramatic; and the differenc
between the epic and the dramatic is this, that in the former th
imagination produces the passion, and in the latter the passion pr
duces the imagination. The interest of epic poetry arises from th
contemplation of certain objects in themselves grand and beautiful: th
interest of dramatic poetry from sympathy with the passions an
pursuits of others; that is, from the practical relations of certai
persons to certain objects, as depending on accident or will.

The Pyramids of Egypt are epic objects; the imagination of the
is necessarily attended with passion; but they have no dramat
interest, till circumstances connect them with some human catastroph
Now, a poem might be constructed almost entirely of such images,
the highest intellectual passion, with little dramatic interest; and
is in this way that Milton has in a great measure constructed h
poem. That is not its fault, but its excellence. The fault is
those who have no idea but of one kind of interest. But this questic
would lead to a longer discussion than we have room for at preser
We shall conclude these extracts from Milton with two passage
which have always appeared to us to be highly affecting, and
contain a fine discrimination of character:

> 'O unexpected stroke, worse than of Death!
> Must I thus leave thee, Paradise? thus leave
> Thee, native soil, these happy walks and shades,
> Fit haunt of Gods? Where I had hope to spend,
> Quiet, though sad, the respite of that day
> That must be mortal to us both? O flowers,
> That never will in other climate grow,

My early visitation and my last
At even, which I bred up with tender hand
From the first opening bud, and gave ye names,
Who now shall rear ye to the sun, or rank
Your tribes, and water from th' ambrosial fount?
Thee, lastly, nuptial bow'r, by me adorn'd
With what to sight or smell was sweet, from thee
How shall I part, and whither wander down
Into a lower world, to this obscure
And wild? how shall we breathe in other air
Less pure, accustom'd to immortal fruits?'

This is the lamentation of *Eve* on being driven out of Paradise. Adam's reflections are in a different strain, and still finer. After expressing his submission to the will of his Maker, he says:

' This most afflicts me, that departing hence
As from his face I shall be hid, depriv'd
His blessed countenance; here I could frequent
With worship place by place where he vouchsaf'd
Presence divine, and to my sons relate,
On this mount he appeared, under this tree
Stood visible, among these pines his voice
I heard, here with him at this fountain talk'd:
So many grateful altars I would rear
Of grassy turf, and pile up every stone
Of lustre from the brook, in memory
Or monument to ages, and thereon
Offer sweet-smelling gums and fruits and flow'rs:
In yonder nether world where shall I seek
His bright appearances or footstep trace?
For though I fled him angry, yet recall'd
To life prolong'd and promis'd race, I now
Gladly behold though but his utmost skirts
Of glory, and far off his steps adore.'

W. H.

OBSERVATIONS ON MR. WORDSWORTH'S POEM THE EXCURSION

THE poem of The *Excursion* resembles that part of the country in which the scene is laid. It has the same vastness and magnificence, with the same nakedness and confusion. It has the same overwhelming, oppressive power. It excites or recalls the same sensations which those who have traversed that wonderful scenery must have felt. We are surrounded with the constant sense and superstitious awe of the collective power of matter, of the gigantic and eternal forms of nature, on which, from the beginning of time, the hand of man has made no impression. Here are no dotted lines, no hedge-row beauties, no box-tree borders, no gravel walks, no square mechanic inclosures; all is left loose and irregular in the rude chaos of aboriginal nature. The boundaries of hill and valley are the poet's only geography, where we wander with him incessantly over deep beds of moss and waving fern, amidst the troops of red-deer and wild animals. Such is the severe simplicity of Mr. Wordsworth's taste, that we doubt whether he would not reject a druidical temple, or time-hallowed ruin as too modern and artificial for his purpose. He only familiarises himself or his readers with a stone, covered with lichens, which has slept in the same spot of ground from the creation of the world, or with the rocky fissure between two mountains caused by thunder, or with a cavern scooped out by the sea. His mind is, as it were, coëval with the primary forms of things; his imagination holds immediately from nature, and 'owes no allegiance' but 'to the elements.'

The *Excursion* may be considered as a philosophical pastoral poem, —as a scholastic romance. It is less a poem on the country, than on the love of the country. It is not so much a description of natural objects, as of the feelings associated with them; not an account of the manners of rural life, but the result of the poet's reflections on it. He does not present the reader with a lively succession of images or incidents, but paints the outgoings of his own heart, the shapings of his own fancy. He may be said to create his own materials; his thoughts are his real subject. His understanding broods over that which is 'without form and void,' and 'makes it pregnant.' He sees all things in himself. He hardly ever avails himself of remarkable objects or situations, but, in general, rejects them as interfering with the workings of his own mind, as disturbing the smooth, deep, majestic current of his own feelings. Thus his descriptions of natural scenery are not brought home distinctly to the naked eye by forms and circumstances, but every object is seen through the medium of innumerable recollections, is clothed with the haze of imagination like a glittering vapour, is obscured with the excess of glory, has the shadowy brightness of a waking dream. The image is lost in the sentiment, as sound in the multiplication of echoes.

> ' And visions, as prophetic eyes avow,
> Hang on each leaf, and cling to every bough.'

In describing human nature, Mr. Wordsworth equally shuns the common 'vantage-grounds of popular story, of striking incident, or fatal catastrophe, as cheap and vulgar modes of producing an effect. He scans the human race as the naturalist measures the earth's zone, without attending to the picturesque points of view, the abrupt inequalities of surface. He contemplates the passions and habits of men, not in their extremes, but in their first elements; their follies and vices, not at their height, with all their embossed evils upon their heads, but as lurking in embryo,—the seeds of the disorder inwoven with our very constitution. He only sympathises with those simple forms of feeling, which mingle at once with his own identity, or with the stream of general humanity. To him the great and the small are the same; the near and the remote; what appears, and what only is. The general and the permanent, like the Platonic ideas, are his only realities. All accidental varieties and individual contrasts are lost in an endless continuity of feeling, like drops of water in the ocean-stream! An intense intellectual egotism swallows up every thing. Even the dialogues introduced in the present volume are soliloquies of the same character, taking different views of the subject. The recluse, the pastor, and the pedlar, are three persons in one poet. We ourselves disapprove of these 'interlocutions between Lucius and Caius' as impertinent babbling, where there is no dramatic distinction of character. But the evident scope and tendency of Mr. Wordsworth's mind is the reverse of dramatic. It resists all change of character, all variety of scenery, all the bustle, machinery, and pantomime of the stage, or of real life,—whatever might relieve, or relax, or change the direction of its own activity, jealous of all competition. The power of his mind preys upon itself. It is as if there were nothing but himself and the universe. He lives in the busy solitude of his own heart; in the deep silence of thought. His imagination lends life and feeling only to 'the bare trees and mountains bare'; peoples the viewless tracts of air, and converses with the silent clouds!

We could have wished that our author had given to his work the form of a didactic poem altogether, with only occasional digressions or allusions to particular instances. But he has chosen to encumber himself with a load of narrative and description, which sometimes hinders the progress and effect of the general reasoning, and which, instead of being inwoven with the text, would have come in better in plain prose as notes at the end of the volume. Mr. Wordsworth, indeed, says finely, and perhaps as truly as finely:

> 'Exchange the shepherd's frock of native grey
> For robes with regal purple tinged; convert
> The crook into a sceptre; give the pomp
> Of circumstance; and here the tragic Muse
> Shall find apt subjects for her highest art.

> Amid the groves, beneath the shadowy hills,
> The generations are prepared ; the pangs,
> The internal pangs, are ready ; the dread strife
> Of poor humanity's afflicted will
> Struggling in vain with ruthless destiny.'

But he immediately declines availing himself of these resources of the rustic moralist : for the priest, who officiates as 'the sad historian of the pensive plain ' says in reply :

> ' Our system is not fashioned to preclude
> That sympathy which you for others ask :
> And I could tell, not travelling for my theme
> Beyond the limits of these humble graves,
> Of strange disasters ; but I pass them by,
> Loth to disturb what Heaven hath hushed to peace.'

There is, in fact, in Mr. Wordsworth's mind an evident repugnance to admit anything that tells for itself, without the interpretation of the poet,—a fastidious antipathy to immediate effect,—a systematic unwillingness to share the palm with his subject. Where, however, he has a subject presented to him, 'such as the meeting soul may pierce,' and to which he does not grudge to lend the aid of his fine genius, his powers of description and fancy seem to be little inferior to those of his classical predecessor, Akenside. Among several others which we might select we give the following passage, describing the religion of ancient Greece :

> ' In that fair clime, the lonely herdsman, stretch'd
> On the soft grass through half a summer's day,
> With music lulled his indolent repose :
> And in some fit of weariness, if he,
> When his own breath was silent, chanced to hear
> A distant strain, far sweeter than the sounds
> Which his poor skill could make, his fancy fetch'd,
> Even from the blazing chariot of the sun,
> A beardless youth, who touched a golden lute,
> And filled the illumined groves with ravishment.
> The nightly hunter, lifting up his eyes
> Towards the crescent moon, with grateful heart
> Called on the lovely wanderer, who bestowed
> That timely light, to share his joyous sport :
> And hence, a beaming Goddess with her Nymphs
> Across the lawn and through the darksome grove,
> (Nor unaccompanied with tuneful notes
> By echo multiplied from rock or cave),
> Swept in the storm of chase, as moon and stars
> Glance rapidly along the clouded heavens,

When winds are blowing strong. The traveller slaked
His thirst from rill, or gushing fount, and thanked
The Naiad. Sun beams, upon distant hills
Gliding apace, with shadows in their train,
Might, with small help from fancy, be transformed
Into fleet Oreads, sporting visibly.
The zephyrs fanning as they passed their wings
Lacked not for love fair objects, whom they wooed
With gentle whisper. Withered boughs grotesque,
Stripped of their leaves and twigs by hoary age,
From depth of shaggy covert peeping forth
In the low vale, or on steep mountain side:
And sometimes intermixed with stirring horns
Of the live deer, or goat's depending beard;
These were the lurking satyrs, a wild brood
Of gamesome Deities! or Pan himself,
The simple shepherd's awe-inspiring God.'

The foregoing is one of a succession of splendid passages equally
enriched with philosophy and poetry, tracing the fictions of Eastern
mythology to the immediate intercourse of the imagination with
Nature, and to the habitual propensity of the human mind to endow
the outward forms of being with life and conscious motion. With
this expansive and animating principle, Mr. Wordsworth has forcibly,
but somewhat severely, contrasted the cold, narrow, lifeless spirit of
modern philosophy:

'How, shall our great discoverers obtain
From sense and reason less than these obtained,
Though far misled? Shall men for whom our age
Unbaffled powers of vision hath prepared,
To explore the world without and world within,
Be joyless as the blind? Ambitious souls—
Whom earth at this late season hath produced
To regulate the moving spheres, and weigh
The planets in the hollow of their hand;
And they who rather dive than soar, whose pains
Have solved the elements, or analysed
The thinking principle—shall they in fact
Prove a degraded race? And what avails
Renown, if their presumption make them such?
Inquire of ancient wisdom; go, demand
Of mighty nature, if 'twas ever meant
That we should pry far off, yet be unraised;
That we should pore, and dwindle as we pore,
Viewing all objects unremittingly
In disconnection dead and spiritless;
And still dividing and dividing still

Break down all grandeur, still unsatisfied
With the perverse attempt, while littleness
May yet become more little ; waging thus
An impious warfare with the very life
Of our own souls ! And if indeed there be
An all-pervading spirit, upon whom
Our dark foundations rest, could he design,
That this magnificent effect of power,
The earth we tread, the sky which we behold
By day, and all the pomp which night reveals,
That these—and that superior mystery,
Our vital frame, so fearfully devised,
And the dread soul within it—should exist
Only to be examined, pondered, searched,
Probed, vexed, and criticised—to be prized
No more than as a mirror that reflects
To proud Self-love her own intelligence ?'

From the chemists and metaphysicians our author turns to the laughing sage of France, Voltaire. 'Poor gentleman, it fares no better with him, for he's a wit.' We cannot, however, agree with Mr. Wordsworth that *Candide* is *dull*. It is, if our author pleases, 'the production of a scoffer's pen,' or it is any thing but dull. It may not be proper in a grave, discreet, orthodox, promising young divine, who studies his opinions in the contraction or distension of his patron's brow, to allow any merit to a work like *Candide* ; but we conceive that it would have been more manly in Mr. Wordsworth, nor do we think it would have hurt the cause he espouses, if he had blotted out the epithet, after it had peevishly escaped him. Whatsoever savours of a little, narrow, inquisitorial spirit, does not sit well on a poet and a man of genius. The prejudices of a philosopher are not natural. There is a frankness and sincerity of opinion, which is a paramount obligation in all questions of intellect, though it may not govern the decisions of the spiritual courts, who may, however, be safely left to take care of their own interests. There is a plain directness and simplicity of understanding, which is the only security against the evils of levity, on the one hand, or of hypocrisy on the other. A speculative bigot is a solecism in the intellectual world. We can assure Mr. Wordsworth, that we should not have bestowed so much serious consideration on a single voluntary perversion of language, but that our respect for his character makes us jealous of his smallest faults !

With regard to his general philippic against the contractedness and egotism of philosophical pursuits, we only object to its not being carried further. We shall not affirm with Rousseau (his authority would perhaps have little weight with Mr. Wordsworth)—'*Tout homme reflechi est mechant*'; but we conceive that the same reasoning which Mr. Wordsworth applies so eloquently and justly to the natural philosopher and metaphysician may be extended to the moralist, the divine, the politician, the orator, the artist, and even the poet. And why so? Because wherever an intense activity is given to any one faculty, it necessarily prevents the due and natural exercise of others. Hence all those professions or pursuits, where the mind is exclusively occupied with the ideas of things as they exist in the imagination or understanding, as they call for the exercise of intellectual activity, and not as they are connected with practical good or evil, must check the genial expansion of the moral sentiments and social affections; must lead to a cold and dry abstraction, as they are found to suspend the animal functions, and relax the bodily frame. Hence the complaint of the want of natural sensibility and constitutional warmth of attachment in those persons who have been devoted to the pursuit of any art or science,—of their restless morbidity of temperament, and indifference to every thing that does not furnish an occasion for the display of their mental superiority and the gratification of their vanity. The philosophical poet himself, perhaps, owes some of his love of nature to the opportunity it affords him of analyzing his own feelings, and contemplating his own powers,—of making every object about him a whole length mirror to reflect his favourite thoughts, and of looking down on the frailties of others in undisturbed leisure, and from a more dignified height.

One of the most interesting parts of this work is that in which the author treats of the French Revolution, and of the feelings connected with it, in ingenuous minds, in its commencement and its progress. The *solitary*,[1] who, by domestic calamities and disappointments, had been cut off from society, and almost from himself, gives the following account of the manner in which he was roused from his melancholy:

> ' From that abstraction I was roused—and how?
> Even as a thoughtful shepherd by a flash
> Of lightning, startled in a gloomy cave
> Of these wild hills. For, lo! the dread Bastile,
> With all the chambers in its horrid towers,
> Fell to the ground: by violence o'erthrown
> Of indignation; and with shouts that drowned
> The crash it made in falling! From the wreck
> A golden palace rose, or seemed to rise,
> The appointed seat of equitable law

---

[1] This word is not English.

And mild paternal sway. The potent shock
I felt ; the transformation I perceived,
As marvellously seized as in that moment,
When, from the blind mist issuing, I beheld
Glory—beyond all glory ever seen,
Dazzling the soul ! Meanwhile prophetic harps
In every grove were ringing, " War shall cease :
Did ye not hear that conquest is abjured ?
Bring garlands, bring forth choicest flowers, to deck
The tree of liberty ! "—My heart rebounded :
My melancholy voice the chorus joined.
Thus was I reconverted to the world ;
Society became my glittering bride,
And airy hopes my children. From the depths
Of natural passion seemingly escaped,
My soul diffused itself in wide embrace
Of institutions and the forms of things.
　　　　　　　　　　——If with noise
And acclamation, crowds in open air
Expressed the tumult of their minds, my voice
There mingled, heard or not. And in still groves,
Where wild enthusiasts tuned a pensive lay
Of thanks and expectation, in accord
With their belief, I sang Saturnian rule
Returned—a progeny of golden years
Permitted to descend, and bless mankind.

　　　.　　　.　　　.　　　.　　　.

Scorn and contempt forbid me to proceed !
But history, time's slavish scribe, will tell
How rapidly the zealots of the cause
Disbanded—or in hostile ranks appeared :
Some, tired of honest service ; these outdone,
Disgusted, therefore, or appalled by aims
Of fiercer zealots. So confusion reigned,
And the more faithful were compelled to exclaim,
As Brutus did to virtue, " Liberty,
I worshipped thee, and find thee but a shade ! "
SUCH RECANTATION HAD FOR ME NO CHARM,
NOR WOULD I BEND TO IT.'

The subject is afterwards resumed, with the same magnanimity
and philosophical firmness :

　　　　　　　　　——'For that other loss,
The loss of confidence in social man,
By the unexpected transports of our age
Carried so high, that every thought which looked
Beyond the temporal destiny of the kind—
To many seemed superfluous ; as no cause
For such exalted confidence could e'er

Exist; so, none is now for such despair.
The two extremes are equally remote
From truth and reason; do not, then, confound
One with the other, but reject them both ;
And choose the middle point, whereon to build
Sound expectations. This doth he advise
Who shared at first the illusion. At this day,
When a Tartarian darkness overspreads
The groaning nations ; when the impious rule,
By will or by established ordinance,
Their own dire agents, and constrain the good
To acts which they abhor; though I bewail
This triumph, yet the pity of my heart
Prevents me not from owning that the law,
By which mankind now suffers, is most just.
For by superior energies; more strict
Affiance in each other; faith more firm
In their unhallowed principles, the bad
Have fairly earned a victory o'er the weak,
The vacillating, inconsistent good.'

In the application of these memorable lines, we should, perhaps, differ a little from Mr. Wordsworth; nor can we indulge with him in the fond conclusion afterwards hinted at, that one day *our* triumph, the triumph of humanity and liberty, may be complete. For this purpose, we think several things necessary which are impossible. It is a consummation which cannot happen till the nature of things is changed, till the many become as united as the *one*, till romantic generosity shall be as common as gross selfishness, till reason shall have acquired the obstinate blindness of prejudice, till the love of power and of change shall no longer goad man on to restless action, till passion and will, hope and fear, love and hatred, and the objects proper to excite them, that is, alternate good and evil, shall no longer sway the bosoms and businesses of men. All things move, not in progress, but in a ceaseless round; our strength lies in our weakness; our virtues are built on our vices; our faculties are as limited as our being; nor can we lift man above his nature more than above the earth he treads. But though we cannot weave over again the airy, unsubstantial dream, which reason and experience have dispelled,

' What though the radiance, which was once so bright,
Be now for ever taken from our sight,
Though nothing can bring back the hour
Of glory in the grass, of splendour in the flower ':—

yet we will never cease, nor be prevented from returning on the wings of imagination to that bright dream of our youth; that glad dawn of the day-star of liberty; that spring-time of the world, in which the hopes and expectations of the human race seemed opening in the same gay career with our own; when France called her children to partake her equal blessings beneath her laughing skies; when the stranger was met in all her villages with dance and festive songs, in celebration of a new and golden era; and when, to the retired and contemplative student, the prospects of human happiness and glory were seen ascending like the steps of Jacob's ladder, in bright and never-ending succession. The dawn of that day was suddenly overcast; that season of hope is past; it is fled with the other dreams of our youth, which we cannot recal, but has left behind it traces, which are not to be effaced by Birth-day and Thanks-giving odes, or the chaunting of *Te Deums* in all the churches of Christendom. To those hopes eternal regrets are due; to those who maliciously and wilfully blasted them, in the fear that they might be accomplished, we feel no less what we owe—hatred and scorn as lasting!

THE SAME SUBJECT CONTINUED

MR. WORDSWORTH'S writings exhibit all the internal power, without the external form of poetry. He has scarcely any of the pomp and decoration and scenic effect of poetry: no gorgeous palaces nor solemn temples awe the imagination; no cities rise ' with glistering spires and pinnacles adorned '; we meet with no knights pricked forth on airy steeds; no hair-breadth 'scapes and perilous accidents by flood or field. Either from the predominant habit of his mind not requiring the stimulus of outward impressions, or from the want of an imagination teeming with various forms, he takes the common every-day events and objects of nature, or rather seeks those that are the most simple and barren of effect; but he adds to them a weight of interest from the resources of his own mind, which makes the most insignificant things serious and even formidable. All other interests are absorbed in the deeper interest of his own thoughts, and find the same level. His mind magnifies the littleness of his subject, and raises its meanness; lends it his strength, and clothes it with borrowed grandeur. With him, a molehill, covered with wild thyme, assumes the importance of 'the great vision of the guarded mount': a puddle is filled with preternatural faces, and agitated with the fiercest storms of passion.

The extreme simplicity which some persons have objected to in Mr. Wordsworth's poetry, is to be found only in the subject and the style: the sentiments are subtle and profound. In the latter respect, his poetry is as much above the common standard or capacity, as in the other it is below it. His poems bear a distant resemblance to some of Rembrandt's landscapes, who, more than any other painter, created the medium through which he saw nature, and out of the stump of an old tree, a break in the sky, and a bit of water, could produce an effect almost miraculous.

Mr. Wordsworth's poems in general are the history of a refined and contemplative mind, conversant only with itself and nature. An intense feeling of the associations of this kind is the peculiar and characteristic feature of all his productions. He has described the love of nature better than any other poet. This sentiment, inly felt in all its force, and sometimes carried to an excess, is the source both of his strength and of his weakness. However we may sympathise with Mr. Wordsworth in his attachment to groves and fields, we cannot extend the same admiration to their inhabitants, or to the manners of country life in general. We go along with him, while he is the subject of his own narrative, but we take leave of him when he makes pedlars and ploughmen his heroes and the interpreters of his sentiments. It is, we think, getting into low company, and company, besides, that we do not like. We take Mr. Wordsworth himself for a great poet, a fine moralist, and a deep philosopher; but if he insists on introducing us to a friend of his, a parish clerk, or the barber of the village, who is as wise as himself, we must be excused if we draw back with some little want of cordial faith. We are satisfied with the friendship which subsisted between *Parson Adams* and *Joseph Andrews*. The author himself lets out occasional hints that all is not as it should be amongst these northern Arcadians. Though, in general, he professes to soften the harsher features of rustic vice, he has given us one picture of depraved and inveterate selfishness, which we apprehend could only be found among the inhabitants of these boasted mountain districts. The account of one of his heroines concludes as follows:

> ' A sudden illness seiz'd her in the strength
> Of life's autumnal season. Shall I tell
> How on her bed of death the matron lay,
> To Providence submissive, so she thought ;
> But fretted, vexed, and wrought upon—almost
> To anger, by the malady that griped
> Her prostrate frame with unrelaxing power,
> As the fierce eagle fastens on the lamb.
> She prayed, she moaned—her husband's sister watched
> Her dreary pillow, waited on her needs ;
> And yet the very sound of that kind foot
> Was anguish to her ears ! " And must she rule
> Sole mistress of this house when I am gone?
> Sit by my fire—possess what I possessed—

Tend what I tended—calling it her own!"
Enough;—I fear too much. Of nobler feeling
Take this example:—One autumnal evening,
While she was yet in prime of health and strength,
I well remember, while I passed her door,
Musing with loitering step, and upward eye
Turned tow'rds the planet Jupiter, that hung
Above the centre of the vale, a voice
Roused me, her voice;—it said, "That glorious star
In its untroubled element will shine
As now it shines, when we are laid in earth,
And safe from all our sorrows." She is safe,
And her uncharitable acts, I trust,
And harsh unkindnesses, are all forgiven;
Though, in this vale, remembered with deep awe!

We think it is pushing our love of the admiration of natural objects a good deal too far, to make it a set-off against a story like the preceding.

All country people hate each other. They have so little comfort, that they envy their neighbours the smallest pleasure or advantage, and nearly grudge themselves the necessaries of life. From not being accustomed to enjoyment, they become hardened and averse to it—stupid, for want of thought—selfish, for want of society. There is nothing good to be had in the country, or, if there is, they will not let you have it. They had rather injure themselves than oblige any one else. Their common mode of life is a system of wretchedness and self-denial, like what we read of among barbarous tribes. You live out of the world. You cannot get your tea and sugar without sending to the next town for it: you pay double, and have it of the worst quality. The small-beer is sure to be sour—the milk skimmed—the meat bad, or spoiled in the cooking. You cannot do a single thing you like; you cannot walk out or sit at home, or write or read, or think or look as if you did, without being subject to impertinent curiosity. The apothecary annoys you with his complaisance; the parson with his superciliousness. If you are poor, you are despised; if you are rich, you are feared and hated. If you do any one a favour, the whole neighbourhood is up in arms; the clamour is like that of a rookery; and the person himself, it is ten to one, laughs at you for your pains, and takes the first opportunity of shewing you that he labours under no uneasy sense of obligation. There is a perpetual round of mischief-making and backbiting for want of any better amusement. There are no shops, no taverns, no theatres, no opera, no concerts, no pictures, no public-buildings, no crowded streets, no noise of coaches, or of courts of law,—neither courtiers nor courtesans, no literary parties, no fashionable routs, no society, no books, or knowledge of books. Vanity and luxury are the civilisers of the world, and sweeteners of human life. Without objects either of pleasure or action, it grows harsh and crabbed: the mind becomes stagnant, the affections callous, and the eye dull. Man left to himself soon degenerates into a very disagreeable person. Ignorance is always bad enough; but rustic ignorance is intolerable. Aristotle has observed, that tragedy purifies the affections by terror and pity. If so, a company of tragedians should be established at the public expence, in every village or hundred, as a better mode of education than either Bell's or Lancaster's. The benefits of knowledge are never so well understood as from seeing the effects of ignorance, in their naked, undisguised state, upon the common country people. Their selfishness and insensibility are perhaps less owing to the hardships and privations, which make them, like people out at sea in a boat, ready to devour one another, than to their having no idea of anything beyond themselves and their immediate sphere of action. They have no knowledge of, and consequently can take no interest in, anything which is not an object of their senses, and of their daily pursuits. They hate all strangers, and have generally a nick-name for the inhabitants of the next village. The two young noblemen in Guzman d'Alfarache, who went to visit their mistresses only a league out of Madrid, were set upon by the peasants, who came round them calling out, '*A wolf.*' Those who have no enlarged or liberal ideas, can have no disinterested or generous sentiments. Persons who are in the habit of reading novels and romances, are compelled to take a deep interest in, and to have their affections strongly excited by, fictitious characters and imaginary situations; their thoughts and feelings are constantly carried out of themselves, to persons they never saw, and things that never existed: history enlarges the mind, by familiarising us with the great vicissitudes of human affairs, and the catastrophes of states and kingdoms; the study of morals accustoms us to refer our actions to a general standard of right and wrong; and abstract reasoning, in general, strengthens the love of truth, and produces an inflexibility of principle which cannot stoop to low trick and cunning. Books, in Lord Bacon's phrase, are 'a discipline of humanity.' Country people have none of these advantages, nor any others to supply the place of them. Having no circulating libraries to exhaust their love of the marvellous, they amuse themselves with fancying the disasters and disgraces of their particular acquaintance. Having no hump-backed *Richard* to excite their wonder and abhorrence, they make themselves a bug-bear of their own, out of the first obnoxious person they can lay their hands on. Not having the fictitious distresses and gigantic crimes of poetry to stimulate their imagination and their passions, they vent their whole stock of spleen, malice, and invention, on their friends and next-door neighbours. They get up a little pastoral drama at home, with fancied events, but real characters. All their spare time is spent in manufacturing and propagating the lie for the day, which does its office, and expires. The next day is spent in the same manner. It is thus that they embellish the simplicity of rural life! The common people in civilised countries are a kind of domesticated savages. They have not the wild imagination, the passions, the fierce energies, or dreadful vicissitudes of the savage tribes, nor have they the leisure, the indolent enjoyments and romantic superstitions, which belonged to the pastoral life in milder climates, and more remote periods of society. They are taken out of a state of nature, without being put in possession of the refinements of art. The customs and institutions of society cramp their imaginations without giving them knowledge. If the inhabitants of the mountainous districts described by Mr. Wordsworth are less gross and sensual than others, they are more selfish. Their egotism becomes more concentrated, as they are more insulated, and their purposes more inveterate, as they have less competition to struggle with. The weight of matter which surrounds them, crushes the finer sympathies. Their minds become hard and cold, like the rocks which they cultivate. The immensity of their mountains makes the human form appear little and insignificant. Men are seen crawling between Heaven and earth, like insects to their graves. Nor do they regard one another more than flies on a wall. Their physiognomy expresses the materialism of their character, which has only one principle—rigid self-will. They move on with their eyes and foreheads fixed, looking neither to the right nor to the left, with a heavy slouch in their gait, and seeming as if nothing would divert them from their path. We do not admire this plodding pertinacity, always directed to the main chance. There is nothing which excites so little sympathy in our minds, as exclusive selfishness. If our theory is wrong, at least it is taken from pretty close observation, and is, we think, confirmed by Mr. Wordsworth's own account.

Of the stories contained in the latter part of the volume, we like that of the Whig and Jacobite friends, and of the good knight, Sir Alfred Irthing, the best. The last reminded us of a fine sketch of a similar character in the beautiful poem of *Hart Leap Well*. To conclude,—if the skill with which the poet had chosen his materials had been equal to the power which he has undeniably exerted over them, if the objects (whether persons or things) which he makes use of as the vehicle of his sentiments, had been such as to convey them in all their depth and force, then the production before us might indeed 'have proved a monument,' as he himself wishes it, worthy of the author, and of his country. Whether, as it is, this very original and powerful performance may not rather remain like one of those stupendous but half-finished structures, which have been suffered to moulder into decay, because the cost and labour attending them exceeded their use or beauty, we feel that it would be presumptuous in us to determine.

CHARACTER OF THE LATE MR. PITT[1]

THE character of Mr. Pitt was, perhaps, one of the most singular that ever existed. With few talents, and fewer virtues, he acquired and preserved, in one of the most trying situations, and in spite of all opposition, the highest reputation for the possession of every moral excellence, and as having carried the attainments of eloquence and wisdom as far as human abilities could go. This he did (strange as it may appear) by a negation (together with the common virtues) of the common vices of human nature, and by the complete negation of every other talent that might interfere with the only ones which he possessed in a supreme degree, and which, indeed, may be made to include the appearance of all others,—an artful use of words, and a certain dexterity of logical arrangement. In these alone his power consisted; and the defect of all other qualities, which usually constitute greatness, contributed to the more complete success of these. Having no strong feelings, no distinct perceptions,—his mind having no link, as it were, to connect it with the world of external nature, every subject presented to him nothing more than a *tabula rasa*, on which he was at liberty to lay whatever colouring of language he pleased; having no general principles, no comprehensive views of things, no moral habits of thinking, no system of action, there was nothing to hinder him from pursuing any particular purpose by any means that offered; having never any plan, he could not be convicted of inconsistency, and his own pride and obstinacy were the only rules of his conduct. Without insight into human nature, without sympathy with the passions of men, or apprehension of their real designs, he seemed perfectly insensible to the consequences of things, and would believe nothing till it actually happened. The fog and haze in which he saw every thing communicated itself to others; and the total indistinctness and uncertainty of his own ideas tended to confound the perceptions of his hearers more effectually than the most

[1] Written in 1806.

ingenious misrepresentation could have done. Indeed, in defending his conduct, he never seemed to consider himself as at all responsible for the success of his measures, or to suppose that future events were in our own power; but that, as the best-laid schemes might fail, and there was no providing against all possible contingencies, this was sufficient excuse for our plunging at once into any dangerous or absurd enterprise without the least regard to consequences. His reserved logic confined itself solely to the *possible* and the *impossible*, and he appeared to regard the *probable* and *improbable*, the only foundation of moral prudence or political wisdom, as beneath the notice of a profound statesman; as if the pride of the human intellect were concerned in never entrusting itself with subjects, where it may be compelled to acknowledge its weakness. Nothing could ever drive him out of his dull forms, and naked generalities; which, as they are susceptible neither of degree nor variation, are therefore equally applicable to every emergency that can happen: and in the most critical aspect of affairs, he saw nothing but the same flimsy web of remote possibilities and metaphysical uncertainty. In his mind, the wholesome pulp of practical wisdom and salutary advice was immediately converted into the dry chaff and husks of a miserable logic. From his manner of reasoning, he seemed not to have believed that the truth of his statements depended on the reality of the facts, but that the facts themselves depended on the order in which he arranged them in words: you would not suppose him to be agitating a serious question, which had real grounds to go upon, but to be declaiming upon an imaginary thesis, proposed as an exercise in the schools. He never set himself to examine the force of the objections that were brought against him, or attempted to defend his measures upon clear, solid grounds of his own; but constantly contented himself with first gravely stating the logical form, or dilemma to which the question reduced itself; and then, after having declared his opinion, proceeded to amuse his hearers by a series of rhetorical common-places, connected together in grave, sonorous, and elaborately constructed periods, without ever shewing their real application to the subject in dispute. Thus, if any member of the opposition disapproved of any measure, and enforced his objections by pointing out the many evils with which it was fraught, or the difficulties attending its execution, his only answer was, 'that it was true there might be inconveniences attending the measure proposed, but we were to remember, that every expedient that could be devised might be said to be nothing more than a choice of difficulties, and that all that human prudence could do, was to consider on which side the advantages lay; that, for his part, he conceived that the present measure was attended with more advantages and fewer disadvantages than any other that could be adopted; that if we were diverted from our object by every appearance of difficulty, the wheels of government would be clogged by endless delays and imaginary grievances; that most of the objections made to the measure appeared to him to be trivial, others of them unfounded and improbable; or that, if a scheme, free from all these objections, could be proposed, it might, after all, prove inefficient; while, in the meantime, a material object remained unprovided for, or the opportunity of action was lost.' This mode of reasoning is admirably described by Hobbes, in speaking of the writings of some of the schoolmen, of whom he says that 'they had learned the trick of imposing what they list upon their readers, and declining the force of true reason by verbal forks, that is, distinctions, which signify nothing, but serve only to astonish the multitude of ignorant men.' That what we have here stated comprehends the whole force of his mind, which consisted solely in this evasive dexterity and perplexing formality, assisted by a copiousness of words and common-place topics, will, we think, be evident to any one who carefully looks over his speeches, undazzled by the reputation or personal influence of the speaker. It will be in vain to look in them for any of the common proofs of human genius or wisdom. He has not left behind him a single memorable saying,—not one profound maxim,—one solid observation,—one forcible description,—one beautiful thought,—one humorous picture,—one affecting sentiment. He has made no addition whatever to the stock of human knowledge. He did not possess any one of those faculties which contribute to the instruction and delight of mankind,—depth of understanding, imagination, sensibility, wit, vivacity, clear and solid judgment. But it may be asked, If these qualities are not to be found in him, where are we to look for them? and we may be required to point out instances of them. We shall answer then, that he had none of the abstract, legislative wisdom, refined sagacity, or rich, impetuous, high-wrought imagination of Burke; the manly eloquence, exact knowledge, vehemence, and natural simplicity of Fox; the ease, brilliancy, and acuteness of Sheridan. It is not merely that he had not all these qualities in the degree that they were severally possessed by his rivals, but he had not any of them in any remarkable degree. His reasoning is a technical arrangement of unmeaning common-places, his eloquence rhetorical, his style monotonous and artificial. If he could pretend to any one excellence more than another, it was to taste in composition. There is certainly nothing low, nothing puerile, nothing far-fetched or abrupt in his speeches; there is a kind of faultless regularity pervading them throughout; but in the confined, formal, passive mode of eloquence which he adopted, it seemed rather more difficult to commit errors than to avoid them. A man who is determined never to move out of the beaten road cannot lose his way. However, habit, joined to the peculiar mechanical memory which he possessed, carried this correctness to a degree which, in an extemporaneous speaker, was almost miraculous; he, perhaps, hardly ever uttered a sentence that was not perfectly regular and connected. In this respect, he not only had the advantage over his own contemporaries, but perhaps no one that ever lived equalled him in this singular faculty. But for this, he would always have passed for a common man; and to this the constant sameness, and, if we may so say, vulgarity of his ideas, must have contributed not a little, as there was nothing to distract his mind from this one object of his unintermitted attention; and as, even in his choice of words, he never aimed at any thing more than a certain general propriety and stately uniformity of style. His talents were exactly fitted for the situation in which he was placed; where it was his business not to overcome others, but to avoid being overcome. He was able to baffle opposition, not from strength or firmness, but from the evasive ambiguity and impalpable nature of his resistance, which gave no hold to the rude grasp of his opponents: no force could bind the loose phantom, and his mind (though 'not matchless, and his pride humbled by such rebuke') soon rose from defeat unhurt,

> ' And in its liquid texture, mortal wound
> Receiv'd no more than can the fluid air.'

ON RELIGIOUS HYPOCRISY

RELIGION either makes men wise and virtuous, or it makes them set up false pretences to both. In the latter case, it makes them hypocrites to themselves as well as others. Religion is, in grosser minds, an enemy to self-knowledge. The consciousness of the presence of an all-powerful Being, who is both the witness and judge of every thought, word, and action, where it does not produce its proper effect, forces the religious man to practise every mode of deceit upon himself with respect to his real character and motives; for it is only by being wilfully blind to his own faults, that he can suppose they will escape the eye of Omniscience. Consequently, the whole business of a religious man's life, if it does not conform to the strict line of his duty, may be said to be to gloss over his errors to himself, and to invent a thousand shifts and palliations, in order to hoodwink the Almighty. While he is sensible of his own delinquency, he knows that it cannot escape the penetration of his invisible Judge; and the distant penalty annexed to every offence, though not sufficient to make him desist from the commission of it, will not suffer him to rest easy, till he has made some compromise with his own conscience as to his motives for committing it. As far as relates to this world, a cunning knave may take a pride in the imposition he practises upon others; and, instead of striving to conceal his true character from himself, may chuckle with inward satisfaction at the folly of those who are not wise enough to detect it. 'But 'tis not so above.' This shallow, skin-deep hypocrisy will not serve the turn of the religious devotee, who is 'compelled to give in evidence against himself,' and who must first become the dupe of his own imposture, before he can flatter himself with the hope of concealment, as children hide their eyes with their hands, and fancy that no one can see them. Religious people often pray very heartily for the forgiveness of a 'multitude of trespasses and sins,' as a mark of their humility, but we never knew them admit any one fault in particular, or acknowledge themselves in the wrong in any instance whatever. The natural jealousy of self-love is in them heightened by the fear of damnation, and they plead *Not Guilty* to every charge brought against them, with all the conscious terrors of a criminal at the bar. It is for this reason that the greatest hypocrites in the world are religious hypocrites.

This quality, as it has been sometimes found united with the clerical character, is known by the name of *Priestcraft*. The Ministers of Religion are perhaps more liable to this vice than any other class of people. They are obliged to assume a greater degree of sanctity, though they have it not, and to screw themselves up to an unnatural pitch of severity and self-denial. They must keep a constant guard over themselves, have an eye always to their own persons, never relax in their gravity, nor give the least scope to their inclinations. A single slip, if discovered, may be fatal to them. Their influence and superiority depend on their pretensions to virtue and piety; and they are tempted to draw liberally on the funds of credulity and ignorance allotted for their convenient support. All this cannot be very friendly to downright simplicity of character. Besides, they are so accustomed to inveigh against the vices of others, that they naturally forget that they have any of their own to correct. They see vice as an object always out of themselves, with which they have no other concern than to denounce and stigmatise it. They are only reminded of it *in the third person*. They as naturally associate sin and its consequences with their flocks as a pedagogue associates a false concord and flogging with his scholars. If we may so express it, they serve as conductors to the lightning of divine indignation, and have only to point the thunders of the law at others. They identify themselves with that perfect system of faith and morals, of which they are the professed teachers, and regard any imputation on their conduct as an indirect attack on the function to which they belong, or as compromising the authority under which they act. It is only the head of the Popish church who assumes the title of *God's Vicegerent upon Earth*; but the feeling is nearly common to all the oracular interpreters of the will of Heaven—from the successor of St. Peter down to the simple, unassuming Quaker, who, disclaiming the imposing authority of title and office, yet fancies himself the immediate organ of a preternatural impulse, and affects to speak only as the spirit moves him.

There is another way in which the formal profession of religion aids hypocrisy, by erecting a secret tribunal, to which those who affect a more than ordinary share of it can (in case of need) appeal from the judgments of men. The religious impostor, reduced to his last shift, and having no other way left to avoid the most 'open and apparent shame,' rejects the fallible decisions of the world, and thanks God that there is one who knows the heart. He is amenable to a higher jurisdiction, and while all is well with Heaven, he can pity the errors, and smile at the malice of his enemies! Whatever cuts men off from their dependence on common opinion or obvious appearances, must open a door to evasion and cunning, by setting up a standard of right and wrong in every one's own breast, of the truth of which nobody can judge but the person himself. There are some fine instances in the old plays and novels (the best commentaries on human nature) of the effect of this principle, in giving the last finishing to the character of duplicity. Miss Harris, in Fielding's *Amelia*, is one of the most striking. Molière's *Tartuffe* is another instance of the facility with which religion may be perverted to the purposes of the most flagrant hypocrisy. It is an impenetrable fastness, to which this worthy person, like so many others, retires without the fear of pursuit. It is an additional disguise, in which he wraps himself up like a cloak. It is a stalking-horse, which is ready on all occasions,—an invisible conscience, which goes about with him,— his good genius, that becomes surety for him in all difficulties,—swears to the purity of his motives,—extricates him out of the most desperate circumstances,—baffles detection, and furnishes a plea to which there is no answer.

The same sort of reasoning will account for the old remark, that persons who are stigmatised as non-conformists to the established eligion, Jews, Presbyterians, etc., are more disposed to this vice han their neighbours. They are inured to the contempt of the world, and steeled against its prejudices : and the same indifference which fortifies them against the unjust censures of mankind, may be converted, as occasion requires, into a screen for the most pitiful conduct. They have no cordial sympathy with others, and, therefore, no sincerity in their intercourse with them. It is the necessity of concealment, in the first instance, that produces, and is, in some measure, an excuse for, the habit of hypocrisy.

Hypocrisy, as it is connected with cowardice, seems to imply weakness of body or want of spirit. The impudence and insensibility which belong to it, ought to suppose robustness of constitution. There is certainly a very successful and formidable class of sturdy, jolly, able-bodied hypocrites, the Friar Johns of the profession. Raphael has represented Elymas the Sorcerer, with a hard iron visage, and large uncouth figure, made up of bones and muscles ; as one not troubled with weak nerves or idle scruples—as one who repelled all sympathy with others—who was not to be jostled out of his course by their censures or suspicions—and who could break with ease through the cobweb snares which he had laid for the credulity of others, without being once entangled in his own delusions. His outward form betrays the hard, unimaginative, self-willed understanding of the sorcerer.   **A.**

ON THE LITERARY CHARACTER

THE following remarks are prefixed to the account of Baron Grimm's Correspondence in a late number of a celebrated Journal :—

'There is nothing more exactly painted in these graphical volumes, than the character of M. Grimm himself ; and the beauty of it is, that, as there is nothing either natural or peculiar about it, it may stand for the character of all the wits and philosophers he frequented. He had more wit, perhaps, and more sound sense and information, than the greatest part of the society in which he lived ; but the leading traits belong to the whole class, and to all classes, indeed, in similar situations, in every part of the world. Whenever there is a very large assemblage of persons who have no other occupation but to amuse themselves, there will infallibly be generated acuteness of intellect, refinement of manners, and good taste in conversation ; and, with the same certainty, all profound thought, and all serious affection, will be discarded from their society.

'The multitude of persons and things that force themselves on the attention in such a scene, and the rapidity with which they succeed each other, and pass away, prevent any one from making a deep or permanent impression; and the mind, having never been tasked to any course of application, and long habituated to this lively succession and variety of objects, comes at last to require the excitement of perpetual change, and to find a multiplicity of friends as indispensable as a multiplicity of amusements. Thus the characteristics of large and polished society come almost inevitably to be, wit and heartlessness —acuteness and perpetual derision. The same impatience of uniformity, and passion for variety, which give so much grace to their conversation, by excluding all tediousness and pertinacious wrangling, make them incapable of dwelling for many minutes on the feelings and concerns of any one individual; while the constant pursuit of little gratifications, and the weak dread of all uneasy sensations, render them equally averse from serious sympathy and deep thought.

'The whole style and tone of this publication affords the most striking illustration of these general remarks. From one end of it to the other, it is a display of the most complete heartlessness, and the most uninterrupted levity. It chronicles the deaths of half the author's acquaintance, and makes jests upon them all; and is much more serious in discussing the merits of an opera-dancer, than in considering the evidence for the being of a God, or the first foundations of morality. Nothing, indeed, can be more just or conclusive than the remark that is forced from M. Grimm himself, upon the utter carelessness, and instant oblivion, that followed the death of one of the most distinguished, active, and amiable members of his coterie: "Tant il est vrai que ce que nous appelons *la société*, est ce qu'il y a de plus léger, plus ingrat, et de plus frivole au monde!"'

These remarks, though shrewd and sensible in themselves, apply rather to the character of M. Grimm and his friends as men of the world, after their initiation into the refined society of Paris and the great world, than as mere men of letters. There is, however, a character which every man of letters has before he comes into society, and which he carries into the world with him, which we shall here attempt to describe.

The weaknesses and vices that arise from a constant intercourse with books, are in certain respects the same with those which arise from daily intercourse with the world; yet each has a character and operation of its own, which may either counteract or aggravate the tendency of the other. The same dissipation of mind, the same listlessness, languor, and indifference, may be produced by both, but they are produced in different ways, and exhibit very different appearances. The defects of the literary character proceed, not from

rivolity and voluptuous indolence, but from the overstrained exertion
of the faculties, from abstraction and refinement. A man without
talents or education might mingle in the same society, might give in
to all the gaiety and foppery of the age, might see the same 'multiplicity of persons and things,' but would not become a wit and a
philosopher for all that. As far as the change of actual objects, the
real variety and dissipation goes, there is no difference between
M. Grimm and a courtier of Francis 1.—between the consummate
philosopher and the giddy girl—between Paris, amidst the barbaric
refinements of the middle of the eighteenth century, and any other
metropolis at any other period. It is in the *ideal* change of objects,
in the *intellectual* dissipation of literature and of literary society, that
we are to seek for the difference. The very same languor and listlessness which, in fashionable life, are owing to the rapid ' succession
of persons and things,' may be found, and even in a more intense
degree, in the most recluse student, who has no knowledge whatever
of the great world, who has never been present at the sallies of a
petit souper, or complimented a lady on presenting her with a bouquet.
It is the province of literature to anticipate the dissipation of real
objects, and to increase it. It creates a fictitious restlessness and
craving after variety, by creating a fictitious world around us, and by
hurrying us, not only through all the mimic scenes of life, but by
plunging us into the endless labyrinths of imagination. Thus the
common indifference produced by the distraction of successive amusements, is superseded by a general indifference to surrounding objects,
to real persons and things, occasioned by the disparity between the
world of our imagination and that without us. The scenes of real
life are not got up in the same style of magnificence ; they want
dramatic illusion and effect. The high-wrought feelings require all
the concomitant and romantic circumstances which fancy can bring
together to satisfy them, and cannot find them in any given object.
M. Grimm was not, by his own account, *born* a lover ; but even
supposing him to have been, in gallantry of temper, a very Amadis,
would it have been necessary that the enthusiasm of a philosopher and
a man of genius should have run the gauntlet of all the *bonnes fortunes*
of Paris to evaporate into insensibility and indifference ? Would not
a Clarissa, a new Eloise, a Cassandra, or a Berenice, have produced
the same mortifying effects on a person of his great critical and acumen
and virtù ? Where, O where would he find the rocks of Meillerie
in the precincts of the Palais Royal, or on what lips would Julia's
kisses grow ? Who, after wandering with Angelica, or having seen
the heavenly face of Una, might not meet with impunity a whole
circle of literary ladies ? Cowley's mistresses reigned by turns in the

poet's fancy, and the beauties of King Charles II. perplex the eye in the preference of their charms as much now as they ever did. One trifling coquette only drives out another; but Raphael's Galatea kills the whole race of pertness and vulgarity at once. After ranging in dizzy mazes, through the regions of imaginary beauty, the mind sinks down, breathless and exhausted, on the earth. In common minds indifference is produced by mixing with the world. Authors and artists bring it into the world with them. The disappointment of the ideal enthusiast is indeed greatest at first, and he grows reconciled to his situation by degrees; whereas the mere man of the world becomes more dissatisfied and fastidious, and more of a misanthrope, the longer he lives.

It is much the same in friendships founded on literary motives. Literary men are not attached to the persons of their friends, but to their minds. They look upon them in the same light as on the books in their library, and read them till they are tired. In casual acquaintances friendship grows out of habit. Mutual kindnesses beget mutual attachment; and numberless little local occurrences in the course of long intimacy, furnish agreeable topics of recollection, and are almost the only sources of conversation among such persons. They have an immediate pleasure in each other's company. But in literature nothing of this kind takes place. Petty and local circumstances are beneath the dignity of philosophy. Nothing will go down but wit or wisdom. The mind is kept in a perpetual state of violent exertion and expectation, and as there cannot always be a fresh supply of stimulus to excite it, as the same remarks or the same *bon mots* come to be often repeated, or others so like them, that we can easily anticipate the effect, and are no longer surprised into admiration, we begin to relax in the frequency of our visits, and the heartiness of our welcome. When we are tired of a book we can lay it down, but we cannot so easily put our friends on the shelf when we grow weary of their society. The necessity of keeping up appearances, therefore, adds to the dissatisfaction on both sides, and at length irritates indifference into contempt.

By the help of arts and science, everything finds an ideal level. Ideas assume the place of realities, and realities sink into nothing. Actual events and objects produce little or no effect on the mind when it has been long accustomed to draw its strongest interest from constant contemplation. It is necessary that it should, as it were, recollect itself—that it should call out its internal resources, and refine upon its own feelings—place the object at a distance, and embellish it at pleasure. By degrees all things are made to serve as hints, and occasions for the exercise of intellectual activity. It was on this

rinciple that the sentimental Frenchman left his Mistress, in order
hat he might think of her. Cicero ceased to mourn for the loss of
is daughter, when he recollected how fine an opportunity it would
fford him to write an eulogy to her memory; and Mr. Shandy
amented over the death of Master Bobby much in the same manner.
The insensibility of Authors, etc., to domestic and private calamities
has been often carried to a ludicrous excess, but it is less than it
ppears to be. The genius of philosophy is not yet *quite* understood.
For instance, the man who might seem at the moment undisturbed
y the death of a wife or mistress, would perhaps never walk out on a
ine evening as long as he lived, without recollecting her; and a
isappointment in love that 'heaves no sigh and sheds no tear,' may
enetrate to the heart, and remain fixed there ever after. *Hæret lateri
ethalis arundo.* The blow is felt only by reflection, the rebound is
atal. Our feelings become more ideal; the impression of the
moment is less violent, but the effect is more general and permanent.
Those whom we love best, take nearly the same rank in our estimation
s the heroine of a favourite novel! Indeed, after all, compared with
he genuine feelings of nature, 'clad in flesh and blood,' with real
assions and affections, conversant about real objects, the life of a
mere man of letters and sentiment appears to be at best but a living
death; a dim twilight existence: a sort of wandering about in an
Elysian fields of our own making; a refined, spiritual, disembodied
tate, like that of the ghosts of Homer's heroes, who, we are told,
would gladly have exchanged situations with the meanest peasant upon
arth! [1]

The moral character of men of letters depends very much upon the
ame principles. All actions are seen through that general medium
which reduces them to individual insignificance. Nothing fills or
ngrosses the mind—nothing seems of sufficient importance to interfere
with our present inclination. Prejudices, as well as attachments, lose
heir hold upon us, and we palter with our duties as we please.
Moral obligations, by being perpetually refined upon, and discussed,
ose their force and efficacy, become mere dry distinctions of the
nderstanding,

> 'Play round the head, but never reach the heart.'

Opposite reasons and consequences balance one another, while appetite

---

[1] Plato's cave, in which he supposes a man to be shut up all his life with his
ack to the light, and to see nothing of the figures of men, or other objects that
ass by, but their shadows on the opposite wall of his cell, so that when he is let
ut and sees the real figures, he is only dazzled and confounded by them, seems an
ngenious satire on the life of a bookworm.

or interest turns the scale. Hence the severe sarcasm of Rousseau
'*Tout homme reflechi est mechant.*' In fact, it must be confessed, that
as all things produce their extremes, so excessive refinement tends to
produce equal grossness. The tenuity of our intellectual desires
leaves a void in the mind which requires to be filled up by coarser
gratification, and that of the senses is always at hand. They alone
always retain their strength. There is not a greater mistake than the
common supposition, that intellectual pleasures are capable of endless
repetition, and physical ones not so. The one, indeed, may be spread
out over a greater surface, they may be dwelt upon and kept in mind
at will, and for that very reason they wear out, and pall by comparison, and require perpetual variety. Whereas the physical gratification
only occupies us at the moment, is, as it were, absorbed in itself, and
forgotten as soon as it is over, and when it returns is *as good as new.*
No one could ever read the same book for any length of time without
being tired of it, but a man is never tired of his meals, however little
variety his table may have to boast. This reasoning is equally true
of all persons who have given much of their time to study and abstracted speculations. Grossness and sensuality have been marked
with no less triumph in the religious devotee than in the professed
philosopher. The perfect joys of heaven do not satisfy the craving
of nature; and the good Canon in Gil Blas might be opposed with
effect to some of the portraits in M. Grimm's Correspondence.

T T

ON COMMON-PLACE CRITICS

'Nor can I think what thoughts they can conceive.'

WE have already given some account of common-place people; we
shall in this number attempt a description of another class of the
community, who may be called (by way of distinction) common-place
critics. The former are a set of people who have no opinions of
their own, and do not pretend to have any; the latter are a set of
people who have no opinions of their own, but who affect to have
one upon every subject you can mention. The former are a very
honest, good sort of people, who are contented to pass for what they
are; the latter are a very pragmatical, troublesome sort of people
who would pass for what they are not, and try to put off their common-place notions in all companies and on all subjects, as something
of their own. They are of both species, the grave and the gay; and
it is hard to say which is the most tiresome.

A common-place critic has something to say upon every occasion and he always tells you either what is not true, or what you knew before, or what is not worth knowing. He is a person who thinks by proxy, and talks by rote. He differs with you, not because he thinks you are in the wrong, but because he thinks somebody else will think so. Nay, it would be well if he stopped here; but he will undertake to misrepresent you by anticipation, lest others should misunderstand you, and will set you right, not only in opinions which you have, but in those which you may be supposed to have. Thus, if you say that *Bottom* the weaver is a character that has not had justice done to it, he shakes his head, is afraid you will be thought extravagant, and wonders you should think the *Midsummer Night's Dream* the finest of all Shakspeare's plays. He judges of matters of taste and reasoning as he does of dress and fashion, by the prevailing tone of good company; and you would as soon persuade him to give up any sentiment that is current there, as to wear the hind part of his coat before. By the best company, of which he is perpetually talking, he means persons who live on their own estates, and other people's ideas. By the opinion of the world, to which he pays and expects you to pay great deference, he means that of a little circle of his own, where he hears and is heard. Again, *good sense* is a phrase constantly in his mouth, by which he does not mean his own sense or that of anybody else, but the opinions of a number of persons who have agreed to take their opinions on trust from others. If any one observes that there is something better than common sense, viz., *uncommon* sense, he thinks this a bad joke. If you object to the opinions of the majority, as often arising from ignorance or prejudice, he appeals from them to the sensible and well-informed; and if you say there may be other persons as sensible and well informed as himself and his friends, he smiles at your presumption. If you attempt to prove anything to him, it is in vain, for he is not thinking of what you say, but of what will be thought of it. The stronger your reasons, the more incorrigible he thinks you; and he looks upon any attempt to expose his gratuitous assumptions as the wandering of a disordered imagination. His notions are like plaster figures cast in a mould, as brittle as they are hollow; but they will break before you can make them give way. In fact, he is the representative of a large part of the community, the shallow, the vain, and indolent, of those who have time to talk, and are not bound to think: and he considers any deviation from the select forms of common-place, or he accredited language of conventional impertinence, as compromising the authority under which he acts in his diplomatic capacity. It is wonderful how this class of people agree with one another; how they herd together in all their opinions; what a tact they have for

folly ; what an instinct for absurdity ; what a sympathy in sentiment ;
how they find one another out by infallible signs, like Freemasons!
The secret of this unanimity and strict accord is, that not any one
of them ever admits any opinion that can cost the least effort of mind
in arriving at, or of courage in declaring it. Folly is as consistent
with itself as wisdom : there is a certain level of thought and sentiment,
which the weakest minds, as well as the strongest, find out as best
adapted to them ; and you as regularly come to the same conclusions,
by looking no farther than the surface, as if you dug to the centre of
the earth ! You know beforehand what a critic of this class will say
on almost every subject the first time he sees you, the next time, the
time after that, and so on to the end of the chapter. The following
list of his opinions may be relied on :—It is pretty certain that before
you have been in the room with him ten minutes, he will give you to
understand that Shakspeare was a great but irregular genius. Again,
he thinks it a question whether any one of his plays, if brought out
now for the first time, would succeed. He thinks that *Macbeth*
would be the most likely, from the music which has been since introduced into it. He has some doubts as to the superiority of the
French School over us in tragedy, and observes, that Hume and Adam
Smith were both of that opinion. He thinks Milton's pedantry a
great blemish in his writings, and that *Paradise Lost* has many prosaic
passages in it. He conceives that genius does not always imply taste,
and that wit and judgment are very different faculties. He considers
Dr. Johnson as a great critic and moralist, and that his Dictionary was
a work of prodigious erudition and vast industry ; but that some of the
anecdotes of him in Boswell are trifling. He conceives that Mr.
Locke was a very original and profound thinker. He thinks Gibbon's
style vigorous but florid. He wonders that the author of *Junius* was
never found out. He thinks Pope's translation of the *Iliad* an improvement on the simplicity of the original, which was necessary to
fit it to the taste of modern readers. He thinks there is a great deal
of grossness in the old comedies ; and that there has been a great
improvement in the morals of the higher classes since the reign of
Charles II. He thinks the reign of Queen Anne the golden period
of our literature, but that, upon the whole, we have no English writer
equal to Voltaire. He speaks of Boccacio as a very licentious
writer, and thinks the wit in Rabelais quite extravagant, though he
never read either of them. He cannot get through Spenser's *Fairy
Queen*, and pronounces all allegorical poetry tedious. He prefers
Smollett to Fielding, and discovers more knowledge of the world
in *Gil Blas* than in *Don Quixote*. Richardson he thinks very minute
and tedious. He thinks the French Revolution has done a great

deal of harm to the cause of liberty; and blames Buonaparte for being so ambitious. He reads the *Edinburgh* and *Quarterly Reviews*, and thinks as they do. He is shy of having an opinion on a new actor or a new singer; for the public do not always agree with the newspapers. He thinks that the moderns have great advantages over the ancients in many respects. He thinks Jeremy Bentham a greater man than Aristotle. He can see no reason why artists of the present day should not paint as well as Raphael or Titian. For instance, he thinks there is something very elegant and classical in Mr. Westall's drawings. He has no doubt that Sir Joshua Reynolds's Lectures were written by Burke. He considers Horne Tooke's account of the conjunction *That* very ingenious, and holds that no writer can be called elegant who uses the present for the subjunctive mood, who says *If it is* for *If it be*. He thinks Hogarth a great master of low, comic humour; and Cobbett a coarse, vulgar writer. He often talks of men of liberal education, and men without education, as if that made much difference. He judges of people by their pretensions; and pays attention to their opinions according to their dress and rank in life. If he meets with a fool, he does not find him out; and if he meets with any one wiser than himself, he does not know what to make of him. He thinks that manners are of great consequence to the common intercourse of life. He thinks it difficult to prove the existence of any such thing as original genius, or to fix a general standard of taste. He does not think it possible to define what wit is. In religion, his opinions are liberal. He considers all enthusiasm as a degree of madness, particularly to be guarded against by young minds; and believes that truth lies in the middle, between the extremes of right and wrong. He thinks that the object of poetry is to please; and that astronomy is a very pleasing and useful study. He thinks all this, and a great deal more, that amounts to nothing. We wonder we have remembered one half of it—

'For true no-meaning puzzles more than wit.'

Though he has an aversion to all new ideas, he likes all new plans and matters-of-fact: the new Schools for All, the Penitentiary, the new Bedlam, the new Steam-Boats, the Gas-Lights, the new Patent Blacking; every thing of that sort but the Bible Society. The Society for the Suppression of Vice he thinks a great nuisance, as every honest man must.

In a word, a common-place critic is the pedant of polite conversation. He refers to the opinion of Lord M. or Lady G. with the same air of significance that the learned pedant does to the authority of Cicero or Virgil; retails the wisdom of the day, as the anecdote-monger does the wit; and carries about with him the sentiments of people of a certain respectability in life, as the dancing-master does their air, or their valets their clothes.   Z.

ON THE CATALOGUE RAISONNÉ OF THE BRITISH INSTITUTION

THE Catalogue Raisonné of the pictures lately exhibited at the British Institution is worthy of notice, both as it is understood to be a declaration of the views of the Royal Academy, and as it contains some erroneous notions with respect to art prevalent in this country. It sets out with the following passages :—

'The first resolution ever framed by the noblemen and gentlemen who met to establish the British Institution, consists of the following sentence, viz. :

'"The *object* of the establishment is to facilitate, by a Public Exhibition, the *Sale* of the productions of *British* artists."

'Now, if the Directors had not felt quite certain as to the result of the present Exhibition, (of the Flemish School), if they had not perfectly satisfied themselves, that, instead of affording any, even the least means of promoting *unfair and invidious comparisons, it would produce abundant matter for exaltation to the living Artist,* can we possibly imagine they, the foster-parents of British Art, would ever have suffered such a display to have taken place? Certainly not. If they had not foreseen and fully provided against *all such injurious results,* by the deep and masterly manœuvre alluded to in our former remarks, is it conceivable that the Directors would have acted in way so counter, so diametrically in opposition to this their fundamental and leading principle? No, No! It is a position which all sense of respect for their consistency will not suffer us to admit, which all feelings of respect for their views forbid us to allow.

'Is it at all to be wondered at, that, in an Exhibition such as this, where nothing *like a patriotic desire* to uphold the arts of their country can possibly have place in the minds of the Directors, we should attribute to them the desire of *holding up the old Masters to derision,* inasmuch as good policy would allow? Is it to be wondered at, that when the Directors have the three-fold prospect, by so doing, of estranging the silly and ignorant Collector from his false and senseless infatuation for the *Black Masters,* of turning his *unjust preference* from Foreign to British Art, and, by affording the living painters a just encouragement, teach them to feel that becoming confidence in the powers, which an acknowledgment of their merits entitles them to? Is it to be wondered at, we say, that a little duplicity should have been practised upon this occasion, that some of our ill-advised Collectors and second-rate picture Amateurs should have been singled out as sheep for the sacrifice, and *thus ingeniously* made to pay unwilling homage *to the talents of their countrymen*, through that very medium by which they had previously been induced *to depreciate them*?'—'If, in our wish to please the Directors, we should, without mercy, damn all that deserves damning, and effectually hide our admiration for those pieces and passages which are truly entitled to admiration, it must be placed entirely to that *patriotic sympathy*, which we feel in common with the Directors, of holding up to the public, as the first and great object, THE PATRONAGE OF MODERN ART.'

Once more:

'Who does not perceive (except those whose eyes are not made for seeing more than they are told by others) that Vandyke's portraits, by the brilliant colour of the velvet hangings, are made to look as if they had been newly fetched home from the clear-starcher, with a double portion of blue in their ruffs? Who does not see, that the angelic females in Rubens's pictures (particularly in that of the Brazen Serpent) labour under a fit of the bile, twice as severe as they would do, if they were not suffering on red velvet? Who does not see, from the same cause, that the landscapes by the same Master are converted into *brown studies*, and that Rembrandt's ladies and gentlemen of fashion look as if they had been on duty for the whole of last week in the Prince Regent's new sewer? *And who, that has any penetration, that has any gratitude, does not see, in seeing all this, the anxious and benevolent solicitude of the Directors to keep the old masters under?*'

So, then, this Writer would think it a matter of lively gratitude, and of exultation in the breasts of living Artists, if the Directors, 'in their anxious and benevolent desire to keep the old Masters under,' had contrived to make Vandyke's pictures look like starch and blue: if they had converted Rubens's pictures into brown studies, or a fit of the bile; or had dragged Rembrandt's through the Prince Regent's sewers. It would have been a great gain, a great triumph to the Academy and to the Art, to have nothing left of all the pleasure or admiration which those painters had hitherto imparted to the world, to find all the excellences which their works had been supposed to possess, and all respect for them in the minds of the public destroyed, and converted into sudden loathing and disgust. This is, according to the Catalogue-writer and his friends, a consummation devoutly to be wished for themselves and for the Art All that is taken from

the old Masters is so much added to the moderns; the marring of Ar
is the making of the Academy. This is the kind of patronage and
promotion of the Fine Arts on which he insists as necessary to keep
up the reputation of living Artists, and to ensure the sale of their
works. There is nothing then in common between the merits of the
old Masters and the doubtful claims of the new: *those* are not ' the
scale by which we can ascend to the love ' of these. The excellence
of the latter are of their own making and of their own seeing; we
must take their own word for them; and not only so, but we must
sacrifice all established principles and all established reputation to
their upstart pretensions, because, if the old pictures are not totally
worthless, their own can be good for nothing. The only chance,
therefore, for the moderns, if the Catalogue-writer is to be believed,
is to decry all the *chef-d'œuvres* of the Art, and to hold up all the
great names in it to derision. If the public once get to relish the
style of the old Masters, they will no longer tolerate theirs. But as
long as the old Masters can be *kept under*, the coloured caricatures of
the moderns, like *Mrs. Peachum's* coloured handkerchiefs, ' will be
of sure sale at their warehouse at Redriff.' The Catalogue-writer
thinks it necessary, in order to raise the Art in this country, to
depreciate all Art in all other times and countries. He thinks that
the way to excite an enthusiastic admiration of genius in the public
is by setting the example of a vulgar and malignant hatred of it in
himself. He thinks to inspire a lofty spirit of emulation in the rising
generation, by shutting his eyes to the excellences of all the finest
models, or by pouring out upon them the overflowings of his gall and
envy, to disfigure them in the eyes of others; so that they may see
nothing in Raphael, in Titian, in Rubens, in Rembrandt, in Vandyke,
in Claude Lorraine, in Leonardo da Vinci, but the low wit and dirty
imagination of a paltry scribbler; and come away from the greatest
monuments of human capacity, without one feeling of excellence in
art, or of beauty or grandeur in nature. Nay, he would persuade us
that this is a great public and private benefit, *viz.*, that there is no
such thing as excellence, as genius, as true fame, except what he and
his anonymous associates arrogate to themselves, with all the profit
and credit of this degradation of genius, this ruin of Art, this obloquy
and contempt heaped on great and unrivalled reputation. He thinks
it a likely mode of producing confidence in the existence and value
of Art, to prove that there never was any such thing, till the last annual
Exhibition of the Royal Academy. He would encourage a disinterested love of Art, and a liberal patronage of it in the great and
opulent, by shewing that the living Artists have no regard, but the most
sovereign and reckless contempt for it, except as it can be made

emporary stalking-horse to their pride and avarice. The writer may have a *patriotic sympathy* with the sale of modern works of Art, but we do not see what sympathy there can be between the buyers and sellers of these works, except in the love of the Art itself. When we find that these patriotic persons would destroy the Art itself to promote the sale of their pictures, we know what to say to them. We are obliged to the zeal of our critic for having set this matter in so clear a light. The public will feel little sympathy with a body of Artists who disclaim all sympathy with all other Artists. They will doubt their pretensions to genius who have no feeling of respect for it in others; they will consider them as bastards, not children of the Art, who would destroy their parent. The public will hardly consent, when the proposition is put to them in this tangible shape, to give up the cause of liberal art and of every liberal sentiment connected with it, and enter, with their eyes open, into a pettifogging cabal to keep the old Masters under, or hold their names up to derision 'as good sport,' merely to gratify the selfish importunity of a gang of sturdy beggars, who demand public encouragement and support, with a claim of settlement in one hand, and a forged certificate of merit in the other. They can only deserve well of the public by deserving well of the Art. Have we taken these men from the plough, from the counter, from the shop-board, from the tap-room and the stable-door, to raise them to fortune, to rank, and distinction in life, for the sake of Art, to give them a chance of doing something in Art like what had been done before them, of promoting and refining the public taste, of setting before them the great models of Art, and by a pure love of truth and beauty, and by patient and disinterested aspirations after it, of rising to the highest excellence, and of making themselves 'a name great above all names'; and do they now turn round upon us, and because they have neglected these high objects of their true calling for pitiful cabals and filling their pockets, insist that we shall league with them in crushing the progress of Art, and the respect attached to all its great efforts? There is no other country in the world in which such a piece of impudent quackery could be put forward with impunity, and still less in which it could be put forward in the garb of patriotism This is the effect of our gross island manners. The Catalogue-writer carries his bear-garden notions of this virtue into the Fine Arts, and would set about destroying Dutch or Italian pictures as he would Dutch shipping or Italian liberty. He goes up to the Rembrandts with the same swaggering Jack-tar airs as he would to a battery of nine-pounders, and snaps his fingers at Raphael as he would at the French. Yet he talks big about the Elgin Marbles, because Mr. Payne Knight has made a slip on that subject; though, to be consistent, he ought to be for pounding them in a mortar, should get his friend the Incendiary to set fire to the room building for them at the British Museum, or should get Mr. Soane to build it. Patriotism and the Fine Arts have nothing to do with one another—because patriotism relates to exclusive advantages, and the advantages of the Fine Arts are not exclusive, but communicable. The physical property of one country cannot be shared without loss by another: the physical force of one country may destroy that of another. These, therefore, are objects of national jealousy and fear of encroachment: for the interests or rights of different countries may be compromised in them. But it is not so in the Fine Arts, which depend upon taste and knowledge. We do not consume the works of Art as articles of food, or clothing, or fuel; but we brood over their *idea*, which is accessible to all, and may be multiplied without end, ' with riches fineless.' Patriotism is ' beastly; subtle as the fox for prey; like warlike as the wolf for what it eats'; but Art is ideal, and therefore liberal. The knowledge or perfection of Art in one age or country is the cause of its existence or perfection in another. Art is the cause of art in other men. Works of genius done by a Dutchman are the cause of genius in an Englishman—are the cause of taste in an Englishman. The patronage of foreign Art is, not to prevent, but to promote Art in England. It does not prevent, but promote taste in England. Art subsists by communication, not by exclusion. The light of art, like that of nature, shines on all alike; and its benefit, like that of the sun, is in being seen and felt. The spirit of art is not the spirit of trade: it is not a question between the grower or consumer of some perishable and personal commodity: but it is a question between human genius and human taste, how much the one can produce for the benefit of mankind, and how much the other can enjoy. It is ' the link of peaceful commerce 'twixt dividable shores.' To take from it this character is to take from it its best privilege, its humanity. Would any one, except our Catalogue-virtuoso, think of destroying or concealing the monuments of Art in past ages, as inconsistent with the progress of taste and civilisation in the present? Would any one find fault with the introduction of the works of Raphael into this country, as if their being done by an Italian confined the benefit to a foreign country, when all the benefit, all the great and lasting benefit, (except the purchase-money, the lasting burden of the Catalogue, and the great test of the value of Art in the opinion of the writer), is instantly communicated to all eyes that behold, and all hearts that can feel them? It is many years ago since we first saw the prints of the Cartoons hung round the parlour of a little inn on the great north road. We were then very young,

nd had not been initiated into the principles of taste and refinement
of the *Catalogue Raisonné*. We had heard of the fame of the
Cartoons, but this was the first time that we had ever been admitted
ace to face into the presence of those divine works. 'How were
we then uplifted!' Prophets and Apostles stood before us, and the
Saviour of the Christian world, with his attributes of faith and
power; miracles were working on the walls; the hand of Raphael
was there, and as his pencil traced the lines, we saw godlike spirits
and lofty shapes descend and walk visibly the earth, but as if their
thoughts still lifted them above the earth. There was that figure
of St. Paul, pointing with noble fervour to 'temples not made with
hands, eternal in the heavens,' and that finer one of Christ in the
boat, whose whole figure seems sustained by meekness and love, and
that of the same person, surrounded by the disciples, like a flock of
sheep listening to the music of some divine shepherd. We knew
not how enough to admire them. If from this transport and
delight there arose in our breasts a wish, a deep aspiration of mingled
hope and fear, to be able one day to do something like them, that
hope has long since vanished; but not with it the love of Art, nor
delight in works of Art, nor admiration of the genius which produces
them, nor respect for fame which rewards and crowns them! Did
we suspect that in this feeling of enthusiasm for the works of Raphael
we were deficient in patriotic sympathy, or that, in spreading it as
far as we could, we did an injury to our country or to living Art?
The very feeling shewed that there was no such distinction in Art,
that her benefits were common, that the power of genius, like the
spirit of the world, is everywhere alike present. And would the
harpies of criticism try to extinguish this common benefit to their
country from a pretended exclusive attachment to their countrymen?
Would they rob their country of the credit of their
professional little-goes and E. O. tables—'cutpurses of the Art, that
from the shelf the precious diadem stole, and put it in their pockets'?
Tired of exposing such folly, we walked out the other day, and saw
a bright cloud resting on the bosom of the blue expanse, which
reminded us of what we had seen in some picture in the Louvre.
We were suddenly roused from our reverie, by recollecting that till
we had answered this catchpenny publication we had no right, without
being liable to a charge of disaffection to our country or treachery
to the Art, to look at nature, or to think of any thing like it in Art, not
of British growth and manufacture!

THE SAME SUBJECT CONTINUED

The Catalogue-writer nicknames the Flemish painters 'the Black Masters.' Either this means that the works of Rubens and Vandyke were originally black pictures, that is, deeply shadowed like those of Rembrandt, which is false, there being no painter who used so little shadow as Vandyke, or so much colour as Rubens; or it must mean that their pictures have turned darker with time, that is, that the art itself is a black art. Is this a triumph for the Academy? Is the defect and decay of Art a subject of exultation to the national genius? Then there is no hope (in this country at least) 'that a great man's memory may outlive him half a year!' Do they calculate that the decomposition and gradual disappearance of the standard works of Art will quicken the demand, and facilitate the sale of modern pictures? Have they no hope of immortality themselves, that they are glad to see the inevitable dissolution of all that has long flourished in splendour and in honour? They are pleased to find, that at the end of near two hundred years, the pictures of Vandyke and Rubens have suffered half as much from time as those of their late President have done in thirty or forty, or their own in the last ten or twelve years. So that the glory of painting is that it does not last for ever: it is this which puts the ancients and the moderns on a level. They hail with undisguised satisfaction the approaches of the slow moulder- ing hand of time in those works which have lasted longest, not anticipating the premature fate of their own. Such is their short- sighted ambition. A picture is with them like the frame it is in, *as good as new*; and the best picture, that which was last painted. They make the weak side of Art the test of its excellence; and though a modern picture of two years standing is hardly fit to be seen, from the general ignorance of the painter in the mechanical as well as other parts of the Art, yet they are sure at any time to get the start of Rubens or Vandyke, by painting a picture against the day of exhibition. We even question whether they would wish to make their own pictures last if they could, and whether they would not destroy their own works as well as those of others, (like chalk figures on the floors), to have new ones bespoke the next day. The Flemish pictures then, except those of Rembrandt, were not originally black; they have not faded in proportion to the length of time they have been painted. All that comes then of the nickname in the Catalogue is, that the pictures of the old Masters have lasted longer than those of the present members of the Royal Academy, and that the latter, it is to be presumed, do not wish their works to last so long, lest they should be called the *Black Masters*. With respect to Rembrandt, this epitaph may be literally true. But, we would ask, whether the style of *chiaro-scuro*, in which Rembrandt painted, is not one fine view of nature and of art? Whether any other painter carried it to the same height of perfection as he did? Whether any other painter ever joined the same depth of shadow with the same clearness? Whether his tones were not as fine as they were true? Whether a more thorough master of his art ever lived? Whether he deserved for this to be nicknamed by the Writer of the Catalogue, or to have his works 'kept under, or himself held up to derision,' by the Patrons and Directors of the British Institution for the support and encouragement of the Fine Arts?

But we have heard it said by a disciple and commentator on the Catalogue, (one would think it was hardly possible to descend lower than the writer himself), that the Directors of the British Institution assume a consequence to themselves, hostile to the pretensions of modern professors, out of the reputation of the old Masters, whom they affect to look upon with wonder, to worship as something preternatural;—that they consider the bare possession of an old picture as a title to distinction, and the respect paid to Art as the highest pretension of the owner. And is this then a subject of complaint with the Academy, that genius is thus thought of, when its claims are once fully established? That those high qualities, which are beyond the estimate of ignorance and selfishness while living, receive their reward from distant ages? Do they not 'feel the future in the instant'? Do they not know, that those qualities which appeal neither to interest nor passion can only find their level with time, and would they annihilate the only pretensions they have? Or have they no conscious affinity with true genius, no claim to the reversion of true fame, no right of succession to this lasting inheritance and final reward of great exertions, which they would therefore destroy, to prevent others from enjoying it? Does all their ambition begin and end in their *patriotic sympathy* with the sale of modern works of Art, and have they no fellow-feeling with the hopes and final destiny of human genius? What poet ever complained of the respect paid to Homer as derogatory to himself? The envy and opposition to established fame is peculiar to the race of modern Artists; and it is to be hoped it will remain so. It is the fault of their education. It is only by a liberal education that we learn to feel respect for the past, or to take an interest in the future. The knowledge of Artists is too often confined to their art, and their views to their own interest. Even in this they are wrong:—in all respects they are wrong. As a mere matter of trade, the prejudice in favour of old pictures does not prevent but assist the sale of modern works of Art. If there was not a prejudice in favour of old pictures, there could be a prejudice in favour of none and none would be sold. The professors seem to think, that for every old picture not sold, one of their own would be. This is a false calculation. The contrary is true. For every old picture not sold one of their own (in proportion) would *not* be sold. The practice of buying pictures is a habit, and it must begin with those pictures which have a character and name, and not with those which have none. 'Depend upon it,' says Mr. Burke in a letter to Barry, 'whatever attracts public attention to the Arts, will in the end be for the benefit of the Artists themselves.' Again, do not the Academicians know, that it is a contradiction in terms, that a man should enjoy the advantages of posthumous fame in his lifetime? Most men cease to be of any consequence at all when they are dead; but it is the privilege of the man of genius to survive himself. But he cannot in the nature of things anticipate this privilege—because in all that appeals to the general intellect of mankind, this appeal is strengthened, as it spreads wider and is acknowledged; because a man cannot unite in himself personally the suffrages of distant ages and nations; because popularity, a newspaper puff, cannot have the certainty of lasting fame; because it does not carry the same weight of sympathy with it; because it cannot have the same interest, the same refinement or grandeur. If Mr. West was equal to Raphael, (which he is not), if Mr. Lawrence was equal to Vandyke or Titian, (which he is not), if Mr Turner was equal to Claude Lorraine, (which he is not), if Mr. Wilkie was equal to Teniers, (which he is not), yet they could not, nor ought they to be thought of in the same manner, because there could not be the same proof of it, nor the same confidence in the opinion of a man and his friends, or of any one generation, as in that of successive generations and the voice of posterity. If it is said that we pass over the faults of the one, and severely scrutinise the excellences of the other; this is also right and necessary, because the one have passed their trial, and the others are upon it. If we forgive or overlook the faults of the ancients, it is because they have dearly earned it at our hands. We ought to have some objects to indulge our enthusiasm upon; and we ought to indulge it upon the highest, and those that are surest of deserving it. Would one of our Academicians expect us to look at his new house in one of the new squares with the same veneration as at Michael Angelo's, which he built with his own hands, as at Tully's villa, or at the tomb of Virgil? We have no doubt they would, but we cannot. Besides, if it were possible to transfer our old prejudices to new candidates, the way to effect this is not by destroying them. If we have no confidence in all that has gone before us, in what has received the sanction of time and the concurring testimony of disinterested judges, are we to believe all of a sudden that excellence has started up in our own times, because it never existed before: are we to take the Artists' own word for their superiority to their predecessors? There is one other plea made by the moderns, 'that they must live,' and the answer to it is, that they do live. An Academician makes his thousand a-year by portrait-painting, and complains that the encouragement given to foreign Art deprives him of the means of subsistence, and prevents him from indulging his genius in works of high history,—'playing at will his virgin fancies wild.'

As to the comparative merits of the ancients and the moderns, it does not admit of a question. The odds are too much in favour of the former, because it is likely that more good pictures were painted in the last three hundred than in the last thirty years. Now, the old pictures are the best remaining out of all that period, setting aside those of living Artists. If they are bad, the Art itself is good for nothing; for they are the best that ever were. They are not good, because they are old; but they have become old, because they are good. The question is not between this and any other generation, but between the present and all preceding generations, whom the Catalogue-writer, in his misguided zeal, undertakes to vilify and 'to keep under, or hold up to derision.' To say that the great names which have come down to us are not worth any thing, is to say that the mountain-tops which we see in the farthest horizon are not so high as the intervening objects. If there had been any greater painters than Vandyke or Rubens, or Raphael or Rembrandt, or N. Poussin or Claude Lorraine, we should have heard of them, we should have seen them in the Gallery, and we should have read a patriotic and disinterested account of them in the *Catalogue Raisonné.* Waiving the unfair and invidious comparison between all former excellence and the concentrated essence of it in the present age, let us ask who, in the last generation of painters, was equal to the old masters? Was it Highmore, or Hayman, or Hudson, or Kneller? Who was the English Raphael, or Rubens, or Vandyke, of that day, to whom the Catalogue-critic would have extended his patriotic sympathy and damning patronage? Kneller, we have been told, was thought superior to Vandyke by the persons of fashion whom he painted. So St. Thomas Apostle seems higher than St. Paul's while you are close under it; but the farther off you go the higher the mighty dome aspires into the skies. What is become of all those great men who flourished in our own time—'like flowers in men's caps, dying or ere they sicken'—Hoppner, Opie, Shee, Loutherbourg, Rigaud, Romney,

Barry, the painters of the Shakspeare Gallery? 'Gone to the vault of all the Capulets,' and their pictures with them, or before them! Shall we put more faith in their successors? Shall we take the words of their friends for their taste and genius? No, we will stick to what we know will stick to us, the 'heirlooms' of the Art, the Black Masters. The picture, for instance, of Charles I. on horseback, which our critic criticises with such heavy drollery, is worth all the pictures that were ever exhibited at the Royal Academy (from the time of Sir Joshua to the present time inclusive) put together. It shews more knowledge and feeling of the Art, more skill and beauty, more sense of what it is in objects that gives pleasure to the eye, with more power to communicate this pleasure to the world. If either this single picture, or all the lumber that has ever appeared at the Academy, were to be destroyed, there could not be a question which, with any Artist or with any judge or lover of Art. So stands the account between ancient and modern Art! By this we may judge of all the rest. The Catalogue-writer makes some strictures in the second part on the Waterloo Exhibition, which he does not think what it ought to be. We wonder he had another word to say on modern Art after seeing it. He should instantly have taken the resolution of *Iago*, 'From this time forth I never will speak more.'

The writer of the *Catalogue Raisonné* has fallen foul of two things which ought to be sacred to Artists and lovers of Art—Genius and Fame. If they are not sacred to them, we do not know to whom they will be sacred. A work such as the present shews that the person who could write it must either have no knowledge or taste for Art, or must be actuated by a feeling of unaccountable malignity towards it. It shews that any body of men by whom it could be set on foot or encouraged are not an Academy of Art. It shews that a country in which such a publication could make its appearance is not the country of the Fine Arts. Does the writer think to prove the genius of his countrymen for Art by proclaiming their utter insensibility and flagitious contempt for all beauty and excellence in the art, except in their own works? No! it is very true that the English are a shopkeeping nation; and the *Catalogue Raisonné* is the proof of it.

Finally, the works of the moderns are not, like those of the Old Masters, a second nature. Oh Art, true likeness of nature, 'balm of hurt minds, great nature's second course, chief nourisher in life's feast,' of what would our Catalogue-mongers deprive us in depriving us of thee and of thy glories, of the lasting works of the great Painters, and of their names no less magnificent, grateful to our hearts as the sound of celestial harmony from other spheres, waking around us (whether heard or not) from youth to age, the stay, the guide and anchor of our purest thoughts; whom, having once seen, we always remember, and who teach us to see all things through them; without whom life would be to begin again, and the earth barren; of Raphael, who lifted the human form half way to heaven; of Titian, who painted the mind in the face, and unfolded the soul of things to the eye; of Rubens, around whose pencil gorgeous shapes thronged numberless, startling us by the novel accidents of form and colour, putting the spirit of motion into the universe, and weaving a gay fantastic round and Bacchanalian dance with nature; of thee, too, Rembrandt, who didst redeem one half of nature from obloquy, from the nickname in the Catalogue, 'smoothing the raven down of darkness till it smiled,' and tinging it with a light like streaks of burnished ore; of these, and more, of whom the world is scarce worthy; and what would they give us in return? Nothing.   W. H.

ON POETICAL VERSATILITY

THE spirit of poetry is in itself favourable to humanity and liberty: but, we suspect, not when its aid is most wanted. The spirit of poetry is not the spirit of mortification or of martyrdom. Poetry dwells in a perpetual Utopia of its own, and is for that reason very ill calculated to make a Paradise upon earth, by encountering the shocks and disappointments of the world. Poetry, like law, is a fiction, only a more agreeable one. It does not create difficulties where they do not exist; but contrives to get rid of them, whether they exist or not. It is not entangled in cobwebs of its own making, but soars above all obstacles. It cannot be 'constrained by mastery.' It has the range of the universe; it traverses the empyrean, and looks down on nature from a higher sphere. When it lights upon the earth, it loses some of its dignity and its use. Its strength is in its wings; its element the air. Standing on its feet, jostling with the crowd, it is liable to be overthrown, trampled on, and defaced; for its wings are of a dazzling brightness, 'heaven's own tinct,' and the least soil upon them shews to disadvantage. Sullied, degraded as we have seen it, we shall not insult over it, but leave it to Time to take out the stains, seeing it is a thing immortal as itself. 'Being so majestical, we should do it wrong to offer it the show of violence.' But the best things, in their abuse, often become the worst; and so it is with poetry when it is diverted from its proper end. Poets live in an ideal world, where they make everything out according to their wishes and fancies. They either find things delightful or make them so. They feign the beautiful and grand out of their own minds, and imagine all things to be, not what they are, but what they ought to be. They are naturally inventors, creators of truth, of love, and beauty: and while they speak to us from the sacred shrine of their own hearts, while they pour out the pure treasures of thought to the world, they cannot be too much admired and applauded : but when, fogetting their high calling, and becoming tools and puppets in the hands of power, they would pass off the gewgaws of corruption and love-tokens of self-interest as the gifts of the Muse, they cannot be too much despised and shunned. We do not like novels founded on facts, nor do we like poets turned courtiers. Poets, it has been said, succeed best in fiction : and they should for the most part stick to it. Invention, not upon an imaginary subject, is a lie: the varnishing over the vices or deformities of actual objects is hypocrisy. Players leave their finery at the stage-door, or they would be hooted ; poets come out into the world with all their bravery on, and yet they would pass for *bona fide* persons. They lend the colours of fancy to whatever they see : whatever they touch becomes gold, though it were lead. With them every Joan is a lady ; and kings and queens are human. Matters of fact they embellish at their will, and reason is the play-thing of their passions, their caprice, or their interest. There is no practice so base of which they will not become the panders : no sophistry of which their understanding may not be made the voluntary dupe. Their only object is to please their fancy. Their souls are effeminate, half man and half woman :—they want fortitude, and are without principle. If things do not turn out according to their wishes, they will make their wishes turn round to things. They can easily overlook whatever they do not like, and make an idol of any thing they please. The object of poetry is to please : this art naturally gives pleasure, and excites admiration. Poets, therefore, cannot do well without sympathy and flattery. It is accordingly very much against the grain that they remain long on the unpopular side of the question. They do not like to be shut out when laurels are to be given away at Court—or places under Government to be disposed of, in romantic situations in the country. They are happy to be reconciled on the first opportunity to prince and people, and to exchange their principles for a pension. They have not always strength of mind to think for themselves, nor courage enough to bear the unjust stigma of the opinions they have taken upon trust from others. Truth alone does not satisfy their pampered appetites without the sauce of praise. To prefer truth to all other things, it requires that the mind should have been at some pains in finding it out, and that we should feel a severe delight in the contemplation of truth, seen by its own clear light, and not as it is reflected in the admiring eyes of the world. A philosopher may perhaps make a shift to be contented with the sober draughts of reason: a poet must have the applause of the world to intoxicate him. Milton was, however, a poet, and an honest man; he was Cromwell's secretary.

T. T

ON ACTORS AND ACTING

PLAYERS are 'the abstracts and brief chronicles of the time'; the motley representatives of human nature. They are the only honest hypocrites. Their life is a voluntary dream; a studied madness. The height of their ambition is to be *beside themselves*. To-day kings, to-morrow beggars, it is only when they are themselves, that they are nothing. Made up of mimic laughter and tears, passing from the extremes of joy or woe at the prompter's call, they wear the livery of other men's fortunes; their very thoughts are not their own. They are, as it were, train-bearers in the pageant of life, and hold a glass up to humanity, frailer than itself. We see ourselves at second-hand in them: they shew us all that we are, all that we wish to be, and all that we dread to be. The stage is an epitome, a bettered likeness of the world, with the dull part left out: and, indeed, with this omission, it is nearly big enough to hold all the rest. What brings the resemblance nearer is, that, as *they* imitate us, we, in our turn, imitate them. How many fine gentlemen do we owe to the stage? How many romantic lovers are mere Romeos in masquerade? How many soft bosoms have heaved with Juliet's sighs? They teach us when to laugh and when to weep, when to love and when to hate, upon principle and with a good grace! Wherever there is a play-house, the world will go on not amiss. The stage not only refines the manners, but it is the best teacher of morals, for it is the truest and most intelligible picture of life. It stamps the image of virtue on the mind by first softening the rude materials of which it is composed, by a sense of pleasure. It regulates the passions by giving a loose to the imagination. It points out the selfish and depraved to our detestation, the amiable and generous to our admiration; and if it clothes the more seductive vices with the borrowed graces of wit and fancy, even those graces operate as a diversion to the coarser poison of experience and bad example, and often prevent or carry off the infection by inoculating the mind with a certain taste and elegance. To shew how little we agree with the common declamations against the immoral tendency of the stage on this score, we will hazard a conjecture, that the acting of the Beggar's Opera a certain number of nights every year since it was first brought out, has done more towards putting down the practice of highway robbery, than all the gibbets that ever were erected. A person, after seeing this piece is too deeply imbued with a sense of humanity, is in too good humour with himself and the rest of the world, to set about cutting throats or rifling pockets. Whatever makes a jest of vice, leaves it too much a matter of indifference for any one in his senses to rush desperately on his ruin for its sake. We suspect that just the contrary effect must be produced by the representation of George Barnwell, which is too much in the style of the Ordinary's sermon to meet with any better success. The mind, in such cases, instead of being deterred by the alarming consequences held out to it, revolts against the denunciation of them as an insult offered to its free-will, and, in a spirit of defiance, returns a practical answer to them, by daring the worst that can happen. The most striking lesson ever read to levity and licentiousness, is in the last act of the Inconstant, where young Mirabel is preserved by the fidelity of his mistress, Orinda, in the disguise of a page, from the hands of assassins, into whose power he has been allured by the temptations of vice and beauty. There never was a rake who did not become in imagination a reformed man, during the representation of the last trying scenes of this admirable comedy.

If the stage is useful as a school of instruction, it is no less so as a source of amusement. It is the source of the greatest enjoyment at the time, and a never-failing fund of agreeable reflection afterwards. The merits of a new play, or of a new actor, are always among the first topics of polite conversation. One way in which public exhibitions contribute to refine and humanise mankind, is by supplying them with ideas and subjects of conversation and interest in common. The progress of civilisation is in proportion to the number of commonplaces current in society. For instance, if we meet with a stranger at an inn or in a stage-coach, who knows nothing but his own affairs, his shop, his customers, his farm, his pigs, his poultry, we can carry on no conversation with him on these local and personal matters : the only way is to let him have all the talk to himself. But if he has fortunately ever seen Mr. Liston act, this is an immediate topic of mutual conversation, and we agree together the rest of the evening in discussing the merits of that inimitable actor, with the same satisfaction as in talking over the affairs of the most intimate friend.

If the stage thus introduces us familiarly to our contemporaries, it also brings us acquainted with former times. It is an interesting revival of past ages, manners, opinions, dresses, persons, and actions,—

whether it carries us back to the wars of York and Lancaster, or half way back to the heroic times of Greece and Rome, in some translation from the French, or quite back to the age of Charles II. in the scenes of Congreve and of Etherege, (the gay Sir George!)—happy age, when kings and nobles led purely ornamental lives; when the utmost stretch of a morning's study went no further than the choice of a sword-knot, or the adjustment of a side-curl; when the soul spoke out in all the pleasing eloquence of dress; and beaux and belles, enamoured of themselves in one another's follies, fluttered like gilded butterflies in giddy mazes through the walks of St. James's Park!

A good company of comedians, a Theatre-Royal judiciously managed, is your true Herald's College; the only Antiquarian Society, that is worth a rush. It is for this reason that there is such an air of romance about players, and that it is pleasanter to see them, even in their own persons, than any of the three learned professions. We feel more respect for John Kemble in a plain coat, than for the Lord Chancellor on the woolsack. He is surrounded, to our eyes, with a greater number of imposing recollections: he is a more reverend piece of formality; a more complicated tissue of costume. We do not know whether to look upon this accomplished actor as Pierre or King John or Coriolanus or Cato or Leontes or the Stranger. But we see in him a stately hieroglyphic of humanity; a living monument of departed greatness, a sombre comment on the rise and fall of kings. We look after him till he is out of sight, as we listen to a story of one of Ossian's heroes, to 'a tale of other times!'

One of the most affecting things we know is to see a favourite actor take leave of the stage. We were present not long ago when Mr. Bannister quitted it. We do not wonder that his feelings were overpowered on the occasion: ours were nearly so too. We remembered him, in the first heyday of our youthful spirits, in the *Prize*, in which he played so delightfully with that fine old croaker Suett, and Madame Storace,—in the farce of *My Grandmother*, in the *Son-in-Law*, in *Autolycus*, and in *Scrub*, in which our satisfaction was at its height. At that time, King and Parsons, and Dodd, and Quick, and Edwin were in the full vigour of their reputation, who are now all gone. We still feel the vivid delight with which we used to see their names in the play-bills, as we went along to the Theatre. Bannister was one of the last of these that remained; and we parted with him as we should with one of our oldest and best friends. The most pleasant feature in the profession of a player, and which, indeed, is peculiar to it, is that we not only admire the talents of those who adorn it, but we contract a personal intimacy with them.

THE ROUND TABLE

There is no class of society whom so many persons regard with affection as actors. We greet them on the stage; we like to meet them in the streets; they almost always recall to us pleasant associations; and we feel our gratitude excited, without the uneasiness of a sense of obligation. The very gaiety and popularity, however, which surround the life of a favourite performer, make the retiring from it a very serious business. It glances a mortifying reflection on the shortness of human life, and the vanity of human pleasures. Something reminds us, that 'all the world's a stage, and all the men and women merely players.'

ON THE SAME

It has been considered as the misfortune of first-rate talents for the stage, that they leave no record behind them except that of vague rumour, and that the genius of a great actor perishes with him, 'leaving the world no copy.' This is a misfortune, or at least an unpleasant circumstance, to actors; but it is, perhaps, an advantage to the stage. It leaves an opening to originality. The stage is always beginning anew; the candidates for theatrical reputation are always setting out afresh, unencumbered by the affectation of the faults or excellences of their predecessors. In this respect, we should imagine that the average quantity of dramatic talent remains more nearly the same than that in any other walk of art In no other instance do the complaints of the degeneracy of the moderns seem so unfounded as in this; and Colley Cibber's account of the regular decline of the stage, from the time of Shakspeare to that of Charles II., and from the time of Charles II. to the beginning of George II. appears quite ridiculous. The stage is a place where genius is sure to come upon its legs, in a generation or two at farthest. In the other arts, (as painting and poetry), it has been contended that what has been well done already, by giving rise to endless vapid imitations, is an obstacle to what might be done well hereafter: that the models or *chef-d'œuvres* of art, where they are accumulated, choke up the path to excellence; and that the works of genius, where they can be rendered permanent and handed down from age to age, not only prevent, but render superfluous, future productions of the same kind. We have not, neither do we want, two Shakspeares, two Miltons, two Raphaels, any more than we require two suns in the same sphere. Even Miss O'Neill stands a little in the way of our recollections of Mrs. Siddons. But Mr. Kean is an excellent substitute for the memory of Garrick, whom we never saw. When an author dies, it is no matter, for his works remain. When a great actor dies, there is a void produced in society, a gap which requires to be filled up. Who does not go to see Kean? Who, if Garrick were alive, would go to see him? At least one or the other must have quitted the stage. We have seen what a ferment has been excited among our living artists by the exhibition of the works of the old Masters at the British Gallery. What would the actors say to it, if, by any spell or power of necromancy, all the celebrated actors, for the last hundred years could be made to appear again on the boards of Covent Garden and Drury-Lane, for the last time, in all their most brilliant parts? What a rich treat to the town, what a feast for the critics, to go and see Betterton, and Booth, and Wilks, and Sandford, and Nokes, and Leigh, and Penkethman, and Bullock, and Estcourt, and Dogget, and Mrs. Barry, and Mrs. Montfort, and Mrs. Oldfield, and Mrs. Bracegirdle, and Mrs. Cibber, and Cibber himself, the prince of coxcombs, and Macklin, and Quin, and Rich, and Mrs. Clive, and Mrs. Pritchard, and Mrs. Abington, and Weston, and Shuter, and Garrick, and all the rest of those who 'gladdened life, and whose deaths eclipsed the gaiety of nations'! We should certainly be there. We should buy a ticket for the season. We should enjoy *our hundred days* again. We should not lose a single night. We would not, for a great deal, be absent from Betterton's Hamlet or his Brutus, or from Booth's Cato, as it was first acted to the contending applause of Whigs and Tories. We should be in the first row when Mrs. Barry (who was kept by Lord Rochester, and with whom Otway was in love) played Monimia or Belvidera; and we suppose we should go to see Mrs. Bracegirdle (with whom all the world was in love) in all her parts. We should then know exactly whether Penkethman's manner of picking a chicken, and Bullock's mode of devouring asparagus, answered to the ingenious account of them in the Tatler; and whether Dogget was equal to Dowton—whether Mrs. Montfort[1] or Mrs. Abington was the finest

[1] The following lively description of this actress is given by Cibber in his Apology :—

'What found most employment for her whole various excellence at once, was the part of Melantha, in Marriage-à-la-mode. Melantha is as finished an impertinent as ever fluttered in a drawing-room, and seems to contain the most complete system of female foppery that could possibly be crowded into the tortured form of a fine lady. Her language, dress, motion, manners, soul, and body, are in a continual hurry to be something more than is necessary or commendable. And though I doubt it will be a vain labour to offer you a just likeness of Mrs. Montfort's action, yet the fantastic impression is still so strong in my memory, that I cannot help saying something, though fantastically, about it. The first ridiculous airs that break from her are upon a gallant never seen before, who delivers her a letter from her father, recommending him to her good graces as an

lady—whether Wilks or Cibber was the best Sir Harry Wildair—whether Macklin was really 'the Jew that Shakspeare drew,' and whether Garrick was, upon the whole, so great an actor as the world have made him out! Many people have a strong desire to pry into the secrets of futurity: for our own parts, we should be satisfied if we had the power to recall the dead, and live the past over again as often as we pleased! Players, after all, have little reason to complain of their hard-earned, short-lived popularity. One thunder of applause from pit, boxes, and gallery, is equal to a whole immortality of posthumous fame: and when we hear an actor, whose modesty is equal to his merit, declare, that he would like to see a dog wag his tail in approbation, what must he feel when he sees the whole house in a roar! Besides, Fame, as if their reputation had been entrusted to her alone, has been particularly careful of the renown of her theatrical favourites: she forgets one by one, and year by year, those who have been great lawyers, great statesmen, and great warriors in their day; but the name of Garrick still survives with the works of Reynolds and of Johnson.

Actors have been accused, as a profession, of being extravagant and dissipated. While they are said to be so as a piece of common cant, they are likely to continue so. But there is a sentence in Shakspeare which should be stuck as a label in the mouths of our beadles and whippers-in of morality: 'The web of our life is of a mingled yarn, good and ill together: our virtues would be proud if our faults whipped them not: and our vices would despair if they were not cherished by our virtues.' With respect to the extravagance of actors, as a traditional character, it is not to be wondered at. They live from hand to mouth: they plunge from want into

honourable lover. Here now, one would think she might naturally shew a little of the sex's decent reserve, though never so slightly covered! No, sir; not a tittle of it; modesty is the virtue of a poor-soul'd country gentlewoman: she is too much a court-lady, to be under so vulgar a confusion: she reads the letter, therefore, with a careless, dropping lip, and an erected brow, humming it hastily over, as if she were impatient to outgo her father's commands, by making a complete conquest of him at once: and that the letter might not embarrass her attack, crack! she crumbles it at once into her palm, and pours upon him her whole artillery of airs, eyes, and motion; down goes her dainty, diving body to the ground, as if she were sinking under the conscious load of her own attractions; then launches into a flood of fine language and compliment, still playing her chest forward in fifty falls and risings, like a swan upon waving water; and, to complete her impertinence, she is so rapidly fond of her own wit, that she will not give her lover leave to praise it: Silent assenting bows, and vain endeavours to speak, are all the share of the conversation he is admitted to, which at last he is relieved from, by her engagement to half a score visits, which she *swims* from him to make, with a promise to return in a twinkling.'—*The Life of Colley Cibber* p. 138.

luxury; they have no means of making money *breed*, and all professions that do not live by turning money into money, or have not a certainty of accumulating it in the end by parsimony, spend it. Uncertain of the future, they make sure of the present moment. This is not unwise. Chilled with poverty, steeped in contempt, they sometimes pass into the sunshine of fortune, and are lifted to the very pinnacle of public favour; yet even there cannot calculate on the continuance of success, but are, 'like the giddy sailor on the mast, ready with every blast to topple down into the fatal bowels of the deep!' Besides, if the young enthusiast, who is smitten with the stage, and with the public as a mistress, were naturally a close *hunks*, he would become or remain a city clerk, instead of turning player. Again, with respect to the habit of convivial indulgence, an actor, to be a good one, must have a great spirit of enjoyment in himself, strong impulses, strong passions, and a strong sense of pleasure: for it is his business to imitate the passions, and to communicate pleasure to others. A man of genius is not a machine. The neglected actor may be excused if he drinks oblivion of his disappointments; the successful one, if he quaffs the applause of the world, and enjoys the friendship of those who are the friends of the favourites of fortune, in draughts of nectar. There is no path so steep as that of fame: no labour so hard as the pursuit of excellence. The intellectual excitement, inseparable from those professions which call forth all our sensibility to pleasure and pain, requires some corresponding physical excitement to support our failure, and not a little to allay the ferment of the spirits attendant on success. If there is any tendency to dissipation beyond this in the profession of a player, it is owing to the prejudices entertained against them, to that spirit of bigotry which in a neighbouring country would deny actors Christian burial after their death, and to that cant of criticism, which, in our own, slurs over their characters, while living, with a half-witted jest.

A London engagement is generally considered by actors as the *ne plus ultra* of their ambition, as 'a consummation devoutly to be wished,' as the great prize in the lottery of their professional life. But this appears to us, who are not in the secret, to be rather the prose termination of their adventurous career: it is the provincial commencement that is the poetical and truly enviable part of it. After that, they have comparatively little to hope or fear. 'The wine of life is drunk, and but the lees remain.' In London, they become gentlemen, and the King's servants: but it is the romantic mixture of the hero and the vagabond that constitutes the essence of the player's life. It is the transition from their real to their assumed characters, from the contempt of the world to the applause of the multitude, that gives its zest to the latter, and raises them as much above common humanity at night, as in the daytime they are depressed below it. 'Hurried from fierce extremes, by contrast made more fierce,'—it is rags and a flock-bed which give their splendour to a plume of feathers and a throne. We should suppose, that if the most admired actor on the London stage were brought to confession on this point, he would acknowledge that all the applause he had received from 'brilliant and overflowing audiences,' was nothing to the light-headed intoxication of unlooked-for success in a barn. In town, actors are criticised: in country-places, they are wondered at, or hooted at: it is of little consequence which, so that the interval is not too long between. For ourselves, we own that the description of the strolling player in Gil Blas, soaking his dry crusts in the well by the roadside, presents to us a perfect picture of human felicity.

W. H.

WHY THE ARTS ARE NOT PROGRESSIVE ?—A FRAGMENT

IT is often made a subject of complaint and surprise, that the arts in this country, and in modern times, have not kept pace with the general progress of society and civilisation in other respects, and it has been proposed to remedy the deficiency by more carefully availing ourselves of the advantages which time and circumstances have placed within our reach, but which we have hitherto neglected, the study of the antique, the formation of academies, and the distribution of prizes.

First, the complaint itself, that the arts do not attain that progressive degree of perfection which might reasonably be expected from them, proceeds on a false notion, for the analogy appealed to in support of the regular advances of art to higher degrees of excellence, totally fails ; it applies to science, not to art. Secondly, the expedients proposed to remedy the evil by adventitious means are only calculated to confirm it. The arts hold immediate communication with nature, and are only derived from that source. When that original impulse no longer exists, when the inspiration of genius is fled, all the attempts to recal it are no better than the tricks of galvanism to restore the dead to life. The arts may be said to resemble Antæus in his struggle with Hercules, who was strangled when he was raised above the ground, and only revived and recovered his strength when he touched his mother earth.

ON THE PROGRESS OF ART

Nothing is more contrary to the fact than the supposition that in what we understand by the *fine arts*, as painting and poetry, relative perfection is only the result of repeated efforts, and that what has been once well done constantly leads to something better. What is mechanical, reducible to rule, or capable of demonstration, is progressive, and admits of gradual improvement: what is not mechanical or definite, but depends on genius, taste, and feeling, very soon becomes stationary or retrograde, and loses more than it gains by transfusion. The contrary opinion is, indeed, a common error, which has grown up, like many others, from transferring an analogy of one kind to something quite distinct, without thinking of the difference in the nature of the things, or attending to the difference of the results. For most persons, finding what wonderful advances have been made in biblical criticism, in chemistry, in mechanics, in geometry, astronomy, etc.—*i.e.*, in things depending on mere inquiry and experiment, or on absolute demonstration, have been led hastily to conclude, that there was a general tendency in the efforts of the human intellect to improve by repetition, and in all other arts and institutions to grow perfect and mature by time. We look back upon the theological creed of our ancestors, and their discoveries in natural philosophy, with a smile of pity; science, and the arts connected with it, have all had their infancy, their youth, and manhood, and seem to have in them no principle of limitation or decay; and, inquiring no farther about the matter, we infer, in the height of our self-congratulation, and in the intoxication of our pride, that the same progress has been, and will continue to be, made in all other things which are the work of man. The fact, however, stares us so plainly in the face, that one would think the smallest reflection must suggest the truth, and overturn our sanguine theories. The greatest poets, the ablest orators, the best painters, and the finest sculptors that the world ever saw, appeared soon after the birth of these arts, and lived in a state of society which was, in other respects, comparatively barbarous. Those arts, which depend on individual genius and incommunicable power, have always leaped at once from infancy to manhood, from the first rude dawn of invention to their meridian height and dazzling lustre, and have in general declined ever after. This is the peculiar distinction and privilege of each, of science and of art; of the one, never to attain its utmost summit of perfection, and of the other, to arrive at it almost at once. Homer, Chaucer, Spenser, Shakspeare, Dante, and Ariosto (Milton alone was of a later age, and not the worse for it), Raphael, Titian, Michael Angelo, Correggio, Cervantes, and Boccaccio—all lived near the beginning of their arts—perfected, and all but created them. These giant sons of genius stand, indeed, upon the earth, but they tower above their fellows, and the long line of their successors does not interpose any thing to obstruct their view, or lessen their brightness. In strength and stature they are unrivalled, in grace and beauty they have never been surpassed. In after-ages, and more refined periods, (as they are called), great men have arisen one by one, as it were by throes and at intervals: though in general the best of these cultivated and artificial minds were of an inferior order, as Tasso and Pope among poets, Guido and Vandyke among painters. But in the earliest stages of the arts, when the first mechanical difficulties had been got over, and the language as it were acquired, they rose by clusters and in constellations, never to rise again.

The arts of painting and poetry are conversant with the world of thought within us, and with the world of sense without us—with what we know, and see, and feel intimately. They flow from the sacred shrine of our own breasts, and are kindled at the living lamp of nature The pulse of the passions assuredly beat as high, the depths and soundings of the human heart were as well understood three thousand years ago, as they are at present; the face of nature and 'the human face divine,' shone as bright then as they have ever done. It is this light, reflected by true genius on art, that marks out its path before it, and sheds a glory round the Muses' feet, like that which 'circled Una's angel face,

'And made a sunshine in the shady place.'

Nature is the soul of art. There is a strength in the imagination that reposes entirely on nature, which nothing else can supply. There is in the old poets and painters a vigour and grasp of mind, a full possession of their subject, a confidence and firm faith, a sublime simplicity, an elevation of thought, proportioned to their depth of feeling, an increasing force and impetus, which moves, penetrates, and kindles all that comes in contact with it, which seems, not theirs, but given to them. It is this reliance on the power of nature which has produced those masterpieces by the Prince of Painters, in which expression is all in all, where one spirit, that of truth, pervades every part, brings down heaven to earth, mingles cardinals and popes with angels and apostles, and yet blends and harmonises the whole by the true touches and intense feeling of what is beautiful and grand in nature. It was the same trust in nature that enabled Chaucer to describe the patient sorrow of Griselda; or the delight of that young beauty in the Flower and the Leaf, shrouded in her bower, and listening, in the morning of the year, to the singing of the nightingale, while her joy rises with the rising song, and gushes out afresh at every pause, and is borne along with the full tide of pleasure, and still increases and repeats and prolongs itself, and knows no ebb. It is thus that Boccaccio, in the divine story of the Hawk, has represented Frederigo Alberigi steadily contemplating his favourite Falcon (the wreck and remnant of his fortune), and glad to see how fat and fair a bird she is, thinking what a dainty repast she would make for his Mistress, who had deigned to visit him in his low cell. So Isabella mourns over her pot of Basile, and never asks for any thing but that. So Lear calls out for his poor fool, and invokes the heavens, for they are old like him. So Titian impressed on the countenance of that young Neapolitan nobleman in the Louvre, a look that never passed away. So Nicolas Poussin describes some shepherds wandering out in a morning of the spring, and coming to a tomb with this inscription, 'I ALSO WAS AN ARCADIAN.'

In general, it must happen in the first stages of the Arts, that as none but those who had a natural genius for them would attempt to practise them, so none but those who had a natural taste for them would pretend to judge of or criticise them. This must be an incalculable advantage to the man of true genius, for it is no other than the privilege of being tried by his peers. In an age when connoisseurship had not become a fashion; when religion, war, and intrigue, occupied the time and thoughts of the great, only those minds of superior refinement would be led to notice the works of art, who had a real sense of their excellence; and in giving way to the powerful bent of his own genius, the painter was most likely to consult the taste of his judges. He had not to deal with pretenders to taste, through vanity, affectation, and idleness. He had to appeal to the higher faculties of the soul; to that deep and innate sensibility to truth and beauty, which required only a proper object to have its enthusiasm excited; and to that independent strength of mind, which, in the midst of ignorance and barbarism, hailed and fostered genius, wherever it met with it. Titian was patronised by Charles v., Count Castiglione was the friend of Raphael. These were true patrons, and true critics; and as there were no others, (for the world, in general, merely looked on and wondered), there can be little doubt, that such a period of dearth of factitious patronage would be the most favourable to the full developement of the greatest talents, and the attainment of the highest excellence.

The diffusion of taste is not the same thing as the improvement of taste; but it is only the former of these objects that is promoted by public institutions and other artificial means. The number of candidates for fame, and of pretenders to criticism, is thus increased beyond all proportion, while the quantity of genius and feeling remains the same; with this difference, that the man of genius is lost in the crowd of competitors, who would never have become such but from encouragement and example; and that the opinion of those few persons whom nature intended for judges, is drowned in the noisy suffrages of shallow smatterers in taste. The principle of universal suffrage, however applicable to matters of government, which concern the common feelings and common interests of society, is by no means applicable to matters of taste, which can only be decided upon by the most refined understandings. The highest efforts of genius, in every walk of art, can never be properly understood by the generality of mankind : There are numberless beauties and truths which lie far beyond their comprehension. It is only as refinement and sublimity are blended with other qualities of a more obvious and grosser nature, that they pass current with the world. Taste is the highest degree of sensibility, or the impression made on the most cultivated and sensible of minds, as genius is the result of the highest powers both of feeling and invention. It may be objected, that the public taste is capable of gradual improvement, because, in the end, the public do justice to works of the greatest merit. This is a mistake. The reputation ultimately, and often slowly affixed to works of genius is stamped upon them by authority, not by popular consent or the common sense of the world. We imagine that the admiration of the works of celebrated men has become common, because the admiration of their names has become so. But does not every ignorant connoisseur pretend the same veneration, and talk with the same vapid assurance of Michael Angelo, though he has never seen even a copy of any of his pictures, as if he had studied them accurately,—merely because Sir Joshua Reynolds has praised him? Is Milton more popular now than when the Paradise Lost was first published? Or does he not rather owe his reputation to the judgment of a few persons in every successive period, accumulating in his favour, and overpowering by its weight the public indifference? Why is Shakspeare popular? Not from his refinement of character or sentiment, so much as from his power of telling a story, the variety and invention, the tragic catastrophe and broad farce of his plays. Spenser is not yet understood. Does not Boccaccio pass to this day for a writer of ribaldry, because his jests and lascivious tales were all that caught the vulgar ear, while the story of the Falcon is forgotten !   W. H.

CHARACTERS OF
SHAKESPEAR'S PLAYS

BIBLIOGRAPHICAL NOTE

Published in 1817 in one 8vo. volume with the following title-page : 'Characters of Shakespear's Plays. By William Hazlitt. London : Printed by C. H. Reynell 21, Piccadilly, for R. Hunter, successor to Mr. Johnson, in St. Paul's Church Yard ; and C. and J. Ollier, Welbeck-Street, Cavendish-Square. 1817.' The second edition was issued in the following year, and the imprint is : 'London Printed for Taylor and Hessey, 93, Fleet Street. 1818.' There are several verbal alterations in the second edition, and one curious *erratum* : 'In *Lear*, p. 173 [p. 269 present edition] dele line "Not an hour more nor less."' In the text of the play these words occur between 'Fourscore and upward' and 'And, to deal plainly.' The second edition also was printed by C. H. Reynell, Broad-street, Golden-square. No further edition was published in Hazlitt's lifetime, and the present issue has consequently been printed from a copy of the second edition ; the proofs, however, have been read with a copy of the first edition, and one or two misprints thereby corrected.

The following announcement appears on the back of the half-title of the second edition : 'This day is published, Lectures on the English Poets, delivered at the Surry Institution, By William Hazlitt. In one vol. 8vo. price 10s. 6d.'

CONTENTS

CHARACTERS OF SHAKESPEAR'S PLAYS

PREFACE

It is observed by Mr. Pope, that

'If ever any author deserved the name of an *original*, it was Shakespear. Homer himself drew not his art so immediately from the fountains of nature; it proceeded through Ægyptian strainers and channels, and came to him not without some tincture of the learning, or some cast of the models, of those before him. The poetry of Shakespear was inspiration indeed: he is not so much an imitator, as an instrument of nature; and it is not so just to say that he speaks from her, as that she speaks through him.

'His *characters* are so much nature herself, that it is a sort of injury to call them by so distant a name as copies of her. Those of other poets have a constant resemblance, which shows that they received them from one another, and were but multipliers of the same image: each picture, like a mock-rainbow, is but the reflection of a reflection. But every single character in Shakespear, is as much an individual, as those in life itself; it is as impossible to find any two alike; and such, as from their relation or affinity in any respect appear most to be twins, will, upon comparison, be found remarkably distinct. To this life and variety of character, we must add the wonderful preservation of it; which is such throughout his plays, that had all the speeches been printed without the very names of the persons, I believe one might have applied them with certainty to every speaker.'

The object of the volume here offered to the public, is to illustrate these remarks in a more particular manner by a reference to each play. A gentleman of the name of Mason, the author of a Treatise on Ornamental Gardening (not Mason the poet), began a work of a similar kind about forty years ago, but he only lived to finish a parallel between the characters of Macbeth and Richard III. which is an exceedingly ingenious piece of analytical criticism. Richardson's Essays include but a few of Shakespear's principal characters. The only work which seemed to supersede the necessity of an attempt like the present was Schlegel's very admirable Lectures on the Drama, which give by far the best account of the plays of Shakespear that has hitherto appeared. The only circumstances in which it was thought not impossible to improve on the manner in which the German critic has executed this part of his design, were in avoiding an appearance of mysticism in his style, not very attractive to the English reader, and in bringing illustrations from particular passages of the plays themselves, of which Schlegel's work, from the extensiveness of his plan, did not admit. We will at the same time confess, that some little jealousy of the character of the national understanding was not without its share in producing the following undertaking, for 'we were piqued' that it should be reserved for a foreign critic to give 'reasons for the faith which we English have in Shakespear.' Certainly no writer among ourselves has shown either the same enthusiastic admiration of his genius, or the same philosophical acuteness in pointing out his characteristic excellences. As we have pretty well exhausted all we had to say upon this subject in the body of the work, we shall here transcribe Schlegel's general account of Shakespear, which is in the following words :—

'Never, perhaps, was there so comprehensive a talent for the delineation of character as Shakespear's. It not only grasps the diversities of rank, sex, and age, down to the dawnings of infancy; not only do the king and the beggar, the hero and the pickpocket, the sage and the idiot speak and act with equal truth; not only does he transport himself to distant ages and foreign nations, and pourtray in the most accurate manner, with only a few apparent violations of costume, the spirit of the ancient Romans, of the French in their wars with the English, of the English themselves during a great part of their history, of the Southern Europeans (in the serious part of many comedies) the cultivated society of that time, and the former rude and barbarous state of the North; his human characters have not only such depth and precision that they cannot be arranged under classes, and are inexhaustible, even in conception :—no—this Prometheus not merely forms men, he opens the gates of the magical world of spirits ; calls up the midnight ghost; exhibits before us his witches amidst their unhallowed mysteries ; peoples the air with sportive fairies and sylphs :— and these beings, existing only in imagination, possess such truth and consistency, that even when deformed monsters like Caliban, he extorts the conviction, that if there should be such beings, they would so conduct themselves. In a word, as he carries with him the most fruitful and daring fancy into the kingdom of nature,—on the other hand, he carrie nature into the regions of fancy, lying beyond the confines of reality We are lost in astonishment at seeing the extraordinary, the wonderful, and the unheard of, in such intimate nearness.

'If Shakespear deserves our admiration for his characters, he is equally deserving of it for his exhibition of passion, taking this word in its widest signification, as including every mental condition, every tone from indifference or familiar mirth to the wildest rage and despair. He gives us the history of minds; he lays open to us, in a single word, a whole series of preceding conditions. His passions do not at first stand displayed to us in all their height, as is the case with so many tragic poets, who, in the language of Lessing, are thorough masters of the legal style of love. He paints, in a most inimitable manner, the gradual progress from the first origin. "He gives," as Lessing says, "a living picture of all the most minute and secret artifices by which a feeling steals into our souls; of all the imperceptible advantages which it there gains; of all the stratagems by which every other passion is made subservient to it, till it becomes the sole tyrant of our desires and our aversions." Of all poets, perhaps, he alone has pourtrayed the mental diseases,—melancholy, delirium, lunacy,—with such inexpressible, and, in every respect, definite truth, that the physician may enrich his observations from them in the same manner as from real cases.

'And yet Johnson has objected to Shakespear, that his pathos is not always natural and free from affectation. There are, it is true, passages, though, comparatively speaking, very few, where his poetry exceeds the bounds of true dialogue, where a too soaring imagination, a too luxuriant wit, rendered the complete dramatic forgetfulness of himself impossible. With this exception, the censure originates only in a fanciless way of thinking, to which everything appears unnatural that does not suit its own tame insipidity. Hence, an idea has been formed of simple and natural pathos, which consists in exclamations destitute of imagery, and nowise elevated above every-day life. But energetical passions electrify the whole of the mental powers, and will, consequently, in highly favoured natures, express themselves in an ingenious and figurative manner. It has been often remarked, that indignation gives wit; and, as despair occasionally breaks out into laughter, it may sometimes also give vent to itself in antithetical comparisons.

'Besides, the rights of the poetical form have not been duly weighed. Shakespear, who was always sure of his object, to move in a sufficiently powerful manner when he wished to do so, has occasionally, by indulging in a freer play, purposely moderated the impressions when too painful, and immediately introduced a musical alleviation of our sympathy. He had not those rude ideas of his art which many moderns seem to have, as if the poet, like the clown in the proverb, must strike twice on the same place. An ancient rhetorician delivered a caution against dwelling too long on the excitation of pity; for nothing, he said, dries so soon as tears; and Shakespear acted conformably to this ingenious maxim, without knowing it.

'The objection, that Shakespear wounds our feelings by the open display of the most disgusting moral odiousness, harrows up the mind unmercifully, and tortures even our senses by the exhibition of the most insupportable and hateful spectacles, is one of much greater importance. He has never, in fact, varnished over wild and bloodthirsty passions with a pleasing exterior,—never clothed crime and want of principle with a false show of greatness of soul; and in that respect he is every way deserving of praise. Twice he has pourtrayed downright villains; and the masterly way in which he has contrived to elude impressions of too painful a nature, may be seen in Iago and Richard the Third. The constant reference to a petty and puny race must cripple the boldness of the poet. Fortunately for his art, Shakespear lived in an age extremely susceptible of noble and tender impressions, but which had still enough of the firmness inherited from a vigorous olden time not to shrink back with dismay from every strong and violent picture. We have lived to see tragedies of which the catastrophe consists in the swoon of an enamoured princess. If Shakespear falls occasionally into the opposite extreme, it is a noble error, originating in the fulness of a gigantic strength: and yet this tragical Titan, who storms the heavens, and threatens to tear the world from off its hinges; who, more terrible than Æschylus, makes our hair stand on end, and congeals our blood with horror, possessed, at the same time, the insinuating loveliness of the sweetest poetry. He plays with love like a child; and his songs are breathed out like melting sighs. He unites in his genius the utmost elevation and the utmost depth; and the most foreign, and even apparently irreconcileable properties subsist in him peaceably together. The world of spirits and nature have laid all their treasures at his feet. In strength a demi-god, in profundity of view a prophet, in all-seeing wisdom a protecting spirit of a higher order, he lowers himself to mortals, as if unconscious of his superiority: and is as open and unassuming as a child.

'Shakespear's comic talent is equally wonderful with that which he has shown in the pathetic and tragic: it stands on an equal elevation, and possesses equal extent and profundity. All that I before wished were, not to admit that the former preponderated. He is highly inventive in comic situations and motives. It will be hardly possible to show whence he has taken any of them; whereas, in the serious part of his drama, he has generally laid hold of something already known. His comic characters are equally true, various, and profound, with his serious. So little is he disposed to caricature, that we may rather say many of his traits are almost too nice and delicate for the stage, that they can only be properly seized by a great actor, and fully understood by a very acute audience. Not only has he delineated many kinds of folly; he has also contrived to exhibit mere stupidity in a most diverting and entertaining manner.'—Vol. ii. p. 145.

We have the rather availed ourselves of this testimony of a foreign critic in behalf of Shakespear, because our own countryman, Dr. Johnson, has not been so favourable to him. It may be said of Shakespear, that 'those who are not for him are against him': for indifference is here the height of injustice. We may sometimes, in order 'to do a great right, do a little wrong.' An overstrained enthusiasm is more pardonable with respect to Shakespear than the want of it; for our admiration cannot easily surpass his genius. We have a high respect for Dr. Johnson's character and understanding, mixed with something like personal attachment: but he was neither a poet nor a judge of poetry. He might in one sense be a judge of poetry as it falls within the limits and rules of prose, but not as it is poetry. Least of all was he qualified to be a judge of Shakespear, who 'alone is high fantastical.' Let those who have a prejudice against Johnson read Boswell's Life of him: as those whom he had prejudiced against Shakespear should read his Irene. We do not say that a man to be a critic must necessarily be a poet: but to be a ood critic, he ought not to be a bad poet. Such poetry as a man deliberately writes, such, and such only will he like. Dr. Johnson's preface to his edition of Shakespear looks like a laborious attempt to bury the characteristic merits of his author under a load of cumbrous phraseology, and to weigh his excellences and defects in equal scales, stuffed full of 'swelling figures and sonorous epithets.' Nor could well be otherwise; Dr. Johnson's general powers of reasoning overlaid his critical susceptibility. All his ideas were cast in a given mould, in a set form: they were made out by rule and system, by climax, inference, and antithesis:—Shakespear's were the reverse. Johnson's understanding dealt only in round numbers: the fractions were lost upon him. He reduced everything to the common standard of conventional propriety; and the most exquisite refinement or sublimity produced an effect on his mind, only as they could be translated into the language of measured prose. To him an excess of beauty was a fault; for it appeared to him like an excrescence; and his imagination was dazzled by the blaze of light. His writings neither shone with the beams of native genius, nor reflected them. The shifting shapes of fancy, the rainbow hues of things, made no impression on him: he seized only on the permanent and tangible. He had no idea of natural objects but 'such as he could measure with a two-foot rule, or tell upon ten fingers': he judged of human nature in the same way, by mood and figure: he saw only the definite, the positive, and the practical, the average forms of things, not their striking differences—their classes, not their degrees. He was a man of strong common sense and practical wisdom, rather than of genius or feeling. He retained the regular, habitual impressions of actual objects, but he could not follow the rapid flights of fancy, or the strong movements of passion. That is, he was to the poet what the painter of still life is to the painter of history. Common sense sympathises with the impressions of things on ordinary minds in ordinary circumstances: genius catches the glancing combinations presented to the eye of fancy, under the influence of passion. It is the province of the didactic reasoner to take cognizance of those results of human nature which are constantly repeated and always the same, which follow one another in regular succession, which are acted upon by large classes of men, and embodied in received customs, laws, language, and institutions; and it was in arranging, comparing, and arguing on these kind of general results, that Johnson's excellence lay. But he could not quit his hold of the common-place and mechanical, and apply the general rule to the particular exception, or shew how the nature of man was modified by the workings of passion, or the infinite fluctuations of thought and accident. Hence he could

G 65

judge neither of the heights nor depths of poetry. Nor is this all
for being conscious of great powers in himself, and those powers
an adverse tendency to those of his author, he would be for settin
up a foreign jurisdiction over poetry, and making criticism a kind
Procrustes' bed of genius, where he might cut down imagination
matter-of-fact, regulate the passions according to reason, and transla
the whole into logical diagrams and rhetorical declamation. Th
he says of Shakespear's characters, in contradiction to what Po
had observed, and to what every one else feels, that each charact
is a species, instead of being an individual. He in fact found th
general species or *didactic* form in Shakespear's characters, which w
all he sought or cared for; he did not find the individual traits,
the *dramatic* distinctions which Shakespear has engrafted on th
general nature, because he felt no interest in them. Shakespear
bold and happy flights of imagination were equally thrown away up
our author. He was not only without any particular fineness
organic sensibility, alive to all the 'mighty world of ear and eye
which is necessary to the painter or musician, but without that i
tenseness of passion, which, seeking to exaggerate whatever excit
the feelings of pleasure or power in the mind, and moulding th
impressions of natural objects according to the impulses of imaginatio
produces a genius and a taste for poetry. According to Dr. Johnso
a mountain is sublime, or a rose is beautiful; for that their name an
definition imply. But he would no more be able to give the descri
tion of Dover cliff in *Lear*, or the description of flowers in *T.
Winter's Tale*, than to describe the objects of a sixth sense; nor d
we think he would have any very profound feeling of the beauty
the passages here referred to. A stately common-place, such
Congreve's description of a ruin in the *Mourning Bride*, would ha
answered Johnson's purpose just as well, or better than the first; an
an indiscriminate profusion of scents and hues would have interfere
less with the ordinary routine of his imagination than Perdita's line
which seem enamoured of their own sweetness—

> ——'Daffodils
> That come before the swallow dares, and take
> The winds of March with beauty; violets dim,
> But sweeter than the lids of Juno's eyes,
> Or Cytherea's breath.'—

No one who does not feel the passion which these objects inspi
can go along with the imagination which seeks to express that passio
and the uneasy sense of delight accompanying it by something sti
more beautiful, and no one can feel this passionate love of natu

thout quick natural sensibility. To a mere literal and formal
prehension, the inimitably characteristic epithet, 'violets *dim*,' must
em to imply a defect, rather than a beauty; and to any one, not
eling the full force of that epithet, which suggests an image like
he sleepy eye of love,' the allusion to 'the lids of Juno's eyes'
ust appear extravagant and unmeaning. Shakespear's fancy lent
ords and images to the most refined sensibility to nature, struggling
r expression: his descriptions are identical with the things them-
lves, seen through the fine medium of passion: strip them of that
nnection, and try them by ordinary conceptions and ordinary rules,
d they are as grotesque and barbarous as you please!—By thus
wering Shakespear's genius to the standard of common-place in-
ntion, it was easy to show that his faults were as great as his
auties; for the excellence, which consists merely in a conformity
rules, is counterbalanced by the technical violation of them.
nother circumstance which led to Dr. Johnson's indiscriminate
aise or censure of Shakespear, is the very structure of his style.
hnson wrote a kind of rhyming prose, in which he was as much
mpelled to finish the different clauses of his sentences, and to
lance one period against another, as the writer of heroic verse is
keep to lines of ten syllables with similar terminations. He no
oner acknowledges the merits of his author in one line than the
riodical revolution of his style carries the weight of his opinion
mpletely over to the side of objection, thus keeping up a perpetual
ternation of perfections and absurdities. We do not otherwise
ow how to account for such assertions as the following:—

'In his tragic scenes, there is always something wanting, but his comedy
ten surpasses expectation or desire. His comedy pleases by the thoughts
d the language, and his tragedy, for the greater part, by incident and
tion. His tragedy seems to be skill, his comedy to be instinct.'

et after saying that 'his tragedy was skill,' he affirms in the next
ge,

'His declamations or set speeches are commonly cold and weak, *for his
wer was the power of nature*: when he endeavoured, like other tragic
riters, to catch opportunities of amplification, and instead of inquiring
hat the occasion demanded, to shew how much his stores of knowledge
uld supply, he seldom escapes without the pity or resentment of his
ader.'

oor Shakespear! Between the charges here brought against him,
' want of nature in the first instance, and of want of skill in the
cond, he could hardly escape being condemned. And again,

'But the admirers of this great poet have most reason to complain when he approaches nearest to his highest excellence, and seems fully resolve to sink them in dejection, or mollify them with tender emotions by t fall of greatness, the danger of innocence, or the crosses of love. Wh he does best, he soon ceases to do. He no sooner begins to move than counteracts himself; and terror and pity, as they are rising in the min are checked and blasted by sudden frigidity.'

In all this, our critic seems more bent on maintaining the equi librium of his style than the consistency or truth of his opinion —If Dr. Johnson's opinion was right, the following observations o Shakespear's Plays must be greatly exaggerated, if not ridiculou If he was wrong, what has been said may perhaps account for h being so, without detracting from his ability and judgment in othe things.

It is proper to add, that the account of the *Midsummer's Night Dream* has appeared in another work.[1]

[1] A few alterations and corrections have been inserted in the present edition.
[Note by W. H. to Second Edition

April 15, 1817.

CHARACTERS OF
SHAKESPEAR'S PLAYS

CYMBELINE

CYMBELINE is one of the most delightful of Shakespear's historical plays. It may be considered as a dramatic romance, in which the most striking parts of the story are thrown into the form of a dialogue, and the intermediate circumstances are explained by the different speakers, as occasion renders it necessary. The action is less concentrated in consequence; but the interest becomes more aerial and refined from the principle of perspective introduced into the subject by the imaginary changes of scene, as well as by the length of time it occupies. The reading of this play is like going a journey with some uncertain object at the end of it, and in which the suspense is kept up and heightened by the long intervals between each action. Though the events are scattered over such an extent of surface, and relate to such a variety of characters, yet the links which bind the different interests of the story together are never entirely broken. The most straggling and seemingly casual incidents are contrived in such a manner as to lead at last to the most complete developement of the catastrophe. The ease and conscious unconcern with which this is effected only makes the skill more wonderful. The business of the plot evidently thickens in the last act: the story moves forward with increasing rapidity at every step; its various ramifications are drawn from the most distant points to the same centre; the principal characters are brought together, and placed in very critical situations; and the fate of almost every person in the drama is made to depend on the solution of a single circumstance—the answer of Iachimo to the question of Imogen respecting the obtaining of the ring from Posthumus   Dr. Johnson is of opinion that Shakespear was generally inattentive to the winding-up of his plots. We think the contrary is true; and we might cite in proof of this remark not only the present play, but the conclusion of *Lear*, of *Romeo and Juliet*, of *Macbeth*, of *Othello*, even of *Hamlet*, and of other plays of less moment, in which the last act is crowded with decisive events brought about by natur and striking means.

The pathos in CYMBELINE is not violent or tragical, but of the mo pleasing and amiable kind. A certain tender gloom overspreads t whole. Posthumus is the ostensible hero of the piece, but its greate charm is the character of Imogen. Posthumus is only interestin from the interest she takes in him; and she is only interesting herse from her tenderness and constancy to her husband. It is the peculi excellence of Shakespear's heroines, that they seem to exist only i their attachment to others. They are pure abstractions of the affec tions. We think as little of their persons as they do themselve because we are let into the secrets of their hearts, which are mor important. We are too much interested in their affairs to stop look at their faces, except by stealth and at intervals. No one eve hit the true perfection of the female character, the sense of weaknes leaning on the strength of its affections for support, so well a Shakespear — no one ever so well painted natural tenderness fre from affectation and disguise—no one else ever so well shewed ho delicacy and timidity, when driven to extremity, grow romantic an extravagant; for the romance of his heroines (in which they abound is only an excess of the habitual prejudices of their sex, scrupulou of being false to their vows, truant to their affections, and taught b the force of feeling when to forego the forms of propriety for th essence of it. His women were in this respect exquisite logicians for there is nothing so logical as passion. They knew their ow minds exactly; and only followed up a favourite purpose, whic they had sworn to with their tongues, and which was engraven o their hearts, into its untoward consequences. They were the prettie little set of martyrs and confessors on record.—Cibber, in speakin of the early English stage, accounts for the want of prominence an theatrical display in Shakespear's female characters from the circum stance, that women in those days were not allowed to play the part of women, which made it necessary to keep them a good deal in th back-ground. Does not this state of manners itself, which prevente their exhibiting themselves in public, and confined them to the rela tions and charities of domestic life, afford a truer explanation of th matter? His women are certainly very unlike stage-heroines; th reverse of tragedy-queens.

We have almost as great an affection for Imogen as she had fo Posthumus; and she deserves it better. Of all Shakespear's wome she is perhaps the most tender and the most artless. Her incredulit in the opening scene with Iachimo, as to her husband's infidelity is much the same as Desdemona's backwardness to believe Othello'

alousy. Her answer to the most distressing part of the picture is
nly, 'My lord, I fear, has forgot Britain.' Her readiness to pardon
achimo's false imputations and his designs against herself, is a good
esson to prudes; and may shew that where there is a real attachment
o virtue, it has no need to bolster itself up with an outrageous or
ffected antipathy to vice. The scene in which Pisanio gives Imogen
is master's letter, accusing her of incontinency on the treacherous
uggestions of Iachimo, is as touching as it is possible for anything
o be :—

> '*Pisanio.* What cheer, Madam?
> *Imogen.* False to his bed! What is it to be false?
> To lie in watch there, and to think on him?
> To weep 'twixt clock and clock? If sleep charge nature,
> To break it with a fearful dream of him,
> And cry myself awake? That's false to 's bed, is it?
> *Pisanio.* Alas, good lady!
> *Imogen.* I false? thy conscience witness, Iachimo,
> Thou didst accuse him of incontinency,
> Thou then look'dst like a villain: now methinks,
> Thy favour's good enough. Some Jay of Italy,
> Whose mother was her painting, hath betray'd him:
> Poor I am stale, a garment out of fashion,
> And for I am richer than to hang by th' walls,
> I must be ript; to pieces with me. Oh,
> Men's vows are women's traitors. All good seeming
> By thy revolt, oh husband, shall be thought
> Put on for villainy: not born where 't grows,
> But worn a bait for ladies.
> *Pisanio.* Good Madam, hear me—
> *Imogen.* Talk thy tongue weary, speak:
> I have heard I am a strumpet, and mine ear,
> Therein false struck, can take no greater wound,
> Nor tent to bottom that.'——

When Pisanio, who had been charged to kill his mistress, puts her
n a way to live, she says,

> 'Why, good fellow,
> What shall I do the while? Where bide? How live?
> Or in my life what comfort, when I am
> Dead to my husband?'

Yet when he advises her to disguise herself in boy's clothes, and
suggests 'a course pretty and full in view,' by which she may 'happily
be near the residence of Posthumus,' she exclaims—

> 'Oh, for such means,
> Though peril to my modesty, not death on 't,
> I would adventure.'

And when **Pisanio**, enlarging on the consequences, tells her she must change

>   ——'Fear and niceness,
> The handmaids of all women, or more truly,
> Woman its pretty self, into a waggish courage,
> Ready in gibes, quick-answer'd, saucy, and
> As quarrellous as the weazel'——

she interrupts him hastily—

> 'Nay, be brief;
> I see into thy end, and am almost
> A man already.'

In her journey thus disguised to Milford-Haven, she loses her guide and her way; and unbosoming her complaints, says beautifully—

>   ——'My dear lord,
> Thou art one of the false ones; now I think on thee,
> My hunger's gone; but even before, I was
> At point to sink for food.'

She afterwards finds, as she thinks, the dead body of Posthumus and engages herself as a footboy to serve a Roman officer, when she has done all due obsequies to him whom she calls her former master—

>   ——'And when
> With wild wood-leaves and weeds I ha' strew'd his grave,
> And on it said a century of pray'rs,
> Such as I can, twice o'er, I'll weep and sigh,
> And leaving so his service, follow you,
> So please you entertain me.'

Now this is the very religion of love. She all along relies little on her personal charms, which she fears may have been eclipsed by some painted Jay of Italy; she relies on her merit, and her merit is in the depth of her love, her truth and constancy. Our admiration of her beauty is excited with as little consciousness as possible on her part. There are two delicious descriptions given of her, one when she is asleep, and one when she is supposed dead. Arviragus thus addresses her—

>   ——'With fairest flowers,
> While summer lasts, and I live here, Fidele,
> I'll sweeten thy sad grave; thou shalt not lack
> The flow'r that's like thy face, pale primrose, nor
> The azur'd hare-bell, like thy veins, no, nor
> The leaf of eglantine, which not to slander,
> Out-sweeten'd not thy breath.'

CYMBELINE

The yellow Iachimo gives another thus, when he steals into her bedchamber:—

> ——'Cytherea,
> How bravely thou becom'st thy bed! Fresh lily,
> And whiter than the sheets! That I might touch——
> But kiss, one kiss——'Tis her breathing that
> Perfumes the chamber thus: the flame o' th' taper
> Bows toward her, and would under-peep her lids
> To see th' enclosed lights now canopied
> Under the windows, white and azure, laced
> With blue of Heav'n's own tinct——on her left breast
> A mole cinque-spotted, like the crimson drops
> I' th' bottom of a cowslip.'

There is a moral sense in the proud beauty of this last image, a rich surfeit of the fancy,—as that well-known passage beginning, 'Me of my lawful pleasure she restrained, and prayed me oft forbearance,' sets a keener edge upon it by the inimitable picture of modesty and self-denial.

The character of Cloten, the conceited, booby lord, and rejected lover of Imogen, though not very agreeable in itself, and at present obsolete, is drawn with much humour and quaint extravagance. The description which Imogen gives of his unwelcome addresses to her— 'Whose love-suit hath been to me as fearful as a siege'—is enough to cure the most ridiculous lover of his folly. It is remarkable that though Cloten makes so poor a figure in love, he is described as assuming an air of consequence as the Queen's son in a council of state, and with all the absurdity of his person and manners, is not without shrewdness in his observations. So true is it that folly is as often owing to a want of proper sentiments as to a want of understanding! The exclamation of the ancient critic—Oh Menander and Nature, which of you copied from the other! would not be misapplied to Shakespear.

The other characters in this play are represented with great truth and accuracy, and as it happens in most of the author's works, there is not only the utmost keeping in each separate character; but in the casting of the different parts, and their relation to one another, there is an affinity and harmony, like what we may observe in the gradations of colour in a picture. The striking and powerful contrasts in which Shakespear abounds could not escape observation; but the use he makes of the principle of analogy to reconcile the greatest diversities of character and to maintain a continuity of feeling throughout, has not been sufficiently attended to. In CYMBELINE, for instance, the principal interest arises out of the unalterable fidelity of Imogen to

*G 65

her husband under the most trying circumstances. Now the other parts of the picture are filled up with subordinate examples of the same feeling, variously modified by different situations, and applied to the purposes of virtue or vice. The plot is aided by the amorous importunities of Cloten, by the persevering determination of Iachimo to conceal the defeat of his project by a daring imposture: the faithful attachment of Pisanio to his mistress is an affecting accompaniment to the whole; the obstinate adherence to his purpose in Bellarius, who keeps the fate of the young princes so long a secret in resentment for the ungrateful return to his former services, the incorrigible wickedness of the Queen, and even the blind uxorious confidence of Cymbeline, are all so many lines of the same story, tending to the same point. The effect of this coincidence is rather felt than observed; and as the impression exists unconsciously in the mind of the reader, so it probably arose in the same manner in the mind of the author, not from design, but from the force of natural association, a particular train of thought suggesting different inflections of the same predominant feeling, melting into, and strengthening one another, like chords in music.

The characters of Bellarius, Guiderius, and Arviragus, and the romantic scenes in which they appear, are a fine relief to the intrigues and artificial refinements of the court from which they are banished. Nothing can surpass the wildness and simplicity of the descriptions of the mountain life they lead. They follow the business of huntsmen, not of shepherds; and this is in keeping with the spirit of adventure and uncertainty in the rest of the story, and with the scenes in which they are afterwards called on to act. How admirably the youthful fire and impatience to emerge from their obscurity in the young princes is opposed to the cooler calculations and prudent resignation of their more experienced counsellor! How well the disadvantages of knowledge and of ignorance, of solitude and society, are placed against each other!

> '*Guiderius.* Out of your proof you speak: we poor unfledg'd
> Have never wing'd from view o' th' nest; nor know not
> What air's from home. Haply this life is best,
> If quiet life is best; sweeter to you
> That have a sharper known; well corresponding
> With your stiff age: but unto us it is
> A cell of ignorance; travelling a-bed,
> A prison for a debtor, that not dares
> To stride a limit.
>   *Arviragus.* What should we speak of
> When we are old as you? When we shall hear
> The rain and wind beat dark December! How,

> In this our pinching cave, shall we discourse
> The freezing hours away ? We have seen nothing.
> We are beastly ; subtle as the fox for prey,
> Like warlike as the wolf for what we eat :
> Our valour is to chase what flies ; our cage
> We make a quire, as doth the prison'd bird,
> And sing our bondage freely.'

The answer of Bellarius to this expostulation is hardly satisfactory ; for nothing can be an answer to hope, or the passion of the mind for unknown good, but experience.—The forest of Arden in *As you like it* can alone compare with the mountain scenes in CYMBELINE : yet how different the contemplative quiet of the one from the enterprising boldness and precarious mode of subsistence in the other ! Shakespear not only lets us into the minds of his characters, but gives a tone and colour to the scenes he describes from the feelings of their supposed inhabitants. He at the same time preserves the utmost propriety of action and passion, and gives all their local accompaniments. If he was equal to the greatest things, he was not above an attention to the smallest. Thus the gallant sportsmen in CYMBELINE have to encounter the abrupt declivities of hill and valley : Touchstone and Audrey jog along a level path. The deer in CYMBELINE are only regarded as objects of prey, ' The game 's a-foot,' etc.—with Jaques they are fine subjects to moralise upon at leisure, ' under the shade of melancholy boughs.'

We cannot take leave of this play, which is a favourite with us, without noticing some occasional touches of natural piety and morality. We may allude here to the opening of the scene in which Bellarius instructs the young princes to pay their orisons to heaven :

> ——'See, boys ! this gate
> Instructs you how t' adore the Heav'ns ; and bows you
> To morning's holy office.
> *Guiderius.* Hail, Heav'n !
> *Arviragus.* Hail, Heav'n !
> *Bellarius.* Now for our mountain-sport, up to yon hill.'

What a grace and unaffected spirit of piety breathes in this passage ! In like manner, one of the brothers says to the other, when about to perform the funeral rites to Fidele,

> ' Nay, Cadwall, we must lay his head to the east ;
> My Father hath a reason for 't '—

—as if some allusion to the doctrines of the Christian faith had been casually dropped in conversation by the old man, and had been no farther inquired into.

Shakespear's morality is introduced in the same simple, unobtrusive manner. Imogen will not let her companions stay away from the chase to attend her when sick, and gives her reason for it—

> 'Stick to your journal course; *the breach of custom*
> *Is breach of all!*'

When the Queen attempts to disguise her motives for procuring the poison from Cornelius, by saying she means to try its effects on 'creatures not worth the hanging,' his answer conveys at once a tacit reproof of her hypocrisy, and a useful lesson of humanity—

> ——'Your Highness
> Shall from this practice but make hard your heart.'

MACBETH

> 'The poet's eye in a fine frenzy rolling
> Doth glance from heaven to earth, from earth to heaven;
> And as imagination bodies forth
> The forms of things unknown, the poet's pen
> Turns them to shape, and gives to airy nothing
> A local habitation and a name.'

MACBETH and *Lear, Othello* and *Hamlet,* are usually reckoned Shakespear's four principal tragedies. *Lear* stands first for the profound intensity of the passion; MACBETH for the wildness of the imagination and the rapidity of the action; *Othello* for the progressive interest and powerful alternations of feeling; *Hamlet* for the refined developement of thought and sentiment. If the force of genius shewn in each of these works is astonishing, their variety is not less so. They are like different creations of the same mind, not one of which has the slightest reference to the rest. This distinctness and originality is indeed the necessary consequence of truth and nature. Shakespear's genius alone appeared to possess the resources of nature. He is 'your only *tragedy-maker*.' His plays have the force of things upon the mind. What he represents is brought home to the bosom as a part of our experience, implanted in the memory as if we had known the places, persons, and things of which he treats. MACBETH is like a record of a preternatural and tragical event. It has the rugged severity of an old chronicle with all that the imagination of the poet can engraft upon traditional belief. The castle of Macbeth, round which 'the air smells wooingly,' and where 'the temple-haunting martlet builds,' has a real subsistence in the mind; the Weïrd Sisters meet us in person on 'the blasted heath'; the 'air-drawn dagger' moves slowly before our eyes; the 'gracious Duncan,' the 'blood-boultered Banquo' stand before us; all that passed through the mind of Macbeth passes, without the loss of a tittle, through ours. All that could actually take place, and all that is only possible to be conceived, what was said and what was done, the workings of passion, the spells of magic, are brought before us with the same absolute truth and vividness.—Shakespear excelled in the openings of his plays: that of MACBETH is the most striking of any. The wildness of the scenery, the sudden shifting of the situations and characters, the bustle, the expectations excited, are equally extraordinary. From the first entrance of the Witches and the description of them when they meet Macbeth,

> ——'What are these
> So wither'd and so wild in their attire,
> That look not like the inhabitants of th' earth
> And yet are on 't?'

the mind is prepared for all that follows.

This tragedy is alike distinguished for the lofty imagination it displays, and for the tumultuous vehemence of the action; and the one is made the moving principle of the other. The overwhelming pressure of preternatural agency urges on the tide of human passion with redoubled force. Macbeth himself appears driven along by the violence of his fate like a vessel drifting before a storm: he reels to and fro like a drunken man; he staggers under the weight of his own purposes and the suggestions of others; he stands at bay with his situation; and from the superstitious awe and breathless suspense into which the communications of the Weïrd Sisters throw him, is hurried on with daring impatience to verify their predictions, and with impious and bloody hand to tear aside the veil which hides the uncertainty of the future. He is not equal to the struggle with fate and conscience. He now 'bends up each corporal instrument to the terrible feat'; at other times his heart misgives him, and he is cowed and abashed by his success. 'The deed, no less than the attempt, confounds him.' His mind is assailed by the stings of remorse, and full of 'preternatural solicitings.' His speeches and soliloquies are dark riddles on human life, baffling solution, and entangling him in their labyrinths. In thought he is absent and perplexed, sudden and desperate in act, from a distrust of his own resolution. His energy springs from the anxiety and agitation of his mind. His blindly rushing forward on the objects of his ambition and revenge, or his recoiling from them, equally betrays the harassed state of his feelings —This part of his character is admirably set off by being brought in connection with that of Lady Macbeth, whose obdurate strength of will and masculine firmness give her the ascendancy over her husband's faultering virtue. She at once seizes on the opportunity that offers for the accomplishment of all their wished-for greatness, and never flinches from her object till all is over. The magnitude of her resolution almost covers the magnitude of her guilt. She is a great bad woman, whom we hate, but whom we fear more than we hate. She does not excite our loathing and abhorrence like Regan and Gonerill. She is only wicked to gain a great end ; and is perhaps more distinguished by her commanding presence of mind and inexorable self-will, which do not suffer her to be diverted from a bad purpose, when once formed, by weak and womanly regrets, than by the hardness of her heart or want of natural affections. The impression which her lofty determination of character makes on the mind of Macbeth is well described where he exclaims,

> ——'Bring forth men children only ;
> For thy undaunted mettle should compose
> Nothing but males ! '

Nor do the pains she is at to 'screw his courage to the sticking place,' the reproach to him, not to be 'lost so poorly in himself,' the assurance that 'a little water clears them of this deed,' show anything but her greater consistency in depravity. Her strong nerved ambition furnishes ribs of steel to 'the sides of his intent'; and she is herself wound up to the execution of her baneful project with the same unshrinking fortitude in crime, that in other circumstances she would probably have shown patience in suffering. The deliberate sacrifice of all other considerations to the gaining 'for their future days and nights sole sovereign sway and masterdom,' by the murder of Duncan, is gorgeously expressed in her invocation on hearing of 'his fatal entrance under her battlements' :—

> ——'Come all you spirits
> That tend on mortal thoughts, unsex me here :
> And fill me, from the crown to th' toe, top-full
> Of direst cruelty ; make thick my blood,
> Stop up the access and passage to remorse,
> That no compunctious visitings of nature
> Shake my fell purpose, nor keep peace between
> The effect and it.   Come to my woman's breasts,
> And take my milk for gall, you murthering ministers,
> Wherever in your sightless substances
> You wait on nature's mischief.   Come, thick night !

And pall thee in the dunnest smoke of hell,
That my keen knife see not the wound it makes,
Nor heav'n peep through the blanket of the dark,
To cry, hold, hold!'——

When she first hears that 'Duncan comes there to sleep' she is so overcome by the news, which is beyond her utmost expectations, that she answers the messenger, 'Thou 'rt mad to say it': and on receiving her husband's account of the predictions of the Witches, conscious of his instability of purpose, and that her presence is necessary to goad him on to the consummation of his promised greatness, she exclaims—

——'Hie thee hither,
That I may pour my spirits in thine ear,
And chastise with the valour of my tongue
All that impedes thee from the golden round,
Which fate and metaphysical aid doth seem
To have thee crowned withal.'

This swelling exultation and keen spirit of triumph, this uncontroulable eagerness of anticipation, which seems to dilate her form and take possession of all her faculties, this solid, substantial flesh and blood display of passion, exhibit a striking contrast to the cold, abstracted, gratuitous, servile malignity of the Witches, who are equally instrumental in urging Macbeth to his fate for the mere love of mischief, and from a disinterested delight in deformity and cruelty. They are hags of mischief, obscene panders to iniquity, malicious from their impotence of enjoyment, enamoured of destruction, because they are themselves unreal, abortive, half-existences—who become sublime from their exemption from all human sympathies and contempt for all human affairs, as Lady Macbeth does by the force of passion! Her fault seems to have been an excess of that strong principle of self-interest and family aggrandisement, not amenable to the common feelings of compassion and justice, which is so marked a feature in barbarous nations and times. A passing reflection of this kind, on the resemblance of the sleeping king to her father, alone prevents her from slaying Duncan with her own hand.

In speaking of the character of Lady Macbeth, we ought not to pass over Mrs. Siddons's manner of acting that part. We can conceive of nothing grander. It was something above nature. It seemed almost as if a being of a superior order had dropped from a higher sphere to awe the world with the majesty of her appearance. Power was seated on her brow, passion emanated from her breast as from a shrine; she was tragedy personified. In coming on in the sleeping-scene, her eyes were open, but their sense was shut. She was like a person bewildered and unconscious of what she did. Her lips moved involuntarily—all her gestures were involuntary and mechanical. She glided on and off the stage like an apparition. To have seen her in that character was an event in every one's life, not to be forgotten.

The dramatic beauty of the character of Duncan, which excites the respect and pity even of his murderers, has been often pointed out. It forms a picture of itself. An instance of the author's power of giving a striking effect to a common reflection, by the manner of introducing it, occurs in a speech of Duncan, complaining of his having been deceived in his opinion of the Thane of Cawdor, at the very moment that he is expressing the most unbounded confidence in the loyalty and services of Macbeth.

> 'There is no art
> To find the mind's construction in the face:
> He was a gentleman, on whom I built
> An absolute trust.
> O worthiest cousin,   (*addressing himself to Macbeth.*)
> The sin of my ingratitude e'en now
> Was great upon me,' etc.

Another passage to show that Shakespear lost sight of nothing that could in any way give relief or heightening to his subject, is the conversation which takes place between Banquo and Fleance immediately before the murder-scene of Duncan.

> '*Banquo.* How goes the night, boy?
> *Fleance.* The moon is down: I have not heard the clock.
> *Banquo.* And she goes down at twelve.
> *Fleance.* I take 't, 'tis later, Sir.
> *Banquo.* Hold, take my sword. There's husbandry in heav'n,
> Their candles are all out.—
> A heavy summons lies like lead upon me,
> And yet I would not sleep: Merciful Powers,
> Restrain in me the cursed thoughts that nature
> Gives way to in repose.'

In like manner, a fine idea is given of the gloomy coming on of evening, just as Banquo is going to be assassinated.

> 'Light thickens and the crow
> Makes wing to the rooky wood.'

> .   .   .   .   .   .

> 'Now spurs the lated traveller apace
> To gain the timely inn.'

MACBETH (generally speaking) is done upon a stronger and more systematic principle of contrast than any other of Shakespear's plays. It moves upon the verge of an abyss, and is a constant struggle between life and death. The action is desperate and the reaction is dreadful. It is a huddling together of fierce extremes, a war of opposite natures which of them shall destroy the other. There is nothing but what has a violent end or violent beginnings. The lights and shades are laid on with a determined hand; the transitions from triumph to despair, from the height of terror to the repose of death, are sudden and startling; every passion brings in its fellow-contrary, and the thoughts pitch and jostle against each other as in the dark. The whole play is an unruly chaos of strange and forbidden things, where the ground rocks under our feet. Shakespear's genius here took its full swing, and trod upon the farthest bounds of nature and passion. This circumstance will account for the abruptness and violent antitheses of the style, the throes and labour which run through the expression, and from defects will turn them into beauties. 'So fair and foul a day I have not seen,' etc. 'Such welcome and unwelcome news together.' 'Men's lives are like the flowers in their caps, dying or ere they sicken.' 'Look like the innocent flower, but be the serpent under it.' The scene before the castle-gate follows the appearance of the Witches on the heath, and is followed by a midnight murder. Duncan is cut off betimes by treason leagued with witchcraft, and Macduff is ripped untimely from his mother's womb to avenge his death. Macbeth, after the death of Banquo, wishes for his presence in extravagant terms, 'To him and all we thirst,' and when his ghost appears, cries out, 'Avaunt and quit my sight,' and being gone, he is 'himself again.' Macbeth resolves to get rid of Macduff, that 'he may sleep in spite of thunder'; and cheers his wife on the doubtful intelligence of Banquo's taking-off with the encouragement—'Then be thou jocund: ere the bat has flown his cloistered flight; ere to black Hecate's summons the shard-born beetle has rung night's yawning peal, there shall be done —a deed of dreadful note.' In Lady Macbeth's speech 'Had he not resembled my father as he slept, I had done 't,' there is murder and filial piety together; and in urging him to fulfil his vengeance against the defenceless king, her thoughts spare the blood neither of infants nor old age. The description of the Witches is full of the same contradictory principle; they 'rejoice when good kings bleed,' they are neither of the earth nor the air, but both; 'they should be women, but their beards forbid it'; they take all the pains possible to lead Macbeth on to the height of his ambition, only to betray him 'in deeper consequence,' and after showing him all the pomp of their art, discover their malignant delight in his disappointed hopes, by that bitter taunt, 'Why stands Macbeth thus amazedly?' We might multiply such instances every where.

The leading features in the character of Macbeth are striking enough, and they form what may be thought at first only a bold, rude, Gothic outline. By comparing it with other characters of the same author we shall perceive the absolute truth and identity which is observed in the midst of the giddy whirl and rapid career of events. Macbeth in Shakespear no more loses his identity of character in the fluctuations of fortune or the storm of passion, than Macbeth in himself would have lost the identity of his person. Thus he is as distinct a being from Richard III. as it is possible to imagine, though these two characters in common hands, and indeed in the hands of any other poet, would have been a repetition of the same general idea, more or less exaggerated. For both are tyrants, usurpers, murderers, both aspiring and ambitious, both courageous, cruel, treacherous. But Richard is cruel from nature and constitution. Macbeth becomes so from accidental circumstances. Richard is from his birth deformed in body and mind, and naturally incapable of good. Macbeth is full of 'the milk of human kindness,' is frank, sociable, generous. He is tempted to the commission of guilt by golden opportunities, by the instigations of his wife, and by prophetic warnings. Fate and metaphysical aid conspire against his virtue and his loyalty. Richard on the contrary needs no prompter, but wades through a series of crimes to the height of his ambition from the ungovernable violence of his temper and a reckless love of mischief. He is never gay but in the prospect or in the success of his villainies: Macbeth is full of horror at the thoughts of the murder of Duncan, which he is with difficulty prevailed on to commit, and of remorse after its perpetration. Richard has no mixture of common humanity in his composition, no regard to kindred or posterity, he owns no fellowship with others, he is 'himself alone.' Macbeth is not destitute of feelings of sympathy, is accessible to pity, is even made in some measure the dupe of his uxoriousness, ranks the loss of friends, of the cordial love of his followers, and of his good name, among the causes which have made him weary of life, and regrets that he has ever seized the crown by unjust means, since he cannot transmit it to his posterity—

> 'For Banquo's issue have I fil'd my mind—
> For them the gracious Duncan have I murther'd,
> To make them kings, the seed of Banquo kings.'

In the agitation of his mind, he envies those whom he has sent to peace. 'Duncan is in his grave; after life's fitful fever he sleeps well.'—It is true, he becomes more callous as he plunges deeper in guilt, 'direness is thus rendered familiar to his slaughterous thoughts,' and he in the end anticipates his wife in the boldness and bloodiness of his enterprises, while she for want of the same stimulus of action, 'is troubled with thick-coming fancies that rob her of her rest,' goes mad and dies. Macbeth endeavours to escape from reflection on his crimes by repelling their consequences, and banishes remorse for the past by the meditation of future mischief. This is not the principle of Richard's cruelty, which displays the wanton malice of a fiend as much as the frailty of human passion. Macbeth is goaded on to acts of violence and retaliation by necessity; to Richard, blood is a pastime.—There are other decisive differences inherent in the two characters. Richard may be regarded as a man of the world, a plotting, hardened knave, wholly regardless of every thing but his own ends, and the means to secure them.—Not so Macbeth. The superstitions of the age, the rude state of society, the local scenery and customs, all give a wildness and imaginary grandeur to his character. From the strangeness of the events that surround him, he is full of amazement and fear; and stands in doubt between the world of reality and the world of fancy. He sees sights not shown to mortal eye, and hears unearthly music. All is tumult and disorder within and without his mind; his purposes recoil upon himself, are broken and disjointed; he is the double thrall of his passions and his evil destiny. Richard is not a character either of imagination or pathos, but of pure self-will. There is no conflict of opposite feelings in his breast. The apparitions which he sees only haunt him in his sleep; nor does he live like Macbeth in a waking dream. Macbeth has considerable energy and manliness of character; but then he is 'subject to all the skyey influences.' He is sure of nothing but the present moment. Richard in the busy turbulence of his projects never loses his self-possession, and makes use of every circumstance that happens as an instrument of his long-reaching designs. In his last extremity we can only regard him as a wild beast taken in the toils: while we never entirely lose our concern for Macbeth; and he calls back all our sympathy by that fine close of thoughtful melancholy—

> 'My way of life is fallen into the sear,
> The yellow leaf; and that which should accompany old age,
> As honour, troops of friends, I must not look to have;
> But in their stead, curses not loud but deep,
> Mouth-honour, breath, which the poor heart
> Would fain deny, and dare not.'

We can conceive a common actor to play Richard tolerably well; we can conceive no one to play Macbeth properly, or to look like a man that had encountered the Weïrd Sisters. All the actors that we have ever seen, appear as if they had encountered them on the boards of Covent-garden or Drury-lane, but not on the heath at Fores, and as if they did not believe what they had seen. The Witches of MACBETH indeed are ridiculous on the modern stage, and we doubt if the Furies of Æschylus would be more respected. The progress of manners and knowledge has an influence on the stage, and will in time perhaps destroy both tragedy and comedy. Filch's picking pockets in the *Beggar's Opera* is not so good a jest as it used to be: by the force of the police and of philosophy, Lillo's murders and the ghosts in Shakespear will become obsolete. At last, there will be nothing left, good nor bad, to be desired or dreaded, on the theatre or in real life.—A question has been started with respect to the originality of Shakespear's Witches, which has been well answered by Mr. Lamb in his notes to the 'Specimens of Early Dramatic Poetry.'

'Though some resemblance may be traced between the charms in MACBETH, and the incantations in this play (the Witch of Middleton), which is supposed to have preceded it, this coincidence will not detract much from the originality of Shakespear. His Witches are distinguished from the Witches of Middleton by essential differences. These are creatures to whom man or woman plotting some dire mischief might resort for occasional consultation. Those originate deeds of blood, and begin bad impulses to men. From the moment that their eyes first meet with Macbeth's, he is spell-bound. That meeting sways his destiny. He can never break the fascination. These Witches can hurt the body; those have power over the soul.—Hecate in Middleton has a son, a low buffoon: the hags of Shakespear have neither child of their own, nor seem to be descended from any parent. They are foul anomalies, of whom we know not whence they are sprung, nor whether they have beginning or ending. As they are without human passions, so they seem to be without human relations. They come with thunder and lightning, and vanish to airy music. This is all we know of them.—Except Hecate, they have no names, which heightens their mysteriousness. The names, and some of the properties which Middleton has given to his hags, excite smiles. The Weïrd Sisters are serious things. Their presence cannot co-exist with mirth. But, in a lesser degree, the Witches of Middleton are fine creations. Their power too is, in some measure, over the mind. They raise jars, jealousies, strifes, *like a thick scurf o'er life*'

JULIUS CÆSAR

JULIUS CÆSAR was one of three principal plays by different authors, pitched upon by the celebrated Earl of Hallifax to be brought out in a splendid manner by subscription, in the year 1707. The other two were the *King and No King* of Fletcher, and Dryden's *Maiden Queen*. There perhaps might be political reasons for this selection, as far as regards our author. Otherwise, Shakespear's JULIUS CÆSAR is not equal as a whole, to either of his other plays taken from the Roman history. It is inferior in interest to *Coriolanus*, and both in interest and power to *Antony and Cleopatra*. It however abounds in admirable and affecting passages, and is remarkable for the profound knowledge of character, in which Shakespear could scarcely fail. If there is any exception to this remark, it is in the hero of the piece himself. We do not much admire the representation here given of Julius Cæsar, nor do we think it answers to the portrait given of him in his Commentaries. He makes several vapouring and rather pedantic speeches, and does nothing. Indeed, he has nothing to do. So far, the fault of the character is the fault of the plot.

The spirit with which the poet has entered at once into the manners of the common people, and the jealousies and heart-burnings of the different factions, is shown in the first scene, where Flavius and Marullus, tribunes of the people, and some citizens of Rome, appear upon the stage.

> '*Flavius.* Thou art a cobler, art thou?
> *Cobler.* Truly, Sir, *all* that I live by, is the *awl*: I meddle with no tradesman's matters, nor woman's matters, but *with-al*, I am indeed, Sir, a surgeon to old shoes; when they are in great danger, I recover them.
> *Flavius.* But wherefore art not in thy shop to-day?
> Why dost thou lead these men about the streets?
> *Cobler.* Truly, Sir, to wear out their shoes, to get myself into more work. But indeed, Sir, we make holiday to see Cæsar, and rejoice in his triumph.'

To this specimen of quaint low humour immediately follows that unexpected and animated burst of indignant eloquence, put into the mouth of one of the angry tribunes.

> '*Marullus.* Wherefore rejoice!—What conquest brings he home?
> What tributaries follow him to Rome,
> To grace in captive-bonds his chariot-wheels?
> Oh you hard hearts, you cruel men of Rome!
> Knew you not Pompey? Many a time and oft

> Have you climb'd up to walls and battlements,
> To towers and windows, yea, to chimney-tops,
> Your infants in your arms, and there have sat
> The live-long day with patient expectation,
> To see great Pompey pass the streets of Rome:
> And when you saw his chariot but appear,
> Have you not made an universal shout,
> That Tyber trembled underneath his banks
> To hear the replication of your sounds,
> Made in his concave shores?
> And do you now put on your best attire?
> And do you now cull out an holiday?
> And do you now strew flowers in his way
> That comes in triumph over Pompey's blood?
> Begone——
> Run to your houses, fall upon your knees,
> Pray to the Gods to intermit the plague,
> That needs must light on this ingratitude.'

The well-known dialogue between Brutus and Cassius, in which the latter breaks the design of the conspiracy to the former, and partly gains him over to it, is a noble piece of high-minded declamation. Cassius's insisting on the pretended effeminacy of Cæsar's character, and his description of their swimming across the Tiber together, 'once upon a raw and gusty day,' are among the finest strokes in it. But perhaps the whole is not equal to the short scene which follows, when Cæsar enters with his train:—

> '*Brutus.* The games are done, and Cæsar is returning.
> *Cassius.* As they pass by, pluck Casca by the sleeve.
> And he will, after his sour fashion, tell you
> What has proceeded worthy note to day.
> *Brutus.* I will do so; but look you, Cassius—
> The angry spot doth glow on Cæsar's brow,
> And all the rest look like a chidden train.
> Calphurnia's cheek is pale; and Cicero
> Looks with such ferret and such fiery eyes,
> As we have seen him in the Capitol,
> Being crost in conference by some senators.
> *Cassius.* Casca will tell us what the matter is.
> *Cæsar.* Antonius——
> *Antony.* Cæsar?
> *Cæsar.* Let me have men about me that are fat,
> Sleek-headed men, and such as sleep a-nights:
> Yon Cassius has a lean and hungry look,
> He thinks too much; such men are dangerous.
> *Antony.* Fear him not, Cæsar, he's not dangerous:
> He is a noble Roman, and well given.

> *Cæsar.* Would he were fatter; but I fear him not:
> Yet if my name were liable to fear,
> I do not know the man I should avoid
> So soon as that spare Cassius. He reads much;
> He is a great observer; and he looks
> Quite through the deeds of men. He loves no plays
> As thou dost, Antony; he hears no music:
> Seldom he smiles, and smiles in such a sort,
> As if he mock'd himself, and scorn'd his spirit,
> That could be mov'd to smile at any thing.
> Such men as he be never at heart's ease,
> Whilst they behold a greater than themselves;
> And therefore are they very dangerous.
> I rather tell thee what is to be fear'd
> Than what I fear; for always I am Cæsar.
> Come on my right hand, for this ear is deaf,
> And tell me truly what thou think'st of him.'

We know hardly any passage more expressive of the genius of Shakespear than this. It is as if he had been actually present, had known the different characters and what they thought of one another, and had taken down what he heard and saw, their looks, words, and gestures, just as they happened.

The character of Mark Antony is farther speculated upon where the conspirators deliberate whether he shall fall with Cæsar. Brutus is against it—

> 'And for Mark Antony, think not of him:
> For he can do no more than Cæsar's arm,
> When Cæsar's head is off.
> *Cassius.* Yet I do fear him:
> For in th' ingrafted love he bears to Cæsar——
> *Brutus.* Alas, good Cassius, do not think of him:
> If he love Cæsar, all that he can do
> Is to himself, take thought, and die for Cæsar:
> And that were much, he should; for he is giv'n
> To sports, to wildness, and much company.
> *Trebonius.* There is no fear in him; let him not die:
> For he will live, and laugh at this hereafter.'

They were in the wrong; and Cassius was right.

The honest manliness of Brutus is however sufficient to find out the unfitness of Cicero to be included in their enterprise, from his affected egotism and literary vanity.

> 'O, name him not: let us not break with him;
> For he will never follow anything,
> That other men begin.'

197

His scepticism as to prodigies and his moralising on the weather—'This disturbed sky is not to walk in'—are in the same spirit of refined imbecility.

Shakespear has in this play and elsewhere shown the same penetration into political character and the springs of public events as into those of every-day life. For instance, the whole design of the conspirators to liberate their country fails from the generous temper and overweening confidence of Brutus in the goodness of their cause and the assistance of others. Thus it has always been. Those who mean well themselves think well of others, and fall a prey to their security. That humanity and honesty which dispose men to resist injustice and tyranny render them unfit to cope with the cunning and power of those who are opposed to them. The friends of liberty trust to the professions of others, because they are themselves sincere, and endeavour to reconcile the public good with the least possible hurt to its enemies, who have no regard to any thing but their own unprincipled ends, and stick at nothing to accomplish them. Cassius was better cut out for a conspirator. His heart prompted his head. His watchful jealousy made him fear the worst that might happen, and his irritability of temper added to his inveteracy of purpose, and sharpened his patriotism. The mixed nature of his motives made him fitter to contend with bad men. The vices are never so well employed as in combating one another. Tyranny and servility are to be dealt with after their own fashion: otherwise, they will triumph over those who spare them, and finally pronounce their funeral panegyric, as Antony did that of Brutus.

> 'All the conspirators, save only he,
> Did that they did in envy of great Cæsar:
> He only in a general honest thought
> And common good to all, made one of them.'

The quarrel between Brutus and Cassius is managed in a masterly way. The dramatic fluctuation of passion, the calmness of Brutus, the heat of Cassius, are admirably described; and the exclamation of Cassius on hearing of the death of Portia, which he does not learn till after their reconciliation, 'How 'scaped I killing when I crost you so?' gives double force to all that has gone before. The scene between Brutus and Portia, where she endeavours to extort the secret of the conspiracy from him, is conceived in the most heroical spirit, and the burst of tenderness in Brutus—

> 'You are my true and honourable wife;
> As dear to me as are the ruddy drops
> That visit my sad heart'—

is justified by her whole behaviour. Portia's breathless impatience to learn the event of the conspiracy, in the dialogue with Lucius, is full of passion. The interest which Portia takes in Brutus and that which Calphurnia takes in the fate of Cæsar are discriminated with the nicest precision. Mark Antony's speech over the dead body of Cæsar has been justly admired for the mixture of pathos and artifice in it: that of Brutus certainly is not so good.

The entrance of the conspirators to the house of Brutus at midnight is rendered very impressive. In the midst of this scene, we meet with one of those careless and natural digressions which occur so frequently and beautifully in Shakespear. After Cassius has introduced his friends one by one, Brutus says—

> 'They are all welcome.
> What watchful cares do interpose themselves
> Betwixt your eyes and night ?
>   *Cassius.* Shall I entreat a word ?   (*They whisper.*)
>   *Decius.* Here lies the east: doth not the day break here ?
>   *Casca.* No.
>   *Cinna.* O pardon, Sir, it doth; and yon grey lines,
> That fret the clouds, are messengers of day.
>   *Casca.* You shall confess, that you are both deceiv'd :
> Here, as I point my sword, the sun arises,
> Which is a great way growing on the south,
> Weighing the youthful season of the year.
> Some two months hence, up higher toward the north
> He first presents his fire, and the high east
> Stands as the Capitol, directly here.'

We cannot help thinking this graceful familiarity better than all the fustian in the world.—The truth of history in JULIUS CÆSAR is very ably worked up with dramatic effect. The councils of generals, the doubtful turns of battles, are represented to the life. The death of Brutus is worthy of him—it has the dignity of the Roman senator with the firmness of the Stoic philosopher. But what is perhaps better than either, is the little incident of his boy, Lucius, falling asleep over his instrument, as he is playing to his master in his tent, the night before the battle. Nature had played him the same forgetful trick once before on the night of the conspiracy. The humanity of Brutus is the same on both occasions.

> ——'It is no matter:
> Enjoy the honey-heavy dew of slumber.
> Thou hast no figures nor no fantasies,
> Which busy care draws in the brains of men.
> Therefore thou sleep'st so sound.'

OTHELLO

It has been said that tragedy purifies the affections by terror and pity. That is, it substitutes imaginary sympathy for mere selfishness. It gives us a high and permanent interest, beyond ourselves, in humanity as such. It raises the great, the remote, and the possible to an equality with the real, the little and the near. It makes man a partaker with his kind. It subdues and softens the stubbornness of his will. It teaches him that there are and have been others like himself, by showing him as in a glass what they have felt, thought, and done. It opens the chambers of the human heart. It leaves nothing indifferent to us that can affect our common nature. It excites our sensibility by exhibiting the passions wound up to the utmost pitch by the power of imagination or the temptation of circumstances; and corrects their fatal excesses in ourselves by pointing to the greater extent of sufferings and of crimes to which they have led others. Tragedy creates a balance of the affections. It makes us thoughtful spectators in the lists of life. It is the refiner of the species; a discipline of humanity. The habitual study of poetry and works of imagination is one chief part of a well-grounded education. A taste for liberal art is necessary to complete the character of a gentleman. Science alone is hard and mechanical. It exercises the understanding upon things out of ourselves, while it leaves the affections unemployed, or engrossed with our own immediate, narrow interests.—OTHELLO furnishes an illustration of these remarks. It excites our sympathy in an extraordinary degree. The moral it conveys has a closer application to the concerns of human life than that of almost any other of Shakespear's plays. 'It comes directly home to the bosoms and business of men.' The pathos in *Lear* is indeed more dreadful and overpowering: but it is less natural, and less of every day's occurrence. We have not the same degree of sympathy with the passions described in *Macbeth*. The interest in *Hamlet* is more remote and reflex. That of OTHELLO is at once equally profound and affecting.

The picturesque contrasts of character in this play are almost as remarkable as the depth of the passion. The Moor Othello, the gentle Desdemona, the villain Iago, the good-natured Cassio, the fool Roderigo, present a range and variety of character as striking and palpable as that produced by the opposition of costume in a picture. Their distinguishing qualities stand out to the mind's eye, so that even when we are not thinking of their actions or sentiments, the idea of their persons is still as present to us as ever. These characters and the images they stamp upon the mind are the farthest asunder possible, the distance between them is immense: yet the compass of knowledge and invention which the poet has shown in embodying these extreme creations of his genius is only greater than the truth and felicity with which he has identified each character with itself, or blended their different qualities together in the same story. What a contrast the character of Othello forms to that of Iago! At the same time, the force of conception with which these two figures are opposed to each other is rendered still more intense by the complete consistency with which the traits of each character are brought out in a state of the highest finishing. The making one black and the other white, the one unprincipled, the other unfortunate in the extreme, would have answered the common purposes of effect, and satisfied the ambition of an ordinary painter of character. Shakespear has laboured the finer shades of difference in both with as much care and skill as if he had had to depend on the execution alone for the success of his design. On the other hand, Desdemona and Æmilia are not meant to be opposed with anything like strong contrast to each other. Both are, to outward appearance, characters of common life, not more distinguished than women usually are, by difference of rank and situation. The difference of their thoughts and sentiments is however laid open, their minds are separated from each other by signs as plain and as little to be mistaken as the complexions of their husbands.

The movement of the passion in Othello is exceedingly different from that of Macbeth. In Macbeth there is a violent struggle between opposite feelings, between ambition and the stings of conscience, almost from first to last: in Othello, the doubtful conflict between contrary passions, though dreadful, continues only for a short time, and the chief interest is excited by the alternate ascendancy of different passions, by the entire and unforeseen change from the fondest love and most unbounded confidence to the tortures of jealousy and the madness of hatred. The revenge of Othello, after it has once taken thorough possession of his mind, never quits it, but grows stronger and stronger at every moment of its delay. The nature of the Moor is noble, confiding, tender, and generous; but his blood is of the most inflammable kind; and being once roused by a sense of his wrongs, he is stopped by no considerations of remorse or pity till he has given a loose to all the dictates of his rage and his despair. It is in working his noble nature up to this extremity through rapid but gradual transitions, in raising passion to its height from the smallest beginnings and in spite of all obstacles, in painting the expiring conflict between love and hatred, tenderness and resentment, jealousy and remorse, in unfolding the strength and the weakness of our nature, in uniting sublimity of thought with the anguish of the keenest woe, in putting in motion the various impulses that agitate this our mortal being, and at last blending them in that noble tide of deep and sustained passion, impetuous but majestic, that 'flows on to the Propontic, and knows no ebb,' that Shakespear has shown the mastery of his genius and of his power over the human heart. The third act of OTHELLO is his finest display, not of knowledge or passion separately, but of the two combined, of the knowledge of character with the expression of passion, of consummate art in the keeping up of appearances with the profound workings of nature, and the convulsive movements of uncontroulable agony, of the power of inflicting torture and of suffering it. Not only is the tumult of passion in Othello's mind heaved up from the very bottom of the soul, but every the slightest undulation of feeling is seen on the surface, as it arises from the impulses of imagination or the malicious suggestions of Iago. The progressive preparation for the catastrophe is wonderfully managed from the Moor's first gallant recital of the story of his love, of 'the spells and witchcraft he had used,' from his unlooked-for and romantic success, the fond satisfaction with which he dotes on his own happiness, the unreserved tenderness of Desdemona and her innocent importunities in favour of Cassio, irritating the suspicions instilled into her husband's mind by the perfidy of Iago, and rankling there to poison, till he loses all command of himself, and his rage can only be appeased by blood. She is introduced, just before Iago begins to put his scheme in practice, pleading for Cassio with all the thoughtless gaiety of friendship and winning confidence in the love of Othello.

'What! Michael Cassio?
That came a wooing with you, and so many a time,
When I have spoke of you dispraisingly,
Hath ta'en your part, to have so much to do
To bring him in?—Why this is not a boon:
'Tis as I should intreat you wear your gloves,
Or feed on nourishing meats, or keep you warm;
Or sue to you to do a peculiar profit
To your person. Nay, when I have a suit,
Wherein I mean to touch your love indeed,
It shall be full of poise, and fearful to be granted.'

Othello's confidence, at first only staggered by broken hints and insinuations, recovers itself at sight of Desdemona; and he exclaims

'If she be false, O then Heav'n mocks itself:
I 'll not believe it.'

But presently after, on brooding over his suspicions by himself, and yielding to his apprehensions of the worst, his smothered jealousy breaks out into open fury, and he returns to demand satisfaction of Iago like a wild beast stung with the envenomed shaft of the hunters. 'Look where he comes,' etc. In this state of exasperation and violence, after the first paroxysms of his grief and tenderness have had their passionate vent in that passionate apostrophe, 'I felt not Cassio's kisses on her lips,' Iago, by false aspersions, and by presenting the most revolting images to his mind,[1] easily turns the storm of passion from himself against Desdemona, and works him up into a trembling agony of doubt and fear, in which he abandons all his love and hopes in a breath.

> 'Now do I see 'tis true. Look here, Iago,
> All my fond love thus do I blow to Heav'n.   'Tis gone.
> Arise black vengeance from the hollow hell;
> Yield up, O love, thy crown and hearted throne
> To tyrannous hate!   Swell bosom with thy fraught ;
> For 'tis of aspicks' tongues.'

From this time, his raging thoughts 'never look back, ne'er ebb to humble love,' till his revenge is sure of its object, the painful regrets and involuntary recollections of past circumstances which cross his mind amidst the dim trances of passion, aggravating the sense of his wrongs, but not shaking his purpose. Once indeed, where Iago shows him Cassio with the handkerchief in his hand, and making sport (as he thinks) of his misfortunes, the intolerable bitterness of his feelings, the extreme sense of shame, makes him fall to praising her accomplishments and relapse into a momentary fit of weakness, 'Yet, oh the pity of it, Iago, the pity of it!' This returning fondness however only serves, as it is managed by Iago, to whet his revenge, and set his heart more against her. In his conversations with Desdemona, the persuasion of her guilt and the immediate proofs of her duplicity seem to irritate his resentment and aversion to her; but in the scene immediately preceding her death, the recollection of his love returns upon him in all its tenderness and force; and after her death, he all at once forgets his wrongs in the sudden and irreparable sense of his loss.

> 'My wife!   My wife!   What wife?   I have no wife.
> Oh insupportable!   Oh heavy hour!'

---

[1] See the passage, beginning—'It is impossible you should see this, were they as prime as goats,' etc.

This happens before he is assured of her innocence; but afterwards his remorse is as dreadful as his revenge has been, and yields only to fixed and death-like despair. His farewell speech, before he kills himself, in which he conveys his reasons to the senate for the murder of his wife, is equal to the first speech in which he gave them an account of his courtship of her, and 'his whole course of love.' Such an ending was alone worthy of such a commencement.

If any thing could add to the force of our sympathy with Othello, or compassion for his fate, it would be the frankness and generosity of his nature, which so little deserve it. When Iago first begins to practise upon his unsuspecting friendship, he answers—

> ——' 'Tis not to make me jealous,
> To say my wife is fair, feeds well, loves company,
> Is free of speech, sings, plays, and dances well;
> Where virtue is, these are most virtuous.
> Nor from my own weak merits will I draw
> The smallest fear or doubt of her revolt,
> For she had eyes and chose me.'

This character is beautifully (and with affecting simplicity) confirmed by what Desdemona herself says of him to Æmilia after she has lost the handkerchief, the first pledge of his love to her.

> ' Believe me, I had rather have lost my purse
> Full of cruzadoes. And but my noble Moor
> Is true of mind, and made of no such baseness,
> As jealous creatures are, it were enough
> To put him to ill thinking.
>   *Æmilia.* Is he not jealous ?
>   *Desdemona.* Who he ? I think the sun where he was born
> Drew all such humours from him.'

In a short speech of Æmilia's, there occurs one of those side-intimations of the fluctuations of passion which we seldom meet with but in Shakespear. After Othello has resolved upon the death of his wife, and bids her dismiss her attendant for the night, she answers,

> ' I will, my Lord.
>   *Æmilia.* How goes it now ? *He looks gentler than he did.*'

Shakespear has here put into half a line what some authors would have spun out into ten set speeches.

The character of Desdemona is inimitable both in itself, and as it appears in contrast with Othello's groundless jealousy, and with the foul conspiracy of which she is the innocent victim. Her beauty and external graces are only indirectly glanced at : we see 'her visage in her mind'; her character every where predominates over her person.

> ' A maiden never bold :
> Of spirit so still and quiet, that her motion
> Blush'd at itself.'

There is one fine compliment paid to her by Cassio, who exclaims triumphantly when she comes ashore at Cyprus after the storm,

> ' Tempests themselves, high seas, and howling winds,
> As having sense of beauty, do omit
> Their mortal natures, letting safe go by
> The divine Desdemona.'

In general, as is the case with most of Shakespear's females, we lose sight of her personal charms in her attachment and devotedness to her husband. 'She is subdued even to the very quality of her lord'; and to Othello's 'honours and his valiant parts her soul and fortunes consecrates.' The lady protests so much herself, and she is as good as her word. The truth of conception, with which timidity and boldness are united in the same character, is marvellous. The extravagance of her resolutions, the pertinacity of her affections, may be said to arise out of the gentleness of her nature. They imply an unreserved reliance on the purity of her own intentions, an entire surrender of her fears to her love, a knitting of herself (heart and soul) to the fate of another. Bating the commencement of her passion, which is a little fantastical and headstrong (though even that may perhaps be consistently accounted for from her inability to resist a rising inclination[1]) her whole character consists in having no will of her own, no prompter but her obedience. Her romantic turn is only a consequence of the domestic and practical part of her disposition ; and instead of following Othello to the wars, she would gladly have 'remained at home a moth of peace,' if her husband could have staid with her. Her resignation and angelic sweetness of temper do not desert her at the last. The scenes in which she laments and tries to account for Othello's estrangement from her are exquisitely beautiful. After he has struck her, and called her names, she says,

> ———' Alas, Iago,
> What shall I do to win my lord again ?
> Good friend, go to him ; for by this light of heaven,
> I know not how I lost him. Here I kneel ;

---

[1] ' *Iago.* Ay, too gentle.
Othello. Nay, that 's certain.'

> If e'er my will did trespass 'gainst his love,
> Either in discourse, or thought, or actual deed,
> Or that mine eyes, mine ears, or any sense
> Delighted them on any other form;
> Or that I do not, and ever did,
> And ever will, though he do shake me off
> To beggarly divorcement, love him dearly,
> Comfort forswear me. Unkindness may do much,
> And his unkindness may defeat my life,
> But never taint my love.
>   *Iago.* I pray you be content: 'tis but his humour.
> The business of the state does him offence.
>   *Desdemona.* If 'twere no other !'——

The scene which follows with Æmilia and the song of the Willow, are equally beautiful, and show the author's extreme power of varying the expression of passion, in all its moods and in all circumstances.

> '*Æmilia.* Would you had never seen him.
>   *Desdemona.* So would not I: my love doth so approve him,
> That even his stubbornness, his checks, his frowns,
> Have grace and favour in them,' etc.

Not the unjust suspicions of Othello, not Iago's unprovoked treachery, place Desdemona in a more amiable or interesting light than the conversation (half earnest, half jest) between her and Æmilia on the common behaviour of women to their husbands. This dialogue takes place just before the last fatal scene. If Othello had overheard it, it would have prevented the whole catastrophe; but then it would have spoiled the play.

The character of Iago is one of the supererogations of Shakespear's genius. Some persons, more nice than wise, have thought this whole character unnatural, because his villainy is *without a sufficient motive.* Shakespear, who was as good a philosopher as he was a poet, thought otherwise. He knew that the love of power, which is another name for the love of mischief, is natural to man. He would know this as well or better than if it had been demonstrated to him by a logical diagram, merely from seeing children paddle in the dirt or kill flies for sport. Iago in fact belongs to a class of character, common to Shakespear and at the same time peculiar to him; whose heads are as acute and active as their hearts are hard and callous. Iago is to be sure an extreme instance of the kind; that is to say, of diseased intellectual activity, with the most perfect indifference to moral good or evil, or rather with a decided preference of the latter, because it falls more readily in with his favourite propensity, gives greater zest to his thoughts and scope to his actions. He is quite or nearly as indifferent to his own fate as to that of others; he runs all risks for a trifling and doubtful advantage; and is himself the dupe and victim of his ruling passion—an insatiable craving after action of the most difficult and dangerous kind. 'Our ancient' is a philosopher, who fancies that a lie that kills has more point in it than an alliteration or an antithesis; who thinks a fatal experiment on the peace of a family a better thing than watching the palpitations in the heart of a flea in a microscope; who plots the ruin of his friends as an exercise for his ingenuity, and stabs men in the dark to prevent *ennui*. His gaiety, such as it is, arises from the success of his treachery; his ease from the torture he has inflicted on others. He is an amateur of tragedy in real life; and instead of employing his invention on imaginary characters, or long-forgotten incidents, he takes the bolder and more desperate course of getting up his plot at home, casts the principal parts among his nearest friends and connections, and rehearses it in downright earnest, with steady nerves and unabated resolution. We will just give an illustration or two.

One of his most characteristic speeches is that immediately after the marriage of Othello.

> '*Roderigo.* What a full fortune does the thick lips owe,
> If he can carry her thus!
>   *Iago.* Call up her father:
> Rouse him (*Othello*) make after him, poison his delight,
> Proclaim him in the streets, incense her kinsmen,
> And tho' he in a fertile climate dwell,
> Plague him with flies: tho' that his joy be joy,
> Yet throw such changes of vexation on it,
> As it may lose some colour.'

In the next passage, his imagination runs riot in the mischief he is plotting, and breaks out into the wildness and impetuosity of real enthusiasm.

> '*Roderigo.* Here is her father's house: I'll call aloud.
>   *Iago.* Do, with like timourous accent and dire yell
> As when, by night and negligence, the fire
> Is spied in populous cities.'

One of his most favourite topics, on which he is rich indeed, and in descanting on which his spleen serves him for a Muse, is the disproportionate match between Desdemona and the Moor. This is a clue to the character of the lady which he is by no means ready to part with. It is brought forward in the first scene, and he recurs to

H 65

it, when in answer to his insinuations against Desdemona, Roderigo says,

> 'I cannot believe that in her—she's full of most blest conditions.
> *Iago.* Bless'd fig's end. The wine she drinks is made of grapes. If she had been blest, she would never have married the Moor.'

And again with still more spirit and fatal effect afterwards, when he turns this very suggestion arising in Othello's own breast to her prejudice.

> '*Othello.* And yet how nature erring from itself—
> *Iago.* Ay, there's the point;—as to be bold with you,
> Not to affect many proposed matches
> Of her own clime, complexion, and degree,' etc

This is probing to the quick. Iago here turns the character of poor Desdemona, as it were, inside out. It is certain that nothing but the genius of Shakespear could have preserved the entire interest and delicacy of the part, and have even drawn an additional elegance and dignity from the peculiar circumstances in which she is placed.— The habitual licentiousness of Iago's conversation is not to be traced to the pleasure he takes in gross or lascivious images, but to his desire of finding out the worst side of everything, and of proving himself an over-match for appearances. He has none of 'the milk of human kindness' in his composition. His imagination rejects every thing that has not a strong infusion of the most unpalatable ingredients; his mind digests only poisons. Virtue or goodness or whatever has the least 'relish of salvation in it,' is, to his depraved appetite, sickly and insipid: and he even resents the good opinion entertained of his own integrity, as if it were an affront cast on the masculine sense and spirit of his character. Thus at the meeting between Othello and Desdemona, he exclaims—'Oh, you are well tuned now: but I'll set down the pegs that make this music, *as honest as I am*'—his character of *bonhommie* not sitting at all easy upon him. In the scenes, where he tries to work Othello to his purpose, he is proportionably guarded, insidious, dark, and deliberate. We believe nothing ever came up to the profound dissimulation and dextrous artifice of the well-known dialogue in the third act, where he first enters upon the execution of his design

> '*Iago.* My noble lord.
> *Othello.* What dost thou say, Iago?
> *Iago.* Did Michael Cassio,
> When you woo'd my lady, know of your love?
> *Othello.* He did from first to last.
> Why dost thou ask?

> *Iago.* But for a satisfaction of my thought,
> No further harm.
> *Othello.* Why of thy thought, Iago ?
> *Iago.* I did not think he had been acquainted with it.
> *Othello.* O yes, and went between us very oft—
> *Iago.* Indeed !
> *Othello.* Indeed ? Ay, indeed. Discern'st thou aught of that ?
> Is he not honest ?
> *Iago.* Honest, my lord ?
> *Othello.* Honest ? Ay, honest.
> *Iago.* My lord, for aught I know.
> *Othello.* What do'st thou think ?
> *Iago.* Think, my lord !
> *Othello.* Think, my lord ! Alas, thou echo'st me,
> As if there was some monster in thy thought
> Too hideous to be shewn.'—

The stops and breaks, the deep workings of treachery under the mask of love and honesty, the anxious watchfulness, the cool earnestness, and if we may so say, the *passion* of hypocrisy, marked in every line, receive their last finishing in that inconceivable burst of pretended indignation at Othello's doubts of his sincerity.

> ' O grace ! O Heaven forgive me !
> Are you a man ? Have you a soul or sense ?
> God be wi' you; take mine office. O wretched fool,
> That lov'st to make thine honesty a vice !
> Oh monstrous world ! Take note, take note, O world !
> To be direct and honest, is not safe.
> I thank you for this profit, and from hence
> I 'll love no friend, since love breeds such offence.'

If Iago is detestable enough when he has business on his hands and all his engines at work, he is still worse when he has nothing to do, and we only see into the hollowness of his heart. His indifference when Othello falls into a swoon, is perfectly diabolical.

> ' *Iago.* How is it, General ? Have you not hurt your head ?
> *Othello.* Do'st thou mock me ?
> *Iago.* I mock you not, by Heaven,' etc.

The part indeed would hardly be tolerated, even as a foil to the virtue and generosity of the other characters in the play, but for its indefatigable industry and inexhaustible resources, which divert the attention of the spectator (as well as his own) from the end he has in view to the means by which it must be accomplished.—Edmund the Bastard in *Lear* is something of the same character, placed in less prominent circumstances. Zanga is a vulgar caricature of it.

TIMON OF ATHENS

TIMON OF ATHENS always appeared to us to be written with as intense a feeling of his subject as any one play of Shakespear. It is one of the few in which he seems to be in earnest throughout, never to trifle nor go out of his way. He does not relax in his efforts, nor lose sight of the unity of his design. It is the only play of our author in which spleen is the predominant feeling of the mind. It is as much a satire as a play: and contains some of the finest pieces of invective possible to be conceived, both in the snarling, captious answers of the cynic Apemantus, and in the impassioned and more terrible imprecations of Timon. The latter remind the classical reader of the force and swelling impetuosity of the moral declamations in *Juvenal*, while the former have all the keenness and caustic severity of the old Stoic philosophers. The soul of Diogenes appears to have been seated on the lips of Apemantus. The churlish profession of misanthropy in the cynic is contrasted with the profound feeling of it in Timon, and also with the soldier-like and determined resentment of Alcibiades against his countrymen, who have banished him, though this forms only an incidental episode in the tragedy.

The fable consists of a single event;—of the transition from the highest pomp and profusion of artificial refinement to the most abject state of savage life, and privation of all social intercourse. The change is as rapid as it is complete; nor is the description of the rich and generous Timon, banqueting in gilded palaces, pampered by every luxury, prodigal of his hospitality, courted by crowds of flatterers, poets, painters, lords, ladies, who—

> ' Follow his strides, his lobbies fill with tendance,
>   Rain sacrificial whisperings in his ear;
>   And through him drink the free air '—

more striking than that of the sudden falling off of his friends and fortune, and his naked exposure in a wild forest digging roots from the earth for his sustenance, with a lofty spirit of self-denial, and bitter scorn of the world, which raise him higher in our esteem than the dazzling gloss of prosperity could do. He grudges himself the means of life, and is only busy in preparing his grave. How forcibly is the difference between what he was, and what he is, described in Apemantus's taunting questions, when he comes to reproach him with the change in his way of life!

> ——'What, think'st thou,
> That the bleak air, thy boisterous chamberlain,
> Will put thy shirt on warm? will these moist trees
> That have outlived the eagle, page thy heels,
> And skip when thou point'st out? will the cold brook,
> Candied with ice, caudle thy morning taste
> To cure thy o'er-night's surfeit? Call the creatures,
> Whose naked natures live in all the spight
> Of wreakful heav'n, whose bare unhoused trunks,
> To the conflicting elements expos'd,
> Answer mere nature, bid them flatter thee.'

The manners are every where preserved with distinct truth. The poet and painter are very skilfully played off against one another, both affecting great attention to the other, and each taken up with his own vanity, and the superiority of his own art. Shakespear has put into the mouth of the former a very lively description of the genius of poetry and of his own in particular.

> ——'A thing slipt idly from me.
> Our poesy is as a gum, which issues
> From whence 'tis nourish'd. The fire i' th' flint
> Shews not till it be struck: our gentle flame
> Provokes itself—and like the current flies
> Each bound it chafes.'

The hollow friendship and shuffling evasions of the Athenian lords, their smooth professions and pitiful ingratitude, are very satisfactorily exposed, as well as the different disguises to which the meanness of self-love resorts in such cases to hide a want of generosity and good faith. The lurking selfishness of Apemantus does not pass unde-tected amidst the grossness of his sarcasms and his contempt for the pretensions of others. Even the two courtezans who accompany Alcibiades to the cave of Timon are very characteristically sketched; and the thieves who come to visit him are also 'true men' in their way.—An exception to this general picture of selfish depravity is found in the old and honest steward Flavius, to whom Timon pays a full tribute of tenderness. Shakespear was unwilling to draw a picture 'ugly all over with hypocrisy.' He owed this character to the good-natured solicitations of his Muse. His mind might well have been said to be the 'sphere of humanity.'

The moral sententiousness of this play equals that of **Lord Bacon's** Treatise on the Wisdom of the Ancients, and is indeed seasoned with greater variety. Every topic of contempt or indignation is here exhausted; but while the sordid licentiousness of Apemantus, which turns every thing to gall and bitterness, shews only the natural virulence of his temper and antipathy to good or evil alike, Timon does not utter an imprecation without betraying the extravagant working of disappointed passion, of love altered to hate. Apemantus sees nothing good in any object, and exaggerates whatever is disgusting: Timon is tormented with the perpetual contrast between things and appearances, between the fresh, tempting outside and the rottenness within, and invokes mischiefs on the heads of mankind proportioned to the sense of his wrongs and of their treacheries. He impatiently cries out, when he finds the gold,

> ' This yellow slave
> Will knit and break religions; bless the accurs'd;
> Make the hoar leprosy ador'd; place thieves,
> And give them title, knee, and approbation,
> With senators on the bench; this is it,
> That makes the wappen'd widow wed again;
> She, whom the spital-house
> Would cast the gorge at, *this embalms and spices*
> *To th' April day again.*'

One of his most dreadful imprecations is that which occurs immediately on his leaving Athens.

> ' Let me look back upon thee, O thou wall,
> That girdlest in those wolves! Dive in the earth,
> And fence not Athens! Matrons, turn incontinent;
> Obedience fail in children; slaves and fools
> Pluck the grave wrinkled senate from the bench,
> And minister in their steads. To general filths
> Convert o' th' instant green virginity!
> Do 't in your parents' eyes. Bankrupts, hold fast;
> Rather than render back, out with your knives,
> And cut your trusters' throats! Bound servants, steal:
> Large-handed robbers your grave masters are
> And pill by law. Maid, to thy master's bed:
> Thy mistress is o' th' brothel. Son of sixteen,
> Pluck the lin'd crutch from thy old limping sire,
> And with it beat his brains out! Fear and piety,
> Religion to the Gods, peace, justice, truth,
> Domestic awe, night-rest, and neighbourhood,
> Instructions, manners, mysteries and trades,
> Degrees, observances, customs and laws,
> Decline to your confounding contraries;
> And let confusion live!—Plagues, incident to men,
> Your potent and infectious fevers heap
> On Athens, ripe for stroke! Thou cold sciatica,
> Cripple our senators, that their limbs may halt
> As lamely as their manners! Lust and liberty

> Creep in the minds and marrows of our youth,
> That 'gainst the stream of virtue they may strive,
> And drown themselves in riot! Itches, blains,
> Sow all th' Athenian bosoms; and their crop
> Be general leprosy: breath infect breath,
> That their society (as their friendship) may
> Be merely poison!'

Timon is here just as ideal in his passion for ill as he had been before in his belief of good. Apemantus was satisfied with the mischief existing in the world, and with his own ill-nature. One of the most decisive intimations of Timon's morbid jealousy of appearances is in his answer to Apemantus, who asks him,

> 'What things in the world can'st thou nearest compare with thy flatterers?
> *Timon.* Women nearest: but men, men are the things themselves.'

Apemantus, it is said, 'loved few things better than to abhor himself.' This is not the case with Timon, who neither loves to abhor himself nor others. All his vehement misanthropy is forced, up-hill work. From the slippery turns of fortune, from the turmoils of passion and adversity, he wishes to sink into the quiet of the grave. On that subject his thoughts are intent, on that he finds time and place to grow romantic. He digs his own grave by the sea-shore; contrives his funeral ceremonies amidst the pomp of desolation, and builds his mausoleum of the elements.

> 'Come not to me again; but say to Athens,
> Timon hath made his everlasting mansion
> Upon the beached verge of the salt flood;
> Which once a-day with his embossed froth
> The turbulent surge shall cover.—Thither come,
> And let my grave-stone be your oracle.'

And again, Alcibiades, after reading his epitaph, says of him,

> 'These well express in thee thy latter spirits:
> Though thou abhorred'st in us our human griefs,
> Scorn'd'st our brain's flow, and those our droplets, which
> From niggard nature fall; yet rich conceit
> Taught thee to make vast Neptune weep for aye
> On thy low grave '——

thus making the winds his funeral dirge, his mourner the murmuring ocean; and seeking in the everlasting solemnities of nature oblivion of the transitory splendour of his life-time.

CORIOLANUS

SHAKESPEAR has in this play shewn himself well versed in history and state-affairs. CORIOLANUS is a store-house of political common-places. Any one who studies it may save himself the trouble of reading Burke's Reflections, or Paine's Rights of Man, or the Debates in both Houses of Parliament since the French Revolution or our own. The arguments for and against aristocracy or democracy, on the privileges of the few and the claims of the many, on liberty and slavery, power and the abuse of it, peace and war, are here very ably handled, with the spirit of a poet and the acuteness of a philosopher. Shakespear himself seems to have had a leaning to the arbitrary side of the question, perhaps from some feeling of contempt for his own origin; and to have spared no occasion of baiting the rabble. What he says of them is very true: what he says of their betters is also very true, though he dwells less upon it.—The cause of the people is indeed but little calculated as a subject for poetry: it admits of rhetoric, which goes into argument and explanation, but it presents no immediate or distinct images to the mind, 'no jutting frieze, buttress, or coigne of vantage' for poetry 'to make its pendant bed and procreant cradle in.' The language of poetry naturally falls in with the language of power. The imagination is an exaggerating and exclusive faculty: it takes from one thing to add to another: it accumulates circumstances together to give the greatest possible effect to a favourite object. The understanding is a dividing and measuring faculty: it judges of things not according to their immediate impression on the mind, but according to their relations to one another. The one is a monopolising faculty, which seeks the greatest quantity of present excitement by inequality and disproportion; the other is a distributive faculty, which seeks the greatest quantity of ultimate good, by justice and proportion. The one is an aristocratical, the other a republican faculty. The principle of poetry is a very anti-levelling principle. It aims at effect, it exists by contrast. It admits of no medium. It is every thing by excess. It rises above the ordinary standard of sufferings and crimes. It presents a dazzling appearance. It shows its head turretted, crowned, and crested. Its front is gilt and blood-stained Before it 'it carries noise, and behind it leaves tears.' It has its altars and its victims, sacrifices, human sacrifices. Kings, priests, nobles, are its train-bearers, tyrants and slaves its executioners.—'Carnage is its daughter.'—Poetry is right-royal. It puts the individual for the species, the one above the infinite many, might before right. A lion hunting a flock of sheep or a herd of wild asses is a more poetical object than they; and we even take part with the lordly beast, because our vanity or some other feeling makes us disposed to place ourselves in the situation of the strongest party. So we feel some concern for the poor citizens of Rome when they meet together to compare their wants and griev- ances, till Coriolanus comes in and with blows and big words drives this set of 'poor rats,' this rascal scum, to their homes and beggary before him. There is nothing heroical in a multitude of miserable rogues not wishing to be starved, or complaining that they are like to be so: but when a single man comes forward to brave their cries and to make them submit to the last indignities, from mere pride and self-will, our admiration of his prowess is immediately converted into contempt for their pusillanimity. The insolence of power is stronger than the plea of necessity. The tame submission to usurped authority or even the natural resistance to it has nothing to excite or flatter the imagination: it is the assumption of a right to insult or oppress others that carries an imposing air of superiority with it. We had rather be the oppressor than the oppressed. The love of power in ourselves and the admiration of it in others are both natural to man: the one makes him a tyrant, the other a slave. Wrong dressed out in pride, pomp, and circumstance, has more attraction than abstract right.—Coriolanus complains of the fickleness of the people: yet, the instant he cannot gratify his pride and obstinacy at their expense, he turns his arms against his country. If his country was not worth defending, why did he build his pride on its defence? He is a con- querer and a hero; he conquers other countries, and makes this a plea for enslaving his own; and when he is prevented from doing so, he leagues with its enemies to destroy his country. He rates the people 'as if he were a God to punish, and not a man of their in- firmity.' He scoffs at one of their tribunes for maintaining their rights and franchises: 'Mark you his absolute *shall*?' not marking his own absolute *will* to take every thing from them, his impatience of the slightest opposition to his own pretensions being in proportion to their arrogance and absurdity. If the great and powerful had the beneficence and wisdom of Gods, then all this would have been well: if with a greater knowledge of what is good for the people, they had as great a care for their interest as they have themselves, if they were seated above the world, sympathising with the welfare, but not feeling the passions of men, receiving neither good nor hurt from them, but bestowing their benefits as free gifts on them, they might then rule over them like another Providence. But this is not the case. Coriolanus is unwilling that the senate should shew their 'cares' for the people, lest their 'cares' should be construed into 'fears,' to the subversion of all due authority; and he is no sooner disappointed in his schemes to deprive the people not only of the cares of the state, but of all power to redress themselves, than Volumnia is made madly to exclaim,

> 'Now the red pestilence strike all trades in Rome,
>   And occupations perish.'

This is but natural: it is but natural for a mother to have more regard for her son than for a whole city; but then the city should be left to take some care of itself. The care of the state cannot, we here see, be safely entrusted to maternal affection, or to the domestic charities of high life. The great have private feelings of their own, to which the interests of humanity and justice must courtesy. Their interests are so far from being the same as those of the community, that they are in direct and necessary opposition to them; their power is at the expense of *our* weakness; their riches of *our* poverty; their pride of *our* degradation; their splendour of *our* wretchedness; their tyranny of *our* servitude. If they had the superior knowledge ascribed to them (which they have not) it would only render them so much more formidable; and from Gods would convert them into Devils. The whole dramatic moral of CORIOLANUS is that those who have little shall have less, and that those who have much shall take all that others have left. The people are poor; therefore they ought to be starved. They are slaves; therefore they ought to be beaten. They work hard; therefore they ought to be treated like beasts of burden. They are ignorant; therefore they ought not to be allowed to feel that they want food, or clothing, or rest, that they are enslaved, oppressed, and miserable. This is the logic of the imagination and the passions; which seek to aggrandize what excites admiration and to heap contempt on misery, to raise power into tyranny, and to make tyranny absolute; to thrust down that which is low still lower, and to make wretches desperate: to exalt magistrates into kings, kings into gods; to degrade subjects to the rank of slaves, and slaves to the condition of brutes. The history of mankind is a romance, a mask, a tragedy, constructed upon the principles of *poetical justice*; it is a noble or royal hunt, in which what is sport to the few is death to the many, and in which the spectators halloo and encourage the strong to set upon the weak, and cry havoc in the chase though they do not share in the spoil. We may depend upon it that what men delight to read in books, they will put in practice in reality.

One of the most natural traits in this play is the difference of the

interest taken in the success of Coriolanus by his wife and mother.
The one is only anxious for his honour; the other is fearful for his
life.

> '*Volumnia.* Methinks I hither hear your husband's drum:
> I see him pluck Aufidius down by th' hair:
> Methinks I see him stamp thus—and call thus—
> Come on, ye cowards; ye were got in fear
> Though you were born in Rome; his bloody brow
> With his mail'd hand then wiping, forth he goes
> Like to a harvest man, that 's task'd to mow
> Or all, or lose his hire.
>   *Virgilia.* His bloody brow! Oh Jupiter, no blood.
>   *Volumnia.* Away, you fool; it more becomes a man
> Than gilt his trophy. The breast of Hecuba,
> When she did suckle Hector, look'd not lovelier
> Than Hector's forehead, when it spit forth blood
> At Grecian swords contending'

When she hears the trumpets that proclaim her son's return, she
says in the true spirit of a Roman matron,

> 'These are the ushers of Martius: before him
> He carries noise, and behind him he leaves tears.
> Death, that dark spirit, in 's nervy arm doth lie,
> Which being advanc'd, declines, and then men die.

Coriolanus himself is a complete character: his love of reputation,
his contempt of popular opinion, his pride and modesty, are consequences of each other. His pride consists in the inflexible sternness
of his will; his love of glory is a determined desire to bear down all
opposition, and to extort the admiration both of friends and foes.
His contempt for popular favour, his unwillingness to hear his own
praises, spring from the same source. He cannot contradict the
praises that are bestowed upon him; therefore he is impatient at
hearing them. He would enforce the good opinion of others by his
actions, but does not want their acknowledgments in words

> 'Pray now, no more: my mother,
> Who has a charter to extol her blood,
> When she does praise me, grieves me.'

His magnanimity is of the same kind. He admires in an enemy
that courage which he honours in himself; he places himself on the
hearth of Aufidius with the same confidence that he would have met
him in the field, and feels that by putting himself in his power, he
takes from him all temptation for using it against him.

In the title-page of CORIOLANUS, it is said at the bottom of the *Dramatis Personæ*, 'The whole history exactly followed, and many of the principal speeches copied from the life of Coriolanus in Plutarch.' It will be interesting to our readers to see how far this is the case. Two of the principal scenes, those between Coriolanus and Aufidius and between Coriolanus and his mother, are thus given in Sir Thomas North's Translation of Plutarch, dedicated to Queen Elizabeth, 1579. The first is as follows :—

'It was even twilight when he entered the city of Antium, and many people met him in the streets, but no man knew him. So he went directly to Tullus Aufidius' house, and when he came thither, he got him up straight to the chimney-hearth, and sat him down, and spake not a word to any man, his face all muffled over. They of the house spying him, wondered what he should be, and yet they durst not bid him rise. For ill-favouredly muffled and disguised as he was, yet there appeared a certain majesty in his countenance and in his silence : whereupon they went to Tullus, who was at supper, to tell him of the strange disguising of this man. Tullus rose presently from the board, and coming towards him, asked him what he was, and wherefore he came. Then Martius unmuffled himself, and after he had paused awhile, making no answer, he said unto himself, If thou knowest me not yet, Tullus, and seeing me, dost not perhaps believe me to be the man I am indeed, I must of necessity discover myself to be that I am. "I am Caius Martius, who hath done to thyself particularly, and to all the Volces generally, great hurt and mischief, which I cannot deny for my surname of Coriolanus that I bear. For I never had other benefit nor recompence of the true and painful service I have done, and the extreme dangers I have been in, but this only surname : a good memory and witness of the malice and displeasure thou shouldest bear me. Indeed the name only remaineth with me; for the rest, the envy and cruelty of the people of Rome have taken from me, by the sufferance of the dastardly nobility and magistrates, who have forsaken me, and let me be banished by the people. This extremity hath now driven me to come as a poor suitor, to take thy chimney-hearth, not of any hope I have to save my life thereby. For if I had feared death, I would not have come hither to put myself in hazard; but pricked forward with desire to be revenged of them that thus have banished me, which now I do begin, in putting my person into the hands of their enemies. Wherefore if thou hast any heart to be wrecked of the injuries thy enemies have done thee, speed thee now, and let my misery serve thy turn, and so use it as my service may be a benefit to the Volces : promising thee, that I will fight with better good will for all you, than I did when I was against you, knowing that they fight more valiantly who know the force of the enemy, than such as have never proved it. And if it be so that thou dare not, and that thou art weary to prove fortune any more, then am I also weary to live any longer And it were no wisdom in thee to save the life of him who hath been heretofore thy mortal enemy, and whose service now can nothing help, nor pleasure thee." Tullus hearing what he said, was a marvellous glad man, and taking him by the hand, he said unto him: "Stand up, O Martius, and be of good cheer, for in proffering thyself unto us, thou doest us great honour: and by this means thou mayest hope also of greater things at all the Volces' hands." So he feasted him for that time, and entertained him in the honourablest manner he could, talking with him of no other matter at that present: but within few days after, they fell to consultation together in what sort they should begin their wars.'

The meeting between Coriolanus and his mother is also nearly the same as in the play.

'Now was Martius set then in the chair of state, with all the honours of a general, and when he had spied the women coming afar off, he marvelled what the matter meant: but afterwards knowing his wife which came foremost, he determined at the first to persist in his obstinate and inflexible rancour. But overcome in the end with natural affection, and being altogether altered to see them, his heart would not serve him to tarry their coming to his chair, but coming down in haste, he went to meet them, and first he kissed his mother, and embraced her a pretty while, then his wife and little children. And nature so wrought with him, that the tears fell from his eyes, and he could not keep himself from making much of them, but yielded to the affection of his blood, as if he had been violently carried with the fury of a most swift-running stream. After he had thus lovingly received them, and perceiving that his mother Volumnia would begin to speak to him, he called the chiefest of the council of the Volces to hear what she would say. Then she spake in this sort: "If we held our peace, my son, and determined not to speak, the state of our poor bodies, and present sight of our raiment, would easily betray to thee what life we have led at home, since thy exile and abode abroad; but think now with thyself, how much more unfortunate than all the women living, we are come hither, considering that the sight which should be most pleasant to all others to behold, spiteful fortune had made most fearful to us: making myself to see my son, and my daughter here her husband, besieging the walls of his native country: so as that which is the only comfort to all others in their adversity and misery, to pray unto the Gods, and to call to them for aid, is the only thing which plungeth us into most deep perplexity. For we cannot, alas, together pray, both for victory to our country, and for safety of thy life also: but a world of grievous curses, yea more than any mortal enemy can heap upon us, are forcibly wrapped up in our prayers. For the bitter sop of most hard choice is offered thy wife and children, to forego one of the two: either to lose the person of thyself, or the nurse of their native country. For myself, my son, I am determined not to tarry till fortune in my lifetime do make an end of this war. For if I cannot persuade thee rather to do good unto both parties, than to overthrow and destroy the one, preferring love and nature before the malice and calamity of wars, thou shalt see, my son, and trust unto it, thou shalt no sooner march forward to assault thy country, but thy foot shall tread upon thy mother's womb, that brought thee first into this world. And I may not defer to see the day, either that my son be led prisoner in triumph by his natural countrymen, or that he himself do triumph of them, and of his natural country. For if it were so, that my request tended to save thy country, in destroying the Volces, I must confess, thou wouldest hardly and doubtfully resolve on that. For as to destroy thy natural country, it is altogether unmeet and unlawful, so were it not just and less honourable to betray those that put their trust in thee. But my only demand consisteth, to make a goal delivery of all evils, which delivereth equal benefit and safety, both to the one and the other, but most honourable for the Volces. For it shall appear, that having victory in their hands, they have of special favour granted us singular graces, peace and amity, albeit themselves have no less part of both than we. Of which good, if so it came to pass, thyself is the only author, and so hast thou the only honour. But if it fail, and fall out contrary, thyself alone deservedly shalt carry the shameful reproach and burthen of either party. So, though the end of war be uncertain, yet this notwithstanding is most certain, that if it be thy chance to conquer, this benefit shalt thou reap of thy goodly conquest, to be chronicled the plague and destroyer of thy country. And if fortune overthrow thee, then the world will say, that through desire to revenge thy private injuries, thou hast for ever undone thy good friends, who did most lovingly and courteously receive thee." Martius gave good ear unto his mother's words, without interrupting her speech at all, and after she had said what she would, he held his peace a pretty while, and answered not a word. Hereupon she began again to speak unto him, and said : "My son, why dost thou not answer me ? Dost thou think it good altogether to give place unto thy choler and desire of revenge, and thinkest thou it not honesty for thee to grant thy mother's request in so weighty a cause ? Dost thou take it honourable for a nobleman to remember the wrongs and injuries done him, and dost not in like case think it an honest nobleman's part to be thankful for the goodness that parents do shew to their children, acknowledging the duty and reverence they ought to bear unto them ? No man living is more bound to shew himself thankful in all parts and respects than thyself; who so universally shewest all ingratitude. Moreover, my son, thou hast sorely taken of thy country, exacting grievous payments upon them, in revenge of the injuries offered thee; besides, thou hast not hitherto shewed thy poor mother any courtesy. And therefore, it is not only honest but due unto me, that without compulsion I should obtain my so just and reasonable request of thee. But since by reason I cannot persuade thee to it, to what purpose do I defer my last hope." And with these words, herself, his wife and children, fell down upon their knees before him : Martius seeing that, could refrain no longer, but went straight and lifted her up, crying out, " Oh mother, what have you done to me ?" And holding her hard by the hand, " Oh mother," said he, "you have won a happy victory for your country, but mortal and unhappy for your son: for I see myself vanquished by you alone." These words being spoken openly, he spake a little apart with his mother and wife, and then let them return again to Rome, for so they did request him; and so remaining in the camp that night, the next morning he dislodged, and marched homeward unto the Volces' country again.'

Shakespear has, in giving a dramatic form to this passage, adhered very closely and properly to the text. He did not think it necessary to improve upon the truth of nature. Several of the scenes in *Julius Cæsar*, particularly Portia's appeal to the confidence of her husband by shewing him the wound she had given herself, and the appearance of the ghost of Cæsar to Brutus, are in like manner, taken from the history.

TROILUS AND CRESSIDA

THIS is one of the most loose and desultory of our author's plays: it rambles on just as it happens, but it overtakes, together with some indifferent matter, a prodigious number of fine things in its way. Troilus himself is no character: he is merely a common lover: but Cressida and her uncle Pandarus are hit off with proverbial truth. By the speeches given to the leaders of the Grecian host, Nestor, Ulysses, Agamemnon, Achilles, Shakespear seems to have known them as well as if he had been a spy sent by the Trojans into the enemy's camp—to say nothing of their affording very lofty examples of didactic eloquence. The following is a very stately and spirited declamation:

> '*Ulysses.* Troy, yet upon her basis, had been down,
> And the great Hector's sword had lack'd a master,
> But for these instances.
> The specialty of rule hath been neglected.
>
> . . . . . .
>
> The heavens themselves, the planets, and this center,
> Observe degree, priority, and place,
> Insisture, course, proportion, season, form,
> Office, and custom, in all line of order:
> And therefore is the glorious planet, Sol,
> In noble eminence, enthron'd and spher'd
> Amidst the other, whose med'cinable eye
> Corrects the ill aspects of planets evil,
> And posts, like the commandment of a king,
> Sans check, to good and bad.   But, when the planets,
> In evil mixture to disorder wander,
> What plagues, and what portents? what mutinies?
> What raging of the sea? shaking of the earth?
> Commotion in the winds? frights, changes, horrors,
> Divert and crack, rend and deracinate
> The unity and married calm of states
> Quite from their fixture!   O, when degree is shaken,
> (Which is the ladder to all high designs)

> The enterprize is sick !   How could communities,
> Degrees in schools, and brotherhoods in cities,
> Peaceful commerce from dividable shores,
> The primogenitive and due of birth,
> Prerogative of age, crowns, sceptres, laurels,
> (But by degree) stand in authentic place ?
> Take but degree away, untune that string,
> And hark what discord follows ! each thing meets
> In mere oppugnancy.   The bounded waters
> Would lift their bosoms higher than the shores,
> And make a sop of all this solid globe:
> Strength would be the lord of imbecility,
> And the rude son would strike his father dead :
> Force would be right; or rather right and wrong
> (Between whose endless jar Justice resides)
> Would lose their names, and so would Justice too.
> Then every thing includes itself in power,
> Power into will, will into appetite ;
> And appetite (an universal wolf,
> So doubly seconded with will and power)
> Must make perforce an universal prey,
> And last eat up himself.   Great Agamemnon,
> This chaos, when degree is suffocate,
> Follows the choking:
> And this neglection of degree it is,
> That by a pace goes backward, in a purpose
> It hath to climb.   The general's disdained
> By him one step below; he, by the next;
> That next, by him beneath : so every step,
> Exampled by the first pace that is sick
> Of his superior, grows to an envious fever
> Of pale and bloodless emulation;
> And 'tis this fever that keeps Troy on foot,
> Not her own sinews.   To end a tale of length,
> Troy in our weakness lives, not in her strength.'

It cannot be said of Shakespear, as was said of some one, that he was 'without o'erflowing full.' He was full, even to o'erflowing. He gave heaped measure, running over. This was his greatest fault. He was only in danger 'of losing distinction in his thoughts' (to borrow his own expression)

> 'As doth a battle when they charge on heaps
> The enemy flying.'

There is another passage, the speech of Ulysses to Achilles, shewing him the thankless nature of popularity, which has a still greater depth of moral observation and richness of illustration than the former. It is long, but worth the quoting. The sometimes giving an entire argument from the unacted plays of our author may with one class of readers have almost the use of restoring a lost passage; and may serve to convince another class of critics, that the poet's genius was not confined to the production of stage effect by preternatural means.—

> '*Ulysses.* Time hath, my lord, a wallet at his back,
> Wherein he puts alms for Oblivion;
> A great-siz'd monster of ingratitudes:
> Those scraps are good deeds past,
> Which are devour'd as fast as they are made,
> Forgot as soon as done. Persev'rance, dear my lord,
> Keeps Honour bright: to have done, is to hang
> Quite out of fashion, like a rusty mail
> In monumental mockery. Take the instant way;
> For Honour travels in a strait so narrow,
> Where one but goes abreast; keep then the path,
> For Emulation hath a thousand sons,
> That one by one pursue; if you give way,
> Or hedge aside from the direct forth right,
> Like to an entered tide, they all rush by,
> And leave you hindmost;——
> Or, like a gallant horse fall'n in first rank,
> O'er-run and trampled on: then what they do in present,
> Tho' less than yours in past must o'ertop yours:
> For Time is like a fashionable host,
> That slightly shakes his parting guest by th' hand,
> And with his arms outstretch'd, as he would fly,
> Grasps in the comer: the welcome ever smiles,
> And farewell goes out sighing. O, let not virtue seek
> Remuneration for the thing it was; for beauty, wit,
> High birth, vigour of bone, desert in service,
> Love, friendship, charity, are subjects all
> To envious and calumniating time:
> One touch of nature makes the whole world kin.
> That all with one consent praise new-born gauds,
> Tho' they are made and moulded of things past.
> The present eye praises the present object.
> Then marvel not, thou great and complete man,
> That all the Greeks begin to worship Ajax;
> Since things in motion sooner catch the eye,
> Than what not stirs. The cry went out on thee,
> And still it might, and yet it may again,
> If thou wouldst not entomb thyself alive,
> And case thy reputation in thy tent.'

The throng of images in the above lines is prodigious; and though they sometimes jostle against one another, they every where raise and carry on the feeling, which is intrinsically true and profound. The debates between the Trojan chiefs on the restoring of Helen are full of knowledge of human motives and character. Troilus enters well into the philosophy of war, when he says in answer to something that falls from Hector,

> 'Why there you touch'd the life of our design:
> Were it not glory that we more affected,
> Than the performance of our heaving spleens,
> I would not wish a drop of Trojan blood
> Spent more in her defence. But, worthy Hector,
> She is a theme of honour and renown,
> A spur to valiant and magnanimous deeds.'

The character of Hector, in a few slight indications which appear of it, is made very amiable. His death is sublime, and shews in a striking light the mixture of barbarity and heroism of the age. The threats of Achilles are fatal; they carry their own means of execution with them.

> 'Come here about me, you my myrmidons,
> Mark what I say.—Attend me where I wheel:
> Strike not a stroke, but keep yourselves in breath;
> And when I have the bloody Hector found,
> Empale him with your weapons round about,
> In fellest manner execute your arms.
> Follow me, sirs, and my proceeding eye.'

He then finds Hector and slays him, as if he had been hunting down a wild beast. There is something revolting as well as terrific in the ferocious coolness with which he singles out his prey: nor does the splendour of the atchievement reconcile us to the cruelty of the means.

The characters of Cressida and Pandarus are very amusing and instructive. The disinterested willingness of Pandarus to serve his friend in an affair which lies next his heart is immediately brought forward. 'Go thy way, Troilus, go thy way; had I a sister were a grace, or a daughter were a goddess, he should take his choice. O admirable man! Paris, Paris is dirt to him, and I warrant Helen, to change, would give money to boot.' This is the language he addresses to his niece: nor is she much behindhand in coming into the plot. Her head is as light and fluttering as her heart. 'It is the prettiest villain, she fetches her breath so short as a new-ta'en sparrow.' Both characters are originals, and quite different from what they are in Chaucer. In Chaucer, Cressida is represented as a grave, sober, considerate personage (a widow—he cannot tell her age, nor whether she has children or no) who has an alternate eye to

her character, her interest, and her pleasure: Shakespear's Cressida
is a giddy girl, an unpractised jilt, who falls in love with Troilus, as
she afterwards deserts him, from mere levity and thoughtlessness of
temper. She may be wooed and won to any thing and from any thing,
at a moment's warning; the other knows very well what she would
be at, and sticks to it, and is more governed by substantial reasons
than by caprice or vanity. Pandarus again, in Chaucer's story, is a
friendly sort of go-between, tolerably busy, officious, and forward in
bringing matters to bear: but in Shakespear he has 'a stamp exclusive
and professional': he wears the badge of his trade; he is a regular
knight of the game. The difference of the manner in which the
subject is treated arises perhaps less from intention, than from the
different genius of the two poets. There is no *double entendre* in the
characters of Chaucer: they are either quite serious or quite comic.
In Shakespear the ludicrous and ironical are constantly blended with
the stately and the impassioned. We see Chaucer's characters as
they saw themselves, not as they appeared to others or might have
appeared to the poet. He is as deeply implicated in the affairs of his
personages as they could be themselves. He had to go a long journey
with each of them, and became a kind of necessary confidant. There
is little relief, or light and shade in his pictures. The conscious
smile is not seen lurking under the brow of grief or impatience.
Every thing with him is intense and continuous—a working out of
what went before.—Shakespear never committed himself to his
characters. He trifled, laughed, or wept with them as he chose.
He has no prejudices for or against them; and it seems a matter of
perfect indifference whether he shall be in jest or earnest. According
to him 'the web of our lives is of a mingled yarn, good and ill
together.' His genius was dramatic, as Chaucer's was historical.
He saw both sides of a question, the different views taken of it
according to the different interests of the parties concerned, and he
was at once an actor and spectator in the scene. If any thing, he is
too various and flexible: too full of transitions, of glancing lights, of
salient points. If Chaucer followed up his subject too doggedly,
perhaps Shakespear was too volatile and heedless. The Muse's
wing too often lifted him from off his feet. He made infinite
excursions to the right and the left.

> ——'He hath done
> Mad and fantastic execution,
> Engaging and redeeming of himself
> With such a careless force and forceless care,
> As if that luck in very spite of cunning
> Bad him win all.'

Chaucer attended chiefly to the real and natural, that is, to the involuntary and inevitable impressions on the mind in given circumstances; Shakespear exhibited also the possible and the fantastical,—not only what things are in themselves, but whatever they might seem to be, their different reflections, their endless combinations. He lent his fancy, wit, invention, to others, and borrowed their feelings in return. Chaucer excelled in the force of habitual sentiment; Shakespear added to it every variety of passion, every suggestion of thought or accident. Chaucer described external objects with the eye of a painter, or he might be said to have embodied them with the hand of a sculptor, every part is so thoroughly made out, and tangible:—Shakespear's imagination threw over them a lustre

—'Prouder than when blue Iris bends.'

Every thing in Chaucer has a downright reality. A simile or a sentiment is as if it were given in upon evidence. In Shakespear the commonest matter-of-fact has a romantic grace about it; or seems to float with the breath of imagination in a freer element. No one could have more depth of feeling or observation than Chaucer, but he wanted resources of invention to lay open the stores of nature or the human heart with the same radiant light that Shakespear has done. However fine or profound the thought, we know what is coming, whereas the effect of reading Shakespear is 'like the eye of vassalage at unawares encountering majesty.' Chaucer's mind was consecutive, rather than discursive. He arrived at truth through a certain process; Shakespear saw every thing by intuition. Chaucer had a great variety of power, but he could do only one thing at once. He set himself to work on a particular subject. His ideas were kept separate, labelled, ticketed and parcelled out in a set form, in pews and compartments by themselves. They did not play into one another's hands. They did not re-act upon one another, as the blower's breath moulds the yielding glass. There is something hard and dry in them. What is the most wonderful thing in Shakespear's faculties is their excessive sociability, and how they gossiped and compared notes together.

We must conclude this criticism; and we will do it with a quotation or two. One of the most beautiful passages in Chaucer's tale is the description of Cresseide's first avowal of her love.

> 'And as the new abashed nightingale,
> That stinteth first when she beginneth sing,
> When that she heareth any herde's tale,
> Or in the hedges any wight stirring,
> And, after, sicker doth her voice outring,

> Right so Cresseide, when that her dread stent,
> Opened her heart, and told him her intent.'

See also the two next stanzas, and particularly that divine one beginning—

> ' Her armes small, her back both straight and soft,' etc.

Compare this with the following speech of Troilus to Cressida in the play :—

> ' O, that I thought it could be in a woman ;
> And if it can, I will presume in you,
> To feed for aye her lamp and flame of love,
> To keep her constancy in plight and youth,
> Out-living beauties outward, with a mind
> That doth renew swifter than blood decays.
> Or, that persuasion could but thus convince me,
> That my integrity and truth to you
> Might be affronted with the match and weight
> Of such a winnow'd purity in love ;
> How were I then uplifted !   But alas,
> I am as true as Truth's simplicity,
> And simpler than the infancy of Truth.'

These passages may not seem very characteristic at first sight, though we think they are so.   We will give two, that cannot be mistaken.   Patroclus says to Achilles,

> ——' Rouse yourselt ; and the weak wanton Cupid
> Shall from your neck unloose his amorous fold,
> And like a dew-drop from the lion's mane,
> Be shook to air.'

Troilus, addressing the God of Day on the approach of the morning that parts him from Cressida, says with much scorn,

> ' What ! proffer'st thou thy light here for to sell ?
> Go sell it them that smallé selés grave.'

If nobody but Shakespear could have written the former, nobody but Chaucer would have thought of the latter.—Chaucer was the most literal of poets, as Richardson was of prose-writers.

ANTONY AND CLEOPATRA

THIS is a very noble play. Though not in the first class of Shakespear's productions, it stands next to them, and is, we think, the finest of his historical plays, that is, of those in which he made poetry the organ of history, and assumed a certain tone of character and sentiment, in conformity to known facts, instead of trusting to his observations of general nature or to the unlimited indulgence of his own fancy. What he has added to the actual story, is upon a par with it. His genius was, as it were, a match for history as well as nature, and could grapple at will with either. The play is full of that pervading comprehensive power by which the poet could always make himself master of time and circumstances. It presents a fine picture of Roman pride and Eastern magnificence: and in the struggle between the two, the empire of the world seems suspended, 'like the swan's down-feather,

> ' That stands upon the swell at full of tide,
> And neither way inclines.'

The characters breathe, move, and live. Shakespear does not stand reasoning on what his characters would do or say, but at once *becomes* them, and speaks and acts for them. He does not present us with groups of stage-puppets or poetical machines making set speeches on human life, and acting from a calculation of problematical motives, but he brings living men and women on the scene, who speak and act from real feelings, according to the ebbs and flows of passion, without the least tincture of pedantry of logic or rhetoric. Nothing is made out by inference and analogy, by climax and antithesis, but every thing takes place just as it would have done in reality, according to the occasion.—The character of Cleopatra is a master-piece. What an extreme contrast it affords to Imogen! One would think it almost impossible for the same person to have drawn both. She is voluptuous, ostentatious, conscious, boastful of her charms, haughty, tyrannical, fickle. The luxurious pomp and gorgeous extravagance of the Egyptian queen are displayed in all their force and lustre, as well as the irregular grandeur of the soul of Mark Antony. Take only the first four lines that they speak as an example of the regal style of love-making.

> ' *Cleopatra.* If it be love indeed, tell me how much?
> *Antony.* There 's beggary in the love that can be reckon'd.
> *Cleopatra.* I 'll set a bourn how far to be belov'd.
> *Antony.* Then must thou needs find out new heav'n, new earth.'

The rich and poetical description of her person beginning—

> 'The barge she sat in, like a burnish'd throne,
>   Burnt on the water; the poop was beaten gold,
>   Purple the sails, and so perfumed, that
>   The winds were love-sick '—

seems to prepare the way for, and almost to justify the subsequent
infatuation of Antony when in the sea-fight at Actium, he leaves the
battle, and 'like a doating mallard' follows her flying sails.

Few things in Shakespear (and we know of nothing in any other
author like them) have more of that local truth of imagination and
character than the passage in which Cleopatra is represented con-
jecturing what were the employments of Antony in his absence—
'He's speaking now, or murmuring—*Where's my serpent of old Nile?*'
Or again, when she says to Antony, after the defeat at Actium, and
his summoning up resolution to risk another fight—'It is my birth-
day; I had thought to have held it poor; but since my lord is
Antony again, I will be Cleopatra.' Perhaps the finest burst of all
is Antony's rage after his final defeat when he comes in, and surprises
the messenger of Cæsar kissing her hand—

> 'To let a fellow that will take rewards,
>   And say God quit you, be familiar with,
>   My play-fellow, your hand; this kingly seal,
>   And plighter of high hearts.'

It is no wonder that he orders him to be whipped; but his low
condition is not the true reason: there is another feeling which lies
deeper, though Antony's pride would not let him shew it, except by
his rage; he suspects the fellow to be Cæsar's proxy.

Cleopatra's whole character is the triumph of the voluptuous, of
the love of pleasure and the power of giving it, over every other
consideration. Octavia is a dull foil to her, and Fulvia a shrew and
shrill-tongued. What a picture do those lines give of her—

> 'Age cannot wither her, nor custom steal
>   Her infinite variety. Other women cloy
>   The appetites they feed, but she makes hungry
>   Where most she satisfies.'

What a spirit and fire in her conversation with Antony's messenger
who brings her the unwelcome news of his marriage with Octavia!
How all the pride of beauty and of high rank breaks out in her
promised reward to him—

> ——'There's gold, and here
>   My bluest veins to kiss ! '—

She had great and unpardonable faults, but the grandeur of her death almost redeems them. She learns from the depth of despair the strength of her affections. She keeps her queen-like state in the last disgrace, and her sense of the pleasurable in the last moments of her life. She tastes a luxury in death. After applying the asp, she says with fondness—

> ' Dost thou not see my baby at my breast,
> That sucks the nurse asleep ?
> As sweet as balm, as soft as air, as gentle.
> Oh Antony ! '

It is worth while to observe that Shakespear has contrasted the extreme magnificence of the descriptions in this play with pictures of extreme suffering and physical horror, not less striking—partly perhaps to place the effeminate character of Mark Antony in a more favourable light, and at the same time to preserve a certain balance of feeling in the mind. Cæsar says, hearing of his rival's conduct at the court of Cleopatra,

> ——' Antony,
> Leave thy lascivious wassels. When thou once
> Wert beaten from Mutina, where thou slew'st
> Hirtius and Pansa, consuls, at thy heel
> Did famine follow, whom thou fought'st against,
> Though daintily brought up, with patience more
> Than savages could suffer. Thou did'st drink
> The stale of horses, and the gilded puddle
> Which beast would cough at. Thy palate then did deign
> The roughest berry on the rudest hedge,
> Yea, like the stag, when snow the pasture sheets,
> The barks of trees thou browsed'st. On the Alps,
> It is reported, thou didst eat strange flesh,
> Which some did die to look on : and all this,
> It wounds thine honour, that I speak it now,
> Was borne so like a soldier, that thy cheek
> So much as lank'd not.'

The passage after Antony's defeat by Augustus, where he is made to say—

> ' Yes, yes ; he at Philippi kept
> His sword e'en like a dancer ; while I struck
> The lean and wrinkled Cassius, and 'twas I
> That the mad Brutus ended '—

is one of those fine retrospections which show us the winding and eventful march of human life. The jealous attention which has been paid to the unities both of time and place has taken away the principle of perspective in the drama, and all the interest which objects derive from distance, from contrast, from privation, from change of fortune, from long-cherished passion; and contrasts our view of life from a strange and romantic dream, long, obscure, and infinite, into a smartly contested, three hours' inaugural disputation on its merits by the different candidates for theatrical applause.

The latter scenes of ANTONY AND CLEOPATRA are full of the changes of accident and passion. Success and defeat follow one another with startling rapidity. Fortune sits upon her wheel more blind and giddy than usual. This precarious state and the approaching dissolution of his greatness are strikingly displayed in the dialogue of Antony with Eros.

> '*Antony.* Eros, thou yet behold'st me?
> *Eros.* Ay, noble lord.
> *Antony.* Sometime we see a cloud that's dragonish,
> A vapour sometime, like a bear or lion,
> A towered citadel, a pendant rock,
> A forked mountain, or blue promontory
> With trees upon 't, that nod unto the world
> And mock our eyes with air. Thou hast seen these signs,
> They are black vesper's pageants.
> *Eros.* Ay, my lord.
> *Antony.* That which is now a horse, even with a thought
> The rack dislimns, and makes it indistinct
> As water is in water.
> *Eros.* It does, my lord.
> *Antony.* My good knave, Eros, now thy captain is
> Even such a body,' etc.

This is, without doubt, one of the finest pieces of poetry in Shakespear. The splendour of the imagery, the semblance of reality, the lofty range of picturesque objects hanging over the world, their evanescent nature, the total uncertainty of what is left behind, are just like the mouldering schemes of human greatness. It is finer than Cleopatra's passionate lamentation over his fallen grandeur, because it is more dim, unstable, unsubstantial. Antony's headstrong presumption and infatuated determination to yield to Cleopatra's wishes to fight by sea instead of land, meet a merited punishment; and the extravagance of his resolutions, increasing with the desperateness of his circumstances, is well commented upon by Œnobarbus.

> ———'I see men's judgments are
> A parcel of their fortunes, and things outward
> Do draw the inward quality after them
> To suffer all alike'

The repentance of Œnobarbus after his treachery to his master is the most affecting part of the play. He cannot recover from the blow which Antony's generosity gives him, and he dies broken-hearted, 'a master-leaver and a fugitive.'

Shakespear's genius has spread over the whole play a richness like the overflowing of the Nile.

HAMLET

THIS is that Hamlet the Dane, whom we read of in our youth, and whom we may be said almost to remember in our after-years; he who made that famous soliloquy on life, who gave the advice to the players, who thought 'this goodly frame, the earth, a steril promontory, and this brave o'er-hanging firmament, the air, this majestical roof fretted with golden fire, a foul and pestilent congregation of vapours'; whom 'man delighted not, nor woman neither'; he who talked with the grave-diggers, and moralised on Yorick's skull; the school-fellow of Rosencrans and Guildenstern at Wittenberg; the friend of Horatio; the lover of Ophelia; he that was mad and sent to England; the slow avenger of his father's death; who lived at the court of Horwendillus five hundred years before we were born, but all whose thoughts we seem to know as well as we do our own, because we have read them in Shakespear.

Hamlet is a name; his speeches and sayings but the idle coinage of the poet's brain. What then, are they not real? They are as real as our own thoughts. Their reality is in the reader's mind. It is *we* who are Hamlet. This play has a prophetic truth, which is above that of history. Whoever has become thoughtful and melancholy through his own mishaps or those of others; whoever has borne about with him the clouded brow of reflection, and thought himself 'too much i' th' sun'; whoever has seen the golden lamp of day dimmed by envious mists rising in his own breast, and could find in the world before him only a dull blank with nothing left remarkable in it; whoever has known 'the pangs of despised love, the insolence of office, or the spurns which patient merit of the unworthy takes'; he who has felt his mind sink within him, and sadness cling to his heart like a malady, who has had his hopes blighted and his youth staggered by the apparitions of strange things; who cannot be well at ease, while he sees evil hovering near him like a spectre; whose powers of action have been eaten up by thought, he to whom the universe seems infinite, and himself nothing; whose bitterness of soul makes him careless of consequences, and who goes to a play as his best resource to shove off, to a second remove, the evils of life by a mock representation of them—this is the true Hamlet.

We have been so used to this tragedy that we hardly know how to criticise it any more than we should know how to describe our own faces. But we must make such observations as we can. It is the one of Shakespear's plays that we think of the oftenest, because it abounds most in striking reflections on human life, and because the distresses of Hamlet are transferred, by the turn of his mind, to the general account of humanity. Whatever happens to him we apply to ourselves, because he applies it so himself as a means of general reasoning. He is a great moraliser; and what makes him worth attending to is, that he moralises on his own feelings and experience. He is not a common-place pedant. If *Lear* is distinguished by the greatest depth of passion, HAMLET is the most remarkable for the ingenuity, originality, and unstudied developement of character. Shakespear had more magnanimity than any other poet, and he has shewn more of it in this play than in any other. There is no attempt to force an interest: every thing is left for time and circumstances to unfold. The attention is excited without effort, the incidents succeed each other as matters of course, the characters think and speak and act just as they might do, if left entirely to themselves. There is no set purpose, no straining at a point. The observations are suggested by the passing scene—the gusts of passion come and go like sounds of music borne on the wind. The whole play is an exact transcript of what might be supposed to have taken place at the court of Denmark, at the remote period of time fixed upon, before the modern refinements in morals and manners were heard of. It would have been interesting enough to have been admitted as a by-stander in such a scene, at such a time, to have heard and witnessed something of what was going on. But here we are more than spectators. We have not only 'the outward pageants and the signs of grief'; but 'we have that within which passes shew.' We read the thoughts of the heart, we catch the passions living as they rise. Other dramatic writers give us very fine versions and paraphrases of nature; but Shakespear, together with his own comments, gives us the original text, that we may judge for ourselves. This is a very great advantage.

The character of Hamlet stands quite by itself. It is not a character marked by strength of will or even of passion, but by refinement of thought and sentiment. Hamlet is as little of the hero as a man can well be: but he is a young and princely novice, full of high enthusiasm and quick sensibility—the sport of circumstances, questioning with fortune and refining on his own feelings, and forced from the natural bias of his disposition by the strangeness of his situation. He seems incapable of deliberate action, and is only hurried into extremities on the spur of the occasion, when he has no time to reflect, as in the scene where he kills Polonius, and again, where he alters the letters which Rosencraus and Guildenstern are taking with them to England, purporting his death. At other times, when he is most bound to act, he remains puzzled, undecided, and sceptical, dallies with his purposes, till the occasion is lost, and finds out some pretence to relapse into indolence and thoughtfulness again. For this reason he refuses to kill the King when he is at his prayers, and by a refinement in malice, which is in truth only an excuse for his own want of resolution, defers his revenge to a more fatal opportunity, when he shall be engaged in some act 'that has no relish of salvation in it.'

> 'He kneels and prays,
> And now I'll do't, and so he goes to heaven,
> And so am I reveng'd: *that would be scann'd.*
> He kill'd my father, and for that,
> I, his sole son, send him to heaven.
> Why this is reward, not revenge.
> Up sword and know thou a more horrid time,
> When he is drunk, asleep, or in a rage.'

He is the prince of philosophical speculators; and because he cannot have his revenge perfect, according to the most refined idea his wish can form, he declines it altogether. So he scruples to trust the suggestions of the ghost, contrives the scene of the play to have surer proof of his uncle's guilt, and then rests satisfied with this confirmation of his suspicions, and the success of his experiment, instead of acting upon it. Yet he is sensible of his own weakness, taxes himself with it, and tries to reason himself out of it.

> 'How all occasions do inform against me,
> And spur my dull revenge! What is a man,
> If his chief good and market of his time
> Be but to sleep and feed? A beast; no more.
> Sure he that made us with such large discourse,
> Looking before and after, gave us not
> That capability and god-like reason
> To rust in us unus'd. Now whether it be
> Bestial oblivion, or some craven scruple
> Of thinking too precisely on th' event,—
> A thought which quarter'd, hath but one part wisdom,
> And ever three parts coward;—I do not know
> Why yet I live to say, this thing's to do;
> Sith I have cause, and will, and strength, and means

To do it. Examples gross as earth exhort me,
Witness this army of such mass and charge,
Led by a delicate and tender prince,
Whose spirit with divine ambition puff'd,
Makes mouths at the invisible event,
Exposing what is mortal and unsure
To all that fortune, death, and danger dare,
Even for an egg-shell. 'Tis not to be great
Never to stir without great argument;
But greatly to find quarrel in a straw,
When honour's at the stake. How stand I then,
That have a father kill'd, a mother stain'd,
Excitements of my reason and my blood,
And let all sleep, while to my shame I see
The imminent death of twenty thousand men,
That for a fantasy and trick of fame,
Go to their graves like beds, fight for a plot
Whereon the numbers cannot try the cause,
Which is not tomb enough and continent
To hide the slain?—O, from this time forth,
My thoughts be bloody or be nothing worth.'

Still he does nothing; and this very speculation on his own infirmity
only affords him another occasion for indulging it. It is not from
any want of attachment to his father or of abhorrence of his murder
that Hamlet is thus dilatory, but it is more to his taste to indulge his
imagination in reflecting upon the enormity of the crime and refining
on his schemes of vengeance, than to put them into immediate practice.
His ruling passion is to think, not to act: and any vague pretext that
flatters this propensity instantly diverts him from his previous purposes.

The moral perfection of this character has been called in question,
we think, by those who did not understand it. It is more interesting
than according to rules; amiable, though not faultless. The ethical
delineations of 'that noble and liberal casuist'[1] (as Shakespear has
been well called) do not exhibit the drab-coloured quakerism of
morality. His plays are not copied either from The Whole Duty
of Man, or from The Academy of Compliments! We confess we
are a little shocked at the want of refinement in those who are
shocked at the want of refinement in Hamlet. The neglect of
punctilious exactness in his behaviour either partakes of the 'licence
of the time,' or else belongs to the very excess of intellectual refinement in the character, which makes the common rules of life, as well
as his own purpose, sit loose upon him. He may be said to be
amenable only to the tribunal of his own thoughts, and is too much

taken up with the airy world of contemplation to lay as much stress as he ought on the practical consequences of things. His habitual principles of action are unhinged and out of joint with the time. His conduct to Ophelia is quite natural in his circumstances. It is that of assumed severity only. It is the effect of disappointed hope, of bitter regrets, of affection suspended, not obliterated, by the distractions of the scene around him! Amidst the natural and preternatural horrors of his situation, he might be excused in delicacy from carrying on a regular courtship. When 'his father's spirit was in arms,' it was not a time for the son to make love in. He could neither marry Ophelia, nor wound her mind by explaining the cause of his alienation, which he durst hardly trust himself to think of. It would have taken him years to have come to a direct explanation on the point. In the harassed state of his mind, he could not have done much otherwise than he did. His conduct does not contradict what he says when he sees her funeral,

> 'I loved Ophelia: forty thousand brothers
> Could not with all their quantity of love
> Make up my sum.'

Nothing can be more affecting or beautiful than the Queen's apostrophe to Ophelia on throwing the flowers into the grave.

> ——'Sweets to the sweet, farewell.
> I hop'd thou should'st have been my Hamlet's wife:
> I thought thy bride-bed to have deck'd, sweet maid,
> And not have strew'd thy grave.'

Shakespear was thoroughly a master of the mixed motives of human character, and he here shews us the Queen, who was so criminal in some respects, not without sensibility and affection in other relations of life.—Ophelia is a character almost too exquisitely touching to be dwelt upon. Oh rose of May, oh flower too soon faded! Her love, her madness, her death, are described with the truest touches of tenderness and pathos. It is a character which nobody but Shakespear could have drawn in the way that he has done, and to the conception of which there is not even the smallest approach, except in some of the old romantic ballads.[1] Her brother,

---

[1] In the account of her death, a friend has pointed out an instance of the poet's exact observation of nature :—

> 'There is a willow growing o'er a brook,
> That shews its hoary leaves i' th' glassy stream.'

The inside of the leaves of the willow, next the water, is of a whitish colour, and the reflection would therefore be 'hoary.'

Laertes, is a character we do not like so well: he is too hot and choleric, and somewhat rhodomontade. Polonius is a perfect character in its kind; nor is there any foundation for the objections which have been made to the consistency of this part. It is said that he acts very foolishly and talks very sensibly. There is no inconsistency in that. Again, that he talks wisely at one time and foolishly at another; that his advice to Laertes is very excellent, and his advice to the King and Queen on the subject of Hamlet's madness very ridiculous. But he gives the one as a father, and is sincere in it; he gives the other as a mere courtier, a busy-body, and is accordingly officious, garrulous, and impertinent. In short, Shakespear has been accused of inconsistency in this and other characters, only because he has kept up the distinction which there is in nature, between the understandings and the moral habits of men, between the absurdity of their ideas and the absurdity of their motives. Polonius is not a fool, but he makes himself so. His folly, whether in his actions or speeches, comes under the head of impropriety of intention.

We do not like to see our author's plays acted, and least of all, HAMLET. There is no play that suffers so much in being transferred to the stage. Hamlet himself seems hardly capable of being acted. Mr. Kemble unavoidably fails in this character from a want of ease and variety. The character of Hamlet is made up of undulating lines; it has the yielding flexibility of 'a wave o' th' sea.' Mr. Kemble plays it like a man in armour, with a determined inveteracy of purpose, in one undeviating straight line, which is as remote from the natural grace and refined susceptibility of the character, as the sharp angles and abrupt starts which Mr. Kean introduces into the part. Mr. Kean's Hamlet is as much too splenetic and rash as Mr. Kemble's is too deliberate and formal. His manner is too strong and pointed. He throws a severity, approaching to virulence, into the common observations and answers. There is nothing of this in Hamlet. He is, as it were, wrapped up in his reflections, and only *thinks aloud*. There should therefore be no attempt to impress what he says upon others by a studied exaggeration of emphasis or manner; no *talking at* his hearers. There should be as much of the gentleman and scholar as possible infused into the part, and as little of the actor. A pensive air of sadness should sit reluctantly upon his brow, but no appearance of fixed and sullen gloom. He is full of weakness and melancholy, but there is no harshness in his nature. He is the most amiable of misanthropes.

THE TEMPEST

THERE can be little doubt that Shakespear was the most universal genius that ever lived. 'Either for tragedy, comedy, history, pastoral, pastoral-comical, historical-pastoral, scene individable or poem unlimited, he is the only man. Seneca cannot be too heavy, nor Plautus too light for him.' He has not only the same absolute command over our laughter and our tears, all the resources of passion, of wit, of thought, of observation, but he has the most unbounded range of fanciful invention, whether terrible or playful, the same insight into the world of imagination that he has into the world of reality ; and over all there presides the same truth of character and nature, and the same spirit of humanity. His ideal beings are as true and natural as his real characters; that is, as consistent with themselves, or if we suppose such beings to exist at all, they could not act, speak, or feel otherwise than as he makes them. He has invented for them a language, manners, and sentiments of their own, from the tremendous imprecations of the Witches in *Macbeth*, when they do 'a deed without a name,' to the sylph-like expressions of Ariel, who 'does his spiriting gently'; the mischievous tricks and gossiping of Robin Goodfellow, or the uncouth gabbling and emphatic gesticulations of Caliban in this play.

The TEMPEST is one of the most original and perfect of Shakespear's productions, and he has shewn in it all the variety of his powers. It is full of grace and grandeur. The human and imaginary characters, the dramatic and the grotesque, are blended together with the greatest art, and without any appearance of it. Though he has here given 'to airy nothing a local habitation and a name,' yet that part which is only the fantastic creation of his mind, has the same palpable texture, and coheres 'semblably' with the rest. As the preternatural part has the air of reality, and almost haunts the imagination with a sense of truth, the real characters and events partake of the wildness of a dream. The stately magician, Prospero, driven from his dukedom, but around whom (so potent is his art) airy spirits throng numberless to do his bidding; his daughter Miranda ('worthy of that name') to whom all the power of his art points, and who seems the goddess of the isle; the princely Ferdinand, cast by fate upon the haven of his happiness in this idol of his love; the delicate Ariel; the savage Caliban, half brute, half demon; the drunken ship's crew—are all connected parts of the story, and can hardly be spared from the place they fill. Even the local scenery is of a piece and character with the subject. Prospero's enchanted island seems to have risen up out of

he sea; the airy music, the tempest-tost vessel, the turbulent waves,
ll have the effect of the landscape background of some fine picture.
Shakespear's pencil is (to use an allusion of his own) 'like the dyer's
and, subdued to what it works in.' Every thing in him, though it
artakes of 'the liberty of wit,' is also subjected to 'the law' of the
understanding. For instance, even the drunken sailors, who are made
reeling-ripe, share, in the disorder of their minds and bodies, in the
tumult of the elements, and seem on shore to be as much at the mercy
f chance as they were before at the mercy of the winds and waves.
These fellows with their sea-wit are the least to our taste of any part
f the play: but they are as like drunken sailors as they can be, and
re an indirect foil to Caliban, whose figure acquires a classical dignity
n the comparison.

The character of Caliban is generally thought (and justly so) to be
ne of the author's master-pieces. It is not indeed pleasant to see
his character on the stage any more than it is to see the god Pan
ersonated there. But in itself it is one of the wildest and most
bstracted of all Shakespear's characters, whose deformity whether of
ody or mind is redeemed by the power and truth of the imagination
isplayed in it. It is the essence of grossness, but there is not a
article of vulgarity in it. Shakespear has described the brutal mind
f Caliban in contact with the pure and original forms of nature; the
character grows out of the soil where it is rooted, uncontrouled,
uncouth and wild, uncramped by any of the meannesses of custom.
t is 'of the earth, earthy.' It seems almost to have been dug out
f the ground, with a soul instinctively superadded to it answering to
ts wants and origin. Vulgarity is not natural coarseness, but conventional coarseness, learnt from others, contrary to, or without an
ntire conformity of natural power and disposition; as fashion is the
common-place affectation of what is elegant and refined without any
eeling of the essence of it. Schlegel, the admirable German critic
n Shakespear, observes that Caliban is a poetical character, and
always speaks in blank verse.' He first comes in thus:

> '*Caliban.* As wicked dew as e'er my mother brush'd
> With raven's feather from unwholesome fen,
> Drop on you both: a south-west blow on ye,
> And blister you all o'er!
> *Prospero.* For this, be sure, to-night thou shalt have cramps,
> Side-stitches that shall pen thy breath up; urchins
> Shall for that vast of night that they may work,
> All exercise on thee: thou shalt be pinched
> As thick as honey-combs, each pinch more stinging
> Than bees that made them.

I 65

> *Caliban.* I must eat my dinner.
> This island's mine by Sycorax my mother,
> Which thou tak'st from me. When thou camest first,
> Thou stroak'dst me, and mad'st much of me; would'st give me
> Water with berries in 't; and teach me how
> To name the bigger light and how the less
> That burn by day and night; and then I lov'd thee,
> And shew'd thee all the qualities o' th' isle,
> The fresh springs, brine-pits, barren place and fertile:
> Curs'd be I that I did so! All the charms
> Of Sycorax, toads, beetles, bats, light on you!
> For I am all the subjects that you have,
> Who first was mine own king; and here you sty me
> In this hard rock, whiles you do keep from me
> The rest o' th' island.'

And again, he promises Trinculo his services thus, if he will free him from his drudgery.

> 'I 'll shew thee the best springs; I 'll pluck thee berries,
> I 'll fish for thee, and get thee wood enough.
> I pr'ythee let me bring thee where crabs grow,
> And I with my long nails will dig thee pig-nuts:
> Shew thee a jay's nest, and instruct thee how
> To snare the nimble marmozet: I 'll bring thee
> To clust'ring filberds; and sometimes I 'll get thee
> Young scamels from the rock.'

In conducting Stephano and Trinculo to Prospero's cell, Caliban shews the superiority of natural capacity over greater knowledge and greater folly; and in a former scene, when Ariel frightens them with his music, Caliban to encourage them accounts for it in the eloquent poetry of the senses.

> —' Be not afraid, the isle is full of noises,
> Sounds, and sweet airs, that give delight and hurt not.
> Sometimes a thousand twanging instruments
> Will hum about mine ears, and sometimes voices,
> That if I then had waked after long sleep,
> Would make me sleep again; and then in dreaming,
> The clouds methought would open, and shew riches
> Ready to drop upon me: when I wak'd,
> I cried to dream again.'

This is not more beautiful than it is true. The poet here shews us the savage with the simplicity of a child, and makes the strange monster amiable. Shakespear had to paint the human animal rude and without choice in its pleasures, but not without the sense leasure or some germ of the affections. Master Barnardine in *Measure for Measure*, the savage of civilized life, is an admirable hilosophical counterpart to Caliban.

Shakespear has, as it were by design, drawn off from Caliban the lements of whatever is ethereal and refined, to compound them in he unearthly mould of Ariel. Nothing was ever more finely conceived than this contrast between the material and the spiritual, he gross and delicate. Ariel is imaginary power, the swiftness of hought personified. When told to make good speed by Prospero, e says, 'I drink the air before me.' This is something like Puck's oast on a similar occasion, 'I'll put a girdle round about the earth n forty minutes.' But Ariel differs from Puck in having a fellow eeling in the interests of those he is employed about. How exquisite s the following dialogue between him and Prospero!

> ' *Ariel.* Your charm so strongly works 'em,
> That if you now beheld them, your affections
> Would become tender.
>   *Prospero.* Dost thou think so, spirit?
>   *Ariel.* Mine would, sir, were I human.
>   *Prospero.* And mine shall.
> Hast thou, which art but air, a touch, a feeling
> Of their afflictions, and shall not myself,
> One of their kind, that relish all as sharply,
> Passion'd as they, be kindlier moved than thou art?'

It has been observed that there is a peculiar charm in the songs ntroduced in Shakespear, which, without conveying any distinct mages, seem to recall all the feelings connected with them, like natches of half-forgotten music heard indistinctly and at intervals. There is this effect produced by Ariel's songs, which (as we are old) seem to sound in the air, and as if the person playing them were invisible. We shall give one instance out of many of this general power.

' *Enter* FERDINAND ; *and* ARIEL *invisible, playing and singing.*

ARIEL'S SONG.

> Come unto these yellow sands,
>   And then take hands;
> Curt'sied when you have, and kiss'd,
>   (The wild waves whist;)
> Foot it featly here and there;
>   And sweet sprites the burden bear.
>   [*Burden dispersedly.*

Hark, hark! bowgh-wowgh: the watch-dogs bark,
            Bowgh-wowgh.
Ariel. Hark, hark! I hear
            The strain of strutting chanticleer
            Cry cock-a-doodle-doo.

Ferdinand. Where should this music be? i' the air or the earth?
It sounds no more: and sure it waits upon
Some god o' th' island. Sitting on a bank
Weeping against the king my father's wreck,
This music crept by me upon the waters,
Allaying both their fury and my passion
With its sweet air; thence I have follow'd it,
Or it hath drawn me rather:—but 'tis gone.—
No, it begins again.

ARIEL'S SONG.

Full fathom five thy father lies,
        Of his bones are coral made:
Those are pearls that were his eyes,
        Nothing of him that doth fade,
But doth suffer a sea change,
Into something rich and strange.
Sea-nymphs hourly ring his knell—
Hark! now I hear them, ding-dong bell.

                                [Burden ding-dong.

Ferdinand. The ditty does remember my drown'd father.
This is no mortal business, nor no sound
That the earth owes: I hear it now above me.'—

The courtship between Ferdinand and Miranda is one of the chief
beauties of this play. It is the very purity of love. The pretended
interference of Prospero with it heightens its interest, and is in
character with the magician, whose sense of preternatural power
makes him arbitrary, tetchy, and impatient of opposition.

The TEMPEST is a finer play than the *Midsummer Night's Dream,*
which has sometimes been compared with it; but it is not so fine a
poem. There are a greater number of beautiful passages in the latter.
Two of the most striking in the TEMPEST are spoken by Prospero.
The one is that admirable one when the vision which he has conjured
up disappears, beginning 'The cloud-capp'd towers, the gorgeous
palaces,' etc., which has been so often quoted, that every school-boy
knows it by heart; the other is that which Prospero makes in
abjuring his art.

'Ye elves of hills, brooks, standing lakes, and groves,
    And ye that on the sands with printless foot
    Do chase the ebbing Neptune, and do fly him

When he comes back; you demi-puppets, that
By moon-shine do the green sour ringlets make,
Whereof the ewe not bites; and you whose pastime
Is to make midnight mushrooms, that rejoice
To hear the solemn curfew, by whose aid
(Weak masters tho' ye be) I have be-dimm'd
The noon-tide sun, call'd forth the mutinous winds,
And 'twixt the green sea and the azur'd vault
Set roaring war; to the dread rattling thunder
Have I giv'n fire, and rifted Jove's stout oak
With his own bolt; the strong-bas'd promontory
Have I made shake, and by the spurs pluck'd up
The pine and cedar: graves at my command
Have wak'd their sleepers; oped, and let 'em forth
By my so potent art. But this rough magic
I here abjure; and when I have requir'd
Some heavenly music, which even now I do,
(To work mine end upon their senses that
This airy charm is for) I'll break my staff,
Bury it certain fadoms in the earth,
And deeper than did ever plummet sound,
I'll drown my book.'—

We must not forget to mention among other things in this play,
that Shakespear has anticipated nearly all the arguments on the
Utopian schemes of modern philosophy.

> '*Gonzalo.* Had I the plantation of this isle, my lord—
> *Antonio.* He'd sow it with nettle-seed.
> *Sebastian.* Or docks or mallows.
> *Gonzalo.* And were the king on 't, what would I do?
> *Sebastian.* 'Scape being drunk, for want of wine.
> *Gonzalo.* I' the commonwealth I would by contraries
Execute all things: for no kind of traffic
Would I admit; no name of magistrate;
Letters should not be known; wealth, poverty,
And use of service, none; contract, succession,
Bourn, bound of land, tilth, vineyard, none;
No use of metal, corn, or wine, or oil;
No occupation, all men idle, all,
And women too; but innocent and pure:
No sovereignty.
> *Sebastian.* And yet he would be king on 't.
> *Antonio.* The latter end of his commonwealth forgets the
> beginning.
> *Gonzalo.* All things in common nature should produce
Without sweat or endeavour. Treason, felony,
Sword, pike, knife, gun, or need of any engine
Would I not have; but nature should bring forth,

> Of its own kind, all foizon, all abundance
> To feed my innocent people !
>> *Sebastian.* No marrying 'mong his subjects ?
>> *Antonio.* None, man ; all idle ; whores and knaves.
>> *Gonzalo.* I would with such perfection govern, sir,
> To excel the golden age.
>> *Sebastian.* Save his majesty ! '

THE MIDSUMMER NIGHT'S DREAM

BOTTOM the Weaver is a character that has not had justice done
him. He is the most romantic of mechanics. And what a list of
companions he has—Quince the Carpenter, Snug the Joiner, Flute
the Bellows-mender, Snout the Tinker, Starveling the Tailor ; and
then again, what a group of fairy attendants, Puck, Peaseblossom,
Cobweb, Moth, and Mustard-seed ! It has been observed that
Shakespear's characters are constructed upon deep physiological
principles ; and there is something in this play which looks very like
it. Bottom the Weaver, who takes the lead of

> 'This crew of patches, rude mechanicals,
> That work for bread upon Athenian stalls,'

follows a sedentary trade, and he is accordingly represented as conceited, serious, and fantastical. He is ready to undertake any thing
and every thing, as if it was as much a matter of course as the motion
of his loom and shuttle. He is for playing the tyrant, the lover, the
lady, the lion. 'He will roar that it shall do any man's heart good
to hear him ' ; and this being objected to as improper, he still has a
resource in his good opinion of himself, and 'will roar you an 'twere
any nightingale.' Snug the Joiner is the moral man of the piece,
who proceeds by measurement and discretion in all things. You see
him with his rule and compasses in his hand 'Have you the lion's
part written ? Pray you, if it be, give it me, for I am slow of study.'
—'You may do it extempore,' says Quince, 'for it is nothing but
roaring.' Starveling the Tailor keeps the peace, and objects to the
lion and the drawn sword. 'I believe we must leave the killing out
when all's done.' Starveling, however, does not start the objections
himself, but seconds them when made by others, as if he had not
spirit to express his fears without encouragement. It is too much
to suppose all this intentional : but it very luckily falls out so. Nature
includes all that is implied in the most subtle analytical distinctions ;
and the same distinctions will be found in Shakespear. Bottom, who

not only chief actor, but stage-manager for the occasion, has a device to obviate the danger of frightening the ladies: 'Write me a prologue, and let the prologue seem to say, we will do no harm with our swords, and that Pyramus is not killed indeed; and for better assurance, tell them that I, Pyramus, am not Pyramus, but Bottom the Weaver: this will put them out of fear.' Bottom seems to have understood the subject of dramatic illusion at least as well as any modern essayist. If our holiday mechanic rules the roast among his fellows, he is no less at home in his new character of an ass, 'with amiable cheeks, and fair large ears.' He instinctively acquires a most learned taste, and grows fastidious in the choice of dried peas and bottled hay. He is quite familiar with his new attendants, and assigns them their parts with all due gravity. 'Monsieur Cobweb, good Monsieur, get your weapon in your hand, and kill me a red-hipt humble bee on the top of a thistle, and, good Monsieur, bring me the honey-bag.' What an exact knowledge is here shewn of natural history!

Puck, or Robin Goodfellow, is the leader of the fairy band. He is the Ariel of the MIDSUMMER NIGHT'S DREAM; and yet as unlike as can be to the Ariel in *The Tempest*. No other poet could have made two such different characters out of the same fanciful materials and situations. Ariel is a minister of retribution, who is touched with the sense of pity at the woes he inflicts. Puck is a mad-cap sprite, full of wantonness and mischief, who laughs at those whom he mis-leads—'Lord, what fools these mortals be!' Ariel cleaves the air, and executes his mission with the zeal of a winged messenger; Puck is borne along on his fairy errand like the light and glittering gossamer before the breeze. He is, indeed, a most Epicurean little gentleman, dealing in quaint devices, and faring in dainty delights Prospero and his world of spirits are a set of moralists: but with Oberon and his fairies we are launched at once into the empire of the butterflies. How beautifully is this race of beings contrasted with the men and women actors in the scene, by a single epithet which Titania gives to the latter, 'the human mortals!' It is astonishing that Shakespear should be considered, not only by foreigners, but by many of our own critics, as a gloomy and heavy writer, who painted nothing but 'gorgons and hydras, and chimeras dire.' His subtlety exceeds that of all other dramatic writers, insomuch that a celebrated person of the present day said that he regarded him rather as a metaphysician than a poet. His delicacy and sportive gaiety are infinite. In the MIDSUMMER NIGHT'S DREAM alone, we should imagine, there is more sweetness and beauty of description than in the whole range of French poetry put together. What we mean is this, that we will produce out of that single play ten passages, to which we do not think any ten passages in the works of the French poets can be opposed, displaying equal fancy and imagery. Shall we mention the remonstrance of Helena to Hermia, or Titania's description of her fairy train, or her disputes with Oberon about the Indian boy, or Puck's account of himself and his employments, or the Fairy Queen's exhortation to the elves to pay due attendance upon her favourite, Bottom; or Hippolita's description of a chace, or Theseus's answer? The two last are as heroical and spirited as the others are full of lusciou tenderness. The reading of this play is like wandering in a grove by moonlight: the descriptions breathe a sweetness like odours thrown from beds of flowers.

Titania's exhortation to the fairies to wait upon Bottom, which is remarkable for a certain cloying sweetness in the repetition of the rhymes, is as follows:—

> 'Be kind and courteous to this gentleman.
> Hop in his walks, and gambol in his eyes,
> Feed him with apricocks and dewberries,
> With purple grapes, green figs and mulberries;
> The honey-bags steal from the humble bees,
> And for night tapers crop their waxen thighs,
> And light them at the fiery glow-worm's eyes,
> To have my love to bed, and to arise:
> And pluck the wings from painted butterflies,
> To fan the moon-beams from his sleeping eyes;
> Nod to him, elves, and do him courtesies.'

The sounds of the lute and of the trumpet are not more distinct than the poetry of the foregoing passage, and of the conversation between Theseus and Hippolita.

> '*Theseus.* Go, one of you, find out the forester,
> For now our observation is perform'd;
> And since we have the vaward of the day,
> My love shall hear the music of my hounds.
> Uncouple in the western valley, go,
> Dispatch, I say, and find the forester.
> We will, fair Queen, up to the mountain's top,
> And mark the musical confusion
> Of hounds and echo in conjunction.
>   *Hippolita.* I was with Hercules and Cadmus once,
> When in a wood of Crete they bay'd the bear
> With hounds of Sparta; never did I hear
> Such gallant chiding. For besides the groves,
> The skies, the fountains, every region near
> Seem'd all one mutual cry. I never heard
> So musical a discord, such sweet thunder.

> *Theseus.* My hounds are bred out of the Spartan kind,
> So flew'd, so sanded, and their heads are hung
> With ears that sweep away the morning dew;
> Crook-knee'd and dew-lap'd, like Thessalian bulls,
> Slow in pursuit, but matched in mouth like bells,
> Each under each.   A cry more tuneable
> Was never halloo'd to, nor cheer'd with horn,
> In Crete, in Sparta, nor in Thessaly:
> Judge when you hear.'—

Even Titian never made a hunting-piece of a *gusto* so fresh and lusty, and so near the first ages of the world as this.—

It had been suggested to us, that the MIDSUMMER NIGHT'S DREAM would do admirably to get up as a Christmas after-piece; and our prompter proposed that Mr. Kean should play the part of Bottom, as worthy of his great talents.   He might, in the discharge of his duty, offer to play the lady like any of our actresses that he pleased, the lover or the tyrant like any of our actors that he pleased, and the lion like 'the most fearful wild-fowl living.'   The carpenter, the tailor, and joiner, it was thought, would hit the galleries.   The young ladies in love would interest the side-boxes; and Robin Goodfellow and his companions excite a lively fellow-feeling in the children from school.   There would be two courts, an empire within an empire, the Athenian and the Fairy King and Queen, with their attendants, and with all their finery.   What an opportunity for processions, for the sound of trumpets and glittering of spears!   What a fluttering of urchins' painted wings; what a delightful profusion of gauze clouds and airy spirits floating on them!

Alas the experiment has been tried, and has failed; not through the fault of Mr. Kean, who did not play the part of Bottom, nor of Mr. Liston, who did, and who played it well, but from the nature of things.   The MIDSUMMER NIGHT'S DREAM, when acted, is converted from a delightful fiction into a dull pantomime.   All that is finest in the play is lost in the representation.   The spectacle was grand: but the spirit was evaporated, the genius was fled.—Poetry and the stage do not agree well together.   The attempt to reconcile them in this instance fails not only of effect, but of decorum.   The *ideal* can have no place upon the stage, which is a picture without perspective; everything there is in the fore-ground.   That which was merely an airy shape, a dream, a passing thought, immediately becomes an unmanageable reality.   Where all is left to the imagination (as is the case in reading) every circumstance, near or remote, has an equal chance of being kept in mind, and tells according to the mixed impression of all that has been suggested.   But the imagination cannot sufficiently qualify the actual impressions of the senses. Any offence given to the eye is not to be got rid of by explanation. Thus Bottom's head in the play is a fantastic illusion, produced by magic spells: on the stage it is an ass's head, and nothing more; certainly a very strange costume for a gentleman to appear in. Fancy cannot be embodied any more than a simile can be painted; and it is as idle to attempt it as to personate *Wall* or *Moonshine*. Fairies are not incredible, but fairies six feet high are so. Monsters are not shocking, if they are seen at a proper distance. When ghosts appear at mid-day, when apparitions stalk along Cheapside, then may the MIDSUMMER NIGHT'S DREAM be represented without injury at Covent Garden or at Drury Lane. The boards of a theatre and the regions of fancy are not the same thing.

ROMEO AND JULIET

ROMEO AND JULIET is the only tragedy which Shakespear has written entirely on a love-story. It is supposed to have been his first play, and it deserves to stand in that proud rank. There is the buoyant spirit of youth in every line, in the rapturous intoxication of hope, and in the bitterness of despair. It has been said of ROMEO AND JULIET by a great critic, that ' whatever is most intoxicating in the odour of a southern spring, languishing in the song of the nightingale, or voluptuous in the first opening of the rose, is to be found in this poem.' The description is true; and yet it does not answer to our idea of the play. For if it has the sweetness of the rose, it has its freshness too; if it has the languor of the nightingale's song, it has also its giddy transport; if it has the softness of a southern spring, it is as glowing and as bright. There is nothing of a sickly and sentimental cast. Romeo and Juliet are in love, but they are not love-sick. Every thing speaks the very soul of pleasure, the high and healthy pulse of the passions: the heart beats, the blood circulates and mantles throughout. Their courtship is not an insipid interchange of sentiments lip-deep, learnt at second-hand from poems and plays,—made up of beauties of the most shadowy kind, of 'fancies wan that hang the pensive head,' of evanescent smiles, and sighs that breathe not, of delicacy that shrinks from the touch, and feebleness that scarce supports itself, an elaborate vacuity of thought, and an artificial dearth of sense, spirit, truth, and nature! It is the reverse of all this. It is Shakespear all over, and Shakespear when he was young.

ROMEO AND JULIET

We have heard it objected to ROMEO AND JULIET, that it is founded on an idle passion between a boy and a girl, who have scarcely seen and can have but little sympathy or rational esteem for one another, who have had no experience of the good or ills of life, and whose raptures or despair must be therefore equally groundless and fantastical. Whoever objects to the youth of the parties in this play as 'too unripe and crude' to pluck the sweets of love, and wishes to see a first-love carried on into a good old age, and the passions taken at the rebound, when their force is spent, may find all this done in the *Stranger* and in other German plays, where they do things by contraries, and trans-pose nature to inspire sentiment and create philosophy. Shakespear proceeded in a more strait-forward, and, we think, effectual way. He did not endeavour to extract beauty from wrinkles, or the wild throb of passion from the last expiring sigh of indifference. He did not 'gather grapes of thorns nor figs of thistles.' It was not his way. But he has given a picture of human life, such as it is in the order of nature. He has founded the passion of the two lovers not on the pleasures they had experienced, but on all the pleasures they had *not* experienced. All that was to come of life was theirs. At that untried source of promised happiness they slaked their thirst, and the first eager draught made them drunk with love and joy. They were in full possession of their senses and their affections. Their hopes were of air, their desires of fire. Youth is the season of love, because the heart is then first melted in tenderness from the touch of novelty, and kindled to rapture, for it knows no end of its enjoyments or its wishes. Desire has no limit but itself. Passion, the love and expec-tation of pleasure, is infinite, extravagant, inexhaustible, till experience comes to check and kill it. Juliet exclaims on her first interview with Romeo—

> 'My bounty is as boundless as the sea,
> My love as deep.'

And why should it not? What was to hinder the thrilling tide of pleasure, which had just gushed from her heart, from flowing on without stint or measure, but experience which she was yet without? What was to abate the transport of the first sweet sense of pleasure, which her heart and her senses had just tasted, but indifference which she was yet a stranger to? What was there to check the ardour of hope, of faith, of constancy, just rising in her breast, but disappoint-ment which she had not yet felt! As are the desires and the hopes of youthful passion, such is the keenness of its disappointments, and their baleful effect. Such is the transition in this play from the highest bliss to the lowest despair, from the nuptial couch to an untimely grave. The only evil that even in apprehension befalls the two lovers is the loss of the greatest possible felicity, yet this loss is fatal to both, for they had rather part with life than bear the thought of surviving all that had made life dear to them. In all this, Shakespear has but followed nature, which existed in his time, as well as now. The modern philosophy, which reduces the whole theory of the mind to habitual impressions, and leaves the natural impulses of passion and imagination out of the account, had not then been discovered; or if it had, would have been little calculated for the uses of poetry.

It is the inadequacy of the same false system of philosophy to account for the strength of our earliest attachments, which has led Mr. Wordsworth to indulge in the mystical visions of Platonism in his Ode on the Progress of Life. He has very admirably described the vividness of our impressions in youth and childhood, and how 'they fade by degrees into the light of common day,' and he ascribes the change to the supposition of a pre-existent state, as if our early thoughts were nearer heaven, reflections of former trails of glory, shadows of our past being. This is idle. It is not from the knowledge of the past that the first impressions of things derive their gloss and splendour, but from our ignorance of the future, which fills the void to come with the warmth of our desires, with our gayest hopes, and brightest fancies. It is the obscurity spread before it that colours the prospect of life with hope, as it is the cloud which reflects the rainbow. There is no occasion to resort to any mystical union and transmission of feeling through different states of being to account for the romantic enthusiasm of youth; nor to plant the root of hope in the grave, nor to derive it from the skies. Its root is in the heart of man: it lifts its head above the stars. Desire and imagination are inmates of the human breast. The heaven 'that lies about us in our infancy' is only a new world, of which we know nothing but what we wish it to be, and believe all that we wish. In youth and boyhood, the world we live in is the world of desire, and of fancy: it is experience that brings us down to the world of reality. What is it that in youth sheds a dewy light round the evening star? That makes the daisy look so bright? That perfumes the hyacinth? That embalms the first kiss of love? It is the delight of novelty, and the seeing no end to the pleasure that we fondly believe is still in store for us. The heart revels in the luxury of its own thoughts, and is unable to sustain the weight of hope and love that presses upon it.—The effects of the passion of love alone might have dissipated Mr. Wordsworth's theory, if he means any thing more by it than an ingenious and poetical allegory. *That* at least is not a link in the chain let down from other worlds; 'the purple light of love' is not a dim reflection of the smiles of celestial bliss. It does not appear till the middle of life, and then seems like 'another morn risen on mid-day.' In this respect the soul comes into the world 'in utter nakedness.' Love waits for the ripening of the youthful blood. The sense of pleasure precedes the love of pleasure, but with the sense of pleasure, as soon as it is felt, come thronging infinite desires and hopes of pleasure, and love is mature as soon as born. It withers and it dies almost as soon!

This play presents a beautiful *coup-d'œil* of the progress of human life. In thought it occupies years, and embraces the circle of the affections from childhood to old age. Juliet has become a great girl, a young woman since we first remember her a little thing in the idle prattle of the nurse. Lady Capulet was about her age when she became a mother, and old Capulet somewhat impatiently tells his younger visitors,

> ——'I 've seen the day,
> That I have worn a visor, and could tell
> A whispering tale in a fair lady's ear,
> Such as would please : 'tis gone, 'tis gone, 'tis gone.'

Thus one period of life makes way for the following, and one generation pushes another off the stage. One of the most striking passages to show the intense feeling of youth in this play is Capulet's invitation to Paris to visit his entertainment.

> 'At my poor house, look to behold this night
> Earth-treading stars that make dark heav'n light;
> Such comfort as do lusty young men feel
> When well-apparel'd April on the heel
> Of limping winter treads, even such delight
> Among fresh female-buds shall you this night
> Inherit at my house.'

The feelings of youth and of the spring are here blended together like the breath of opening flowers. Images of vernal beauty appear to have floated before the author's mind, in writing this poem, in profusion. Here is another of exquisite beauty, brought in more by accident than by necessity. Montague declares of his son smit with a hopeless passion, which he will not reveal—

> 'But he, his own affection's counsellor,
> Is to himself so secret and so close,
> So far from sounding and discovery,
> As is the bud bit with an envious worm,
> Ere he can spread his sweet leaves to the air,
> Or dedicate his beauty to the sun.'

This casual description is as full of passionate beauty as when Romeo dwells in frantic fondness on 'the white wonder of his Juliet's hand.' The reader may, if he pleases, contrast the exquisite pastoral simplicity of the above lines with the gorgeous description of Juliet when Romeo first sees her at her father's house, surrounded by company and artificial splendour.

> 'What lady 's that which doth enrich the hand
> Of yonder knight ?
> O she doth teach the torches to burn bright ;
> Her beauty hangs upon the cheek of night,
> Like a rich jewel in an Æthiop's ear.'

It would be hard to say which of the two garden scenes is the finest, that where he first converses with his love, or takes leave of her the morning after their marriage. Both are like a heaven upon earth ; the blissful bowers of Paradise let down upon this lower world. We will give only one passage of these well known scenes to shew the perfect refinement and delicacy of Shakespear's conception of the female character. It is wonderful how Collins, who was a critic and a poet of great sensibility, should have encouraged the common error on this subject by saying—'But stronger Shakespear felt for man alone.'

The passage we mean is Juliet's apology for her maiden boldness.

> 'Thou know'st the mask of night is on my face ;
> Else would a maiden blush bepaint my cheek
> For that which thou hast heard me speak to-night.
> Fain would I dwell on form, fain, fain deny
> What I have spoke—but farewel compliment :
> Dost thou love me ? I know thou wilt say, ay,
> And I will take thee at thy word—Yet if thou swear'st,
> Thou may'st prove false ; at lovers' perjuries
> They say Jove laughs. Oh gentle Romeo,
> If thou dost love, pronounce it faithfully ;
> Or if thou think I am too quickly won,
> I 'll frown and be perverse, and say thee nay,
> So thou wilt woo : but else not for the world.
> In truth, fair Montague, I am too fond ;
> And therefore thou may'st think my 'haviour light ;
> But trust me, gentleman, I 'll prove more true
> Than those that have more cunning to be strange.
> I should have been more strange, I must confess
> But that thou over-heard'st, ere I was ware,
> My true love's passion ; therefore pardon me,
> And not impute this yielding to light love,
> Which the dark night hath so discovered.'

In this and all the rest, her heart, fluttering between pleasure, hope, and fear, seems to have dictated to her tongue, and ‘ calls true love spoken simple modesty.’ Of the same sort, but bolder in virgin innocence, is her soliloquy after her marriage with Romeo.

> ‘ Gallop apace, you fiery-footed steeds,
> Towards Phœbus’ mansion; such a waggoner
> As Phaëton would whip you to the west,
> And bring in cloudy night immediately.
> Spread thy close curtain, love-performing night;
> That run-aways’ eyes may wink; and Romeo
> Leap to these arms, untalked of, and unseen !——
> Lovers can see to do their amorous rites
> By their own beauties : or if love be blind,
> It best agrees with night.—Come, civil night,
> Thou sober-suited matron, all in black,
> And learn me how to lose a winning match,
> Play’d for a pair of stainless maidenhoods :
> Hold my unmann’d blood bating in my cheeks,
> With thy black mantle; till strange love, grown bold,
> Thinks true love acted, simple modesty.
> Come night !—Come, Romeo ! come, thou day in night;
> For thou wilt lie upon the wings of night
> Whiter than new snow on a raven’s back.——
> Come, gentle night; come, loving, black-brow’d night,
> Give me my Romeo : and when he shall die,
> Take him and cut him out in little stars,
> And he will make the face of heaven so fine,
> That all the world shall be in love with night,
> And pay no worship to the garish sun.——
> O, I have bought the mansion of a love,
> But not possess’d it; and though I am sold,
> Not yet enjoy’d : so tedious is this day,
> As is the night before some festival
> To an impatient child, that hath new robes,
> And may not wear them.’

We the rather insert this passage here, inasmuch as we have no doubt it has been expunged from the Family Shakespear. Such critics do not perceive that the feelings of the heart sanctify, without disguising, the impulses of nature. Without refinement themselves, they confound modesty with hypocrisy. Not so the German critic, Schlegel. Speaking of ROMEO AND JULIET, he says, ‘ It was reserved for Shakespear to unite purity of heart and the glow of imagination, sweetness and dignity of manners and passionate violence, in one ideal picture.’ The character is indeed one of perfect truth and sweetness It has nothing forward, nothing coy, nothing affected or coquettish about it;—it is a pure effusion of nature. It is as frank as it is modest, for it has no thought that it wishes to conceal   It reposes in conscious innocence on the strength of its affections.   Its delicacy does not consist in coldness and reserve, but in combining warmth of imagination and tenderness of heart with the most voluptuous sensibility.   Love is a gentle flame that rarifies and expands her whole being.   What an idea of trembling haste and airy grace, borne upon the thoughts of love, does the Friar's exclamation give of her, as she approaches his cell to be married—

> 'Here comes the lady.   Oh, so light of foot
> Will ne'er wear out the everlasting flint:
> A lover may bestride the gossamer,
> That idles in the wanton summer air,
> And yet not fall, so light is vanity.'

The tragic part of this character is of a piece with the rest.   It is the heroic founded on tenderness and delicacy.   Of this kind are her resolution to follow the Friar's advice, and the conflict in her bosom between apprehension and love when she comes to take the sleeping poison.   Shakespear is blamed for the mixture of low characters. If this is a deformity, it is the source of a thousand beauties.   One instance is the contrast between the guileless simplicity of Juliet's attachment to her first love, and the convenient policy of the nurse in advising her to marry Paris, which excites such indignation in her mistress.   'Ancient damnation! oh most wicked fiend,' etc.

Romeo is Hamlet in love.   There is the same rich exuberance of passion and sentiment in the one, that there is of thought and sentiment in the other.   Both are absent and self-involved, both live out of themselves in a world of imagination.   Hamlet is abstracted from every thing; Romeo is abstracted from every thing but his love, and lost in it.   His 'frail thoughts dally with faint surmise,' and are fashioned out of the suggestions of hope, 'the flatteries of sleep.'   He is himself only in his Juliet; she is his only reality, his heart's true home and idol.   The rest of the world is to him a passing dream. How finely is this character pourtrayed where he recollects himself on seeing Paris slain at the tomb of Juliet!—

> 'What said my man, when my betossed soul
> Did not attend him as we rode?   I think
> He told me Paris should have married Juliet.'

And again, just before he hears the sudden tidings of her death—

> 'If I may trust the flattery of sleep,
> My dreams presage some joyful news at hand;

My bosom's lord sits lightly on his throne,
And all this day an unaccustom'd spirit
Lifts me above the ground with cheerful thoughts.
I dreamt my lady came and found me dead,
(Strange dream! that gives a dead man leave to think)
And breath'd such life with kisses on my lips,
That I reviv'd and was an emperour.
Ah me! how sweet is love itself possess'd,
When but love's shadows are so rich in joy!'

Romeo's passion for Juliet is not a first love: it succeeds and drives out his passion for another mistress, Rosaline, as the sun hides the stars. This is perhaps an artifice (not absolutely necessary) to give us a higher opinion of the lady, while the first absolute surrender of her heart to him enhances the richness of the prize. The commencement, progress, and ending of his second passion are however complete in themselves, not injured if they are not bettered by the first. The outline of the play is taken from an Italian novel; but the dramatic arrangement of the different scenes between the lovers, the more than dramatic interest in the progress of the story, the developement of the characters with time and circumstances, just according to the degree and kind of interest excited, are not inferior to the expression of passion and nature. It has been ingeniously remarked among other proofs of skill in the contrivance of the fable, that the improbability of the main incident in the piece, the administering of the sleeping-potion, is softened and obviated from the beginning by the introduction of the Friar on his first appearance culling simples and descanting on their virtues. Of the passionate scenes in this tragedy, that between the Friar and Romeo when he is told of his sentence of banishment, that between Juliet and the Nurse when she hears of it, and of the death of her cousin Tybalt (which bear no proportion in her mind, when passion after the first shock of surprise throws its weight into the scale of her affections) and the last scene at the tomb, are among the most natural and overpowering. In all of these it is not merely the force of any one passion that is given, but the slightest and most unlooked-for transitions from one to another, the mingling currents of every different feeling rising up and prevailing in turn, swayed by the master-mind of the poet, as the waves undulate beneath the gliding storm. Thus when Juliet has by her complaints encouraged the Nurse to say, 'Shame come to Romeo,' she instantly repels the wish, which she had herself occasioned, by answering—

'Blister'd be thy tongue
For such a wish! He was not born to shame.

> Upon his brow shame is ashamed to sit,
> For 'tis a throne where honour may be crown'd
> Sole monarch of the universal earth !
> O, what a beast was I to chide him so ?
> *Nurse.* Will you speak well of him that kill'd your cousin ?
> *Juliet.* Shall I speak ill of him that is my husband ?
> Ah my poor lord, what tongue shall smooth thy name,
> When I, thy three-hours' wife, have mangled it ?'

And then follows on the neck of her remorse and returning fondness,
that wish treading almost on the brink of impiety, but still held back
by the strength of her devotion to her lord, that 'father, mother, nay,
or both were dead,' rather than Romeo banished. If she requires
any other excuse, it is in the manner in which Romeo echoes her
frantic grief and disappointment in the next scene at being banished
from her.—Perhaps one of the finest pieces of acting that ever was
witnessed on the stage, is Mr. Kean's manner of doing this scene
and his repetition of the word, *Banished.* He treads close indeed
upon the genius of his author.

A passage which this celebrated actor and able commentator on
Shakespear (actors are the best commentators on the poets) did not
give with equal truth or force of feeling was the one which Romeo
makes at the tomb of Juliet, before he drinks the poison.

> ———' Let me peruse this face—
> Mercutio's kinsman ! noble county Paris !
> What said my man, when my betossed soul
> Did not attend him as we rode ? I think,
> He told me Paris should have married Juliet :
> Said he not so ? or did I dream it so ?
> Or am I mad, hearing him talk of Juliet,
> To think it was so ?——O, give me thy hand,
> One writ with me in sour misfortune's book !
> I 'll bury thee in a triumphant grave——
> For here lies Juliet.

> ———O, my love ! my wife !
> Death that hath suck'd the honey of thy breath,
> Hath had no power yet upon thy beauty :
> Thou art not conquer'd ; beauty's ensign yet
> Is crimson in thy lips, and in thy cheeks,
> And Death's pale flag is not advanced there.——
> Tybalt, ly'st thou there in thy bloody sheet ?
> O, what more favour can I do to thee,
> Than with that hand that cut thy youth in twain,
> To sunder his that was thine enemy ?
> Forgive me, cousin ! Ah, dear Juliet,
> Why art thou yet so fair ! Shall I believe

That unsubstantial death is amorous;
And that the lean abhorred monster keeps
Thee here in dark to be his paramour!
For fear of that, I will stay still with thee;
And never from this palace of dim night
Depart again: here, here will I remain
With worms that are thy chamber-maids; O, here
Will I set up my everlasting rest;
And shake the yoke of inauspicious stars
From this world-wearied flesh.—Eyes, look your last!
Arms, take your last embrace! and lips, O you,
The doors of breath, seal with a righteous kiss
A dateless bargain to engrossing death!——
Come, bitter conduct, come unsavoury guide!
Thou desperate pilot, now at once run on
The dashing rocks my sea-sick weary bark!
Here's to my love!—[*Drinks.*] O, true apothecary!
Thy drugs are quick.—Thus with a kiss I die.'

The lines in this speech, describing the loveliness of Juliet, who is supposed to be dead, have been compared to those in which it is said of Cleopatra after her death, that she looked ' as she would take another Antony in her strong toil of grace '; and a question has been started which is the finest, that we do not pretend to decide. We can more easily decide between Shakespear and any other author, than between him and himself.—Shall we quote any more passages to shew his genius or the beauty of ROMEO AND JULIET? At that rate, we might quote the whole. The late Mr. Sheridan, on being shewn a volume of the Beauties of Shakespear, very properly asked—' But where are the other eleven?' The character of Mercutio in this play is one of the most mercurial and spirited of the productions of Shakespear's comic muse.

LEAR

WE wish that we could pass this play over, and say nothing about it. All that we can say must fall far short of the subject; or even of what we ourselves conceive of it. To attempt to give a description of the play itself or of its effect upon the mind, is mere impertinence: yet we must say something.—It is then the best of all Shakespear's plays, for it is the one in which he was the most in earnest. He was here fairly caught in the web of his own imagination. The passion which he has taken as his subject is that which strikes its root deepest into the human heart; of which the bond is the hardest to be unloosed; and the cancelling and tearing to pieces of which gives the greatest revulsion to the frame. This depth of nature, this force of passion, this tug and war of the elements of our being, this firm faith in filial piety, and the giddy anarchy and whirling tumult of the thoughts at finding this prop failing it, the contrast between the fixed, immoveable basis of natural affection, and the rapid, irregular starts of imagination, suddenly wrenched from all its accustomed holds and resting-places in the soul, this is what Shakespear has given, and what nobody else but he could give. So we believe.—The mind of Lear, staggering between the weight of attachment and the hurried movements of passion, is like a tall ship driven about by the winds, buffetted by the furious waves, but that still rides above the storm, having its anchor fixed in the bottom of the sea; or it is like the sharp rock circled by the eddying whirlpool that foams and beats against it, or like the solid promontory pushed from its basis by the force of an earthquake.

The character of Lear itself is very finely conceived for the purpose. It is the only ground on which such a story could be built with the greatest truth and effect. It is his rash haste, his violent impetuosity, his blindness to every thing but the dictates of his passions or affections, that produces all his misfortunes, that aggravates his impatience of them, that enforces our pity for him. The part which Cordelia bears in the scene is extremely beautiful: the story is almost told in the first words she utters. We see at once the precipice on which the poor old king stands from his own extravagant and credulous importunity, the indiscreet simplicity of her love (which, to be sure, has a little of her father's obstinacy in it) and the hollowness of her sisters' pretensions. Almost the first burst of that noble tide of passion, which runs through the play, is in the remonstrance of Kent to his royal master on the injustice of his sentence against his youngest daughter—'Be Kent unmannerly, when Lear is mad!' This manly plainness, which draws down on him the displeasure of the unadvised king, is worthy of the fidelity with which he adheres to his fallen fortunes. The true character of the two eldest daughters, Regan and Gonerill (they are so thoroughly hateful that we do not even like to repeat their names) breaks out in their answer to Cordelia who desires them to treat their father well—'Prescribe not us our duties' —their hatred of advice being in proportion to their determination to do wrong, and to their hypocritical pretensions to do right. Their deliberate hypocrisy adds the last finishing to the odiousness of their characters. It is the absence of this detestable quality that is the only relief in the character of Edmund the Bastard, and that at times reconciles us to him. We are not tempted to exaggerate the guilt of his conduct, when he himself gives it up as a bad business, and writes himself down 'plain villain.' Nothing more can be said about it. His religious honesty in this respect is admirable. One speech of his is worth a million. His father, Gloster, whom he has just deluded with a forged story of his brother Edgar's designs against his life, accounts for his unnatural behaviour and the strange depravity of the times from the late eclipses in the sun and moon. Edmund, who is in the secret, says when he is gone—'This is the excellent foppery of the world, that when we are sick in fortune (often the surfeits of our own behaviour) we make guilty of our disasters the sun, the moon, and stars: as if we were villains on necessity; fools by heavenly compulsion; knaves, thieves, and treacherous by spherical predominance; drunkards, liars, and adulterers by an enforced obedience of planetary influence; and all that we are evil in, by a divine thrusting on. An admirable evasion of whore-master man, to lay his goatish disposition on the charge of a star! My father compounded with my mother under the Dragon's tail, and my nativity was under Ursa Major: so that it follows, I am rough and lecherous. Tut! I should have been what I am, had the maidenliest star in the firmament twinkled on my bastardising.'—The whole character, its careless, light-hearted villainy, contrasted with the sullen, rancorous malignity of Regan and Gonerill, its connection with the conduct of the under-plot, in which Gloster's persecution of one of his sons and the ingratitude of another, form a counterpart to the mistakes and misfortunes of Lear,—his double amour with the two sisters, and the share which he has in bringing about the fatal catastrophe, are all managed with an uncommon degree of skill and power.

It has been said, and we think justly, that the third act of *Othello* and the three first acts of LEAR, are Shakespear's great master-pieces in the logic of passion: that they contain the highest examples not only of the force of individual passion, but of its dramatic vicissitudes and striking effects arising from the different circumstances and characters of the persons speaking. We see the ebb and flow of the feeling, its pauses and feverish starts, its impatience of opposition, its accumulating force when it has time to recollect itself, the manner in which it avails itself of every passing word or gesture, its haste to repel insinuation, the alternate contraction and dilatation of the soul, and all 'the dazzling fence of controversy' in this mortal combat with poisoned weapons, aimed at the heart, where each wound is fatal. We have seen in *Othello*, how the unsuspecting frankness and impetuous passions of the Moor are played upon and exasperated by the artful dexterity of Iago. In the present play, that which aggravates the sense of sympathy in the reader, and of uncontroulable anguish in the swoln heart of Lear, is the petrifying indifference, the cold, calculating, obdurate selfishness of his daughters. His keen passions seem whetted on their stony hearts. The contrast would be too painful, the shock too great, but for the intervention of the Fool, whose well-timed levity comes in to break the continuity of feeling when it can no longer be borne, and to bring into play again the fibres of the heart just as they are growing rigid from over-strained excitement. The imagination is glad to take refuge in the half-comic, half-serious comments of the Fool, just as the mind under the extreme anguish of a surgical operation vents itself in sallies of wit. The character was also a grotesque ornament of the barbarous times, in which alone the tragic ground-work of the story could be laid. In another point of view it is indispensable, inasmuch as while it is a diversion to the too great intensity of our disgust, it carries the pathos to the highest pitch of which it is capable, by shewing the pitiable weakness of the old king's conduct and its irretrievable consequences in the most familiar point of view. Lear may well 'beat at the gate which let his folly in,' after, as the Fool says, 'he has made his daughters his mothers.' The character is dropped in the third act to make room for the entrance of Edgar as Mad Tom, which well accords with the increasing bustle and wildness of the incidents; and nothing can be more complete than the distinction between Lear's real and Edgar's assumed madness, while the resemblance in the cause of their distresses, from the severing of the nearest ties of natural affection, keeps up a unity of interest. Shakespear's mastery over his subject, if it was not art, was owing to a knowledge of the connecting links of the passions, and their effect upon the mind, still more wonderful than any systematic adherence to rules, and that anticipated and outdid all the efforts of the most refined art, not inspired and rendered instinctive by genius.

One of the most perfect displays of dramatic power is the first interview between Lear and his daughter, after the designed affronts upon him, which till one of his knights reminds him of them, his sanguine temperament had led him to overlook. He returns with his train from hunting, and his usual impatience breaks out in his first words, 'Let me not stay a jot for dinner; go, get it ready.' He then encounters the faithful Kent in disguise, and retains him in his service; and the first trial of his honest duty is to trip up the heels of the officious Steward who makes so prominent and despicable a figure through the piece On the entrance of Gonerill the following dialogue takes place:—

    '*Lear*. How now, daughter? what makes that frontlet on?
Methinks, you are too much of late i' the frown.

LEAR

Fool. Thou wast a pretty fellow, when thou had'st no need to care for her frowning; now thou art an O without a figure: I am better than thou art now; I am a fool, thou art nothing.——Yes, forsooth, I will hold my tongue; [*To Gonerill*], so your face bids me, though you say nothing. Mum, mum.

> He that keeps nor crust nor crum,
> Weary of all, shall want some.——

That 's a sheal'd peascod!   [*Pointing to Lear.*

    Gonerill. Not only, sir, this your all-licens'd fool,
But other of your insolent retinue
Do hourly carp and quarrel; breaking forth
In rank and not-to-be-endured riots.
I had thought, by making this well known unto you,
To have found a safe redress; but now grow fearful,
By what yourself too late have spoke and done,
That you protect this course, and put it on
By your allowance; which if you should, the fault
Would not 'scape censure, nor the redresses sleep,
Which in the tender of a wholesome weal,
Might in their working do you that offence,
(Which else were shame) that then necessity
Would call discreet proceeding.

    Fool. For you trow, nuncle,

> The hedge sparrow fed the cuckoo so long,
> That it had its head bit off by its young.

So out went the candle, and we were left darkling.

    Lear. Are you our daughter?

    Gonerill. Come, sir,
I would, you would make use of that good wisdom
Whereof I know you are fraught; and put away
These dispositions, which of late transform you
From what you rightly are.

    Fool. May not an ass know when the cart draws the horse?
——Whoop, Jug, I love thee.

    Lear. Does any here know me?—Why, this is not Lear:
Does Lear walk thus? speak thus?——Where are his eyes?
Either his notion weakens, or his discernings
Are lethargy'd——Ha! waking?—'Tis not so.——
Who is it that can tell me who I am?—Lear's shadow?
I would learn that: for by the marks
Of sov'reignty, of knowledge, and of reason,
I should be false persuaded I had daughters.——
Your name, fair gentlewoman?

    Gonerill. Come, sir:
This admiration is much o' the favour
Of other your new pranks. I do beseech you
To understand my purposes aright:

As you are old and reverend, you should be wise :
Here do you keep a hundred knights and squires ;
Men so disorder'd, so debauch'd, and bold,
That this our court, infected with their manners,
Shews like a riotous inn : epicurism and lust
Make it more like a tavern, or a brothel,
Than a grac'd palace.   The shame itself doth speak
For instant remedy : be then desir'd
By her, that else will take the thing she begs,
A little to disquantity your train ;
And the remainder, that shall still depend,
To be such men as may besort your age,
And know themselves and you.
    Lear. Darkness and devils !——
Saddle my horses ; call my train together.——
Degenerate bastard ! I 'll not trouble thee ;
Yet have I left a daughter.
    Gonerill. You strike my people ; and your disorder'd rabble
Make servants of their betters.

Enter ALBANY.

    Lear. Woe, that too late repents—O, sir, are you come ?
Is it your will ? speak, sir.—Prepare my horses.——
                                 [*To Albany*
Ingratitude ! thou marble-hearted fiend,
More hideous, when thou shew'st thee in a child,
Than the sea-monster !
    Albany. Pray, sir, be patient.
    Lear. Detested kite ! thou liest.   [*To Gonerill.*
My train are men of choice and rarest parts,
That all particulars of duty know ;
And in the most exact regard support
The worships of their name.——O most small fault,
How ugly didst thou in Cordelia shew !
Which, like an engine, wrench'd my frame of nature
From the fixt place ; drew from my heart all love,
And added to the gall.   O Lear, Lear, Lear !
Beat at the gate, that let thy folly in,   [*Striking his head.*
And thy dear judgment out !——Go, go, my people !
    Albany. My lord, I am guiltless, as I am ignorant
Of what hath mov'd you.
    Lear. It may be so, my lord——
Hear, nature, hear ! dear goddess, hear !
Suspend thy purpose, if thou didst intend
To make this creature fruitful !
Into her womb convey sterility ;
Dry up in her the organs of increase ;
And from her derogate body never spring

A babe to honour her !   If she must teem,
Create her child of spleen : that it may live,
To be a thwart disnatur'd torment to her !
Let it stamp wrinkles in her brow of youth ;
With cadent tears fret channels in her cheeks ;
Turn all her mother's pains, and benefits,
To laughter and contempt ; that she may feel
How sharper than a serpent's tooth it is
To have a thankless child !——Away, away !   [*Exit.*
  Albany. Now, gods, that we adore, whereof comes this ?
  Gonerill. Never afflict yourself to know the cause ;
But let his disposition have that scope
That dotage gives it.

Re-enter LEAR.

  Lear. What, fifty of my followers at a clap !
Within a fortnight !
  Albany. What 's the matter, sir ?
  Lear. I 'll tell thee ; life and death ! I am asham'd
That thou hast power to shake my manhood thus :
                              [*To Gonerill.*
That these hot tears, which break from me perforce,
Should make thee worth them.——Blasts and fogs upon thee !
The untented woundings of a father's curse
Pierce every sense about thee !——Old fond eyes
Beweep this cause again, I 'll pluck you out ;
And cast you, with the waters that you lose,
To temper clay.——Ha ! is it come to this ?
Let it be so :——Yet have I left a daughter,
Who, I am sure, is kind and comfortable ;
When she shall hear this of thee, with her nails
She 'll flea thy wolfish visage.   Thou shalt find,
That I 'll resume the shape, which thou dost think
I have cast off for ever.

              [*Exeunt Lear, Kent, and Attendants.'*

This is certainly fine : no wonder that Lear says after it, 'O let
me not be mad, not mad, sweet heavens,' feeling its effects by anticipation ; but fine as is this burst of rage and indignation at the first
blow aimed at his hopes and expectations, it is nothing near so fine
as what follows from his double disappointment, and his lingering
efforts to see which of them he shall lean upon for support and find
comfort in, when both his daughters turn against his age and weakness.   It is with some difficulty that Lear gets to speak with his
daughter Regan, and her husband, at Gloster's castle.   In concert
with Gonerill they have left their own home on purpose to avoid
him.   His apprehensions are first alarmed by this circumstance, and

when Gloster, whose guests they are, urges the fiery temper of the Duke of Cornwall as an excuse for not importuning him a second time, Lear breaks out—

> 'Vengeance! Plague! Death! Confusion!——
> Fiery? What quality? Why, Gloster, Gloster,
> I'd speak with the Duke of Cornwall, and his wife.'

Afterwards, feeling perhaps not well himself, he is inclined to admit their excuse from illness, but then recollecting that they have set his messenger (Kent) in the stocks, all his suspicions are roused again and he insists on seeing them.

> '*Enter* CORNWALL, REGAN, GLOSTER, *and Servants.*
>
>   *Lear.* Good-morrow to you both.
>   *Cornwall.* Hail to your grace!   [*Kent is set at liberty.*
>   *Regan.* I am glad to see your highness.
>   *Lear.* Regan, I think you are; I know what reason
> I have to think so: if thou should'st not be glad,
> I would divorce me from thy mother's tomb,
> Sepulch'ring an adultress.——O, are you free?   [*To Kent.*
> Some other time for that.——Beloved Regan,
> Thy sister's naught: O Regan, she hath tied
> Sharp-tooth'd unkindness, like a vulture, here——
>   [*Points to his heart.*
> I can scarce speak to thee; thou 'lt not believe,
> Of how deprav'd a quality——O Regan!
>   *Regan.* I pray you, sir, take patience; I have hope
> You less know how to value her desert,
> Than she to scant her duty.
>   *Lear.* Say, how is that?
>   *Regan.* I cannot think my sister in the least
> Would fail her obligation; if, sir, perchance,
> She have restrain'd the riots of your followers,
> 'Tis on such ground, and to such wholesome end,
> As clears her from all blame.
>   *Lear.* My curses on her!
>   *Regan.* O, sir, you are old;
> Nature in you stands on the very verge
> Of her confine: you should be rul'd, and led
> By some discretion, that discerns your state
> Better than you yourself: therefore, I pray you,
> That to our sister you do make return;
> Say, you have wrong'd her, sir.
>   *Lear.* Ask her forgiveness?
> Do you but mark how this becomes the use?
> *Dear daughter, I confess that I am old;*

LEAR

Age is unnecessary ; on my knees I beg,
That you'll vouchsafe me raiment, bed, and food.

    Regan. Good sir, no more ; these are unsightly tricks:
Return you to my sister.

    Lear. Never, Regan :
She hath abated me of half my train ;
Look'd blank upon me ; struck me with her tongue,
Most serpent-like, upon the very heart :——
All the stor'd vengeances of heaven fall
On her ungrateful top ! Strike her young bones,
You taking airs, with lameness !

    Cornwall. Fie, sir, fie !

    Lear. You nimble lightnings, dart your blinding flames
Into her scornful eyes ! Infect her beauty,
You fen-suck'd fogs, drawn by the powerful sun,
To fall, and blast her pride !

    Regan. O the blest gods !
So will you wish on me, when the rash mood is on.

    Lear. No, Regan, thou shalt never have my curse ;
Thy tender-hefted nature shall not give
Thee o'er to harshness ; her eyes are fierce, but thine
Do comfort, and not burn : 'Tis not in thee
To grudge my pleasures, to cut off my train,
To bandy hasty words, to scant my sizes,
And, in conclusion, to oppose the bolt
Against my coming in : thou better know'st
The offices of nature, bond of childhood,
Effects of courtesy, dues of gratitude ;
Thy half o' the kingdom thou hast not forgot,
Wherein I thee endow'd.

    Regan. Good sir, to the purpose.   [*Trumpets within.*

    Lear. Who put my man i' the stocks ?

    Cornwall. What trumpet 's that ?

Enter Stewara.

    Regan. I know 't, my sister's : this approves her letter,
That she would soon be here.—Is your lady come ?

    Lear. This is a slave, whose easy-borrow'd pride
Dwells in the fickle grace of her he follows :——
Out, Varlet, from my sight !

    Cornwall. What means your grace ?

    Lear. Who stock'd my servant ? Regan, I have good hope
Thou did'st not know on 't.——Who comes here ? O heavens,

Enter GONERILL.

If you do love old men, if your sweet sway
Allow obedience, if yourselves are old,
Make it your cause ; send down, and take my part !—

Art not asham'd to look upon this beard ?—   [*To Gonerill*
O, Regan, wilt thou take her by the hand ?
   Gonerill. Why not by the hand, sir ? How have I offended ?
All 's not offence, that indiscretion finds,
And dotage terms so.
   Lear. O, sides, you are too tough !
Will you yet hold ?—How came my man i' the stocks ?
   Cornwall. I set him there, sir : but his own disorders
Deserv'd much less advancement.
   Lear. You ! did you ?
   Regan. I pray you, father, being weak, seem so.
If, till the expiration of your month,
You will return and sojourn with my sister,
Dismissing half your train, come then to me ;
I am now from home, and out of that provision
Which shall be needful for your entertainment.
   Lear. Return to her, and fifty men dismiss'd ?
No, rather I abjure all roofs, and choose
To be a comrade with the wolf and owl——
To wage against the enmity o' the air,
Necessity's sharp pinch !——Return with her !
Why, the hot-blooded France, that dowerless took
Our youngest born, I could as well be brought
To knee his throne, and squire-like pension beg
To keep base life afoot.——Return with her !
Persuade me rather to be slave and sumpter
To this detested groom.   [*Looking on the Steward.*
   Gonerill. At your choice, sir.
   Lear. Now, I pr'ythee, daughter, do not make me mad ;
I will not trouble thee, my child ; farewell :
We 'll no more meet, no more see one another :——
But yet thou art my flesh, my blood, my daughter ;
Or, rather, a disease that 's in my flesh,
Which I must needs call mine : thou art a bile,
A plague-sore, an embossed carbuncle,
In my corrupted blood. But I 'll not chide thee ,
Let shame come when it will, I do not call it :
I did not bid the thunder-bearer shoot,
Nor tell tales of thee to high-judging Jove :
Mend when thou canst ; be better, at thy leisure :
I can be patient ; I can stay with Regan,
I, and my hundred knights.
   Regan. Not altogether so, sir ;
I look'd not for you yet, nor am provided
For your fit welcome : Give ear, sir, to my sister ;
For those that mingle reason with your passion
Must be content to think you old, and so——
But she knows what she does.
   Lear. Is this well spoken now ?

Regan. I dare avouch it, sir : What, fifty followers
Is it not well ? What should you need of more ?
Yea, or so many ? Sith that both charge and danger
Speak 'gainst so great a number ? How, in one house,
Should many people, under two commands,
Hold amity ? 'Tis hard, almost impossible.

Gonerill. Why might not you, my lord, receive attendance
From those that she calls servants, or from mine ?

Regan. Why not, my lord ? If then they chanc'd to slack you,
We would controul them : if you will come to me
(For now I spy a danger) I entreat you
To bring but five-and-twenty ; to no more
Will I give place, or notice.

Lear. I gave you all——

Regan. And in good time you gave it.

Lear. Made you my guardians, my depositaries ;
But kept a reservation to be follow'd
With such a number : what, must I come to you
With five-and-twenty, Regan ! said you so ?

Regan. And speak it again, my lord : no more with me.

Lear. Those wicked creatures yet do look well-favour'd,
When others are more wicked ; not being the worst,
Stands in some rank of praise :——I 'll go with thee ;

                                                [*To Gonerill.*

Thy fifty yet doth double five-and-twenty,
And thou art twice her love.

Gonerill. Hear me, my lord ;
What need you five-and-twenty, ten, or five,
To follow in a house, where twice so many
Have a command to tend you ?

Regan. What need one ?

Lear. O, reason not the need : our basest beggars
Are in the poorest thing superfluous :
Allow not nature more than nature needs,
Man's life is cheap as beast's : thou art a lady ;
If only to go warm were gorgeous,
Why, nature needs not what thou gorgeous wear'st ;
Which scarcely keeps thee warm.——But, for true need——
You heavens, give me that patience which I need !
You see me here, you gods ; a poor old man,
As full of grief as age ; wretched in both !
If it be you that stir these daughters' hearts
Against their father, fool me not so much
To bear it tamely ; touch me with noble anger !
O, let no woman's weapons, water-drops,
Stain my man's cheeks !——No, you unnatural hags,
I will have such revenges on you both,
That all the world shall——I will do such things——
What they are, yet I know not ; but they shall be

The terrors of the earth.   You think, I 'll weep :
No, I 'll not weep :——
I have full cause of weeping ; but this heart
Shall break into a hundred thousand flaws,
Or e'er I 'll weep :——O, fool, I shall go mad !——
                              [*Exeunt Lear, Gloster, Kent, and Fool.*

If there is any thing in any author like this yearning of the heart,
these throes of tenderness, this profound expression of all that can
be thought and felt in the most heart-rending situations, we are glad
of it ; but it is in some author that we have not read.

The scene in the storm, where he is exposed to all the fury of
the elements, though grand and terrible, is not so fine, but the moralising scenes with Mad Tom, Kent, and Gloster, are upon a par with
the former.   His exclamation in the supposed trial-scene of his
daughters, 'See the little dogs and all, Tray, Blanch, and Sweet-
heart, see they bark at me,' his issuing his orders, 'Let them anato-
mize Regan, see what breeds about her heart,' and his reflection
when he sees the misery of Edgar, 'Nothing but his unkind daughters
could have brought him to this,' are in a style of pathos, where the
extremest resources of the imagination are called in to lay open the
deepest movements of the heart, which was peculiar to Shakespear
In the same style and spirit is his interrupting the Fool who asks
'whether a madman be a gentleman or a yeoman,' by answering
'A king, a king.'——

The indirect part that Gloster takes in these scenes where his
generosity leads him to relieve Lear and resent the cruelty of his
daughters, at the very time that he is himself instigated to seek the
life of his son, and suffering under the sting of his supposed ingratitude, is a striking accompaniment to the situation of Lear.   Indeed,
the manner in which the threads of the story are woven together
is almost as wonderful in the way of art as the carrying on the tide
of passion, still varying and unimpaired, is on the score of nature.
Among the remarkable instances of this kind are Edgar's meeting
with his old blind father ; the deception he practises upon him when
he pretends to lead him to the top of Dover-cliff—'Come on, sir,
here 's the place,' to prevent his ending his life and miseries together ;
his encounter with the perfidious Steward whom he kills, and his
finding the letter from Gonerill to his brother upon him which leads
to the final catastrophe, and brings the wheel of Justice 'full circle
home' to the guilty parties.   The bustle and rapid succession of
events in the last scenes is surprising.   But the meeting between Lear
and Cordelia is by far the most affecting part of them.   It has all
the wildness of poetry, and all the heart-felt truth of nature.   The

previous account of her reception of the news of his unkind treatment, her involuntary reproaches to her sisters, 'Shame, ladies,
shame,' Lear's backwardness to see his daughter, the picture of the
desolate state to which he is reduced, 'Alack, 'tis he; why he was
met even now, as mad as the vex'd sea, singing aloud,' only prepare
the way for and heighten our expectation of what follows, and
assuredly this expectation is not disappointed when through the
tender care of Cordelia he revives and recollects her.

> '*Cordelia.* How does my royal lord? How fares your
>   majesty!
>   *Lear.* You do me wrong, to take me out o' the grave:
> Thou art a soul in bliss; but I am bound
> Upon a wheel of fire, that mine own tears
> Do scald like molten lead.
>   *Cordelia.* Sir, do you know me?
>   *Lear.* You are a spirit I know: when did you die?
>   *Cordelia.* Still, still, far wide!
>   *Physician.* He's scarce awake; let him alone awhile.
>   *Lear.* Where have I been? Where am I?—Fair day-
>   light?——
> I am mightily abus'd.—I should even die with pity,
> To see another thus.—I know not what to say.——
> I will not swear these are my hands:—let's see;
> I feel this pin prick. 'Would I were assured
> Of my condition.
>   *Cordelia.* O, look upon me, sir,
> And hold your hands in benediction o'er me :——
> No, sir, you must not kneel.
>   *Lear.* Pray, do not mock me:
> I am a very foolish fond old man,
> Fourscore and upward;
> And, to deal plainly,
> I fear, I am not in my perfect mind.
> Methinks, I shou'd know you, and know this man;
> Yet I am doubtful: for I am mainly ignorant
> What place this is; and all the skill I have
> Remembers not these garments; nor I know not
> Where I did lodge last night: do not laugh at me;
> For, as I am a man, I think this lady
> To be my child Cordelia.
>   *Cordelia.* And so I am, I am!'

Almost equal to this in awful beauty is their consolation of each
other when, after the triumph of their enemies, they are led to prison.

> '*Cordelia.* We are not the first,
> Who, with best meaning, have incurr'd the worst.

> For thee, oppressed king, am I cast down;
> Myself could else out-frown false fortune's frown.—
> Shall we not see these daughters, and these sisters?
>   *Lear.* No, no, no, no! Come, let's away to prison:
> We two alone will sing like birds i' the cage:
> When thou dost ask me blessing, I'll kneel down,
> And ask of thee forgiveness: so we'll live,
> And pray, and sing, and tell old tales, and laugh
> At gilded butterflies, and hear poor rogues
> Talk of court news; and we'll talk with them too—
> Who loses, and who wins; who's in, who's out;—
> And take upon us the mystery of things,
> As if we were God's spies: and we'll wear out,
> In a wall'd prison, packs and sects of great ones,
> That ebb and flow by the moon.
>   *Edmund.* Take them away.
>   *Lear.* Upon such sacrifices, my Cordelia,
> The gods themselves throw incense.'

The concluding events are sad, painfully sad; but their pathos is extreme. The oppression of the feelings is relieved by the very interest we take in the misfortunes of others, and by the reflections to which they give birth. Cordelia is hanged in prison by the orders of the bastard Edmund, which are known too late to be counter-manded, and Lear dies broken-hearted, lamenting over her.

> '*Lear.* And my poor fool is hang'd! No, no, no life:
> Why should a dog, a horse, a rat, have life,
> And thou no breath at all? O, thou wilt come no more,
> Never, never, never, never, never!——
> Pray you, undo this button: thank you, sir.'

He dies, and indeed we feel the truth of what Kent says on the occasion—

> 'Vex not his ghost: O, let him pass! he hates him,
> That would upon the rack of this rough world
> Stretch him out longer.'

Yet a happy ending has been contrived for this play, which is approved of by Dr. Johnson and condemned by Schlegel. A better authority than either, on any subject in which poetry and feeling are concerned, has given it in favour of Shakespear, in some remarks on the acting of Lear, with which we shall conclude this account:

'The LEAR of Shakespear cannot be acted. The contemptible machinery with which they mimic the storm which he goes out in, is not more inadequate to represent the horrors of the real elements than any actor can be to represent Lear. The greatness of Lear is not in corporal dimension, but in intellectual; the explosions of his passions are terrible as a volcano: they are storms turning up and disclosing to the bottom that rich sea, his mind, with all its vast riches. It is his mind which is laid bare. This case of flesh and blood seems too insignificant to be thought on ; even as he himself neglects it. On the stage we see nothing but corporal infirmities and weakness, the impotence of rage; while we read it, we see not Lear, but we are Lear;—we are in his mind; we are sustained by a grandeur, which baffles the malice of daughters and storms; in the aberrations of his reason, we discover a mighty irregular power of reasoning, immethod-ised from the ordinary purposes of life, but exerting its powers, as the wind blows where it listeth, at will on the corruptions and abuses of mankind. What have looks or tones to do with that sublime identification of his age with that of *the heavens themselves*, when in his reproaches to them for conniving at the injustice of his children, he reminds them that "they themselves are old !" What gesture shall we appropriate to this ? What has the voice or the eye to do with such things ? But the play is beyond all art, as the temperings with it shew : it is too hard and stony : it must have love-scenes, and a happy ending. It is not enough that Cordelia is a daughter, she must shine as a lover too. Tate has put his hook in the nostrils of this Leviathan, for Garrick and his followers, the shewmen of the scene, to draw it about more easily. A happy ending !—as if the living martyrdom that Lear had gone through,—the flaying of his feelings alive, did not make a fair dismissal from the stage of life the only decorous thing for him. If he is to live and be happy after, if he could sustain this world's burden after, why all this pudder and preparation—why torment us with all this unnecessary sympathy ? As if the childish pleasure of getting his gilt robes and sceptre again could tempt him to act over again his misused station,—as if at his years and with his experience, any thing was left but to die.' [1]

Four things have struck us in reading LEAR :

1. That poetry is an interesting study, for this reason, that it relates to whatever is most interesting in human life. Whoever therefore has a contempt for poetry, has a contempt for himself and humanity.

2. That the language of poetry is superior to the language of painting ; because the strongest of our recollections relate to feelings, not to faces.

3. That the greatest strength of genius is shewn in describing the strongest passions : for the power of the imagination, in works of invention, must be in proportion to the force of the natural impressions, which are the subject of them.

4. That the circumstance which balances the pleasure against the

---

[1] See an article, called *Theatralia*, in the second volume of the *Reflector*, by Charles Lamb.

pain in tragedy is, that in proportion to the greatness of the evil, is our sense and desire of the opposite good excited; and that our sympathy with actual suffering is lost in the strong impulse given to our natural affections, and carried away with the swelling tide of passion, that gushes from and relieves the heart.

RICHARD II

RICHARD II. is a play little known compared with *Richard III.* which last is a play that every unfledged candidate for theatrical fame chuses to strut and fret his hour upon the stage in; yet we confess that we prefer the nature and feeling of the one to the noise and bustle of the other; at least, as we are so often forced to see it acted. In RICHARD II. the weakness of the king leaves us leisure to take a greater interest in the misfortunes of the man. After the first act, in which the arbitrariness of his behaviour only proves his want of resolution, we see him staggering under the unlooked-for blows of fortune, bewailing his loss of kingly power, not preventing it, sinking under the aspiring genius of Bolingbroke, his authority trampled on, his hopes failing him, and his pride crushed and broken down under insults and injuries, which his own misconduct had provoked, but which he has not courage or manliness to resent. The change of tone and behaviour in the two competitors for the throne according to their change of fortune, from the capricious sentence of banishment passed by Richard upon Bolingbroke, the suppliant offers and modest pretensions of the latter on his return to the high and haughty tone with which he accepts Richard's resignation of the crown after the loss of all his power, the use which he makes of the deposed king to grace his triumphal progress through the streets of London, and the final intimation of his wish for his death, which immediately finds a servile executioner, is marked throughout with complete effect and without the slightest appearance of effort. The steps by which Bolingbroke mounts the throne are those by which Richard sinks into the grave We feel neither respect nor love for the deposed monarch; for he is as wanting in energy as in principle: but we pity him, for he pities himself. His heart is by no means hardened against himself, but bleeds afresh at every new stroke of mischance, and his sensibility, absorbed in his own person, and unused to misfortune, is not only tenderly alive to its own sufferings, but without the fortitude to bear them. He is, however, human in his distresses; for to feel pain, and sorrow, weakness, disappointment, remorse and anguish, is the lot of humanity, and we sympathize with him accordingly. The sufferings of the man make us forget that he ever was a king.

The right assumed by sovereign power to trifle at its will with the happiness of others as a matter of course, or to remit its exercise as a matter of favour, is strikingly shewn in the sentence of banishment so unjustly pronounced on Bolingbroke and Mowbray, and in what Bolingbroke says when four years of his banishment are taken off, with as little reason.

> 'How long a time lies in one little word!
> Four lagging winters and four wanton springs
> End in a word: such is the breath of kings.'

A more affecting image of the loneliness of a state of exile can hardly be given than by what Bolingbroke afterwards observes of his having 'sighed his English breath in foreign clouds'; or than that conveyed in Mowbray's complaint at being banished for life.

> 'The language I have learned these forty years,
> My native English, now I must forego;
> And now my tongue's use is to me no more
> Than an unstringed viol or a harp,
> Or like a cunning instrument cas'd up,
> Or being open, put into his hands
> That knows no touch to tune the harmony.
> I am too old to fawn upon a nurse,
> Too far in years to be a pupil now.'—

How very beautiful is all this, and at the same time how very *English* too!

RICHARD II. may be considered as the first of that series of English historical plays, in which 'is hung armour of the invincible knights of old,' in which their hearts seem to strike against their coats of mail, where their blood tingles for the fight, and words are but the harbingers of blows. Of this state of accomplished barbarism the appeal of Bolingbroke and Mowbray is an admirable specimen. Another of these 'keen encounters of their wits,' which serve to whet the talkers' swords, is where Aumerle answers in the presence of Bolingbroke to the charge which Bagot brings against him of being an accessory in Gloster's death.

> '*Fitzwater*. If that thy valour stand on sympathies,
> There is my gage, Aumerle, in gage to thine;
> By that fair sun that shows me where thou stand'st,
> I heard thee say, and vauntingly thou spak'st it,

That thou wert cause of noble Gloster's death.
If thou deny'st it twenty times thou liest,
And I will turn thy falsehood to thy heart
Where it was forged, with my rapier's point.
   Aumerle. Thou dar'st not, coward, live to see the day.
   Fitzwater. Now, by my soul, I would it were this hour,
   Aumerle. Fitzwater, thou art damn'd to hell for this.
   Percy. Aumerle, thou liest ; his honour is as true,
In this appeal, as thou art all unjust ;
And that thou art so, there I throw my gage
To prove it on thee, to the extremest point
Of mortal breathing.   Seize it, if thou dar'st.
   Aumerle. And if I do not, may my hands rot off,
And never brandish more revengeful steel
Over the glittering helmet of my foe.
Who sets me else ? By heav'n, I 'll throw at all.
I have a thousand spirits in my breast,
To answer twenty thousand such as you.
   Surry. My lord Fitzwater, I remember well
The very time Aumerle and you did talk.
   Fitzwater. My lord, 'tis true : you were in presence then :
And you can witness with me, this is true.
   Surry. As false, by heav'n, as heav'n itself is true.
   Fitzwater. Surry, thou liest.
   Surry. Dishonourable boy,
That lie shall lye so heavy on my sword,
That it shall render vengeance and revenge,
Till thou the lie-giver and that lie rest
In earth as quiet as thy father's skull.
In proof whereof, there is mine honour's pawn :
Engage it to the trial, if thou dar'st.
   Fitzwater. How fondly dost thou spur a forward horse :
If I dare eat or drink, or breathe or live,
I dare meet Surry in a wilderness,
And spit upon him, whilst I say he lies,
And lies, and lies: there is my bond of faith,
To tie thee to thy strong correction.
As I do hope to thrive in this new world,
Aumerle is guilty of my true appeal.'

The truth is, that there is neither truth nor honour in all these noble persons: they answer words with words, as they do blows with blows, in mere self defence: nor have they any principle whatever but that of courage in maintaining any wrong they dare commit, or any falsehood which they find it useful to assert. How different were these noble knights and 'barons bold' from their more refined descendants in the present day, who, instead of deciding questions of right by brute force, refer everything to convenience fashion, and good breeding! In point of any abstract love of truth or justice, they are just the same now that they were then.

The characters of old John of Gaunt and of his brother York, uncles to the King, the one stern and foreboding, the other honest, good-natured, doing all for the best, and therefore doing nothing, are well kept up. The speech of the former, in praise of England, is one of the most eloquent that ever was penned. We should perhaps hardly be disposed to feed the pampered egotism of our countrymen by quoting this description, were it not that the conclusion of it (which looks prophetic) may qualify any improper degree of exultation.

> 'This royal throne of kings, this sceptered isle,
> This earth of Majesty, this seat of Mars,
> This other Eden, demi-Paradise,
> This fortress built by nature for herself
> Against infection and the hand of war;
> This happy breed of men, this little world,
> This precious stone set in the silver sea,
> Which serves it in the office of a wall,
> Or as a moat defensive to a house
> Against the envy of less happy lands:
> This blessed plot, this earth, this realm, this England,
> This nurse, this teeming womb of royal kings,
> Fear'd for their breed and famous for their birth,
> Renowned for their deeds as far from home,
> (For Christian service and true chivalry)
> As is the sepulchre in stubborn Jewry
> Of the world's ransom, blessed Mary's son;
> This land of such dear souls, this dear dear land,
> Dear for her reputation through the world,
> Is now leas'd out (I die pronouncing it)
> Like to a tenement or pelting farm.
> England bound in with the triumphant sea,
> Whose rocky shore beats back the envious surge
> Of wat'ry Neptune, is bound in with shame,
> With inky-blots and rotten parchment bonds.
> That England that was wont to conquer others,
> Hath made a shameful conquest of itself.'

The character of Bolingbroke, afterwards Henry IV. is drawn with a masterly hand :—patient for occasion, and then steadily availing himself of it, seeing his advantage afar off, but only seizing on it when he has it within his reach, humble, crafty, bold, and aspiring, encroaching by regular but slow degrees, building power on opinion, and cementing opinion by power. His disposition is first unfolded

by Richard himself, who however is too self-willed and secure to
make a proper use of his knowledge.

> 'Ourself and Bushy, Bagot here and Green,
> Observed his courtship of the common people:
> How he did seem to dive into their hearts,
> With humble and familiar courtesy,
> What reverence he did throw away on slaves;
> Wooing poor craftsmen with the craft of smiles,
> And patient under-bearing of his fortune,
> As 'twere to banish their affections with him.
> Off goes his bonnet to an oyster-wench;
> A brace of draymen bid God speed him well,
> And had the tribute of his supple knee,
> With thanks my countrymen, my loving friends;
> As were our England in reversion his,
> And he our subjects' next degree in hope.'

Afterwards, he gives his own character to Percy, in these words:

> 'I thank thee, gentle Percy, and be sure
> I count myself in nothing else so happy,
> As in a soul rememb'ring my good friends;
> And as my fortune ripens with thy love,
> It shall be still thy true love's recompense.'

We know how he afterwards kept his promise. His bold assertion
of his own rights, his pretended submission to the king, and the
ascendancy which he tacitly assumes over him without openly claim-
ing it, as soon as he has him in his power, are characteristic traits
of this ambitious and politic usurper. But the part of Richard
himself gives the chief interest to the play. His folly, his vices, his
misfortunes, his reluctance to part with the crown, his fear to keep
it, his weak and womanish regrets, his starting tears, his fits of hectic
passion, his smothered majesty, pass in succession before us, and make
a picture as natural as it is affecting. Among the most striking
touches of pathos are his wish 'O that I were a mockery king of
snow to melt away before the sun of Bolingbroke,' and the incident
of the poor groom who comes to visit him in prison, and tells him
how 'it yearned his heart that Bolingbroke upon his coronation-day
rode on Roan Barbary.' We shall have occasion to return hereafter
to the character of Richard II. in speaking of Henry VI. There is
only one passage more, the description of his entrance into London
with Bolingbroke, which we should like to quote here, if it had not
been so used and worn out, so thumbed and got by rote, so praised
and painted; but its beauty surmounts all these considerations.

'*Duchess.* My lord, you told me you would tell the rest,
When weeping made you break the story off
Of our two cousins coming into London.
   York. Where did I leave?
   Duchess. At that sad stop, my lord,
Where rude misgovern'd hands, from window tops,
Threw dust and rubbish on king Richard's head.
   York. Then, as I said, the duke, great Bolingbroke,
Mounted upon a hot and fiery steed,
Which his aspiring rider seem'd to know,
With slow, but stately pace, kept on his course,
While all tongues cried—God save thee, Bolingbroke!
You would have thought the very windows spake,
So many greedy looks of young and old
Through casements darted their desiring eyes
Upon his visage; and that all the walls,
With painted imag'ry, had said at once—
Jesu preserve thee! welcome, Bolingbroke!
Whilst he, from one side to the other turning,
Bare-headed, lower than his proud steed's neck,
Bespake them thus—I thank you, countrymen:
And thus still doing thus he pass'd along.
   Duchess. Alas, poor Richard! where rides he the while?
   York. As in a theatre, the eyes of men,
After a well-grac'd actor leaves the stage,
Are idly bent on him that enters next,
Thinking his prattle to be tedious:
Even so, or with much more contempt, men's eyes
Did scowl on Richard; no man cried God save him!
No joyful tongue gave him his welcome home:
But dust was thrown upon his sacred head!
Which with such gentle sorrow he shook off—
His face still combating with tears and smiles,
The badges of his grief and patience—
That had not God, for some strong purpose, steel'd
The hearts of men, they must perforce have melted,
And barbarism itself have pitied him.'

HENRY IV

IN TWO PARTS

IF Shakespear's fondness for the ludicrous sometimes led to faults in
his tragedies (which was not often the case) he has made us amends
by the character of Falstaff. This is perhaps the most substantial
comic character that ever was invented. Sir John carries a most
portly presence in the mind's eye; and in him, not to speak it

profanely, 'we behold the fulness of the spirit of wit and humour bodily.' We are as well acquainted with his person as his mind, and his jokes come upon us with double force and relish from the quantity of flesh through which they make their way, as he shakes his fat sides with laughter, or 'lards the lean earth as he walks along.' Other comic characters seem, if we approach and handle them, to resolve themselves into air, 'into thin air'; but this is embodied and palpable to the grossest apprehension: it lies 'three fingers deep upon the ribs,' it plays about the lungs and the diaphragm with all the force of animal enjoyment. His body is like a good estate to his mind, from which he receives rents and revenues of profit and pleasure in kind, according to its extent, and the richness of the soil. Wit is often a meagre substitute for pleasurable sensation; an effusion of spleen and petty spite at the comforts of others, from feeling none in itself. Falstaff's wit is an emanation of a fine constitution; an exuberance of good-humour and good-nature; an overflowing of his love of laughter and good-fellowship; a giving vent to his heart's ease, and over-contentment with himself and others. He would not be in character, if he were not so fat as he is; for there is the greatest keeping in the boundless luxury of his imagination and the pampered self-indulgence of his physical appetites. He manures and nourishes his mind with jests, as he does his body with sack and sugar. He carves out his jokes, as he would a capon or a haunch of venison, where there is *cut and come again*; and pours out upon them the oil of gladness. His tongue drops fatness, and in the chambers of his brain 'it snows of meat and drink.' He keeps up perpetual holiday and open house, and we live with him in a round of invitations to a rump and dozen.—Yet we are not to suppose that he was a mere sensualist. All this is as much in imagination as in reality. His sensuality does not engross and stupify his other faculties, but 'ascends me into the brain, clears away all the dull, crude vapours that environ it, and makes it full of nimble, fiery, and delectable shapes.' His imagination keeps up the ball after his senses have done with it. He seems to have even a greater enjoyment of the freedom from restraint, of good cheer, of his ease, of his vanity, in the ideal exaggerated description which he gives of them, than in fact. He never fails to enrich his discourse with allusions to eating and drinking, but we never see him at table. He carries his own larder about with him, and he is himself 'a tun of man.' His pulling out the bottle in the field of battle is a joke to shew his contempt for glory accompanied with danger, his systematic adherence to his Epicurean philosophy in the most trying circumstances. Again, such is his deliberate exaggeration of his own vices, that it does not seem quite certain whether the account of his hostess's bill, found in his pocket, with such an out-of-the-way charge for capons and sack with only one halfpenny-worth of bread, was not put there by himself as a trick to humour the jest upon his favourite propensities, and as a conscious caricature of himself. He is represented as a liar, a braggart, a coward, a glutton, etc. and yet we are not offended but delighted with him; for he is all these as much to amuse others as to gratify himself. He openly assumes all these characters to shew the humourous part of them. The unrestrained indulgence of his own ease, appetites, and convenience, has neither malice nor hypocrisy in it. In a word, he is an actor in himself almost as much as upon the stage, and we no more object to the character of Falstaff in a moral point of view than we should think of bringing an excellent comedian, who should represent him to the life, before one of the police offices. We only consider the number of pleasant lights in which he puts certain foibles (the more pleasant as they are opposed to the received rules and necessary restraints of society) and do not trouble ourselves about the consequences resulting from them, for no mischievous consequences do result. Sir John is old as well as fat, which gives a melancholy retrospective tinge to the character; and by the disparity between his inclinations and his capacity for enjoyment, makes it still more ludicrous and fantastical.

The secret of Falstaff's wit is for the most part a masterly presence of mind, an absolute self-possession, which nothing can disturb. His repartees are involuntary suggestions of his self-love; instinctive evasions of every thing that threatens to interrupt the career of his triumphant jollity and self-complacency. His very size floats him out of all his difficulties in a sea of rich conceits; and he turns round on the pivot of his convenience, with every occasion and at a moment's warning. His natural repugnance to every unpleasant thought or circumstance, of itself makes light of objections, and provokes the most extravagant and licentious answers in his own justification. His indifference to truth puts no check upon his invention, and the more improbable and unexpected his contrivances are, the more happily does he seem to be delivered of them, the anticipation of their effect acting as a stimulus to the gaiety of his fancy. The success of one adventurous sally gives him spirits to undertake another: he deals always in round numbers, and his exaggerations and excuses are 'open, palpable, monstrous as the father that begets them.' His dissolute carelessness of what he says discovers itself in the first dialogue with the Prince.

'*Falstaff.* By the lord, thou say'st true, lad; and is not mine hostess of the tavern a most sweet wench?

*K 65

P. Henry. As the honey of Hibla, my old lad of the castle , and is not a buff-jerkin a most sweet robe of durance ?

Falstaff. How now, how now, mad wag, what in thy quips and thy quiddities ? what a plague have I to do with a buff-jerkin ?

P. Henry. Why, what a pox have I to do with mine hostess of the tavern ? '

In the same scene he afterwards affects melancholy, from pure satisfaction of heart, and professes reform, because it is the farthest thing in the world from his thoughts. He has no qualms of conscience, and therefore would as soon talk of them as of anything else when the humour takes him.

'*Falstaff.* But Hal, I pr'ythee trouble me no more with vanity. I would to God thou and I knew where a commodity of good names were to be bought : an old lord of council rated me the other day in the street about you, sir; but I mark'd him not, and yet he talked very wisely, and in the street too.

P. Henry. Thou didst well, for wisdom cries out in the street, and no man regards it.

Falstaff. O, thou hast damnable iteration, and art indeed able to corrupt a saint. Thou hast done much harm unto me, Hal ; God forgive thee for it. Before I knew thee, Hal, I knew nothing, and now I am, if a man should speak truly, little better than one of the wicked. I must give over this life, and I will give it over, by the lord ; an I do not, I am a villain. I 'll be damn'd for never a king's son in Christendom.

P. Henry. Where shall we take a purse to-morrow, Jack ?

Falstaff. Where thou wilt, lad, I 'll make one ; an I do not, call me villain, and baffle me.

P. Henry. I see good amendment of life in thee, from praying to purse-taking.

Falstaff. Why, Hal, 'tis my vocation, Hal. 'Tis no sin for a man to labour in his vocation.'

Of the other prominent passages, his account of his pretended resistance to the robbers, 'who grew from four men in buckram into eleven ' as the imagination of his own valour increased with his relating it, his getting off when the truth is discovered by pretending he knew the Prince, the scene in which in the person of the old king he lectures the prince and gives himself a good character, the soliloquy on honour, and description of his new-raised recruits, his meeting with the chief justice, his abuse of the Prince and Poins, who overhear him, to Doll Tearsheet, his reconciliation with Mrs. Quickly who has arrested him for an old debt, and whom he persuades to pawn her plate to lend him ten pounds more, and the scenes with Shallow and Silence, are all inimitable. Of all of them, the scene in which

HENRY IV.

Falstaff plays the part, first, of the King, and then of Prince Henry, is the one that has been the most often quoted. We must quote it once more in illustration of our remarks.

'*Falstaff.* Harry, I do not only marvel where thou spendest thy time, but also how thou art accompanied: for though the camomile, the more it is trodden on, the faster it grows, yet youth, the more it is wasted, the sooner it wears. That thou art my son, I have partly thy mother's word, partly my own opinion; but chiefly, a villainous trick of thine eye, and a foolish hanging of thy nether lip, that doth warrant me. If then thou be son to me, here lies the point;——Why, being son to me, art thou so pointed at? Shall the blessed sun of heaven prove a micher, and eat blackberries? A question not to be ask'd. Shall the son of England prove a thief, and take purses? a question not to be ask'd. There is a thing, Harry, which thou hast often heard of, and it is known to many in our land by the name of pitch: this pitch, as ancient writers do report, doth defile; so doth the company thou keepest: for, Harry, now I do not speak to thee in drink, but in tears; not in pleasure, but in passion; not in words only, but in woes also:—and yet there is a virtuous man, whom I have often noted in thy company, but I know not his name.

P. Henry. What manner of man, an it like your majesty?

Falstaff. A goodly portly man, i'faith, and a corpulent; of a cheerful look, a pleasing eye, and a most noble carriage; and, as I think, his age some fifty, or, by'r-lady, inclining to threescore; and now I do remember me, his name is Falstaff: if that man should be lewdly given, he deceiveth me; for, Harry, I see virtue in his looks. If then the fruit may be known by the tree, as the tree by the fruit, then peremptorily I speak it, there is virtue in that Falstaff: him keep with, the rest banish. And tell me now, thou naughty varlet, tell me, where hast thou been this month?

P. Henry. Dost thou speak like a king? Do thou stand for me, and I'll play my father.

Falstaff. Depose me? if thou dost it half so gravely, so majestically, both in word and matter, hang me up by the heels for a rabbit-sucker, or a poulterer's hare.

P. Henry. Well, here I am set.

Falstaff. And here I stand:—judge, my masters.

P. Henry. Now, Harry, whence come you?

Falstaff. My noble lord, from Eastcheap.

P. Henry. The complaints I hear of thee are grievous.

Falstaff. S'blood, my lord, they are false:—nay, I'll tickle ye for a young prince, i'faith.

P. Henry. Swearest thou, ungracious boy? henceforth ne'er look on me. Thou art violently carried away from grace: there is a devil haunts thee, in the likeness of a fat old man; a tun of man is thy companion. Why dost thou converse with that trunk of humours, that bolting-hutch of beastliness, that swoln parcel of dropsies, that huge bombard of sack, that stuft cloak-bag of guts, that roasted Manning-tree ox with the pudding in his belly, that reverend vice, that grey iniquity, that father ruffian, that vanity in years? wherein is he good, but to taste sack and drink it? wherein neat and cleanſy, but to carve a capon and eat it? wherein cunning, but in craft? wherein crafty, but in villainy? wherein villainous, but in all things? wherein worthy, but in nothing?

Falstaff. I would, your grace would take me with you; whom means your grace?

P. Henry. That villainous, abominable mis-leader ot youth, Falstaff, that old white-bearded Satan.

Falstaff. My lord, the man I know.

P. Henry. I know thou dost.

Falstaff. But to say, I know more harm in him than in myself, were to say more than I know. That he is old (the more the pity) his white hairs do witness it: but that he is (saving your reverence) a whore-master, that I utterly deny. If sack and sugar be a fault, God help the wicked! if to be old and merry be a sin, then many an old host that I know is damned: if to be fat be to be hated, then Pharaoh's lean kine are to be loved. No, my good lord; banish Peto, banish Bardolph, banish Poins: but for sweet Jack Falstaff, kind Jack Falstaff, true Jack Falstaff, valiant Jack Falstaff, and therefore more valiant, being as he is, old Jack Falstaff, banish not him thy Harry's company; banish plump Jack, and banish all the world.

P. Henry. I do, I will.

[*Knocking; and Hostess and Bardolph go out.*

Re-enter BARDOLPH, *running.*

Bardolph. O, my lord, my lord; the sheriff, with a most monstrous watch, is at the door.

Falstaff. Out, you rogue! play out the play: I have much to say in the behalf of that Falstaff.'

One of the most characteristic descriptions of Sir John is that which Mrs. Quickly gives of him when he asks her 'What is the gross sum that I owe thee?'

'*Hostess.* Marry, if thou wert an honest man, thyself, and the money too. Thou didst swear to me upon a parcel-gilt goblet, sitting in my Dolphin-chamber, at the round table, by a sea-coal fire on Wednesday in Whitsun-week, when the prince broke thy head for likening his father to a singing man of Windsor; thou didst swear to me then, as I was washing thy wound, to marry me, and make me my lady thy wife. Canst thou deny it? Did not goodwife Keech, the butcher's wife, come in then, and call me gossip Quickly? coming in to borrow a mess of vinegar; telling us, she had a good dish of prawns; whereby thou didst desire to eat some; whereby I told thee, they were ill for a green wound? And didst thou not, when she was gone down stairs, desire me to be no more so familiarity with such poor people; saying, that ere long they should call me madam? And didst thou not kiss me, and bid me fetch thee thirty shillings? I put thee now to thy book-oath; deny it, if thou canst.'

This scene is to us the most convincing proof of Falstaff's power of gaining over the good will of those he was familiar with, except indeed

Bardolph's somewhat profane exclamation on hearing the account of his death, 'Would I were with him, wheresoe'er he is, whether in heaven or hell.'

One of the topics of exulting superiority over others most common in Sir John's mouth is his corpulence and the exterior marks of good living which he carries about him, thus 'turning his vices into commodity.' He accounts for the friendship between the Prince and Poins, from 'their legs being both of a bigness'; and compares Justice Shallow to 'a man made after supper of a cheese-paring.' There cannot be a more striking gradation of character than that between Falstaff and Shallow, and Shallow and Silence. It seems difficult at first to fall lower than the squire; but this fool, great as he is, finds an admirer and humble foil in his cousin Silence. Vain of his acquaintance with Sir John, who makes a butt of him, he exclaims, 'Would, cousin Silence, that thou had'st seen that which this knight and I have seen!'—'Aye, Master Shallow, we have heard the chimes at midnight,' says Sir John. To Falstaff's observation 'I did not think Master Silence had been a man of this mettle,' Silence answers, 'Who, I? I have been merry twice and once ere now.' What an idea is here conveyed of a prodigality of living? What good husbandry and economical self-denial in his pleasures? What a stock of lively recollections? It is curious that Shakespear has ridiculed in Justice Shallow, who was 'in some authority under the king,' that disposition to unmeaning tautology which is the regal infirmity of later times, and which, it may be supposed, he acquired from talking to his cousin Silence, and receiving no answers.

'*Falstaff.* You have here a goodly dwelling, and a rich.

Shallow. Barren, barren, barren; beggars all, beggars all, Sir John: marry, good air. Spread Davy, spread Davy. Well said, Davy.

Falstaff. This Davy serves you for good uses.

Shallow. A good varlet, a good varlet, a very good varlet. By the mass, I have drank too much sack at supper. A good varlet. Now sit down, now sit down. Come, cousin.'

The true spirit of humanity, the thorough knowledge of the stuff we are made of, the practical wisdom with the seeming fooleries in the whole of the garden-scene at Shallow's country-seat, and just before in the exquisite dialogue between him and Silence on the death of old Double, have no parallel any where else. In one point of view, they are laughable in the extreme; in another they are equally affecting, if it is affecting to shew *what a little thing is human life,* what a poor forked creature man is!

The heroic and serious part of these two plays founded on the story of Henry iv. is not inferior to the comic and farcical. The characters of Hotspur and Prince Henry are two of the most beautiful and dramatic, both in themselves and from contrast, that ever were drawn. They are the essence of chivalry. We like Hotspur the best upon the whole, perhaps because he was unfortunate.—The characters of their fathers, Henry iv. and old Northumberland, are kept up equally well. Henry naturally succeeds by his prudence and caution in keeping what he has got; Northumberland fails in his enterprise from an excess of the same quality, and is caught in the web of his own cold, dilatory policy. Owen Glendower is a masterly character. It it as bold and original as it is intelligible and thoroughly natural. The disputes between him and Hotspur are managed with infinite address and insight into nature. We cannot help pointing out here some very beautiful lines, where Hotspur describes the fight between Glendower and Mortimer.

> ——'When on the gentle Severn's sedgy bank,
> In single opposition hand to hand,
> He did confound the best part of an hour
> In changing hardiment with great Glendower:
> Three times they breath'd, and three times did they drink,
> Upon agreement, of swift Severn's flood;
> Who then affrighted with their bloody looks,
> Ran fearfully among the trembling reeds,
> And hid his crisp head in the hollow bank,
> Blood-stained with these valiant combatants.'

The peculiarity and the excellence of Shakespear's poetry is, that it seems as if he made his imagination the hand-maid of nature, and nature the plaything of his imagination. He appears to have been all the characters, and in all the situations he describes. It is as if either he had had all their feelings, or had lent them all his genius to express themselves. There cannot be stronger instances of this than Hotspur's rage when Henry iv. forbids him to speak of Mortimer, his insensibility to all that his father and uncle urge to calm him, and his fine abstracted apostrophe to honour, 'By heaven methinks it were an easy leap to pluck bright honour from the moon,' etc. After all, notwithstanding the gallantry, generosity, good temper, and idle freaks of the mad-cap Prince of Wales, we should not have been sorry, if Northumberland's force had come up in time to decide the fate of the battle at Shrewsbury; at least, we always heartily sympathise with Lady Percy's grief, when she exclaims,

> 'Had my sweet Harry had but half their numbers,
> To-day might I (hanging on Hotspur's neck)
> Have talked of Monmouth's grave.'

HENRY V.

The truth is, that we never could forgive the Prince's treatment of Falstaff; though perhaps Shakespear knew what was best, according to the history, the nature of the times, and of the man. We speak only as dramatic critics. Whatever terror the French in those days might have of Henry v. yet, to the readers of poetry at present, Falstaff is the better man of the two. We think of him and quote him oftener

HENRY V.

HENRY v. is a very favourite monarch with the English nation, and he appears to have been also a favourite with Shakespear, who labours hard to apologise for the actions of the king, by shewing us the character of the man, as 'the king of good fellows.' He scarcely deserves this honour. He was fond of war and low company :—we know little else of him. He was careless, dissolute, and ambitious ;— idle, or doing mischief. In private, he seemed to have no idea of the common decencies of life, which he subjected to a kind of regal licence; in public affairs, he seemed to have no idea of any rule of right or wrong, but brute force, glossed over with a little religious hypocrisy and archiepiscopal advice. His principles did not change with his situation and professions. His adventure on Gadshill was a prelude to the affair of Agincourt, only a bloodless one; Falstaff was a puny prompter of violence and outrage, compared with the pious and politic Archbishop of Canterbury, who gave the king *carte blanche*, in a genealogical tree of his family, to rob and murder in circles of latitude and longitude abroad—to save the possessions of the church at home. This appears in the speeches in Shakespear, where the hidden motives that actuate princes and their advisers in war and policy are better laid open than in speeches from the throne or woolsack. Henry, because he did not know how to govern his own kingdom, determined to make war upon his neighbours. Because his own title to the crown was doubtful, he laid claim to that of France. Because he did not know how to exercise the enormous power, which had just dropped into his hands, to any one good purpose, he immediately undertook (a cheap and obvious resource of sovereignty) to do all the mischief he could. Even if absolute monarchs had the wit to find out objects of laudable ambition, they could only 'plume up their wills' in adhering to the more sacred formula of the royal prerogative, 'the right divine of kings to govern wrong,' because will is only then triumphant when it is opposed to the will of others, because the pride of power is only then shewn, not when it consults the rights and interests of others, but when it insults and tramples on all justice and all humanity. Henry declares his resolution 'when France is his, to bend it to his awe, or break it all to pieces'—a resolution worthy of a conqueror, to destroy all that he cannot enslave; and what adds to the joke, he lays all the blame of the consequences of his ambition on those who will not submit tamely to his tyranny. Such is the history of kingly power, from the beginning to the end of the world;—with this difference, that the object of war formerly, when the people adhered to their allegiance, was to depose kings; the object latterly, since the people swerved from their allegiance, has been to restore kings, and to make common cause against mankind. The object of our late invasion and conquest of France was to restore the legitimate monarch, the descendant of Hugh Capet, to the throne: Henry v. in his time made war on and deposed the descendant of this very Hugh Capet, on the plea that he was a usurper and illegitimate. What would the great modern catspaw of legitimacy and restorer of divine right have said to the claim of Henry and the title of the descendants of Hugh Capet? Henry v. it is true, was a hero, a King of England, and the conqueror of the king of France. Yet we feel little love or admiration for him. He was a hero, that is, he was ready to sacrifice his own life for the pleasure of destroying thousands of other lives: he was a king of England, but not a constitutional one, and we only like kings according to the law; lastly, he was a conqueror of the French king, and for this we dislike him less than if he had conquered the French people. How then do we like him? We like him in the play. There he is a very amiable monster, a very splendid pageant. As we like to gaze at a panther or a young lion in their cages in the Tower, and catch a pleasing horror from their glistening eyes, their velvet paws, and dreadless roar, so we take a very romantic, heroic, patriotic, and poetical delight in the boasts and feats of our younger Harry, as they appear on the stage and are confined to lines of ten syllables; where no blood follows the stroke that wounds our ears, where no harvest bends beneath horses' hoofs, no city flames, no little child is butchered, no dead men's bodies are found piled on heaps and festering the next morning—in the orchestra!

So much for the politics of this play; now for the poetry. Perhaps one of the most striking images in all Shakespear is that given of war in the first lines of the Prologue.

> 'O for a muse of fire, that would ascend
> The brightest heaven of invention,
> A kingdom for a stage, princes to act,
> And monarchs to behold the swelling scene!

> Then should the warlike Harry, like himself,
> Assume the port of Mars, and *at his heels*
> *Leash'd in like hounds, should famine, sword, and fire*
> *Crouch for employment.*'

Rubens, if he had painted it, would not have improved upon this simile.

The conversation between the Archbishop of Canterbury and the Bishop of Ely, relating to the sudden change in the manners of Henry v. is among the well-known *Beauties* of Shakespear. It is indeed admirable both for strength and grace. It has sometimes occurred to us that Shakespear, in describing 'the reformation' of the Prince, might have had an eye to himself—

> 'Which is a wonder how his grace should glean it,
> Since his addiction was to courses vain,
> His companies unletter'd, rude and shallow,
> His hours fill'd up with riots, banquets, sports,
> And never noted in him any study,
> Any retirement, any sequestration
> From open haunts and popularity.
>   *Ely.* The strawberry grows underneath the nettle,
> And wholesome berries thrive and ripen best
> Neighbour'd by fruit of baser quality:
> And so the prince obscur'd his contemplation
> Under the veil of wildness, which no doubt
> Grew like the summer-grass, fastest by night,
> Unseen, yet crescive in his faculty.'

This at least is as probable an account of the progress of the poet's mind as we have met with in any of the Essays on the Learning of Shakespear.

Nothing can be better managed than the caution which the king gives the meddling Archbishop, not to advise him rashly to engage in the war with France, his scrupulous dread of the consequences of that advice, and his eager desire to hear and follow it.

> 'And God forbid, my dear and faithful lord,
> That you should fashion, wrest, or bow your reading.
> Or nicely charge your understanding soul
> With opening titles miscreate, whose right
> Suits not in native colours with the truth.
> For God doth know how many now in health
> Shall drop their blood, in approbation
> Of what your reverence shall incite us to.
> Therefore take heed how you impawn your person,
> How you awake our sleeping sword of war;

> We charge you in the name of God, take heed.
> For never two such kingdoms did contend
> Without much fall of blood, whose guiltless drops
> Are every one a woe, a sore complaint
> 'Gainst him, whose wrong gives edge unto the swords
> That make such waste in brief mortality.
> Under this conjuration, speak, my lord ;
> For we will hear, note, and believe in heart,
> That what you speak, is in your conscience wash'd,
> As pure as sin with baptism.'

Another characteristic instance of the blindness of human nature to every thing but its own interests, is the complaint made by the king of 'the ill neighbourhood' of the Scot in attacking England when she was attacking France.

> 'For once the eagle England being in prey,
> To her unguarded nest the weazel Scot
> Comes sneaking, and so sucks her princely eggs.

It is worth observing that in all these plays, which give an admirable picture of the spirit of the *good old times*, the moral inference does not at all depend upon the nature of the actions, but on the dignity or meanness of the persons committing them. 'The eagle England' has a right 'to be in prey,' but 'the weazel Scot' has none 'to come sneaking to her nest,' which she has left to pounce upon others. Might was right, without equivocation or disguise, in that heroic and chivalrous age. The substitution of right for might, even in theory, is among the refinements and abuses of modern philosophy.

A more beautiful rhetorical delineation of the effects of subordination in a commonwealth can hardly be conceived than the following :—

> 'For government, though high and low and lower,
> Put into parts, doth keep in one consent,
> Congruing in a full and natural close,
> Like music.
> ——Therefore heaven doth divide
> The state of man in divers functions,
> Setting endeavour in continual motion ;
> To which is fixed, as an aim or butt,
> Obedience : for so work the honey-bees ;
> Creatures that by a rule in nature, teach
> The art of order to a peopled kingdom.
> They have a king, and officers of sorts :
> Where some, like magistrates, correct at home
> Others, like merchants, venture trade abroad ;

Others, like soldiers, armed in their stings,
Make boot upon the summer's velvet buds ;
Which pillage they with merry march bring home
To the tent-royal of their emperor ;
Who, busied in his majesty, surveys
The singing mason building roofs of gold ;
The civil citizens kneading up the honey ;
The poor mechanic porters crowding in
Their heavy burthens at his narrow gate ;
The sad-eyed justice, with his surly hum,
Delivering o'er to executors pale
The lazy yawning drone.   I this infer,—
That many things, having full reference
To one consent, may work contrariously :
As many arrows, loosed several ways,
Come to one mark ;
As many ways meet in one town ;
As many fresh streams meet in one salt sea ;
As many lines close in the dial's centre ;
So may a thousand actions, once a-foot,
End in one purpose, and be all well borne
Without defeat.'

HENRY V. is but one of Shakespear's second-rate plays.   Yet by quoting passages, like this, from his second-rate plays alone, we might make a volume 'rich with his praise,'

' As is the oozy bottom of the sea
With sunken wrack and sumless treasuries.

Of this sort are the king's remonstrance to Scroop, Grey, and Cambridge, on the detection of their treason, his address to the soldiers at the siege of Harfleur, and the still finer one before the battle of Agincourt, the description of the night before the battle, and the reflections on ceremony put into the mouth of the king.

' O hard condition ; twin-born with greatness,
Subjected to the breath of every fool,
Whose sense no more can feel but his own wringing !
What infinite heart's ease must kings neglect,
That private men enjoy ; and what have kings,
That privates have not too, save ceremony ?
Save general ceremony ?
And what art thou, thou idol ceremony ?
What kind of God art thou, that suffer'st more
Of mortal griefs, than do thy worshippers ?
What are thy rents ? what are thy comings-in ?
O ceremony, shew me but thy worth !
What is thy soul, O adoration ?

Art thou aught else but place, degree, and form,
Creating awe and fear in other men ?
Wherein thou art less happy, being feared,
Than they in fearing.
What drink'st thou oft, instead of homage sweet,
But poison'd flattery ?   O, be sick, great greatness,
And bid thy ceremony give thee cure !
Think'st thou, the fiery fever will go out
With titles blown from adulation ?
Will it give place to flexure and low bending ?
Can'st thou, when thou command'st the beggar's knee,
Command the health of it ?   No, thou proud dream,
That play'st so subtly with a king's repose,
I am a king, that find thee : and I know,
'Tis not the balm, the sceptre, and the ball,
The sword, the mace, the crown imperial,
The enter-tissu'd robe of gold and pearl,
The farsed title running 'fore the king,
The throne he sits on, nor the tide of pomp
That beats upon the high shore of this world,
No, not all these, thrice-gorgeous ceremony,
Not all these, laid in bed majestical,
Can sleep so soundly as the wretched slave ;
Who, with a body fill'd, and vacant mind,
Gets him to rest, cramm'd with distressful bread,
Never sees horrid night, the child of hell :
But like a lacquey, from the rise to set,
Sweats in the eye of Phœbus, and all night
Sleeps in Elysium ; next day, after dawn,
Doth rise, and help Hyperion to his horse ;
And follows so the ever-running year
With profitable labour, to his grave :
And, but for ceremony, such a wretch,
Winding up days with toil, and nights with sleep,
Has the forehand and vantage of a king.
The slave, a member of the country's peace,
Enjoys it ; but in gross brain little wots,
What watch the king keeps to maintain the peace,
Whose hours the peasant best advantages.'

Most of these passages are well known : there is one, which we do not remember to have seen noticed, and yet it is no whit inferior to the rest in heroic beauty.   It is the account of the deaths of York and Suffolk.

' *Exeter.* The duke of York commends him to your majesty.
K. Henry. Lives he, good uncle ? thrice within this hour,
I saw him down ; thrice up again, and fighting ;
From helmet to the spur all blood he was.

Exeter. In which array (brave soldier) doth he lie,
Larding the plain : and by his bloody side
(Yoke-fellow to his honour-owing wounds)
The noble earl of Suffolk also lies.
Suffolk first died : and York, all haggled o'er,
Comes to him, where in gore he lay insteep'd,
And takes him by the beard ; kisses the gashes,
That bloodily did yawn upon his face ;
And cries aloud—*Tarry, dear cousin Suffolk !*
My soul shall thine keep company to heaven :
Tarry, sweet soul, for mine, then fly a-breast ;
As, in this glorious and well-foughten field,
We kept together in our chivalry !
Upon these words I came, and cheer'd him up :
He smil'd me in the face, raught me his hand,
And, with a feeble gripe, says—*Dear my lord,*
Commend my service to my sovereign.
So did he turn, and over Suffolk's neck
He threw his wounded arm, and kiss'd his lips ;
And so, espous'd to death, with blood he seal'd
A testament of noble-ending love.'

But we must have done with splendid quotations. The behaviour of the king, in the difficult and doubtful circumstances in which he is placed, is as patient and modest as it is spirited and lofty in his prosperous fortune. The character of the French nobles is also very admirably depicted ; and the Dauphin's praise of his horse shews the vanity of that class of persons in a very striking point of view. Shakespear always accompanies a foolish prince with a satirical courtier, as we see in this instance. The comic parts of HENRY V. are very inferior to those of *Henry IV.* Falstaff is dead, and without him, Pistol, Nym, and Bardolph, are satellites without a sun. Fluellen the Welchman is the most entertaining character in the piece. He is good-natured, brave, choleric, and pedantic. His parallel between Alexander and Harry of Monmouth, and his desire to have ' some disputations ' with Captain Macmorris on the discipline of the Roman wars, in the heat of the battle, are never to be forgotten. His treatment of Pistol is as good as Pistol's treatment of his French prisoner. There are two other remarkable prose passages in this play : the conversation of Henry in disguise with the three centinels on the duties of a soldier, and his courtship of Katherine in broken French. We like them both exceedingly, though the first savours perhaps too much of the king, and the last too little of the lover.

HENRY VI.

IN THREE PARTS

DURING the time of the civil wars of York and Lancaster, England was a perfect bear-garden, and Shakespear has given us a very lively picture of the scene. The three parts of HENRY VI. convey a picture of very little else; and are inferior to the other historical plays. They have brilliant passages; but the general ground-work is comparatively poor and meagre, the style 'flat and unraised.' There are few lines like the following:—

> ' Glory is like a circle in the water;
> Which never ceaseth to enlarge itself,
> Till by broad spreading it disperse to nought.'

The first part relates to the wars in France after the death of Henry v. and the story of the Maid of Orleans. She is here almost as scurvily treated as in Voltaire's Pucelle. Talbot is a very magnificent sketch: there is something as formidable in this portrait of him, as there would be in a monumental figure of him or in the sight of the armour which he wore. The scene in which he visits the Countess of Auvergne, who seeks to entrap him, is a very spirited one, and his description of his own treatment while a prisoner to the French not less remarkable.

> ' *Salisbury.* Yet tell'st thou not how thou wert entertain'd.
>   *Talbot.* With scoffs and scorns, and contumelious taunts.
> In open market-place produced they me,
> To be a public spectacle to all.
> Here, said they, is the terror of the French,
> The scarecrow that affrights our children so.
> Then broke I from the officers that led me,
> And with my nails digg'd stones out of the ground,
> To hurl at the beholders of my shame.
> My grisly countenance made others fly,
> None durst come near for fear of sudden death.
> In iron walls they deem'd me not secure:
> So great a fear my name amongst them spread,
> That they suppos'd I could rend bars of steel,
> And spurn in pieces posts of adamant.
> Wherefore a guard of chosen shot I had:
> They walk'd about me every minute-while;
> And if I did but stir out of my bed,
> Ready they were to shoot me to the heart.'

HENRY VI.

The second part relates chiefly to the contests between the nobles during the minority of Henry, and the death of Gloucester, the good Duke Humphrey. The character of Cardinal Beaufort is the most prominent in the group: the account of his death is one of our author's master-pieces. So is the speech of Gloucester to the nobles on the loss of the provinces of France by the King's marriage with Margaret of Anjou. The pretensions and growing ambition of the Duke of York, the father of Richard III. are also very ably developed. Among the episodes, the tragi-comedy of Jack Cade, and the detection of the impostor Simcox are truly edifying.

The third part describes Henry's loss of his crown: his death takes place in the last act, which is usually thrust into the common acting play of *Richard III.* The character of Gloucester, afterwards King Richard, is here very powerfully commenced, and his dangerous designs and long-reaching ambition are fully described in his soliloquy in the third act, beginning, 'Aye, Edward will use women honourably.' Henry VI. is drawn as distinctly as his highspirited Queen, and notwithstanding the very mean figure which Henry makes as a King, we still feel more respect for him than for his wife.

We have already observed that Shakespear was scarcely more remarkable for the force and marked contrasts of his characters than for the truth and subtlety with which he has distinguished those which approached the nearest to each other. For instance, the soul of Othello is hardly more distinct from that of Iago than that of Desdemona is shewn to be from Æmilia's; the ambition of Macbeth is as distinct from the ambition of Richard III. as it is from the meekness of Duncan; the real madness of Lear is as different from the feigned madness of Edgar [1] as from the babbling of the fool; the contrast between wit and folly in Falstaff and Shallow is not more characteristic though more obvious than the gradations of folly, loquacious or reserved, in Shallow and Silence; and again, the gallantry of Prince Henry is as little confounded with that of Hotspur as with the cowardice of Falstaff, or as the sensual and philosophic cowardice of the Knight is with the pitiful and cringing cowardice of Parolles. All these several personages were as different in Shakespear as they would have been in themselves: his imagination borrowed from the life, and every circumstance, object, motive, passion, operated there as it would in reality, and produced a world of men and women as distinct, as true and as various as those that

---

[1] There is another instance of the same distinction in Hamlet and Ophelia. Hamlet's pretended madness would make a very good real madness in any other author.

exist in nature. The peculiar property of Shakespear's imagination was this truth, accompanied with the unconsciousness of nature: indeed, imagination to be perfect must be unconscious, at least in production; for nature is so.—We shall attempt one example more in the characters of Richard II. and Henry VI.

The characters and situations of both these persons were so nearly alike, that they would have been completely confounded by a common-place poet. Yet they are kept quite distinct in Shakespear. Both were kings, and both unfortunate. Both lost their crowns owing to their mismanagement and imbecility; the one from a thoughtless, wilful abuse of power, the other from an indifference to it. The manner in which they bear their misfortunes corresponds exactly to the causes which led to them. The one is always lamenting the loss of his power which he has not the spirit to regain; the other seems only to regret that he had ever been king, and is glad to be rid of the power, with the trouble; the effeminacy of the one is that of a voluptuary, proud, revengeful, impatient of contradiction, and inconsolable in his misfortunes; the effeminacy of the other is that of an indolent, good-natured mind, naturally averse to the turmoils of ambition and the cares of greatness, and who wishes to pass his time in monkish indolence and contemplation.—Richard bewails the loss of the kingly power only as it was the means of gratifying his pride and luxury; Henry regards it only as a means of doing right, and is less desirous of the advantages to be derived from possessing it than afraid of exercising it wrong. In knighting a young soldier, he gives him ghostly advice—

> 'Edward Plantagenet, arise a knight,
> And learn this lesson, draw thy sword in right.'

Richard II. in the first speeches of the play betrays his real character. In the first alarm of his pride, on hearing of Bolingbroke's rebellion, before his presumption has met with any check, he exclaims—

> 'Mock not my senseless conjuration, lords:
> This earth shall have a feeling, and these stones
> Prove armed soldiers, ere her native king
> Shall faulter under proud rebellious arms.
>
> . . . . .
>
> Not all the water in the rough rude sea
> Can wash the balm from an anointed king;
> The breath of worldly man cannot depose
> The Deputy elected by the Lord.
> For every man that Bolingbroke hath prest,

> To lift sharp steel against our golden crown,
> Heaven for his Richard hath in heavenly pay
> A glorious angel; then if angels fight,
> Weak men must fall; for Heaven still guards the right.'

Yet, notwithstanding this royal confession of faith, on the very first news of actual disaster, all his conceit of himself as the peculiar favourite of Providence vanishes into air.

> ' But now the blood of twenty thousand men
> Did triumph in my face, and they are fled.
> All souls that will be safe fly from my side;
> For time hath set a blot upon my pride.'

Immediately after, however, recollecting that 'cheap defence' of the divinity of kings which is to be found in opinion, he is for arming his name against his enemies.

> ' Awake, thou coward Majesty, thou sleep'st;
> Is not the King's name forty thousand names?
> Arm, arm, my name: a puny subject strikes
> At thy great glory.'

King Henry does not make any such vapouring resistance to the loss of his crown, but lets it slip from off his head as a weight which he is neither able nor willing to bear; stands quietly by to see the issue of the contest for his kingdom, as if it were a game at push-pin, and is pleased when the odds prove against him.

When Richard first hears of the death of his favourites, Bushy, Bagot, and the rest, he indignantly rejects all idea of any further efforts, and only indulges in the extravagant impatience of his grief and his despair, in that fine speech which has been so often quoted :—

> ' *Aumerle.* Where is the duke my father, with his power?
> *K. Richard.* No matter where: of comfort no man speak:
> Let 's talk of graves, of worms, and epitaphs,
> Make dust our paper, and with rainy eyes
> Write sorrow in the bosom of the earth!
> Let 's chuse executors, and talk of wills:
> And yet not so—for what can we bequeath,
> Save our deposed bodies to the ground?
> Our lands, our lives, and all are Bolingbroke's,
> And nothing can we call our own but death,
> And that small model of the barren earth,
> Which serves as paste and cover to our bones.
> For heaven's sake let us sit upon the ground,
> And tell sad stories of the death of Kings:
> How some have been depos'd, some slain in war;

> Some haunted by the ghosts they dispossess'd;
> Some poison'd by their wives, some sleeping kill'd;
> All murder'd:—for within the hollow crown,
> That rounds the mortal temples of a king,
> Keeps death his court: and there the antic sits,
> Scoffing his state, and grinning at his pomp!
> Allowing him a breath, a little scene
> To monarchize, be fear'd, and kill with looks;
> Infusing him with self and vain conceit—
> As if this flesh, which walls about our life,
> Were brass impregnable; and, humour'd thus,
> Comes at the last, and, with a little pin,
> Bores through his castle wall, and—farewell king!
> Cover your heads, and mock not flesh and blood
> With solemn reverence; throw away respect,
> Tradition, form, and ceremonious duty,
> For you have but mistook me all this while:
> I live on bread like you, feel want, taste grief,
> Need friends, like you;—subjected thus,
> How can you say to me—I am a king?'

There is as little sincerity afterwards in his affected resignation to his fate, as there is fortitude in this exaggerated picture of his misfortunes before they have happened.

When Northumberland comes back with the message from Bolingbroke, he exclaims, anticipating the result,—

> 'What must the king do now? Must he submit?
> The king shall do it: must he be depos'd?
> The king shall be contented: must he lose
> The name of king? O' God's name let it go.
> I'll give my jewels for a set of beads;
> My gorgeous palace for a hermitage;
> My gay apparel for an alms-man's gown;
> My figur'd goblets for a dish of wood;
> My sceptre for a palmer's walking staff;
> My subjects for a pair of carved saints,
> And my large kingdom for a little grave—
> A little, little grave, an obscure grave.'

How differently is all this expressed in King Henry's soliloquy, during the battle with Edward's party:—

> 'This battle fares like to the morning's war,
> When dying clouds contend with growing light,
> What time the shepherd blowing of his nails,
> Can neither call it perfect day or night.
> Here on this mole-hill will I sit me down;

To whom God will, there be the victory!
For Margaret my Queen and Clifford too
Have chid me from the battle, swearing both
They prosper best of all when I am thence.
Would I were dead, if God's good will were so.
For what is in this world but grief and woe ?
O God ! methinks it were a happy life
To be no better than a homely swain,
To sit upon a hill as I do now,
To carve out dials quaintly, point by point,
Thereby to see the minutes how they run :
How many make the hour full complete,
How many hours bring about the day,
How many days will finish up the year,
How many years a mortal man may live.
When this is known, then to divide the times ;
So many hours must I tend my flock,
So many hours must I take my rest,
So many hours must I contemplate,
So many hours must I sport myself ;
So many days my ewes have been with young,
So many weeks ere the poor fools will yean,
So many months ere I shall shear the fleece :
So many minutes, hours, weeks, months, and years
Past over, to the end they were created,
Would bring white hairs unto a quiet grave.
Ah ! what a life were this ! how sweet, how lovely !
Gives not the hawthorn bush a sweeter shade
To shepherds looking on their silly sheep,
Than doth a rich embroidered canopy
To kings that fear their subjects' treachery ?
O yes it doth, a thousand fold it doth.
And to conclude, the shepherds' homely curds,
His cold thin drink out of his leather bottle,
His wonted sleep under a fresh tree's shade,
All which secure and sweetly he enjoys,
Is far beyond a prince's delicates,
His viands sparkling in a golden cup,
His body couched in a curious bed,
When care, mistrust, and treasons wait on him.'

This is a true and beautiful description of a naturally quiet and contented disposition, and not, like the former, the splenetic effusion of disappointed ambition.

In the last scene of *Richard II.* his despair lends him courage : he beats the keeper, slays two of his assassins, and dies with imprecations in his mouth against Sir Pierce Exton, who 'had staggered his royal person.' Henry, when he is seized by the deer-stealers, only reads them a moral lecture on the duty of allegiance and the sanctity of an oath; and when stabbed by Gloucester in the tower, reproaches him with his crimes, but pardons him his own death.

RICHARD III

RICHARD III. may be considered as properly a stage-play: it belongs to the theatre, rather than to the closet. We shall therefore criticise it chiefly with a reference to the manner in which we have seen it performed. It is the character in which Garrick came out: it was the second character in which Mr. Kean appeared, and in which he acquired his fame. Shakespear we have always with us: actors we have only for a few seasons; and therefore some account of them may be acceptable, if not to our cotemporaries, to those who come after us, if 'that rich and idle personage, Posterity,' should deign to look into our writings.

It is possible to form a higher conception of the character of Richard than that given by Mr. Kean: but we cannot imagine any character represented with greater distinctness and precision, more perfectly *articulated* in every part. Perhaps indeed there is too much of what is technically called execution. When we first saw this celebrated actor in the part, we thought he sometimes failed from an exuberance of manner, and dissipated the impression of the general character by the variety of his resources. To be complete, his delineation of it should have more solidity, depth, sustained and impassioned feeling, with somewhat less brilliancy, with fewer glancing lights, pointed transitions, and pantomimic evolutions.

The Richard of Shakespear is towering and lofty; equally impetuous and commanding; haughty, violent, and subtle; bold and treacherous; confident in his strength as well as in his cunning; raised high by his birth, and higher by his talents and his crimes; a royal usurper, a princely hypocrite, a tyrant, and a murderer of the house of Plantagenet.

> 'But I was born so high:
> Our aery buildeth in the cedar's top,
> And dallies with the wind, and scorns the sun.'

The idea conveyed in these lines (which are indeed omitted in the miserable medley acted for RICHARD III.) is never lost sight of by Shakespear, and should not be out of the actor's mind for a moment.

RICHARD III.

The restless and sanguinary Richard is not a man striving to be great, but to be greater than he is; conscious of his strength of will, his power of intellect, his daring courage, his elevated station; and making use of these advantages to commit unheard-of crimes, and to shield himself from remorse and infamy.

If Mr. Kean does not entirely succeed in concentrating all the lines of the character, as drawn by Shakespear, he gives an animation, vigour, and relief to the part which we have not seen equalled. He is more refined than Cooke; more bold, varied, and original than Kemble in the same character. In some parts he is deficient in dignity, and particularly in the scenes of state business, he has by no means an air of artificial authority. There is at times an aspiring elevation, an enthusiastic rapture in his expectations of attaining the crown, and at others a gloating expression of sullen delight, as if he already clenched the bauble, and held it in his grasp. The courtship scene with Lady Anne is an admirable exhibition of smooth and smiling villainy. The progress of wily adulation, of encroaching humility, is finely marked by his action, voice and eye. He seems, like the first Tempter, to approach his prey, secure of the event, and as if success had smoothed his way before him. The late Mr. Cooke's manner of representing this scene was more vehement, hurried, and full of anxious uncertainty. This, though more natural in general, was less in character in this particular instance. Richard should woo less as a lover than as an actor—to shew his mental superiority, and power of making others the playthings of his purposes. Mr. Kean's attitude in leaning against the side of the stage before he comes forward to address Lady Anne, is one of the most graceful and striking ever witnessed on the stage. It would do for Titian to paint. The frequent and rapid transition of his voice from the expression of the fiercest passion to the most familiar tones of conversation was that which gave a peculiar grace of novelty to his acting on his first appearance. This has been since imitated and caricatured by others, and he himself uses the artifice more sparingly than he did. His bye-play is excellent. His manner of bidding his friends ' Good night,' after pausing with the point of his sword, drawn slowly backward and forward on the ground, as if considering the plan of the battle next day, is a particularly happy and natural thought. He gives to the two last acts of the play the greatest animation and effect. He fills every part of the stage; and makes up for the deficiency of his person by what has been sometimes objected to as an excess of action. The concluding scene in which he is killed by Richmond is the most brilliant of the whole. He fights at last like one drunk with wounds; and the attitude in which he stands with his hands stretched out, after his sword is wrested from him, has a preternatural and terrific grandeur, as if his will could not be disarmed, and the very phantoms of his despair had power to kill.—Mr. Kean has since in a great measure effaced the impression of his Richard III. by the superior efforts of his genius in Othello (his master-piece), in the murder-scene in Macbeth, in Richard II., in Sir Giles Overreach, and lastly in Oroonoko; but we still like to look back to his first performance of this part, both because it first assured his admirers of his future success, and because we bore our feeble but, at that time, not useless testimony to the merits of this very original actor, on which the town was considerably divided for no other reason than because they *were* original.

The manner in which Shakespear's plays have been generally altered or rather mangled by modern mechanists, is a disgrace to the English stage. The patch-work RICHARD III. which is acted under the sanction of his name, and which was manufactured by Cibber, is a striking example of this remark.

The play itself is undoubtedly a very powerful effusion of Shakespear's genius. The ground-work of the character of Richard, that mixture of intellectual vigour with moral depravity, in which Shakespear delighted to shew his strength — gave full scope as well as temptation to the exercise of his imagination. The character of his hero is almost every where predominant, and marks its lurid track throughout. The original play is however too long for representation, and there are some few scenes which might be better spared than preserved, and by omitting which it would remain a complete whole. The only rule, indeed, for altering Shakespear is to retrench certain passages which may be considered either as superfluous or obsolete, but not to add or transpose any thing. The arrangement and developement of the story, and the mutual contrast and combination of the *dramatis personæ*, are in general as finely managed as the developement of the characters or the expression of the passions.

This rule has not been adhered to in the present instance. Some of the most important and striking passages in the principal character have been omitted, to make room for idle and misplaced extracts from other plays; the only intention of which seems to have been to make the character of Richard as odious and disgusting as possible. It is apparently for no other purpose than to make Gloucester stab King Henry on the stage, that the fine abrupt introduction of the character in the opening of the play is lost in the tedious whining morality of the uxorious king (taken from another play);—we say *tedious*, because it interrupts the business of the scene, and loses its beauty and effect by having no intelligible connection with the previous

3OO

character of the mild, well-meaning monarch. The passages which the unfortunate Henry has to recite are beautiful and pathetic in themselves, but they have nothing to do with the world that Richard has to ' bustle in.' In the same spirit of vulgar caricature is the scene between Richard and Lady Anne (when his wife) interpolated without any authority, merely to gratify this favourite propensity to disgust and loathing. With the same perverse consistency, Richard, after his last fatal struggle, is raised up by some Galvanic process, to utter the imprecation, without any motive but pure malignity, which Shakespear has so properly put into the mouth of Northumberland on hearing of Percy's death. To make room for these worse than needless additions, many of the most striking passages in the real play have been omitted by the foppery and ignorance of the prompt-book critics. We do not mean to insist merely on passages which are fine as poetry and to the reader, such as Clarence's dream, etc. but on those which are important to the understanding of the character, and peculiarly adapted for stage-effect. We will give the following as instances among several others. The first is the scene where Richard enters abruptly to the queen and her friends to defend himself :—

> '*Gloucester.* They do me wrong, and I will not endure it.
> Who are they that complain unto the king,
> That I forsooth am stern, and love them not ?
> By holy Paul, they love his grace but lightly,
> That fill his ears with such dissentious rumours :
> Because I cannot flatter and look fair,
> Smile in men's faces, smooth, deceive, and cog,
> Duck with French nods, and apish courtesy,
> I must be held a rancorous enemy.
> Cannot a plain man live, and think no harm,
> But thus his simple truth must be abus'd
> With silken, sly, insinuating Jacks ?
>   *Gray.* To whom in all this presence speaks your grace ?
>   *Gloucester.* To thee, that hast nor honesty nor grace ;
> When have I injur'd thee, when done thee wrong ?
> Or thee ? or thee ? or any of your faction ?
> A plague upon you all ! '

Nothing can be more characteristic than the turbulent pretensions to meekness and simplicity in this address. Again, the versatility and adroitness of Richard is admirably described in the following ironical conversation with Brakenbury :—

> · *Brakenbury.* I beseech your graces both to pardon me.
> His majesty hath straitly given in charge,
> That no man shall have private conference,
> Of what degree soever, with your brother.

Gloucester. E'en so, and please your worship, Brakenbury.
You may partake of any thing we say:
We speak no treason, man—we say the king
Is wise and virtuous, and his noble queen
Well strook in years, fair, and not jealous.
We say that Shore's wife hath a pretty foot,
A cherry lip,
A bonny eye, a passing pleasing tongue;
That the queen's kindred are made gentlefolks.
How say you, sir?   Can you deny all this?
    Brakenbury. With this, my lord, myself have nought to do.
    Gloucester. What, fellow, naught to do with mistress Shore?
I tell you, sir, he that doth naught with her,
Excepting one, were best to do it secretly alone.
    Brakenbury. What one, my lord?
    Gloucester. Her husband, knave—would'st thou betray me?'

The feigned reconciliation of Gloucester with the queen's kinsmen is also a master-piece. One of the finest strokes in the play, and which serves to shew as much as any thing the deep, plausible manners of Richard, is the unsuspecting security of Hastings, at the very time when the former is plotting his death, and when that very appearance of cordiality and good-humour on which Hastings builds his confidence arises from Richard's consciousness of having betrayed him to his ruin. This, with the whole character of Hastings, is omitted.

Perhaps the two most beautiful passages in the original play are the farewell apostrophe of the queen to the Tower, where the children are shut up from her, and Tyrrel's description of their death. We will finish our quotations with them.

    ' *Queen.* Stay, yet look back with me unto the Tower;
Pity, you ancient stones, those tender babes,
Whom envy hath immured within your walls;
Rough cradle for such little pretty ones,
Rude, rugged nurse, old sullen play-fellow,
For tender princes!'

The other passage is the account of their death by Tyrrel:—

'Dighton and Forrest, whom I did suborn
To do this piece of ruthless butchery,
Albeit they were flesh'd villains, bloody dogs,—
Melting with tenderness and mild compassion,
Wept like to children in their death's sad story:
O thus! quoth Dighton, lay the gentle babes;
Thus, thus, quoth Forrest, girdling one another
Within their innocent alabaster arms;
Their lips were four red roses on a stalk,

And in that summer beauty kissed each other ;
A book of prayers on their pillow lay,
Which once, quoth Forrest, almost changed my mind :
But oh the devil !—there the villain stopped ;
When Dighton thus told on—we smothered
The most replenished sweet work of nature,
That from the prime creation ere she framed.'

These are some of those wonderful bursts of feeling, done to the life, to the very height of fancy and nature, which our Shakespear alone could give. We do not insist on the repetition of these last passages as proper for the stage : we should indeed be loth to trust them in the mouth of almost any actor : but we should wish them to be retained in preference at least to the fantoccini exhibition of the young princes, Edward and York, bandying childish wit with their uncle

HENRY VIII.

THIS play contains little action or violence of passion, yet it has considerable interest of a more mild and thoughtful cast, and some of the most striking passages in the author's works. The character of Queen Katherine is the most perfect delineation of matronly dignity, sweetness, and resignation, that can be conceived. Her appeals to the protection of the king, her remonstrances to the cardinals, her conversations with her women, shew a noble and generous spirit accompanied with the utmost gentleness of nature. What can be more affecting than her answer to Campeius and Wolsey, who come to visit her as pretended friends.

——'Nay, forsooth, my friends,
They that must weigh out my afflictions,
They that my trust must grow to, live not here ;
They are, as all my comforts are, far hence,
In mine own country, lords.'

Dr. Johnson observes of this play, that 'the meek sorrows and virtuous distress of Katherine have furnished some scenes, which may be justly numbered among the greatest efforts of tragedy. But the genius of Shakespear comes in and goes out with Katherine. Every other part may be easily conceived and easily written.' This is easily said ; but with all due deference to so great a reputed authority as that of Johnson, it is not true. For instance, the scene of Buckingham led to execution is one of the most affecting and natural in Shakespear, and one to which there is hardly an approach in any other author. Again, the character of Wolsey, the description of his pride and of his fall, are inimitable, and have, besides their gorgeousness of effect, a pathos, which only the genius of Shakespear could lend to the distresses of a proud, bad man, like Wolsey. There is a sort of child-like simplicity in the very helplessness of his situation, arising from the recollection of his past overbearing ambition. After the cutting sarcasms of his enemies on his disgrace, against which he bears up with a spirit conscious of his own superiority, he breaks out into that fine apostrophe—

> 'Farewell, a long farewell, to all my greatness !
> This is the state of man; to-day he puts forth
> The tender leaves of hope, to-morrow blossoms,
> And bears his blushing honours thick upon him ;
> The third day comes a frost, a killing frost;
> And—when he thinks, good easy man, full surely
> His greatness is a ripening—nips his root,
> And then he falls, as I do. I have ventur'd,
> Like little wanton boys that swim on bladders
> These many summers in a sea of glory;
> But far beyond my depth : my high-blown pride
> At length broke under me; and now has left me,
> Weary and old with service, to the mercy
> Of a rude stream, that must for ever hide me.
> Vain pomp and glory of the world, I hate ye !
> I feel my heart new open'd : O how wretched
> Is that poor man, that hangs on princes' favours.
> There is betwixt that smile we would aspire to,
> That sweet aspect of princes, and our ruin,
> More pangs and fears than war and women have ;
> And when he falls, he falls like Lucifer,
> Never to hope again !'—

There is in this passage, as well as in the well-known dialogue with Cromwell which follows, something which stretches beyond commonplace ; nor is the account which Griffiths gives of Wolsey's death less Shakespearian ; and the candour with which Queen Katherine listens to the praise of ' him whom of all men while living she hated most ' adds the last graceful finishing to her character.

Among other images of great individual beauty might be mentioned the description of the effect of Ann Boleyn's presenting herself to the crowd at her coronation.

> ——'While her grace sat down
> To rest awhile, some half an hour or so,
> In a rich chair of state, opposing freely

> The beauty of her person to the people.
> Believe me, sir, she is the goodliest woman
> That ever lay by man. Which when the people
> Had the full view of, *such a noise arose*
> *As the shrouds make at sea in a stiff tempest,*
> *As loud and to as many tunes.'*

The character of Henry VIII. is drawn with great truth and spirit. It is like a very disagreeable portrait, sketched by the hand of a master. His gross appearance, his blustering demeanour, his vulgarity, his arrogance, his sensuality, his cruelty, his hypocrisy, his want of common decency and common humanity, are marked in strong lines. His traditional peculiarities of expression complete the reality of the picture. The authoritative expletive, 'Ha!' with which he intimates his indignation or surprise, has an effect like the first startling sound that breaks from a thunder-cloud. He is of all the monarchs in our history the most disgusting: for he unites in himself all the vices of barbarism and refinement, without their virtues. Other kings before him (such as Richard III.) were tyrants and murderers out of ambition or necessity: they gained or established unjust power by violent means: they destroyed their enemies, or those who barred their access to the throne or made its tenure insecure. But Henry VIII.'s power is most fatal to those whom he loves: he is cruel and remorseless to pamper his luxurious appetites: bloody and voluptuous; an amorous murderer; an uxorious debauchee. His hardened insensibility to the feelings of others is strengthened by the most profligate self-indulgence. The religious hypocrisy, under which he masks his cruelty and his lust, is admirably displayed in the speech in which he describes the first misgivings of his conscience and its increasing throes and terrors, which have induced him to divorce his queen. The only thing in his favour in this play is his treatment of Cranmer: there is also another circumstance in his favour, which is his patronage of Hans Holbein.—It has been said of Shakespear—'No maid could live near such a man.' It might with as good reason be said—'No king could live near such a man.' His eye would have penetrated through the pomp of circumstance and the veil of opinion. As it is, he has represented such persons to the life—his plays are in this respect the glass of history—he has done them the same justice as if he had been a privy counsellor all his life, and in each successive reign. Kings ought never to be seen upon the stage. In the abstract, they are very disagreeable characters: it is only while living that they are 'the best of kings.' It is their power, their splendour, it is the apprehension of the personal consequences of their favour or their hatred that dazzles the imagination and suspends the judgment of their favourites or their vassals; but death cancels the bond of allegiance and of interest; and seen *as they were*, their power and their pretensions look monstrous and ridiculous. The charge brought against modern philosophy as inimical to loyalty is unjust, because it might as well be brought against other things. No reader of history can be a lover of kings. We have often wondered that Henry viii. as he is drawn by Shakespear, and as we have seen him represented in all the bloated deformity of mind and person, is not hooted from the English stage.

KING JOHN

KING JOHN is the last of the historical plays we shall have to speak of; and we are not sorry that it is. If we are to indulge our imaginations, we had rather do it upon an imaginary theme; if we are to find subjects for the exercise of our pity and terror, we prefer seeking them in fictitious danger and fictitious distress. It gives a *soreness* to our feelings of indignation or sympathy, when we know that in tracing the progress of sufferings and crimes, we are treading upon real ground, and recollect that the poet's dream '*denoted a foregone conclusion*'—irrevocable ills, not conjured up by fancy, but placed beyond the reach of poetical justice. That the treachery of King John, the death of Arthur, the grief of Constance, had a real truth in history, sharpens the sense of pain, while it hangs a leaden weight on the heart and the imagination. Something whispers us that we have no right to make a mock of calamities like these, or to turn the truth of things into the puppet and plaything of our fancies. 'To consider thus' may be 'to consider too curiously'; but still we think that the actual truth of the particular events, in proportion as we are conscious of it, is a drawback on the pleasure as well as the dignity of tragedy.

KING JOHN has all the beauties of language and all the richness of the imagination to relieve the painfulness of the subject. The character of King John himself is kept pretty much in the background; it is only marked in by comparatively slight indications. The crimes he is tempted to commit are such as are thrust upon him rather by circumstances and opportunity than of his own seeking: he is here represented as more cowardly than cruel, and as more contemptible than odious. The play embraces only a part of his history. There are however few characters on the stage that excite more disgust and loathing. He has no intellectual grandeur or strength of character to shield him from the indignation which his immediate conduct provokes: he stands naked and defenceless, in that respect, to the worst we can think of him: and besides, we are impelled to put the very worst construction on his meanness and cruelty by the tender picture of the beauty and helplessness of the object of it, as well as by the frantic and heart-rending pleadings of maternal despair. We do not forgive him the death of Arthur, because he had too late revoked his doom and tried to prevent it; and perhaps because he has himself repented of his black design, our *moral sense* gains courage to hate him the more for it. We take him at his word, and think his purposes must be odious indeed, when he himself shrinks back from them. The scene in which King John suggests to Hubert the design of murdering his nephew is a master-piece of dramatic skill, but it is still inferior, very inferior to the scene between Hubert and Arthur, when the latter learns the orders to put out his eyes. If any thing ever was penned, heart-piercing, mixing the extremes of terror and pity, of that which shocks and that which soothes the mind, it is this scene. We will give it entire, though perhaps it is tasking the reader's sympathy too much.

'*Enter* HUBERT *and Executioner.*

Hubert. Heat me these irons hot, and look you stand
Within the arras; when I strike my foot
Upon the bosom of the ground, rush forth
And bind the boy, which you shall find with me,
Fast to the chair: be heedful: hence, and watch.
  Executioner. I hope your warrant will bear out the deed.
  Hubert. Uncleanly scruples! fear not you; look to 't.—
Young lad, come forth; I have to say with you.

Enter ARTHUR.

Arthur. Good morrow, Hubert.
  Hubert. Morrow, little Prince.
  Arthur. As little prince (having so great a title
To be more prince) as may be. You are sad.
  Hubert. Indeed I have been merrier.
  Arthur. Mercy on me!
Methinks no body should be sad but I;
Yet I remember when I was in France,
Young gentlemen would be as sad as night,
Only for wantonness. By my Christendom,
So were I out of prison, and kept sheep,
I should be merry as the day is long.
And so I would be here, but that I doubt
My uncle practises more harm to me.
He is afraid of me, and I of him.

Is it my fault that I was Geoffrey's son?
Indeed it is not, and I would to heav'n
I were your son, so you would love me, Hubert.
  Hubert. If I talk to him, with his innocent prate
He will awake my mercy, which lies dead ;
Therefore I will be sudden, and dispatch.   *[Aside.*
  Arthur. Are you sick, Hubert? you look pale to-day?
In sooth, I would you were a little sick,
That I might sit all night and watch with you.
Alas, I love you more than you do me.
  Hubert. His words do take possession of my bosom.
Read here, young Arthur—   *[Shewing a paper.*
How now, foolish rheum,   *[Aside.*
Turning dis-piteous torture out of door !
I must be brief, lest resolution drop
Out at mine eyes in tender womanish tears.—
Can you not read it? Is it not fair writ?
  Arthur. Too fairly, Hubert, for so foul effect.
Must you with irons burn out both mine eyes?
  Hubert. Young boy, I must.
  Arthur. And will you?
  Hubert. And I will.
  Arthur. Have you the heart? When your head did but ache,
I knit my handkerchief about your brows,
(The best I had, a princess wrought it me)
And I did never ask it you again ;
And with my hand at midnight held your head;
And like the watchful minutes to the hour,
Still and anon chear'd up the heavy time,
Saying, what lack you? and where lies your grief?
Or, what good love may I perform for you?
Many a poor man's son would have lain still,
And ne'er have spoke a loving word to you;
But you at your sick service had a prince.
Nay, you may think my love was crafty love,
And call it cunning. Do, and if you will :
If heav'n be pleas'd that you must use me ill,
Why then you must——Will you put out mine eyes?
These eyes, that never did, and never shall,
So much as frown on you?
  Hubert. I've sworn to do it;
And with hot irons must I burn them out.
  Arthur. Oh if an angel should have come to me,
And told me Hubert should put out mine eyes,
I would not have believ'd a tongue but Hubert's.
  Hubert. Come forth; do as I bid you.   *[Stamps, and the men enter*
  Arthur. O save me, Hubert, save me! my eyes are out
Ev'n with the fierce looks of these bloody men.
  Hubert. Give me the iron, I say, and bind him here.

KING JOHN

Arthur. Alas, what need you be so boist'rous rough?
I will not struggle, I will stand stone-still.
For heav'n's sake, Hubert, let me not be bound!
Nay, hear me, Hubert! drive these men away,
And I will sit as quiet as a lamb:
I will not stir, nor wince, nor speak a word,
Nor look upon the iron angrily:
Thrust but these men away, and I'll forgive you,
Whatever torment you do put me to.

    Hubert. Go, stand within; let me alone with him.

    Executioner. I am best pleas'd to be from such a deed.   [*Exit.*

    Arthur. Alas, I then have chid away my friend.
He hath a stern look, but a gentle heart;
Let him come back, that his compassion may
Give life to yours.

    Hubert. Come, boy, prepare yourself.

    Arthur. Is there no remedy?

    Hubert. None, but to lose your eyes.

    Arthur. O heav'n! that there were but a mote in yours,
A grain, a dust, a gnat, a wand'ring hair,
Any annoyance in that precious sense!
Then, feeling what small things are boist'rous there,
Your vile intent must needs seem horrible.

    Hubert. Is this your promise? go to, hold your tongue.

    Arthur. Let me not hold my tongue; let me not, Hubert;
Or, Hubert, if you will, cut out my tongue,
So I may keep mine eyes. O spare mine eyes!
Though to no use, but still to look on you.
Lo, by my troth, the instrument is cold,
And would not harm me.

    Hubert. I can heat it, boy.

    Arthur. No, in good sooth, the fire is dead with grief,
Being create for comfort, to be us'd
In undeserv'd extremes; see else yourself,
There is no malice in this burning coal;
The breath of heav'n hath blown its spirit out,
And strew'd repentant ashes on its head.

    Hubert. But with my breath I can revive it, boy.

    Arthur. All things that you shall use to do me wrong,
Deny their office; only you do lack
That mercy which fierce fire and iron extend,
Creatures of note for mercy-lacking uses.

    Hubert. Well, see to live; I will not touch thine eyes
For all the treasure that thine uncle owns:
Yet I am sworn, and I did purpose, boy,
With this same very iron to burn them out.

    Arthur. O, now you look like Hubert. All this while
You were disguised.

    Hubert. Peace; no more. Adieu,

Your uncle must not know but you are dead.
I'll fill these dogged spies with false reports:
And, pretty child, sleep doubtless and secure,
That Hubert, for the wealth of all the world,
Will not offend thee.
    Arthur. O heav'n! I thank you, Hubert.
    Hubert. Silence, no more; go closely in with me;
Much danger do I undergo for thee.   *[Exeunt.'*

His death afterwards, when he throws himself from his prison walls, excites the utmost pity for his innocence and friendless situation, and well justifies the exaggerated denunciations of Falconbridge to Hubert, whom he suspects wrongfully of the deed.

   'There is not yet so ugly a fiend of hell
   As thou shalt be, if thou did'st kill this child.
   —If thou did'st but consent
   To this most cruel act, do but despair:
   And if thou want'st a cord, the smallest thread
   That ever spider twisted from her womb
   Will strangle thee; a rush will be a beam
   To hang thee on: or would'st thou drown thyself,
   Put but a little water in a spoon,
   And it shall be as all the ocean,
   Enough to stifle such a villain up.'

The excess of maternal tenderness, rendered desperate by the fickleness of friends and the injustice of fortune, and made stronger in will, in proportion to the want of all other power, was never more finely expressed than in Constance. The dignity of her answer to King Philip, when she refuses to accompany his messenger, 'To me and to the state of my great grief, let kings assemble,' her indignant reproach to Austria for deserting her cause, her invocation to death, 'that love of misery,' however fine and spirited, all yield to the beauty of the passage, where, her passion subsiding into tenderness, she addresses the Cardinal in these words:—

   'Oh father Cardinal, I have heard you say
   That we shall see and know our friends in heav'n:
   If that be, I shall see my boy again,
   For since the birth of Cain, the first male child,
   To him that did but yesterday suspire,
   There was not such a gracious creature born.
   But now will canker-sorrow eat my bud,
   And chase the native beauty from his cheek,
   And he will look as hollow as a ghost,
   As dim and meagre as an ague's fit,
   And so he'll die; and rising so again,

When I shall meet him in the court of heav'n,
I shall not know him ; therefore never, never
Must I behold my pretty Arthur more.
    K. Philip. You are as fond of grief as of your child.
    Constance. Grief fills the room up of my absent child :
Lies in his bed, walks up and down with me ;
Puts on his pretty looks, repeats his words,
Remembers me of all his gracious parts ;
Stuffs out his vacant garments with his form.
Then have I reason to be fond of grief.'

The contrast between the mild resignation of Queen Katherine to her own wrongs, and the wild, uncontroulable affliction of Constance for the wrongs which she sustains as a mother, is no less naturally conceived than it is ably sustained throughout these two wonderful characters.

The accompaniment of the comic character of the Bastard was well chosen to relieve the poignant agony of suffering, and the cold cowardly policy of behaviour in the principal characters of this play. Its spirit, invention, volubility of tongue and forwardness in action, are unbounded. *Aliquando sufflaminandus erat,* says Ben Jonson of Shakespear. But we should be sorry if Ben Jonson had been his licenser. We prefer the heedless magnanimity of his wit infinitely to all Jonson's laborious caution. The character of the Bastard's comic humour is the same in essence as that of other comic characters in Shakespear ; they always run on with good things and are never exhausted ; they are always daring and successful. They have words at will, and a flow of wit like a flow of animal spirits. The difference between Falconbridge and the others is that he is a soldier, and brings his wit to bear upon action, is courageous with his sword as well as tongue, and stimulates his gallantry by his jokes, his enemies feeling the sharpness of his blows and the sting of his sarcasms at the same time. Among his happiest sallies are his descanting on the composition of his own person, his invective against 'commodity, tickling commodity,' and his expression of contempt for the Arch-duke of Austria, who had killed his father, which begins in jest but ends in serious earnest. His conduct at the siege of Angiers shews that his resources were not confined to verbal retorts.—The same exposure of the policy of courts and camps, of kings, nobles, priests, and cardinals, takes place here as in the other plays we have gone through, and we shall not go into a disgusting repetition.

This, like the other plays taken from English history, is written in a remarkably smooth and flowing style, very different from some of the tragedies, *Macbeth*, for instance. The passages consist of a

    *L 65

series of single lines, not running into one another. This peculiarity
in the versification, which is most common in the three parts of
Henry VI. has been assigned as a reason why those plays were not
written by Shakespear. But the same structure of verse occurs in
his other undoubted plays, as in *Richard II.* and in KING JOHN.
The following are instances :—

> ' That daughter there of Spain, the lady Blanch,
> Is near to England ; look upon the years
> Of Lewis the dauphin, and that lovely maid.
> If lusty love should go in quest of beauty,
> Where should he find it fairer than in Blanch ?
> If zealous love should go in search of virtue,
> Where should he find it purer than in Blanch ?
> If love ambitious sought a match of birth,
> Whose veins bound richer blood than lady Blanch?
> Such as she is, in beauty, virtue, birth,
> Is the young dauphin every way complete :
> If not complete of, say he is not she ;
> And she again wants nothing, to name want,
> If want it be not, that she is not he.
> He is the half part of a blessed man,
> Left to be finished by such as she ;
> And she a fair divided excellence,
> Whose fulness of perfection lies in him.
> O, two such silver currents, when they join,
> Do glorify the banks that bound them in :
> And two such shores to two such streams made one,
> Two such controuling bounds, shall you be, kings,
> To these two princes, if you marry them.'

Another instance, which is certainly very happy as an example
of the simple enumeration of a number of particulars, is Salisbury's
remonstrance against the second crowning of the king.

> Therefore to be possessed with double pomp,
> To guard a title that was rich before ;
> To gild refined gold, to paint the lily,
> To throw a perfume on the violet,
> To smooth the ice, to add another hue
> Unto the rainbow, or with taper light
> To seek the beauteous eye of heav'n to garnish :
> Is wasteful and ridiculous excess.'

TWELFTH NIGHT; OR, WHAT YOU WILL

THIS is justly considered as one of the most delightful of Shakespear's comedies. It is full of sweetness and pleasantry. It is perhaps too good-natured for comedy. It has little satire, and no spleen. It aims at the ludicrous rather than the ridiculous. It makes us laugh at the follies of mankind, not despise them, and still less bear any ill-will towards them. Shakespear's comic genius resembles the bee rather in its power of extracting sweets from weeds or poisons, than in leaving a sting behind it. He gives the most amusing exaggeration of the prevailing foibles of his characters, but in a way that they themselves, instead of being offended at, would almost join in to humour; he rather contrives opportunities for them to shew themselves off in the happiest lights, than renders them contemptible in the perverse construction of the wit or malice of others.—There is a certain stage of society in which people become conscious of their peculiarities and absurdities, affect to disguise what they are, and set up pretensions to what they are not. This gives rise to a corresponding style of comedy, the object of which is to detect the disguises of self-love, and to make reprisals on these preposterous assumptions of vanity, by marking the contrast between the real and the affected character as severely as possible, and denying to those, who would impose on us for what they are not, even the merit which they have. This is the comedy of artificial life, of wit and satire, such as we see it in Congreve, Wycherley, Vanbrugh, etc. To this succeeds a state of society from which the same sort of affectation and pretence are banished by a greater knowledge of the world or by their successful exposure on the stage; and which by neutralising the materials of comic character, both natural and artificial, leaves no comedy at all—but *the sentimental*. Such is our modern comedy. There is a period in the progress of manners anterior to both these, in which the foibles and follies of individuals are of nature's planting, not the growth of art or study; in which they are therefore unconscious of them themselves, or care not who knows them, if they can but have their whim out; and in which, as there is no attempt at imposition, the spectators rather receive pleasure from humouring the inclinations of the persons they laugh at, than wish to give them pain by exposing their absurdity. This may be called the comedy of nature, and it is the comedy which we generally find in Shakespear.—Whether the analysis here given be just or not, the spirit of his comedies is evidently

313

quite distinct from that of the authors above mentioned, as it is in it essence the same with that of Cervantes, and also very frequently c Molière, though he was more systematic in his extravagance tha Shakespear. Shakespear's comedy is of a pastoral and poetical cast Folly is indigenous to the soil, and shoots out with native, happy unchecked luxuriance. Absurdity has every encouragement afforde it; and nonsense has room to flourish in. Nothing is stunted by th churlish, icy hand of indifference or severity. The poet runs riot i a conceit, and idolises a quibble. His whole object is to turn th meanest or rudest objects to a pleasurable account. The relish whic he has of a pun, or of the quaint humour of a low character, does n interfere with the delight with which he describes a beautiful imag or the most refined love. The clown's forced jests do not spoil th sweetness of the character of Viola; the same house is big enough hold Malvolio, the Countess, Maria, Sir Toby, and Sir Andre Ague-cheek. For instance, nothing can fall much lower than th last character in intellect or morals: yet how are his weaknesse nursed and dandled by Sir Toby into something 'high fantastical when on Sir Andrew's commendation of himself for dancing an fencing, Sir Toby answers—'Wherefore are these things hid Wherefore have these gifts a curtain before them? Are they like take dust like mistress Moll's picture? Why dost thou not go t church in a galliard, and come home in a coranto? My very wal should be a jig! I would not so much as make water but in cinque-pace. What dost thou mean? Is this a world to hide virtu in? I did think by the excellent constitution of thy leg, it wa framed under the star of a galliard!'—How Sir Toby, Sir Andrew and the Clown afterwards *chirp over their cups*, how they 'rouse th night-owl in a catch, able to draw three souls out of one weaver! What can be better than Sir Toby's unanswerable answer to Malvoli 'Dost thou think, because thou art virtuous, there shall be no mor cakes and ale?'—In a word, the best turn is given to every thin instead of the worst. There is a constant infusion of the romanti and enthusiastic, in proportion as the characters are natural an sincere: whereas, in the more artificial style of comedy, every thin gives way to ridicule and indifference, there being nothing left b affectation on one side, and incredulity on the other.—Much as w like Shakespear's comedies, we cannot agree with Dr. Johnson th they are better than his tragedies; nor do we like them half so wel If his inclination to comedy sometimes led him to trifle with t seriousness of tragedy, the poetical and impassioned passages are t best parts of his comedies. The great and secret charm of TWELFT NIGHT is the character of Viola. Much as we like catches and cak

nd ale, there is something that we like better. We have a friendship
or Sir Toby; we patronise Sir Andrew; we have an understanding
with the Clown, a sneaking kindness for Maria and her rogueries; we
eel a regard for Malvolio, and sympathise with his gravity, his smiles,
his cross garters, his yellow stockings, and imprisonment in the stocks.
But there is something that excites in us a stronger feeling than all
his—it is Viola's confession of her love.

> '*Duke.* What's her history?
> *Viola. A blank, my lord, she never told her love*
> She let concealment, like a worm i' th' bud,
> Feed on her damask cheek: she pin'd in thought,
> And with a green and yellow melancholy,
> She sat like Patience on a monument,
> Smiling at grief. *Was not this love indeed?*
> We men may say more, swear more, but indeed,
> Our shews are more than will; for still we prove
> Much in our vows, but little in our love.
> *Duke.* But died thy sister of her love, my boy?
> *Viola.* I am all the daughters of my father's house,
> And all the brothers too;—and yet I know not.'—

Shakespear alone could describe the effect of his own poetry.

> ' Oh, it came o'er the ear like the sweet south
> That breathes upon a bank of violets,
> Stealing and giving odour.'

What we so much admire here is not the image of Patience on a
monument, which has been generally quoted, but the lines before and
after it. 'They give a very echo to the seat where love is throned.'
How long ago it is since we first learnt to repeat them; and still, still
they vibrate on the heart, like the sounds which the passing wind
draws from the trembling strings of a harp left on some desert shore!
There are other passages of not less impassioned sweetness. Such is
Olivia's address to Sebastian, whom she supposes to have already
deceived her in a promise of marriage

> ' Blame not this haste of mine: if you mean well,
> Now go with me and with this holy man
> Into the chantry by: there before him,
> And underneath that consecrated roof,
> Plight me the full assurance of your faith,
> *That my most jealous and too doubtful soul*
> *May live at peace.*'

We have already said something of Shakespear's songs. One of

315

the most beautiful of them occurs in this play, with a preface of his own to it

> '*Duke.* O fellow, come, the song we had last night.
> Mark it, Cesario, it is old and plain;
> The spinsters and the knitters in the sun,
> And the free maids that weave their thread with bones,
> Do use to chaunt it: it is silly sooth,
> And dallies with the innocence of love,
> Like the old age.

SONG.

> Come away, come away, death,
> And in sad cypress let me be laid;
> Fly away, fly away, breath;
> I am slain by a fair cruel maid.
> My shroud of white, stuck all with yew,
> O prepare it;
> My part of death no one so true
> Did share it.
>
> Not a flower, not a flower sweet,
> On my black coffin let there be strewn;
> Not a friend, not a friend greet
> My poor corpse, where my bones shall be thrown:
> A thousand thousand sighs to save,
> Lay me, O! where
> Sad true-love never find my grave,
> To weep there.'

Who after this will say that Shakespear's genius was only fitted for comedy? Yet after reading other parts of this play, and particularly the garden-scene where Malvolio picks up the letter, if we were to say that his genius for comedy was less than his genius for tragedy, it would perhaps only prove that our own taste in such matters is more saturnine than mercurial.

Enter MARIA.

Sir Toby. Here comes the little villain:—How now, my nettle of India!

Maria. Get ye all three into the box-tree: Malvolio's coming down this walk: he has been yonder i' the sun, practising behaviour to his own shadow this half hour: observe him, for the love of mockery; for I know this letter will make a contemplative idiot of him. Close, in the name of jesting! Lie thou there; for here come's the trout that must be caught with tickling. [*They hide themselves. Maria throws down a letter, and Exit*

Enter MALVOLIO.

Malvolio. 'Tis but fortune; all is fortune. Maria once told me, she did affect me ; and I have heard herself come thus near, that, should she fancy, it should be one of my complexion. Besides, she uses me with a more exalted respect than any one else that follows her. What should I think on't ?

Sir Toby. Here's an over-weening rogue !

Fabian. O, peace ! Contemplation makes a rare turkey-cock of him ; how he jets under his advanced plumes !

Sir Andrew. 'Slight, I could so beat the rogue :—

Sir Toby. Peace, I say.

Malvolio. To be count Malvolio ;—

Sir Toby. Ah, rogue !

Sir Andrew. Pistol him, pistol him.

Sir Toby. Peace, peace !

Malvolio. There is example for't ; the lady of the Strachy married the yeoman of the wardrobe.

Sir Andrew. Fie on him, Jezebel !

Fabian. O, peace ! now he's deeply in ; look, how imagination blows him.

Malvolio. Having been three months married to her, sitting in my chair of state,——

Sir Toby. O for a stone bow, to hit him in the eye !

Malvolio. Calling my officers about me, in my branch'd velvet gown ; having come from a day-bed, where I have left Olivia sleeping.

Sir Toby. Fire and brimstone !

Fabian. O peace, peace !

Malvolio. And then to have the humour of state : and after a demure travel of regard,——telling them, I know my place, as I would they should do theirs,—to ask for my kinsman Toby.——

Sir Toby. Bolts and shackles !

Fabian. O, peace, peace, peace ! now, now.

Malvolio. Seven of my people, with an obedient start, make out for him ; I frown the while ; and, perchance, wind up my watch, or play with some rich jewel. Toby approaches ; curtsies there to me.

Sir Toby. Shall this fellow live ?

Fabian. Though our silence be drawn from us with cares, yet peace.

Malvolio. I extend my hand to him thus, quenching my familiar smile with an austere regard to controul.

Sir Toby. And does not Toby take you a blow o' the lips then ?

Malvolio. Saying—Cousin Toby, my fortunes having cast me on your niece, give me this prerogative of speech ;—

Sir Toby. What, what ?

Malvolio. You must amend your drunkenness.

Fabian. Nay, patience, or we break the sinews of our plot.

Malvolio. Besides, you waste the treasure of your time with a foolish knight—

Sir Andrew. That's me, I warrant you.

Malvolio. One Sir Andrew——

Sir Andrew. I knew, 'twas I ; for many do call me fool.

Malvolio. What employment have we here ? *[Taking up the letter.'*

317

The letter and his comments on it are equally good. If poor Malvolio's treatment afterwards is a little hard, poetical justice is done in the uneasiness which Olivia suffers on account of her mistaken attachment to Cesario, as her insensibility to the violence of the Duke's passion is atoned for by the discovery of Viola's concealed love of him.

THE TWO GENTLEMEN OF VERONA

THIS is little more than the first outlines of a comedy loosely sketched in. It is the story of a novel dramatised with very little labour or pretension; yet there are passages of high poetical spirit, and of inimitable quaintness of humour, which are undoubtedly Shakespear's, and there is throughout the conduct of the fable a careless grace and felicity which marks it for his. One of the editors (we believe M: Pope) remarks in a marginal note to the TWO GENTLEMEN OF VERONA—

'It is observable (I know not for what cause) that the style of this comedy is less figurative, and more natural and unaffected than the greater part of this author's, though supposed to be one of the first he wrote.'

Yet so little does the editor appear to have made up his mind upon this subject, that we find the following note to the very next (the second) scene.

'This whole scene, like many others in these plays (some of which I believe were written by Shakespear, and others interpolated by the players) is composed of the lowest and most trifling conceits, to be accounted for only by the gross taste of the age he lived in: *Populo ut placerent*. I wish I had authority to leave them out, but I have done all I could, set a mark of reprobation upon them, throughout this edition.'

It is strange that our fastidious critic should fall so soon from praising to reprobating. The style of the familiar parts of this comedy is indeed made up of conceits—low they may be for what we know, but then they are not poor, but rich ones. The scene of Launce with his dog (not that in the second, but that in the fourth act) is a perfect treat in the way of farcical drollery and invention; nor do we think Speed's manner of proving his master to be in love deficient in wit or sense, though the style may be criticised as not simple enough for the modern taste.

'*Valentine*. Why, how know you that I am in love?
Speed. Marry, by these special marks: first, you have learned, like Sir Protheus, to wreathe your arms like a malcontent, to relish a love-song

like a robin-red-breast, to walk alone like one that had the pestilence, to sigh like a school-boy that had lost his ABC, to weep like a young wench that had buried her grandam, to fast like one that takes diet, to watch like one that fears robbing, to speak puling like a beggar at Hallowmas. You were wont, when you laughed, to crow like a cock; when you walked, to walk like one of the lions; when you fasted, it was presently after dinner; when you looked sadly, it was for want of money; and now you are meta-morphosed with a mistress, that when I look on you, I can hardly think you my master.'

The tender scenes in this play, though not so highly wrought as in some others, have often much sweetness of sentiment and expression. There is something pretty and playful in the conversation of Julia with her maid, when she shews such a disposition to coquetry about receiving the letter from Protheus; and her behaviour afterwards and her disappointment, when she finds him faithless to his vows, remind us at a distance of Imogen's tender constancy. Her answer to Lucetta, who advises her against following her lover in disguise, is a beautiful piece of poetry.

> *Lucetta.* I do not seek to quench your love's hot fire,
> But qualify the fire's extremest rage,
> Lest it should burn above the bounds of reason.
>   *Julia.* The more thou damm'st it up, the more it burns,
> The current that with gentle murmur glides,
> Thou know'st, being stopp'd, impatiently doth rage;
> But when his fair course is not hindered,
> He makes sweet music with th' enamell'd stones,
> Giving a gentle kiss to every sedge
> He overtaketh in his pilgrimage:
> And so by many winding nooks he strays,
> With willing sport, to the wild ocean.[1]
> Then let me go, and hinder not my course;
> I'll be as patient as a gentle stream,
> And make a pastime of each weary step,
> Till the last step have brought me to my love,
> And there I'll rest, as after much turmoil,
> A blessed soul doth in Elysium.'

If Shakespear indeed had written only this and other passages in the Two GENTLEMEN OF VERONA, he would *almost* have deserved Milton's praise of him—

> 'And sweetest Shakespear, Fancy's child,
> Warbles his native wood-notes wild.'

But as it is, he deserves rather more praise than this.

---

[1] The river wanders at its own sweet will.—WORDSWORTH.

THE MERCHANT OF VENICE

THIS is a play that in spite of the change of manners and prejudices still holds undisputed possession of the stage. Shakespear's malignant has outlived Mr. Cumberland's benevolent Jew. In proportion as Shylock has ceased to be a popular bugbear, 'baited with the rabble's curse,' he becomes a half-favourite with the philosophical part of the audience, who are disposed to think that Jewish revenge is at least as good as Christian injuries. Shylock is *a good hater*; 'a man no less sinned against than sinning.' If he carries his revenge too far, yet he has strong grounds for 'the lodged hate he bears Anthonio,' which he explains with equal force of eloquence and reason. He seems the depositary of the vengeance of his race; and though the long habit of brooding over daily insults and injuries has crusted over his temper with inveterate misanthropy, and hardened him against the contempt of mankind, this adds but little to the triumphant pretensions of his enemies. There is a strong, quick, and deep sense of justice mixed up with the gall and bitterness of his resentment. The constant apprehension of being burnt alive, plundered, banished, reviled, and trampled on, might be supposed to sour the most forbearing nature, and to take something from that 'milk of human kindness,' with which his persecutors contemplated his indignities. The desire of revenge is almost inseparable from the sense of wrong; and we can hardly help sympathising with the proud spirit, hid beneath his 'Jewish gaberdine,' stung to madness by repeated undeserved provocations, and labouring to throw off the load of obloquy and oppression heaped upon him and all his tribe by one desperate act of 'lawful' revenge, till the ferociousness of the means by which he is to execute his purpose, and the pertinacity with which he adheres to it, turn us against him; but even at last, when disappointed of the sanguinary revenge with which he had glutted his hopes, and exposed to beggary and contempt by the letter of the law on which he had insisted with so little remorse, we pity him, and think him hardly dealt with by his judges. In all his answers and retorts upon his adversaries, he has the best not only of the argument but of the question, reasoning on their own principles and practice. They are so far from allowing of any measure of equal dealing, of common justice or humanity between themselves and the Jew, that even when they come to ask a favour of him, and Shylock reminds them that 'on such a day they spit upon him, another spurned him, another called him dog, and for these curtesies request he 'll lend them so much monies'—

Anthonio, his old enemy, instead of any acknowledgment of the shrewdness and justice of his remonstrance, which would have been preposterous in a respectable Catholic merchant in those times, threatens him with a repetition of the same treatment—

> ' I am as like to call thee so again,
> To spit on thee again, to spurn thee too.'

After this, the appeal to the Jew's mercy, as if there were any common principle of right and wrong between them, is the rankest hypocrisy, or the blindest prejudice; and the Jew's answer to one of Anthonio's friends, who asks him what his pound of forfeit flesh is good for, is irresistible—

To bait fish withal; it it will feed nothing else, it will feed my revenge. He hath disgrac'd me, and hinder'd me of half a million, laughed at my losses, mock'd at my gains, scorn'd my nation, thwarted my bargains, cool'd my friends, heated mine enemies; and what's his reason? I am a Jew. Hath not a Jew eyes; hath not a Jew hands, organs, dimensions, senses, affections, passions; fed with the same food, hurt with the same weapons, subject to the same diseases, healed by the same means, warmed and cooled by the same winter and summer that a Christian is? If you prick us, do we not bleed? If you tickle us, do we not laugh? If you poison us, do we not die? And if you wrong us, shall we not revenge? If we are like you in the rest, we will resemble you in that. If a Jew wrong a Christian, what is his humility? revenge. If a Christian wrong a Jew, what should his sufferance be by Christian example? why revenge. The villainy you teach me I will execute, and it shall go hard but I will better the instruction.'

The whole of the trial-scene, both before and after the entrance of Portia, is a master-piece of dramatic skill. The legal acuteness, the passionate declamations, the sound maxims of jurisprudence, the wit and irony interspersed in it, the fluctuations of hope and fear in the different persons, and the completeness and suddenness of the catastrophe, cannot be surpassed. Shylock, who is his own counsel, defends himself well, and is triumphant on all the general topics that are urged against him, and only fails through a legal flaw. Take the following as an instance:—

> ' *Shylock*. What judgment shall I dread, doing no wrong?
> You have among you many a purchas'd slave,
> Which like your asses, and your dogs, and mules,
> You use in abject and in slavish part,
> Because you bought them:—shall I say to you,
> Let them be free, marry them to your heirs?
> Why sweat they under burdens? let their beds
> Be made as soft as yours, and let their palates

> Be season'd with such viands? you will answer,
> The slaves are ours:—so do I answer you:
> The pound of flesh, which I demand of him,
> Is dearly bought, is mine, and I will have it:
> If you deny me, fie upon your law!
> There is no force in the decrees of Venice:
> I stand for judgment: answer; shall I have it?'

The keenness of his revenge awakes all his faculties; and he beats back all opposition to his purpose, whether grave or gay, whether of wit or argument, with an equal degree of earnestness and self-possession. His character is displayed as distinctly in other less prominent parts of the play, and we may collect from a few sentences the history of his life—his descent and origin, his thrift and domestic economy, his affection for his daughter, whom he loves next to his wealth, his courtship and his first present to Leah, his wife! 'I would not have parted with it' (the ring which he first gave her) 'for a wilderness of monkies!' What a fine Hebraism is implied in this expression!

Portia is not a very great favourite with us; neither are we in love with her maid, Nerissa. Portia has a certain degree of affectation and pedantry about her, which is very unusual in Shakespear's women, but which perhaps was a proper qualification for the office of a 'civil doctor,' which she undertakes and executes so successfully. The speech about Mercy is very well; but there are a thousand finer ones in Shakespear. We do not admire the scene of the caskets: and object entirely to the Black Prince, Morocchius. We should like Jessica better if she had not deceived and robbed her father, and Lorenzo, if he had not married a Jewess, though he thinks he has a right to wrong a Jew. The dialogue between this newly-married couple by moonlight, beginning 'On such a night,' etc. is a collection of classical elegancies. Launcelot, the Jew's man, is an honest fellow. The dilemma in which he describes himself placed between his 'conscience and the fiend,' the one of which advises him to run away from his master's service and the other to stay in it, is exquisitely humourous.

Gratiano is a very admirable subordinate character. He is the jester of the piece: yet one speech of his, in his own defence, contains a whole volume of wisdom.

> '*Anthonio.* I hold the world but as the world, Gratiano,
> A stage, where every one must play his part;
> And mine a sad one.
>   *Gratiano.* Let me play the fool:
> With mirth and laughter let old wrinkles come;

And let my liver rather heat with wine,
Than my heart cool with mortifying groans.
Why should a man, whose blood is warm within,
Sit like his grandsire cut in alabaster?
Sleep when he wakes? and creep into the jaundice
By being peevish? I tell thee what, Anthonio—
I love thee, and it is my love that speaks;—
There are a sort of men, whose visages
Do cream and mantle like a standing pond:
And do a wilful stillness entertain,
With purpose to be drest in an opinion
Of wisdom, gravity, profound conceit;
As who should say, *I am Sir Oracle,*
And when I ope my lips, let no dog bark!
O, my Anthonio, I do know of these,
That therefore only are reputed wise,
For saying nothing; who, I am sure,
If they should speak, would almost damn those ears,
Which hearing them, would call their brothers, fools.
I'll tell thee more of this another time:
But fish not with this melancholy bait,
For this fool's gudgeon, this opinion.'

Gratiano's speech on the philosophy of love, and the effect of habit in taking off the force of passion, is as full of spirit and good sense. The graceful winding up of this play in the fifth act, after the tragic business is despatched, is one of the happiest instances of Shakespear's knowledge of the principles of the drama. We do not mean the pretended quarrel between Portia and Nerissa and their husbands about the rings, which is amusing enough, but the conversation just before and after the return of Portia to her own house, beginning 'How sweet the moonlight sleeps upon this bank,' and ending 'Peace! how the moon sleeps with Endymion, and would not be awaked.' There is a number of beautiful thoughts crowded into that short space, and linked together by the most natural transitions.

When we first went to see Mr. Kean in Shylock, we expected to see, what we had been used to see, a decrepid old man, bent with age and ugly with mental deformity, grinning with deadly malice, with the venom of his heart congealed in the expression of his countenance, sullen, morose, gloomy, inflexible, brooding over one idea, that of his hatred, and fixed on one unalterable purpose, that of his revenge. We were disappointed, because we had taken our idea from other actors, not from the play. There is no proof there that Shylock is old, but a single line, 'Bassanio and *old* Shylock, both stand forth,'—which does not imply that he is infirm with age—and the circumstance that he has a daughter marriageable, which does not imply that he is old at all. It would be too much to say that his body should be made crooked and deformed to answer to his mind, which is bowed down and warped with prejudices and passion. That he has but one idea, is not true; he has more ideas than any other person in the piece; and if he is intense and inveterate in the pursuit of his purpose, he shews the utmost elasticity, vigour, and presence of mind, in the means of attaining it. But so rooted was our habitual impression of the part from seeing it caricatured in the representation, that it was only from a careful perusal of the play itself that we saw our error. The stage is not in general the best place to study our author's characters in. It is too often filled with traditional common-place conceptions of the part, handed down from sire to son, and suited to the taste of *the great vulgar and the small*.—''Tis an unweeded garden: things rank and gross do merely gender in it!' If a man of genius comes once in an age to clear away the rubbish, to make it fruitful and wholesome, they cry, ''Tis a bad school: it may be like nature, it may be like Shakespear, but it is not like us.' Admirable critics!

THE WINTER'S TALE

WE wonder that Mr. Pope should have entertained doubts of the genuineness of this play. He was, we suppose, shocked (as a certain critic suggests) at the Chorus, Time, leaping over sixteen years with his crutch between the third and fourth act, and at Antigonus's landing with the infant Perdita on the sea-coast of Bohemia. These slips or blemishes however do not prove it not to be Shakespear's; for he was as likely to fall into them as any body; but we do not know any body but himself who could produce the beauties. The *stuff* of which the tragic passion is composed, the romantic sweetness, the comic humour, are evidently his. Even the crabbed and tortuous style of the speeches of Leontes, reasoning on his own jealousy, beset with doubts and fears, and entangled more and more in the thorny labyrinth, bears every mark of Shakespear's peculiar manner of conveying the painful struggle of different thoughts and feelings, labouring for utterance, and almost strangled in the birth. For instance:—

> 'Ha' not you seen, Camillo?
> (But that's past doubt; you have, or your eye-glass
> Is thicker than a cuckold's horn) or heard,
> (For to a vision so apparent, rumour
> Cannot be mute) or thought (for cogitation

THE WINTER'S TALE

> Resides not within man that does not think)
> My wife is slippery? If thou wilt, confess,
> Or else be impudently negative,
> To have nor eyes, nor ears, nor thought.'—

Here Leontes is confounded with his passion, and does not know which way to turn himself, to give words to the anguish, rage, and apprehension, which tug at his breast. It is only as he is worked up into a clearer conviction of his wrongs by insisting on the grounds of his unjust suspicions to Camillo, who irritates him by his opposition, that he bursts out into the following vehement strain of bitter indignation: yet even here his passion staggers, and is as it were oppressed with its own intensity.

> ' Is whispering nothing?
> Is leaning cheek to cheek? is meeting noses?
> Kissing with inside lip? stopping the career
> Of laughter with a sigh? (a note infallible
> Of breaking honesty!) horsing foot on foot?
> Skulking in corners? wishing clocks more swift?
> Hours, minutes? the noon, midnight? and all eyes
> Blind with the pin and web, but theirs; theirs only,
> That would, unseen, be wicked? is this nothing?
> Why then the world, and all that's in't, is nothing,
> The covering sky is nothing, Bohemia's nothing,
> My wife is nothing!'

The character of Hermione is as much distinguished by its saint-like resignation and patient forbearance, as that of Paulina is by her zealous and spirited remonstrances against the injustice done to the queen, and by her devoted attachment to her misfortunes. Hermione's restoration to her husband and her child, after her long separation from them, is as affecting in itself as it is striking in the representation. Camillo, and the old shepherd and his son, are subordinate but not uninteresting instruments in the developement of the plot, and though last, not least, comes Autolycus, a very pleasant, thriving rogue; and (what is the best feather in the cap of all knavery) he escapes with impunity in the end.

THE WINTER'S TALE is one of the best-acting of our author's plays. We remember seeing it with great pleasure many years ago. It was on the night that King took leave of the stage, when he and Mrs. Jordan played together in the after-piece of the Wedding-day. Nothing could go off with more *éclat*, with more spirit, and grandeur of effect. Mrs. Siddons played Hermione, and in the last scene acted the painted statue to the life—with true monumental dignity and noble passion; Mr. Kemble, in Leontes, worked himself up into a very fine classical phrensy; and Bannister, as Autolycus, roared as loud for pity as a sturdy beggar could do who felt none of the pain he counterfeited, and was sound of wind and limb. We shall never see these parts so acted again; or if we did, it would be in vain. Actors grow old, or no longer surprise us by their novelty. But true poetry, like nature, is always young; and we still read the courtship of Florizel and Perdita, as we welcome the return of spring, with the same feelings as ever.

> '*Florizel.* Thou dearest Perdita,
> With these forc'd thoughts, I pr'ythee, darken not
> The mirth o' the feast: or, I 'll be thine, my fair,
> Or not my father's: for I cannot be
> Mine own, nor any thing to any, if
> I be not thine. To this I am most constant,
> Tho' destiny say, No. Be merry, gentle;
> Strangle such thoughts as these, with any thing
> That you behold the while. Your guests are coming:
> Lift up your countenance; as it were the day
> Of celebration of that nuptial, which
> We two have sworn shall come.
>   *Perdita.* O lady fortune,
> Stand you auspicious!

> #### Enter Shepherd, Clown, MOPSA, DORCAS, Servants; with POLIXENES, and CAMILLO, disguised.

> *Florizel.* See, your guests approach.
> Address yourself to entertain them sprightly,
> And let 's be red with mirth.
>   *Shepherd.* Fie, daughter! when my old wife liv'd, upon
> This day, she was both pantler, butler, cook;
> Both dame and servant: welcom'd all, serv'd all:
> Would sing her song, and dance her turn: now here
> At upper end o' the table, now i' the middle:
> On his shoulder, and his: her face o' fire
> With labour; and the thing she took to quench it
> She would to each one sip. You are retir'd,
> As if you were a feasted one, and not
> The hostess of the meeting. Pray you, bid
> These unknown friends to us welcome; for it is
> A way to make us better friends, more known.
> Come, quench your blushes; and present yourself
> That which you are, mistress o' the feast. Come on,
> And bid us welcome to your sheep-shearing,
> As your good flock shall prosper.
>   *Perdita.* Sir, welcome!   [*To Polixenes and Camillo.*
> It is my father's will I should take on me
> The hostess-ship o' the day: you 're welcome, sir!

Give me those flowers there, Dorcas.——Reverend sirs,
For you there's rosemary and rue; these keep
Seeming, and savour, all the winter long:
Grace and remembrance be unto you both,
And welcome to our shearing!

Polixenes. Shepherdess,
(A fair one are you) well you fit our ages
With flowers of winter.

Perdita. Sir, the year growing ancient,
Not yet on summer's death, nor on the birth
Of trembling winter, the fairest flowers o' the season
Are our carnations, and streak'd gilly-flowers,
Which some call nature's bastards: of that kind
Our rustic garden's barren; and I care not
To get slips of them.

Polixenes. Wherefore, gentle maiden,
Do you neglect them?

Perdita. For I have heard it said
There is an art, which, in their piedness, shares
With great creating nature.

Polixenes. Say, there be:
Yet nature is made better by no mean,
But nature makes that mean: so, o'er that art
Which you say, adds to nature, is an art
That nature makes. You see, sweet maid, we marry
A gentler scyon to the wildest stock;
And make conceive a bark of baser kind
By bud of nobler race. This is an art
Which does mend nature, change it rather: but
The art itself is nature.

Perdita. So it is.[1]

Polixenes. Then make your garden rich in gilly-flowers,
And do not call them bastards.

Perdita. I'll not put
The dibble in earth, to set one slip of them;[1]
No more than, were I painted, I would wish
This youth should say, 'twere well; and only therefore
Desire to breed by me.— Here's flowers for you;
Hot lavender, mints, savoury, marjoram;
The marigold, that goes to bed with the sun,
And with him rises, weeping: these are flowers
Of middle summer, and, I think, they are given
To men of middle age. You are very welcome.

Camillo. I should leave grazing, were I of your flock,
And only live by gazing.

Perdita. Out, alas!
You'd be so lean, that blasts of January

---

[1] The lady, we here see, gives up the argument, but keeps her mind.

Would blow you through and through. Now my fairest friends,
I would I had some flowers o' the spring, that might
Become your time of day; and your's, and your's,
That wear upon your virgin branches yet
Your maiden-heads growing: O Proserpina,
For the flowers now, that, frighted, thou let'st fall
From Dis's waggon! daffodils,
That come before the swallow dares, and take
The winds of March with beauty: violets dim,
But sweeter than the lids of Juno's eyes,
Or Cytherea's breath; pale primroses,
That die unmarried, ere they can behold
Bright Phœbus in his strength (a malady
Most incident to maids); bold oxlips, and
The crown-imperial; lilies of all kinds,
The fleur-de-lis being one! O, these I lack
To make you garlands of; and my sweet friend
To strow him o'er and o'er.

   Florizel. What, like a corse?

   Perdita. No, like a bank, for love to lie and play on;
Not like a corse; or if—not to be buried,
But quick, and in mine arms. Come take your flowers;
Methinks, I play as I have seen them do
In Whitsun pastorals: sure this robe of mine
Does change my disposition.

   Florizel. What you do,
Still betters what is done. When you speak, sweet,
I'd have you do it ever: when you sing,
I'd have you buy and sell so; so, give alms;
Pray, so; and for the ordering your affairs,
To sing them too. When you do dance, I wish you
A wave o' the sea, that you might ever do
Nothing but that: move still, still so,
And own no other function. Each your doing,
So singular in each particular,
Crowns what you're doing in the present deeds,
That all your acts are queens.

   Perdita. O Doricles,
Your praises are too large; but that your youth
And the true blood, which peeps forth fairly through it,
Do plainly give you out an unstained shepherd;
With wisdom I might fear, my Doricles,
You woo'd me the false way.

   Florizel. I think you have
As little skill to fear, as I have purpose
To put you to't. But come, our dance, I pray;
Your hand, my Perdita: so turtles pair,
That never mean to part.

   Perdita. I'll swear for 'em.

ALL'S WELL THAT ENDS WELL

> *Polixenes.* This is the prettiest low-born lass that ever
> Ran on the green-sward ; nothing she does, or seems,
> But smacks of something greater than herself,
> Too noble for this place.
> > *Camillo.* He tells her something
> That makes her blood look out : good sooth she is
> The queen of curds and cream.'

This delicious scene is interrupted by the father of the prince dis-covering himself to Florizel, and haughtily breaking off the intended match between his son and Perdita. When Polixenes goes out, Perdita says,

> ' Even here undone :
> I was not much afraid ; for once or twice
> I was about to speak ; and tell him plainly,
> The self-same sun that shines upon his court,
> Hides not his visage from our cottage, but
> Looks on 't alike. Wilt please you, sir, be gone ?   [*To Florizel.*
> I told you what would come of this. Beseech you,
> Of your own state take care : this dream of mine,
> Being now awake, I 'll queen it no inch farther,
> But milk my ewes and weep.'

As Perdita, the supposed shepherdess, turns out to be the daughter of Hermione, and a princess in disguise, both feelings of the pride of birth and the claims of nature are satisfied by the fortunate event of the story, and the fine romance of poetry is reconciled to the strictest court-etiquette.

ALL 'S WELL THAT ENDS WELL

ALL 'S WELL THAT ENDS WELL is one of the most pleasing of our author's comedies. The interest is however more of a serious than of a comic nature. The character of Helen is one of great sweetness and delicacy. She is placed in circumstances of the most critical kind, and has to court her husband both as a virgin and a wife : yet the most scrupulous nicety of female modesty is not once violated. There is not one thought or action that ought to bring a blush into her cheeks, or that for a moment lessens her in our esteem. Perhaps the romantic attachment of a beautiful and virtuous girl to one placed above her hopes by the circumstances of birth and fortune, was never so exquisitely expressed as in the reflections which she utters when young Roussillon leaves his mother's house, under whose protection she has been brought up with him, to repair to the French king's court.

> '*Helena.* Oh, were that all—I think not on my father,
> And these great tears grace his remembrance more
> Than those I shed for him. What was he like?
> I have forgot him. My imagination
> Carries no favour in it, but Bertram's.
> I am undone, there is no living, none
> If Bertram be away. It were all one
> That I should love a bright particular star,
> And think to wed it; he is so above me:
> In his bright radiance and collateral light
> Must I be comforted, not in his sphere.
> Th' ambition in my love thus plagues itself;
> The hind that would be mated by the lion,
> Must die for love. 'Twas pretty, tho' a plague,
> To see him every hour, to sit and draw
> His arched brows, his hawking eye, his curls
> In our heart's table: heart too capable
> Of every line and trick of his sweet favour.
> But now he's gone, and my idolatrous fancy
> Must sanctify his relics.'

The interest excited by this beautiful picture of a fond and innocent heart is kept up afterwards by her resolution to follow him to France, the success of her experiment in restoring the king's health, her demanding Bertram in marriage as a recompense, his leaving her in disdain, her interview with him afterwards disguised as Diana, a young lady whom he importunes with his secret addresses, and their final reconciliation when the consequences of her stratagem and the proofs of her love are fully made known. The persevering gratitude of the French king to his benefactress, who cures him of a languishing distemper by a prescription hereditary in her family, the indulgent kindness of the Countess, whose pride of birth yields, almost without a struggle, to her affection for Helen, the honesty and uprightness of the good old lord Lafeu, make very interesting parts of the picture. The wilful stubbornness and youthful petulance of Bertram are also very admirably described. The comic part of the play turns on the folly, boasting, and cowardice of Parolles, a parasite and hanger-on of Bertram's, the detection of whose false pretensions to bravery and honour forms a very amusing episode. He is first found out by the old lord Lafeu, who says, 'The soul of this man is in his clothes'; and it is proved afterwards that his heart is in his tongue, and that both are false and hollow. The adventure of 'the bringing off of his drum' has become proverbial as a satire on all ridiculous and bluster ing undertakings which the person never means to perform: nor can any thing be more severe than what one of the bye-standers remarks upon what Parolles says of himself, 'Is it possible he should know what he is, and be that he is?' Yet Parolles himself gives the best solution of the difficulty afterwards when he is thankful to escape with his life and the loss of character; for, so that he can live on, he is by no means squeamish about the loss of pretensions, to which he had sense enough to know he had no real claim, and which he had assumed only as a means to live.

> '*Parolles.* Yet I am thankful: if my heart were great,
> 'Twould burst at this. Captain I 'll be no more,
> But I will eat and drink, and sleep as soft
> As captain shall. Simply the thing I am
> Shall make me live: who knows himself a braggart,
> Let him fear this; for it shall come to pass,
> That every braggart shall be found an ass.
> Rust sword, cool blushes, and Parolles live
> Safest in shame; being fool'd, by fool'ry thrive;
> There 's place and means for every man alive.
> I 'll after them.'

The story of ALL'S WELL THAT ENDS WELL, and of several others of Shakespear's plays, is taken from Boccacio. The poet has dramatised the original novel with great skill and comic spirit, and has preserved all the beauty of character and sentiment without *improving upon* it, which was impossible. There is indeed in Boccacio's serious pieces a truth, a pathos, and an exquisite refinement of sentiment, which is hardly to be met with in any other prose writer whatever. Justice has not been done him by the world. He has in general passed for a mere narrator of lascivious tales or idle jests. This character probably originated in his obnoxious attacks on the monks, and has been kept up by the grossness of mankind, who revenged their own want of refinement on Boccacio, and only saw in his writings what suited the coarseness of their own tastes. But the truth is, that he has carried sentiment of every kind to its very highest purity and perfection By sentiment we would here understand the habitual workings of some one powerful feeling, where the heart reposes almost entirely upon itself, without the violent excitement of opposing duties or untoward circumstances. In this way, nothing ever came up to the story of Frederigo Alberigi and his Falcon. The perseverance in attachment, the spirit of gallantry and generosity displayed in it, has no parallel in the history of heroical sacrifices. The feeling is so unconscious too, and involuntary, is brought out in such small, unlooked-for, and unostentatious circumstances, as to show it to have been woven into the very nature and soul of the author. The story of Isabella is scarcely less fine, and is more affecting in the circumstances and in the catastrophe. Dryden has done justice to the impassioned eloquence of the Tancred and Sigismunda; but has not given an adequate idea of the wild preternatural interest of the story of Honoria. Cimon and Iphigene is by no means one of the best, notwithstanding the popularity of the subject. The proof of unalterable affection given in the story of Jeronymo, and the simple touches of nature and picturesque beauty in the story of the two holiday lovers, who were poisoned by tasting of a leaf in the garden at Florence, are perfect master-pieces. The epithet of Divine was well bestowed on this great painter of the human heart. The invention implied in his different tales is immense: but we are not to infer that it is all his own. He probably availed himself of all the common traditions which were floating in his time, and which he was the first to appropriate. Homer appears the most original of all authors—probably for no other reason than that we can trace the plagiarism no farther. Boccacio has furnished subjects to numberless writers since his time, both dramatic and narrative. The story of Griselda is borrowed from his Decameron by Chaucer; as is the Knight's Tale (Palamon and Arcite) from his poem of the Theseid.

LOVE'S LABOUR'S LOST

IF we were to part with any of the author's comedies, it should be this. Yet we should be loth to part with Don Adriano de Armado, that mighty potentate of nonsense, or his page, that handful of wit; with Nathaniel the curate, or Holofernes the school-master, and their dispute after dinner on 'the golden cadences of poesy'; with Costard the clown, or Dull the constable. Biron is too accomplished a character to be lost to the world, and yet he could not appear without his fellow courtiers and the king: and if we were to leave out the ladies, the gentlemen would have no mistresses. So that we believe we may let the whole play stand as it is, and we shall hardly venture to 'set a mark of reprobation on it.' Still we have some objections to the style, which we think savours more of the pedantic spirit of Shakespear's time than of his own genius; more of controversial divinity, and the logic of Peter Lombard, than of the inspiration of the Muse. It transports us quite as much to the manners of the court, and the quirks of courts of law, as to the scenes of nature or the fairy-land of his own imagination. Shakespear has set himself to imitate the tone of polite conversation then prevailing among the fair, the witty, and the learned, and he has imitated it but too faithfully. It is as if the hand of Titian had been employed to give grace to the curls of a full-bottomed periwig, or Raphael had attempted to give expression to the tapestry figures in the House of Lords. Shakespear has put an excellent description of this fashionable jargon into the mouth of the critical Holofernes 'as too picked, too spruce, too affected, too odd, as it were, too peregrinate, as I may call it'; and nothing can be more marked than the difference when he breaks loose from the trammels he had imposed on himself, 'as light as bird from brake,' and speaks in his own person. We think, for instance, that in the following soliloquy the poet has fairly got the start of Queen Elizabeth and her maids of honour :—

> '*Biron.* O! and I torsooth in love,
> I that have been love's whip;
> A very beadle to an amorous sigh:
> A critic; nay, a night-watch constable,
> A domineering pedant o'er the boy,
> Than whom no mortal more magnificent.
> This wimpled, whining, purblind, wayward boy,
> This signior Junio, giant dwarf, Dan Cupid,
> Regent of love-rhymes, lord of folded arms,
> Th' anointed sovereign of sighs and groans:
> Liege of all loiterers and malecontents,
> Dread prince of plackets, king of codpieces,
> Sole imperator, and great general
> Of trotting parators (O my little heart!)
> And I to be a corporal of his field,
> And wear his colours like a tumbler's hoop?
> What? I love! I sue! I seek a wife!
> A woman, that is like a German clock,
> Still a repairing; ever out of frame;
> And never going aright, being a watch,
> And being watch'd, that it may still go right?
> Nay, to be perjur'd, which is worst of all:
> And among three to love the worst of all,
> A whitely wanton with a velvet brow,
> With two pitch balls stuck in her face for eyes;
> Ay, and by heav'n, one that will do the deed,
> Though Argus were her eunuch and her guard;
> And I to sigh for her! to watch for her!
> To pray for her! Go to; it is a plague
> That Cupid will impose for my neglect
> Of his almighty dreadful little might.
> Well, I will love, write, sigh, pray, sue, and groan:
> Some men must love my lady, and some Joan.'

The character of Biron drawn by Rosaline and that which Biron gives of Boyet are equally happy. The observations on the use and abuse of study, and on the power of beauty to quicken the understanding as well as the senses, are excellent. The scene which has the greatest dramatic effect is that in which Biron, the king, Longaville, and Dumain, successively detect each other and are detected in their breach of their vow and in their profession of attachment to their several mistresses, in which they suppose themselves to be overheard by no one. The reconciliation between these lovers and their sweethearts is also very good, and the penance which Rosaline imposes on Biron, before he can expect to gain her consent to marry him, full of propriety and beauty.

> '*Rosaline.* Oft have I heard of you, my lord Biron,
> Before I saw you: and the world's large tongue
> Proclaims you for a man replete with mocks;
> Full of comparisons, and wounding flouts;
> Which you on all estates will execute,
> That lie within the mercy of your wit.
> To weed this wormwood from your faithful brain;
> And therewithal to win me, if you please,
> (Without the which I am not to be won)
> You shall this twelvemonth term from day to day
> Visit the speechless sick, and still converse
> With groaning wretches; and your task shall be,
> With all the fierce endeavour of your wit,
> T' enforce the pained impotent to smile.
>   *Biron.* To move wild laughter in the throat of death?
> It cannot be: it is impossible:
> Mirth cannot move a soul in agony.
>   *Rosaline.* Why, that's the way to choke a gibing spirit,
> Whose influence is begot of that loose grace,
> Which shallow laughing hearers give to fools:
> A jest's prosperity lies in the ear
> Of him that hears it; never in the tongue
> Of him that makes it: then, if sickly ears,
> Deaf'd with the clamours of their own dear groans,
> Will hear your idle scorns, continue then,
> And I will have you, and that fault withal;
> But, if they will not, throw away that spirit,
> And I shall find you empty of that fault,
> Right joyful of your reformation.
>   *Biron.* A twelvemonth? Well, befall what will befall,
> I'll jest a twelvemonth in an hospital'

The famous cuckoo-song closes the play: but we shall add no mo
criticisms: 'the words of Mercury are harsh after the songs of Apollo

MUCH ADO ABOUT NOTHING

THIS admirable comedy used to be frequently acted till of late years. Mr. Garrick's Benedick was one of his most celebrated characters; and Mrs. Jordan, we have understood, played Beatrice very delightfully. The serious part is still the most prominent here, as in other instances that we have noticed. Hero is the principal figure in the piece, and leaves an indelible impression on the mind by her beauty, her tenderness, and the hard trial of her love. The passage in which Claudio first makes a confession of his affection towards her, conveys as pleasing an image of the entrance of love into a youthful bosom as can well be imagined.

> 'Oh, my lord,
> When you went onward with this ended action,
> I look'd upon her with a soldier's eye,
> That lik'd, but had a rougher task in hand
> Than to drive liking to the name of love;
> But now I am return'd, and that war-thoughts
> Have left their places vacant; in their rooms
> Come thronging soft and delicate desires,
> All prompting me how fair young Hero is,
> Saying, I lik'd her ere I went to wars.'

In the scene at the altar, when Claudio, urged on by the villain Don John, brings the charge of incontinence against her, and as it were divorces her in the very marriage-ceremony, her appeals to her own conscious innocence and honour are made with the most affecting simplicity.

> '*Claudio.* No, Leonato,
> I never tempted her with word too large,
> But, as a brother to his sister, shew'd
> Bashful sincerity, and comely love.
>> *Hero.* And seem'd I ever otherwise to you?
>> *Claudio.* Out on thy seeming, I will write against it:
> You seem to me as Dian in her orb,
> As chaste as is the bud ere it be blown;
> But you are more intemperate in your blood
> Than Venus, or those pamper'd animals
> That rage in savage sensuality.
>> *Hero.* Is my lord well, that he doth speak so wide?
>> *Leonato.* Are these things spoken, or do I but dream?
>> *John.* Sir, they are spoken, and these things are true.
>> *Benedick.* This looks not like a nuptial.
>> *Hero.* True! O God!'

The justification of Hero in the end, and her restoration to the confidence and arms of her lover, is brought about by one of those temporary consignments to the grave of which Shakespear seems to have been fond. He has perhaps explained the theory of this predilection in the following lines :—

> '*Friar.* She dying, as it must be so maintain'd,
> Upon the instant that she was accus'd,
> Shall be lamented, pity'd, and excus'd,
> Of every hearer : for it so falls out,
> That what we have we prize not to the worth,
> While we enjoy it ; but being lack'd and lost,
> Why then we rack the value ; then we find
> The virtue, that possession would not shew us
> Whilst it was ours.—So will it fare with Claudio ;
> When he shall hear she dy'd upon his words,
> The idea of her love shall sweetly creep
> Into his study of imagination ;
> And every lovely organ of her life
> Shall come apparel'd in more precious habit,
> More moving. delicate, and full of life,
> Into the eye and prospect of his soul,
> Than when she liv'd indeed.'

The principal comic characters in MUCH ADO ABOUT NOTHING, Benedick and Beatrice, are both essences in their kind. His character as a woman-hater is admirably supported, and his conversion to matrimony is no less happily effected by the pretended story of Beatrice's love for him. It is hard to say which of the two scenes is the best, that of the trick which is thus practised on Benedick, or that in which Beatrice is prevailed on to take pity on him by over-hearing her cousin and her maid declare (which they do on purpose) that he is dying of love for her. There is something delightfully picturesque in the manner in which Beatrice is described as coming to hear the plot which is contrived against herself—

> 'For look where Beatrice, like a lapwing, runs
> Close by the ground, to hear our conference.'

In consequence of what she hears (not a word of which is true) she exclaims when these good-natured informants are gone,

> ' What fire is in mine ears ? Can this be true ?
> Stand I condemn'd for pride and scorn so much ?
> Contempt, farewell ! and maiden pride adieu !
> No glory lives behind the back of such.

And, Benedick, love on, I will requite thee ;
    Taming my wild heart to thy loving hand ;
If thou dost love, my kindness shall incite thee
    To bind our loves up in an holy band :
For others say thou dost deserve ; and I
    Believe it better than reportingly.'

And Benedick, on his part, is equally sincere in his repentance with equal reason, after he has heard the grey-beard, Leonato, and his friend, 'Monsieur Love,' discourse of the desperate state of his supposed inamorata.

'This can be no trick ; the conference was sadly borne.—They have the truth of this from Hero. They seem to pity the lady ; it seems her affections have the full bent. Love me ! why, it must be requited. I hear how I am censur'd : they say, I will bear myself proudly, if I perceive the love come from her ; they say too, that she will rather die than give any sign of affection.—I did never think to marry : I must not seem proud :—happy are they that hear their detractions, and can put them to mending. They say, the lady is fair ; 'tis a truth, I can bear them witness : and virtuous ;—'tis so, I cannot reprove it : and wise—but for loving me : —by my troth it is no addition to her wit ;—nor no great argument of her folly, for I will be horribly in love with her.—I may chance to have some odd quirks and remnants of wit broken on me, because I have rail'd so long against marriage : but doth not the appetite alter ? A man loves the meat in his youth, that he cannot endure in his age.—Shall quips, and sentences, and these paper bullets of the brain, awe a man from the career of his humour ? No : the world must be peopled. When I said, I would die a bachelor, I did not think I should live till I were marry'd.—Here comes Beatrice : by this day, she 's a fair lady : I do spy some marks of love in her.

The beauty of all this arises from the characters of the persons so entrapped. Benedick is a professed and staunch enemy to marriage, and gives very plausible reasons for the faith that is in him. And as to Beatrice, she persecutes him all day with her jests (so that he could hardly think of being troubled with them at night) she not only turns him but all other things into jest, and is proof against everything serious.

'*Hero.* Disdain and scorn ride sparkling in her eyes,
Misprising what they look on ; and her wit
Values itself so highly, that to her
All matter else seems weak : she cannot love,
Nor take no shape nor project of affection,
She is so self-endeared.
    Ursula. Sure, I think so ;
And therefore, certainly, it were not good
She knew his love, lest she make sport at it.

> *Hero.* Why, you speak truth: I never yet saw man,
> How wise, how noble, young, how rarely featur'd,
> But she would spell him backward: if fair-fac'd,
> She 'd swear the gentleman should be her sister;
> If black, why, nature, drawing of an antick,
> Made a foul blot: if tall, a lance ill-headed;
> If low, an agate very vilely cut:
> If speaking, why, a vane blown with all winds;
> If silent, why, a block moved with none.
> So turns she every man the wrong side out;
> And never gives to truth and virtue that
> Which simpleness and merit purchaseth.'

These were happy materials for Shakespear to work on, and he has made a happy use of them. Perhaps that middle point of comedy was never more nicely hit in which the ludicrous blends with the tender, and our follies, turning round against themselves in support of our affections, retain nothing but their humanity.

Dogberry and Verges in this play are inimitable specimens of quaint blundering and misprisions of meaning; and are a standing record of that formal gravity of pretension and total want of common understanding, which Shakespear no doubt copied from real life, and which in the course of two hundred years appear to have ascended from the lowest to the highest offices in the state.

AS YOU LIKE IT

SHAKESPEAR has here converted the forest of Arden into another Arcadia, where they 'fleet the time carelessly, as they did in the golden world.' It is the most ideal of any of this author's plays. It is a pastoral drama, in which the interest arises more out of the sentiments and characters than out of the actions or situations. It is not what is done, but what is said, that claims our attention. Nursed in solitude, 'under the shade of melancholy boughs,' the imagination grows soft and delicate, and the wit runs riot in idleness, like a spoiled child, that is never sent to school. Caprice and fancy reign and revel here, and stern necessity is banished to the court. The mild sentiments of humanity are strengthened with thought and leisure; the echo of the cares and noise of the world strikes upon the ear of those 'who have felt them knowingly,' softened by time and distance. 'They hear the tumult, and are still.' The very air of the place seems to breathe a spirit of philosophical poetry: to stir the thoughts, to touch the heart with pity, as the drowsy forest rustles to the sighing gale. Never was there such beautiful moralising, equally free from pedantry or petulance.

> ' And this their life, exempt from public haunts,
> Finds tongues in trees, books in the running brooks,
> Sermons in stones, and good in every thing.'

Jaques is the only purely contemplative character in Shakespear. He thinks, and does nothing. His whole occupation is to amuse his mind, and he is totally regardless of his body and his fortunes. He is the prince of philosophical idlers; his only passion is thought; he sets no value upon any thing but as it serves as food for reflection. He can 'suck melancholy out of a song, as a weasel sucks eggs'; the motley fool, 'who morals on the time,' is the greatest prize he meets with in the forest. He resents Orlando's passion for Rosalind as some disparagement of his own passion for abstract truth; and leaves the Duke, as soon as he is restored to his sovereignty, to seek his brother out who has quitted it, and turned hermit.

> —' Out of these convertites
> There is much matter to be heard and learnt.'

Within the sequestered and romantic glades of the forest of Arden, they find leisure to be good and wise, or to play the fool and fall in love. Rosalind's character is made up of sportive gaiety and natural tenderness: her tongue runs the faster to conceal the pressure at her heart. She talks herself out of breath, only to get deeper in love. The coquetry with which she plays with her lover in the double character which she has to support is managed with the nicest address. How full of voluble, laughing grace is all her conversation with Orlando—

> —' In heedless mazes running
> With wanton haste and giddy cunning.'

How full of real fondness and pretended cruelty is her answer to him when he promises to love her ' For ever and a day ! '

'Say a day without the ever: no, no, Orlando, men are April when they woo, December when they wed: maids are May when they are maids, but the sky changes when they are wives: I will be more jealous of thee than a Barbary cock-pigeon over his hen; more clamorous than a parrot against rain; more new-fangled than an ape; more giddy in my desires than a monkey; I will weep for nothing like Diana in the fountain, and I will do that when you are disposed to be merry; I will laugh like a hyen, and that when you are inclined to sleep.

Orlando. But will my Rosalind do so ?
Rosalind. By my life she will do as I do.'

The silent and retired character of Celia is a necessary relief to the provoking loquacity of Rosalind, nor can anything be better conceived or more beautifully described than the mutual affection between the two cousins :—

> —' We still have slept together,
> Rose at an instant, learn'd, play'd, eat together,
> And wheresoe'r we went, like Juno's swans,
> Still we went coupled and inseparable.'

The unrequited love of Silvius for Phebe shews the perversity of this passion in the commonest scenes of life, and the rubs and stops which nature throws in its way, where fortune has placed none. Touchstone is not in love, but he will have a mistress as a subject for the exercise of his grotesque humour, and to shew his contempt for the passion, by his indifference about the person. He is a rare fellow. He is a mixture of the ancient cynic philosopher with the modern buffoon, and turns folly into wit, and wit into folly, just as the fit takes him. His courtship of Audrey not only throws a degree of ridicule on the state of wedlock itself, but he is equally an enemy to the prejudices of opinion in other respects. The lofty tone of enthusiasm, which the Duke and his companions in exile spread over the stillness and solitude of a country life, receives a pleasant shock from Touchstone's sceptical determination of the question.

' *Corin.* And how like you this shepherd's life, Mr. Touchstone ?
Clown. Truly, shepherd, in respect of itself, it is a good life ; but in respect that it is a shepherd's life, it is naught. In respect that it is solitary, I like it very well ; but in respect that it is private, it is a very vile life. Now in respect it is in the fields, it pleaseth me well ; but in respect it is not in the court, it is tedious. As it is a spare life, look you, it fits my humour ; but as there is no more plenty in it, it goes much against my stomach.'

Zimmerman's celebrated work on Solitude discovers only *half* the sense of this passage.

There is hardly any of Shakespear's plays that contains a greater number of passages that have been quoted in books of extracts, or a greater number of phrases that have become in a manner proverbial. If we were to give all the striking passages, we should give half the play. We will only recall a few of the most delightful to the reader's recollection. Such are the meeting between Orlando and Adam, the exquisite appeal of Orlando to the humanity of the Duke and his company to supply him with food for the old man, and their answer, the Duke's description of a country life, and the account of Jaques moralising on the wounded deer, his meeting with Touchstone in the forest, his apology for his own melancholy and his satirical vein, and the well-known speech on the stages of human life, the old song of ' Blow, blow, thou winter's wind,' Rosalind's description of the marks of a lover and of the progress of time with different persons, the picture of the snake wreathed round Oliver's neck while the lioness watches her sleeping prey, and Touchstone's lecture to the shepherd, his defence of cuckolds, and panegyric on the virtues of ' an If.'—All of these are familiar to the reader: there is one passage of equal delicacy and beauty which may have escaped him, and with it we shall close our account of As You Like It. It is Phebe's description of Ganimed at the end of the third act.

> ' Think not I love him, tho' I ask for him ;
> 'Tis but a peevish boy, yet he talks well ;—
> But what care I for words ! yet words do well,
> When he that speaks them pleases those that hear :
> It is a pretty youth ; not very pretty ;
> But sure he 's proud, and yet his pride becomes him ;
> He 'll make a proper man ; the best thing in him
> Is his complexion ; and faster than his tongue
> Did make offence, his eye did heal it up :
> He is not very tall, yet for his years he 's tall ;
> His leg is but so so, and yet 'tis well ;
> There was a pretty redness in his lip,
> A little riper, and more lusty red
> Than that mix'd in his cheek ; 'twas just the difference
> Betwixt the constant red and mingled damask.
> There be some women, Silvius, had they mark'd him
> In parcels as I did, would have gone near
> To fall in love with him : but for my part
> I love him not, nor hate him not ; and yet
> I have more cause to hate him than to love him ;
> For what had he to do to chide at me ?'

THE TAMING OF THE SHREW

The Taming of the Shrew is almost the only one of Shakespear's comedies that has a regular plot, and downright moral. It is full of bustle, animation, and rapidity of action. It shews admirably how self-will is only to be got the better of by stronger will, and how one degree of ridiculous perversity is only to be driven out by another still greater. Petruchio is a madman in his senses ; a very honest fellow, who hardly speaks a word of truth, and succeeds in all his tricks and impostures. He acts his assumed character to the life with the most fantastical extravagance, with complete presence of mind, with untired animal spirits, and without a particle of ill humour from beginning to end.—The situation of poor Katherine, worn out by his incessant persecutions, becomes at last almost as pitiable as it is ludicrous, and it is difficult to say which to admire most, the un-accountableness of his actions, or the unalterableness of his resolutions. It is a character which most husbands ought to study, unless perhaps the very audacity of Petruchio's attempt might alarm them more than his success would encourage them. What a sound must the following speech carry to some married ears !

> 'Think you a little din can daunt my ears?
> Have I not in my time heard lions roar?
> Have I not heard the sea, puff'd up with winds,
> Rage like an angry boar, chafed with sweat?
> Have I not heard great ordnance in the field?
> And heav'n's artillery thunder in the skies?
> Have I not in a pitched battle heard
> Loud larums, neighing steeds, and trumpets clang?
> And do you tell me of a woman's tongue,
> That gives not half so great a blow to hear,
> As will a chesnut in a farmer's fire?'

Not all Petruchio's rhetoric would persuade more than 'some dozen followers' to be of this heretical way of thinking. He unfolds his scheme for the *Taming of the Shrew*, on a principle of contradiction, thus :—

> 'I 'll woo her with some spirit when she comes.
> Say that she rail, why then I 'll tell her plain
> She sings as sweetly as a nightingale;
> Say that she frown, I 'll say she looks as clear
> As morning roses newly wash'd with dew;
> Say she be mute, and will not speak a word,
> Then I 'll commend her volubility,
> And say she uttereth piercing eloquence:
> If she do bid me pack, I 'll give her thanks,
> As though she bid me stay by her a week;
> If she deny to wed, I 'll crave the day,
> When I shall ask the banns, and when be married?'

He accordingly gains her consent to the match, by telling her father that he has got it; disappoints her by not returning at the time he has promised to wed her, and when he returns, creates no small con-sternation by the oddity of his dress and equipage. This, however, is nothing to the astonishment excited by his mad-brained behaviour at the marriage. Here is the account of it by an eye-witness :—

> ' *Gremio.* Tut, she 's a lamb, a dove, a fool to him ;
> I 'll tell you, Sir Lucentio ; when the priest
> Should ask if Katherine should be his wife ?
> Ay, by gogs woons, quoth he ; and swore so loud,
> That, all amaz'd, the priest let fall the book ;
> And as he stooped again to take it up,
> This mad-brain'd bridegroom took him such a cuff,
> That down fell priest and book, and book and priest.
> Now take them up, quoth he, if any list.
>   *Tranio.* What said the wench when he rose up again ?
>   *Gremio.* Trembled and shook ; for why, he stamp'd and swore,
> As if the vicar meant to cozen him.
> But after many ceremonies done,
> He calls for wine ; a health, quoth he ; as if
> He'ad been aboard carousing with his mates
> After a storm ; quaft off the muscadel,
> And threw the sops all in the sexton's face ;
> Having no other cause but that his beard
> Grew thin and hungerly, and seem'd to ask
> His sops as he was drinking. This done, he took
> The bride about the neck, and kiss'd her lips
> With such a clamourous smack, that at their parting
> All the church echoed : and I seeing this,
> Came thence for very shame ; and after me,
> I know, the rout is coming ;—
> Such a mad marriage never was before.'

The most striking and at the same time laughable feature in the character of Petruchio throughout, is the studied approximation to the intractable character of real madness, his apparent insensibility to all external considerations, and utter indifference to every thing but the wild and extravagant freaks of his own self-will. There is no contending with a person on whom nothing makes any impression but his own purposes, and who is bent on his own whims just in proportion as they seem to want common sense. With him a thing's being plain and reasonable is a reason against it. The airs he gives himself are infinite, and his caprices as sudden as they are groundless. The whole of his treatment of his wife at home is in the same spirit of ironical attention and inverted gallantry. Every thing flies before his will, like a conjuror's wand, and he only metamorphoses his wife's temper by metamorphosing her senses and all the objects she sees, at a word's speaking. Such are his insisting that it is the moon and not the sun which they see, etc. This extravagance reaches its most pleasant and poetical height in the scene where, on their return to her father's, they meet old Vincentio, whom Petruchio immediately addresses as a young lady :—

> ' *Petruchio.* Good morrow, gentle mistress, where away ?
> Tell me, sweet Kate, and tell me truly too,
> Hast thou beheld a fresher gentlewoman ?
> Such war of white and red within her cheeks ;
> What stars do spangle heaven with such beauty,
> As those two eyes become that heav'nly face ?
> Fair lovely maid, once more good day to thee :
> Sweet Kate, embrace her for her beauty's sake.
>   *Hortensio.* He 'll make the man mad to make a woman of him.
>   *Katherine.* Young budding virgin, fair and fresh and sweet,
> Whither away, or where is thy abode ?
> Happy the parents of so fair a child ;
> Happier the man whom favourable stars
> Allot thee for his lovely bed-fellow.
>   *Petruchio.* Why, how now, Kate, I hope thou art not mad :
> This is a man, old, wrinkled, faded, wither'd,
> And not a maiden, as thou say'st he is.
>   *Katherine.* Pardon, old father, my mistaken eyes
> That have been so bedazed with the sun
> That everything I look on seemeth green.
> Now I perceive thou art a reverend father.'

The whole is carried off with equal spirit, as if the poet's comic Muse had wings of fire. It is strange how one man could be so many things ; but so it is. The concluding scene, in which trial is made of the obedience of the new-married wives (so triumphantly for Petruchio) is a very happy one.—In some parts of this play there is a little too much about music-masters and masters of philosophy. They were things of greater rarity in those days than they are now. Nothing however can be better than the advice which Tranio gives his master for the prosecution of his studies :—

> ' The mathematics, and the metaphysics,
> Fall to them as you find your stomach serves you :
> No profit grows, where is no pleasure ta'en :
> In brief, sir, study what you most affect.'

We have heard the *Honey-Moon* called ' an elegant Katherine and Petruchio.' We suspect we do not understand this word *elegant* in the sense that many people do. But in our sense of the word, we should call Lucentio's description of his mistress elegant.

> ' Tranio, I saw her coral lips to move,
> And with her breath she did perfume the air :
> Sacred and sweet was all I saw in her.'

When Biondello tells the same Lucentio for his encouragement, ' I knew a wench married in an afternoon as she went to the garden for parsley to stuff a rabbit, and so may you, sir '—there is nothing elegant in this, and yet we hardly know which of the two passages is the best.

The Taming of the Shrew is a play within a play. It is supposed to be a play acted for the benefit of Sly the tinker, who is made to believe himself a lord, when he wakes after a drunken brawl. The character of Sly and the remarks with which he accompanies the play are as good as the play itself. His answer when he is asked how he likes it, ' Indifferent well; 'tis a good piece of work, would 'twere done,' is in good keeping, as if he were thinking of his Saturday night's job. Sly does not change his tastes with his new situation, but in the midst of splendour and luxury still calls out lustily and repeatedly ' for a pot o' the smallest ale.' He is very slow in giving up his personal identity in his sudden advancement.—' I am Christophero Sly, call not me honour nor lordship. I ne'er drank sack in my life: and if you give me any conserves, give me conserves of beef: ne'er ask me what raiment I'll wear, for I have no more doublets than backs, no more stockings than legs, nor no more shoes than feet, nay, sometimes more feet than shoes, or such shoes as my toes look through the over-leather.—What, would you make me mad? Am not I Christophero Sly, old Sly's son of Burton-heath, by birth a pedlar, by education a card-maker, by transmutation a bear-herd, and now by present profession a tinker? Ask Marian Hacket, the fat alewife of Wincot, if she know me not; if she say I am not fourteen-pence on the score for sheer ale, score me up for the lying'st knave in Christendom.'

This is honest. ' The Slies are no rogues,' as he says of himself. We have a great predilection for this representative of the family; and what makes us like him the better is, that we take him to be of kin (not many degrees removed) to Sancho Panza.

MEASURE FOR MEASURE

This is a play as full of genius as it is of wisdom. Yet there is an original sin in the nature of the subject, which prevents us from taking a cordial interest in it. ' The height of moral argument ' which the author has maintained in the intervals of passion or blended with the more powerful impulses of nature, is hardly surpassed in any of his plays. But there is in general a want of passion; the affections

are at a stand; our sympathies are repulsed and defeated in all
directions. The only passion which influences the story is that of
Angelo; and yet he seems to have a much greater passion for
hypocrisy than for his mistress. Neither are we greatly enamoured
of Isabella's rigid chastity, though she could not act otherwise than
she did. We do not feel the same confidence in the virtue that is
'sublimely good' at another's expense, as if it had been put to some
less disinterested trial. As to the Duke, who makes a very imposing and mysterious stage-character, he is more absorbed in his own
plots and gravity than anxious for the welfare of the state; more
tenacious of his own character than attentive to the feelings and
apprehensions of others. Claudio is the only person who feels
naturally; and yet he is placed in circumstances of distress which
almost preclude the wish for his deliverance. Mariana is also in
love with Angelo, whom we hate. In this respect, there may be
said to be a general system of cross-purposes between the feelings
of the different characters and the sympathy of the reader or the
audience. This principle of repugnance seems to have reached its
height in the character of Master Barnardine, who not only sets at
defiance the opinions of others, but has even thrown off all self-
regard,—'one that apprehends death no more dreadfully but as a
drunken sleep; careless, reckless, and fearless of what's past, present,
and to come.' He is a fine antithesis to the morality and the hypocrisy of the other characters of the play. Barnardine is Caliban
transported from Prospero's wizard island to the forests of Bohemia
or the prisons of Vienna. He is the creature of bad habits as Caliban
is of gross instincts. He has however a strong notion of the natural
fitness of things, according to his own sensations—'He has been
drinking hard all night, and he will not be hanged that day'—and
Shakespear has let him off at last. We do not understand why the
philosophical German critic, Schlegel, should be so severe on those
pleasant persons, Lucio, Pompey, and Master Froth, as to call them
'wretches.' They appear all mighty comfortable in their occupations,
and determined to pursue them, 'as the flesh and fortune should
serve.' A very good exposure of the want of self-knowledge and
contempt for others, which is so common in the world, is put into
the mouth of Abhorson, the jailor, when the Provost proposes to
associate Pompey with him in his office—'A bawd, sir? Fie upon
him, he will discredit our mystery.' And the same answer will
serve in nine instances out of ten to the same kind of remark, 'Go
to, sir, you weigh equally; a feather will turn the scale.' Shakespear was in one sense the least moral of all writers; for morality
(commonly so called) is made up of antipathies; and his talent con-

sisted in sympathy with human nature, in all its shapes, degrees, depressions, and elevations. The object of the pedantic moralist is to find out the bad in everything : his was to shew that 'there is some soul of goodness in things evil.' Even Master Barnardine is not left to the mercy of what others think of him ; but when he comes in, speaks for himself, and pleads his own cause, as well as if counsel had been assigned him. In one sense, Shakespear was no moralist at all : in another, he was the greatest of all moralists. He was a moralist in the same sense in which nature is one. He taught what he had learnt from her. He shewed the greatest knowledge of humanity with the greatest fellow-feeling for it.

One of the most dramatic passages in the present play is the interview between Claudio and his sister, when she comes to inform him of the conditions on which Angelo will spare his life.

> *' Claudio.* Let me know the point.
> *Isabella.* O, I do fear thee, Claudio : and I quake,
> Lest thou a feverous life should'st entertain,
> And six or seven winters more respect
> Than a perpetual honour. Dar'st thou die ?
> The sense of death is most in apprehension ;
> And the poor beetle, that we tread upon,
> In corporal sufferance finds a pang as great
> As when a giant dies.
> *Claudio.* Why give you me this shame ?
> Think you I can a resolution fetch
> From flowery tenderness ; if I must die,
> I will encounter darkness as a bride,
> And hug it in mine arms.
> *Isabella.* There spake my brother ! there my father's grave
> Did utter forth a voice ! Yes, thou must die :
> Thou art too noble to conserve a life
> In base appliances. This outward-sainted deputy—
> Whose settled visage and deliberate word
> Nips youth i' the head, and follies doth emmew,
> As faulcon doth the fowl—is yet a devil.
> *Claudio.* The princely Angelo ?
> *Isabella.* Oh, 'tis the cunning livery of hell,
> The damned'st body to invest and cover
> In princely guards ! Dost thou think, Claudio,
> If I would yield him my virginity,
> Thou might'st be freed ?
> *Claudio.* Oh, heavens ! it cannot be.
> *Isabella.* Yes, he would give it thee, for this rank offence,
> So to offend him still : this night 's the time
> That I should do what I abhor to name,
> Or else thou dy'st to-morrow.

> *Claudio.* Thou shalt not do 't.
> *Isabella.* Oh, were it but my life,
> I 'd throw it down for your deliverance
> As frankly as a pin.
> *Claudio.* Thanks, dear Isabel.
> *Isabella.* Be ready, Claudio, for your death to-morrow.
> *Claudio.* Yes.—Has he affections in him,
> That thus can make him bite the law by the nose?
> When he would force it, sure it is no sin;
> Or of the deadly seven it is the least.
> *Isabella.* Which is the least?
> *Claudio.* If it were damnable, he, being so wise,
> Why would he for the momentary trick
> Be perdurably fin'd? Oh, Isabel!
> *Isabella.* What says my brother?
> *Claudio.* Death is a fearful thing.
> *Isabella.* And shamed life a hateful.
> *Claudio.* Aye, but to die, and go we know not where;
> To lie in cold obstruction, and to rot;
> This sensible warm motion to become
> A kneaded clod; and the delighted spirit
> To bathe in fiery floods, or to reside
> In thrilling regions of thick-ribbed ice;
> To be imprison'd in the viewless winds,
> And blown with restless violence round about
> The pendant world; or to be worse than worst
> Of those, that lawless and incertain thoughts
> Imagine howling!—'tis too horrible!
> The weariest and most loathed worldly life,
> That age, ache, penury, and imprisonment
> Can lay on nature, is a paradise
> To what we fear of death.
> *Isabella.* Alas! alas!
> *Claudio.* Sweet sister, let me live:
> What sin you do to save a brother's life,
> Nature dispenses with the deed so far,
> That it becomes a virtue.'

What adds to the dramatic beauty of this scene and the effect of Claudio's passionate attachment to life is, that it immediately follows the Duke's lecture to him, in the character of the Friar, recommending an absolute indifference to it.

> —' Reason thus with life,—
> If I do lose thee, I do lose a thing,
> That none but fools would keep: a breath thou art,
> Servile to all the skyey influences
> That do this habitation, where thou keep'st,
> Hourly afflict: merely, thou art death's fool;

For him thou labour'st by thy flight to shun,
And yet run'st toward him still: thou art not noble;
For all the accommodations, that thou bear'st,
Are nurs'd by baseness: thou art by no means valiant;
For thou dost fear the soft and tender fork
Of a poor worm: thy best of rest is sleep,
And that thou oft provok'st; yet grossly fear'st
Thy death, which is no more. Thou art not thyself;
For thou exist'st on many a thousand grains
That issue out of dust: happy thou art not;
For what thou hast not, still thou striv'st to get;
And what thou hast, forget'st: thou art not certain;
For thy complexion shifts to strange effects,
After the moon: if thou art rich, thou art poor;
For, like an ass, whose back with ingots bows
Thou bear'st thy heavy riches but a journey,
And death unloads thee: friend thou hast none;
For thy own bowels, which do call thee sire,
The mere effusion of thy proper loins,
Do curse the gout, serpigo, and the rheum,
For ending thee no sooner; thou hast nor youth, nor age;
But, as it were, an after-dinner's sleep,
Dreaming on both: for all thy blessed youth
Becomes as aged, and doth beg the alms
Of palsied eld; and when thou art old, and rich,
Thou hast neither heat, affection, limb, nor beauty,
To make thy riches pleasant. What's yet in this,
That bears the name of life? Yet in this life
Lie hid more thousand deaths; yet death we fear,
That makes these odds all even.'

THE MERRY WIVES OF WINDSOR

THE MERRY WIVES OF WINDSOR is no doubt a very amusing play, with a great deal of humour, character, and nature in it: but we should have liked it much better, if any one else had been the hero of it, instead of Falstaff. We could have been contented if Shakespear had not been 'commanded to shew the knight in love.' Wits and philosophers, for the most part, do not shine in that character; and Sir John himself, by no means, comes off with flying colours. Many people complain of the degradation and insults to which Don Quixote is so frequently exposed in his various adventures. But what are the unconscious indignities which he suffers, compared with the sensible mortifications which Falstaff is made to bring upon himself?

What are the blows and buffettings which the Don receives from the staves of the Yanguesian carriers or from Sancho Panza's more hard-hearted hands, compared with the contamination of the buck-basket, the disguise of the fat woman of Brentford, and the horns of Herne the hunter, which are discovered on Sir John's head? In reading the play, we indeed wish him well through all these discomfitures, but it would have been as well if he had not got into them. Falstaff in the MERRY WIVES OF WINDSOR is not the man he was in the two parts of *Henry IV*. His wit and eloquence have left him. Instead of making a butt of others, he is made a butt of by them. Neither is there a single particle of love in him to excuse his follies: he is merely a designing, bare-faced knave, and an unsuccessful one. The scene with Ford as Master Brook, and that with Simple, Slender's man, who comes to ask after the Wise Woman, are almost the only ones in which his old intellectual ascendancy appears. He is like a person recalled to the stage to perform an unaccustomed and ungracious part; and in which we perceive only 'some faint sparks of those flashes of merriment, that were wont to set the hearers in a roar.' But the single scene with Doll Tearsheet, or Mrs. Quickly's account of his desiring 'to eat some of housewife Keach's prawns,' and telling her 'to be no more so familiarity with such people,' is worth the whole of the MERRY WIVES OF WINDSOR put together. Ford's jealousy, which is the main spring of the comic incidents, is certainly very well managed. Page, on the contrary, appears to be somewhat uxorious in his disposition; and we have pretty plain indications of the effect of the characters of the husbands on the different degrees of fidelity in their wives. Mrs. Quickly makes a very lively go-between, both between Falstaff and his Dulcineas, and Anne Page and her lovers, and seems in the latter case so intent on her own interest as totally to overlook the intentions of her employers. Her master, Dr. Caius, the Frenchman, and her fellow-servant Jack Rugby, are very completely described. This last-mentioned person is rather quaintly commended by Mrs. Quickly as 'an honest, willing, kind fellow, as ever servant shall come in house withal, and I warrant you, no tell-tale, nor no breed-bate; his worst fault is, that he is given to prayer; he is something peevish that way; but nobody but has his fault.' The Welch Parson, Sir Hugh Evans (a title which in those days was given to the clergy) is an excellent character in all respects. He is as respectable as he is laughable. He has 'very good discretions, and very odd humours.' The duel-scene with Caius gives him an opportunity to shew his 'cholers and his tremblings of mind,' his valour and his melancholy, in an irresistible manner. In the dialogue, which at his mother's request he holds with his pupil, William Page, to shew his progress in learning, it is hard to say whether the simplicity of the master or the scholar is the greatest. Nym, Bardolph, and Pistol, are but the shadows of what they were; and Justice Shallow himself has little of his consequence left. But his cousin, Slender, makes up for the deficiency. He is a very potent piece of imbecility. In him the pretensions of the worthy Gloucestershire family are well kept up, and immortalised. He and his friend Sackerson and his book of songs and his love of Anne Page and his having nothing to say to her can never be forgotten. It is the only first-rate character in the play : but it is in that class. Shakespear is the only writer who was as great in describing weakness as strength.

THE COMEDY OF ERRORS

This comedy is taken very much from the Menæchmi of Plautus, and is not an improvement on it. Shakespear appears to have bestowed no great pains on it, and there are but a few passages which bear the decided stamp of his genius. He seems to have relied on his author, and on the interest arising out of the intricacy of the plot. The curiosity excited is certainly very considerable, though not of the most pleasing kind. We are teazed as with a riddle, which notwithstanding we try to solve. In reading the play, from the sameness of the names of the two Antipholises and the two Dromios, as well from their being constantly taken for each other by those who see them, it is difficult, without a painful effort of attention, to keep the characters distinct in the mind. And again, on the stage, either the complete similarity of their persons and dress must produce the same perplexity whenever they first enter, or the identity of appearance which the story supposes, will be destroyed. We still, however, having a clue to the difficulty, can tell which is which, merely from the practical contradictions which arise, as soon as the different parties begin to speak ; and we are indemnified for the perplexity and blunders into which we are thrown by seeing others thrown into greater and almost inextricable ones.—This play (among other considerations) leads us not to feel much regret that Shakespear was not what is called a classical scholar. We do not think his *forte* would ever have lain in imitating or improving on what others invented, so much as in inventing for himself, and perfecting what he invented,—not perhaps by the omission of faults, but by the addition of the highest excellencies. His own genius was strong enough to bear him up, and he soared longest and best on unborrowed plumes.—The only passage of a very Shakespearian cast in this comedy is the one in which the Abbess, with admirable characteristic artifice, makes Adriana confess her own misconduct in driving her husband mad.

> ' *Abbess.* How long hath this possession held the man?
> *Adriana.* This week he hath been heavy, sour, sad,
> And much, much different from the man he was;
> But, till this afternoon, his passion
> Ne'er brake into extremity of rage.
> *Abbess.* Hath he not lost much wealth by wreck at sea?
> Bury'd some dear friend? Hath not else his eye
> Stray'd his affection in unlawful love?
> A sin prevailing much in youthful men,
> Who give their eyes the liberty of gazing.
> Which of these sorrows is he subject to?
> *Adriana.* To none of these, except it be the last:
> Namely, some love, that drew him oft from home.
> *Abbess.* You should for that have reprehended him.
> *Adriana.* Why, so I did.
> *Abbess.* But not rough enough.
> *Adriana.* As roughly as my modesty would let me.
> *Abbess.* Haply, in private.
> *Adriana.* And in assemblies too.
> *Abbess.* Aye, but not enough.
> *Adriana.* It was the copy of our conference:
> In bed, he slept not for my urging it;
> At board, he fed not for my urging it;
> Alone it was the subject of my theme;
> In company, I often glanc'd at it;
> Still did I tell him it was vile and bad.
> *Abbess.* And therefore came it that the man was mad:
> The venom'd clamours of a jealous woman
> Poison more deadly than a mad dog's tooth.
> It seems, his sleeps were hinder'd by thy railing:
> And therefore comes it that his head is light.
> Thou say'st his meat was sauc'd with thy upbraidings:
> Unquiet meals make ill digestions,
> Therefore the raging fire of fever bred:
> And what's a fever but a fit of madness?
> Thou say'st his sports were hinder'd by thy brawls:
> Sweet recreation barr'd, what doth ensue,
> But moody and dull melancholy,
> Kinsman to grim and comfortless despair;
> And, at her heels, a huge infectious troop
> Of pale distemperatures, and foes to life?
> In food, in sport, and life-preserving rest

> To be disturb'd, would mad or man or beast:
> The consequence is then, thy jealous fits
> Have scar'd thy husband from the use of wits.
> *Luciana.* She never reprehended him but mildly,
> When he demeaned himself rough, rude, and wildly.—
> Why bear you these rebukes, and answer not?
> *Adriana.* She did betray me to my own reproof.'

Pinch the conjuror is also an excrescence not to be found in Plautus. He is indeed a very formidable anachronism.

> ' They brought one Pinch, a hungry lean-fac'd villain,
> A meer anatomy, a mountebank,
> A thread-bare juggler and a fortune-teller;
> A needy, hollow-ey'd, sharp-looking wretch,
> A living dead man.'

This is exactly like some of the Puritanical portraits to be met with in Hogarth.

DOUBTFUL PLAYS OF SHAKESPEAR

WE shall give for the satisfaction of the reader what the celebrated German critic, Schlegel, says on this subject, and then add a very few remarks of our own.

' All the editors, with the exception of Capell, are unanimous in rejecting *Titus Andronicus* as unworthy of Shakespear, though they always allow it to be printed with the other pieces, as the scape-goat, as it were, of their abusive criticism. The correct method in such an investigation is first to examine into the external grounds, evidences, etc. and to weigh their worth; and then to adduce the internal reasons derived from the quality of the work. The critics of Shakespear follow a course directly the reverse of this; they set out with a preconceived opinion against a piece, and seek, in justification of this opinion, to render the historical grounds suspicious, and to set them aside. *Titus Andronicus* is to be found in the first folio edition of Shakespear's works, which it was known was conducted by Heminge and Condell, for many years his friends and fellow-managers of the same theatre. Is it possible to persuade ourselves that they would not have known if a piece in their repertory did or did not actually belong to Shakespear? And are we to lay to the charge of these honourable men a designed fraud in this single case, when we know that they did not shew themselves so very desirous of scraping everything together which went by the name of Shakespear, but, as it appears, merely gave those plays of which they had manuscripts in hand? Yet the following circumstance is still stronger: George Meres, a contemporary and admirer of Shakespear, mentions *Titus Andronicus* in an enumeration of his works, in the year 1598. Meres was personally acquainted with the poet, and so very intimately, that the latter read over to him his Sonnets before they were printed. I cannot conceive that all the critical scepticism in the world would be sufficient to get over such a testimony.

'This tragedy, it is true, is framed according to a false idea of the tragic, which by an accumulation of cruelties and enormities degenerates into the horrible, and yet leaves no deep impression behind : the story of Tereus and Philomela is heightened and overcharged under other names, and mixed up with the repast of Atreus and Thyestes, and many other incidents. In detail there is no want of beautiful lines, bold images, nay, even features which betray the peculiar conception of Shakespear. Among these we may reckon the joy of the treacherous Moor at the blackness and ugliness of his child begot in adultery ; and in the compassion of Titus Andronicus, grown childish through grief, for a fly which had been struck dead, and his rage afterwards when he imagines he discovers in it his black enemy, we recognize the future poet of *Lear*. Are the critics afraid that Shakespear's fame would be injured, were it established that in his early youth he ushered into the world a feeble and immature work ? Was Rome the less the conqueror of the world because Remus could leap over its first walls ? Let any one place himself in Shakespear's situation at the commencement of his career. He found only a few indifferent models, and yet these met with the most favourable reception, because men are never difficult to please in the novelty of an art before their taste has become fastidious from choice and abundance. Must not this situation have had its influence on him before he learned to make higher demands on himself, and, by digging deeper in his own mind, discovered the richest veins of a noble metal ? It is even highly probable that he must have made several failures before getting into the right path. Genius is in a certain sense infallible, and has nothing to learn ; but art is to be learned, and must be acquired by practice and experience. In Shakespear's acknowledged works we find hardly any traces of his apprenticeship, and yet an apprenticeship he certainly had. This every artist must have, and especially in a period where he has not before him the example of a school already formed. I consider it as extremely probable, that Shakespear began to write for the theatre at a much earlier period than the one which is generally stated, namely, not till after the year 1590. It appears that, as early as the year 1584, when only twenty years of age, he had left his paternal home and repaired to London. Can we imagine that such an active head would remain idle for six whole years without making any attempt to emerge by his talents from an uncongenial situation ? That in the dedication of the poem of Venus and Adonis he calls it, 'the first heir of his invention,' proves nothing against the supposition. It was the first which he printed ; he might have composed it at an earlier period ; perhaps, also, he did not include theatrical labours, as they then possessed but little literary dignity. The earlier Shakespear began to compose for the theatre, the less are we enabled to consider the immaturity and imperfection of a work as a proof of its spuriousness in opposition to historical evidence, if we only find in it prominent features of his mind. Several of the works rejected as spurious, may still have been produced in the period betwixt *Titus Andronicus*, and the earliest of the acknowledged pieces.

'At last, Steevens published seven pieces ascribed to Shakespear in two supplementary volumes. It is to be remarked, that they all appeared in print in Shakespear's life-time, with his name prefixed at full length. They are the following :—

' 1. *Locrine.* The proofs of the genuineness of this piece are not altogether unambiguous; the grounds for doubt, on the other hand, are entitled to attention. However, this question is immediately connected with that respecting *Titus Andronicus,* and must be at the same time resolved in the affirmative or negative.

' 2. *Pericles, Prince of Tyre.* This piece was acknowledged by Dryden, but as a youthful work of Shakespear. It is most undoubtedly his, and it has been admitted into several of the late editions. The supposed imperfections originate in the circumstance, that Shakespear here handled a childish and extravagant romance of the old poet Gower, and was unwilling to drag the subject out of its proper sphere. Hence he even introduces Gower himself, and makes him deliver a prologue entirely in his antiquated language and versification. This power of assuming so foreign a manner is at least no proof of helplessness.

' 3. *The London Prodigal.* If we are not mistaken, Lessing pronounced this piece to be Shakespear's, and wished to bring it on the German stage.

' 4. *The Puritan; or, the Widow of Watling Street.* One of my literary friends, intimately acquainted with Shakespear, was of opinion that the poet must have wished to write a play for once in the style of Ben Jonson, and that in this way we must account for the difference between the present piece and his usual manner. To follow out this idea however would lead to a very nice critical investigation.

' 5. *Thomas, Lord Cromwell.*

' 6. *Sir John Oldcastle—First Part.*

' 7. *A Yorkshire Tragedy.*

'The three last pieces are not only unquestionably Shakespear's, but in my opinion they deserve to be classed among his best and maturest works.—Steevens admits at last, in some degree, that they are Shakespear's, as well as the others, excepting *Locrine,* but he speaks of all of them with great contempt, as quite worthless productions. This condemnatory sentence is not however in the slightest degree convincing, nor is it supported by critical acumen. I should like to see how such a critic would, of his own natural suggestion, have decided on Shakespear's acknowledged master-pieces, and what he would have thought of praising in them, had the public opinion not imposed on him the duty of admiration. *Thomas, Lord Cromwell,* and *Sir John Oldcastle,* are biographical dramas, and models in this species: he first is linked, from its subject, to *Henry the Eighth,* and the second to *Henry the Fifth.* The second part of *Oldcastle* is wanting; I know not whether a copy of the old edition has been discovered in England, or whether it is lost. *The Yorkshire Tragedy* is a tragedy in one act, a dramatised tale of murder: the tragical effect is overpowering, and it is extremely important to see how poetically Shakespear could handle such a subject.

'There have been still farther ascribed to him :—1st. *The Merry Devil of Edmonton,* a comedy in one act, printed in Dodsley's old plays. This has certainly some appearances in its favour. It contains a merry landlord, who bears a great similarity to the one in the *Merry Wives of Windsor*. However, at all events, though an ingenious, it is but a hasty sketch. 2d. *The Accusation of Paris.* 3d. *The Birth of Merlin.* 4th. *Edward the Third.* 5th. *The Fair Emma.* 6th. *Mucedorus.* 7th. *Arden of Feversham.* I have never seen any of these, and cannot therefore say anything respecting them. From the passages cited, I am led to conjecture that the subject of *Mucedorus* is the popular story of Valentine and Orson; a beautiful subject which Lope de Vega has also taken for a play. *Arden of Feversham* is said to be a tragedy on the story of a man, from whom the poet was descended by the mother's side. If the quality of the piece is not too directly at variance with this claim, the circumstance would afford an additional probability in its favour. For such motives were not foreign to Shakespear: he treated Henry the Seventh, who bestowed lands on his forefathers for services performed by them, with a visible partiality.

'Whoever takes from Shakespear a play early ascribed to him, and confessedly belonging to his time, is unquestionably bound to answer, with some degree of probability, this question: who has then written it? Shakespear's competitors in the dramatic walk are pretty well known, and if those of them who have even acquired a considerable name, a Lilly, a Marlow, a Heywood, are still so very far below him, we can hardly imagine that the author of a work, which rises so high beyond theirs, would have remained unknown.'—*Lectures on Dramatic Literature*, vol. ii. page 252.

We agree to the truth of this last observation, but not to the justice of its application to some of the plays here mentioned. It is true that Shakespear's best works are very superior to those of Marlow, or Heywood, but it is not true that the best of the doubtful plays above enumerated are superior or even equal to the best of theirs. *The Yorkshire Tragedy*, which Schlegel speaks of as an undoubted production of our author's, is much more in the manner of Heywood than of Shakespear. The effect is indeed overpowering, but the mode of producing it is by no means poetical. The praise which Schlegel gives to *Thomas, Lord Cromwell*, and to *Sir John Oldcastle*, is altogether exaggerated. They are very indifferent compositions, which have not the slightest pretensions to rank with *Henry V.* or *Henry VIII.* We suspect that the German critic was not very well acquainted with the dramatic contemporaries of Shakespear, or aware of their general merits; and that he accordingly mistakes a resemblance in style and manner for an equal degree of excellence. Shakespear differed from the other writers of his age not in the mode of treating his subjects, but in the grace and power which he displayed in them. The reason assigned by a literary friend of Schlegel's for supposing *The Puritan; or, the Widow of Watling Street*, to be Shakespear's, viz. that it is in the style of Ben Jonson, that is to say, in a style just the reverse of his own, is not very satisfactory to a plain English understanding. *Locrine*, and *The London Prodigal*, if they were Shakespear's at all, must have been among the sins of his youth. *Arden of Feversham* contains several striking passages, but the passion which they express is rather that of a sanguine temperament than of a lofty imagination; and in this respect they approximate more nearly to the style of other writers of the time than to Shakespear's. *Titus Andronicus* is certainly as unlike Shakespear's usual style as it is possible. It is an accumulation of vulgar physical horrors, in which the power exercised by the poet bears no proportion to the repugnance excited by the subject. The character of Aaron the Moor is the only thing which shews any originality of conception; and the scene in which he expresses his joy 'at the blackness and ugliness of his child begot in adultery,' the only one worthy of Shakespear. Even this is worthy of him only in the display of power, for it gives no pleasure. Shakespear managed these things differently. Nor do we think it a sufficient answer to say that this was an embryo or crude production of the author. In its kind it is full grown, and its features decided and overcharged. It is not like a first imperfect essay, but shews a confirmed habit, a systematic preference of violent effect to everything else. There are occasional detached images of great beauty and delicacy, but these were not beyond the powers of other writers then living. The circumstance which inclines us to reject the external evidence in favour of this play being Shakespear's is, that the grammatical construction is constantly false and mixed up with vulgar abbreviations, a fault that never occurs in any of his genuine plays. A similar defect, and the halting measure of the verse are the chief objections to *Pericles of Tyre*, if we except the far-fetched and complicated absurdity of the story. The movement of the thoughts and passions has something in it not unlike Shakespear, and several of the descriptions are either the original hints of passages which Shakespear has ingrafted on his other plays, or are imitations of them by some contemporary poet. The most memorable idea in it is in Marina's speech, where she compares the world to 'a lasting storm, hurrying her from her friends.'

POEMS AND SONNETS

OUR idolatry of Shakespear (not to say our admiration) ceases with his plays. In his other productions, he was a mere author, though not a common author. It was only by representing others, that he became himself. He could go out of himself, and express the soul of Cleopatra; but in his own person, he appeared to be always waiting for the prompter's cue. In expressing the thoughts of others, he seemed inspired; in expressing his own, he was a mechanic. The licence of an assumed character was necessary to restore his genius to the privileges of nature, and to give him courage to break through the tyranny of fashion, the trammels of custom. In his plays, he was 'as broad and casing as the general air': in his poems, on the contrary, he appears to be 'cooped, and cabined in' by all the technicalities of art, by all the petty intricacies of thought and language, which poetry had learned from the controversial jargon of the schools, where words had been made a substitute for things. There was, if we mistake not, something of modesty, and a painful sense of personal propriety at the bottom of this. Shakespear's imagination, by identifying itself with the strongest characters in the most trying circumstances, grappled at once with nature, and trampled the littleness of art under his feet: the rapid changes of situation, the wide range of the universe, gave him life and spirit, and afforded full scope to his genius; but returned into his closet again, and having assumed the badge of his profession, he could only labour in his vocation, and conform himself to existing models. The thoughts, the passions, the words which the poet's pen, 'glancing from heaven to earth, from earth to heaven,' lent to others, shook off the fetters of pedantry and affectation; while his own thoughts and feelings, standing by themselves, were seized upon as lawful prey, and tortured to death according to the established rules and practice of the day. In a word, we do not like Shakespear's poems, because we like his plays: the one, in all their excellencies, are just the reverse of the other. It has been the fashion of late to cry up our author's poems, as equal to his plays: this is the desperate cant of modern criticism. We would ask, was there the slightest comparison between Shakespear, and either Chaucer or Spenser, as mere poets? Not any.—The two poems of Venus and Adonis and of Tarquin and Lucrece appear to us like a couple of ice-houses. They are about as hard, as glittering, and as cold. The author seems all the time to be thinking of his verses, and not of his subject,—not of what his characters would feel, but of what he shall say; and as it must happen in all such cases, he always puts into their mouths those things which they would be the last to think of, and which it shews the greatest ingenuity in him to find out. The whole is laboured, up-hill work. The poet is perpetually singling out the difficulties of the art to make an exhibition of his strength and skill in wrestling with them. He is making perpetual trials of them as if his mastery over them were doubted. The images, which are often striking, are generally applied to things which they are the least like: so that they do not blend with the poem, but seem stuck upon it, like splendid patch-work, or remain quite distinct from it, like detached substances, painted and varnished over. A beautiful thought is sure to be lost in an endless commentary upon it. The speakers are like persons who have both leisure and inclination to make riddles on their own situation, and to twist and turn every object or incident into acrostics and anagrams. Everything is spun out into allegory; and a digression is always preferred to the main story. Sentiment is built up upon plays of words; the hero or heroine feels, not from the impulse of passion, but from the force of dialectics. There is besides a strange attempt to substitute the language of painting for that of poetry, to make us *see* their feelings in the faces of the persons; and again, consistently with this, in the description of the picture in Tarquin and Lucrece, those circumstances are chiefly insisted on, which it would be impossible to convey except by words. The invocation to opportunity in the Tarquin and Lucrece is full of thoughts and images, but at the same time it is over-loaded by them. The concluding stanza expresses all our objections to this kind of poetry :—

> ' Oh ! idle words, servants to shallow fools ;
> Unprofitable sounds, weak arbitrators ;
> Busy yourselves in skill-contending schools ;
> Debate when leisure serves with dull debaters ;
> To trembling clients be their mediators :
> For me I force not argument a straw,
> Since that my case is past all help of law.'

The description of the horse in Venus and Adonis has been particularly admired, and not without reason :—

> ' Round hoof'd, short jointed, fetlocks shag and long,
> Broad breast, full eyes, small head, and nostril wide,
> High crest, short ears, strait legs, and passing strong,
> Thin mane, thick tail, broad buttock, tender hide,
> Look what a horse should have, he did not lack,
> Save a proud rider on so proud a back.'

Now this inventory of perfections shews great knowledge of the horse; and is good matter-of-fact poetry. Let the reader but compare it with a speech in the *Midsummer Night's Dream* where Theseus describes his hounds—

> ' And their heads are hung
> With ears that sweep away the morning dew '—

and he will perceive at once what we mean by the difference between Shakespear's own poetry, and that of his plays. We prefer the

Passionate Pilgrim very much to the Lover's Complaint. It has been doubted whether the latter poem is Shakespear's.

Of the Sonnets we do not well know what to say. The subject of them seems to be somewhat equivocal; but many of them are highly beautiful in themselves, and interesting as they relate to the state of the personal feelings of the author. The following are some of the most striking :—

CONSTANCY

'Let those who are in favour with their stars,
Of public honour and proud titles boast,
Whilst I, whom fortune of such triumph bars,
Unlook'd for joy in that I honour most.
Great princes' favourites their fair leaves spread,
But as the marigold in the sun's eye;
And in themselves their pride lies buried,
For at a frown they in their glory die.
The painful warrior famous'd for fight,
After a thousand victories once foil'd,
Is from the book of honour razed quite,
And all the rest forgot for which he toil'd:
　　Then happy I, that love and am belov'd,
　　Where I may not remove, nor be remov'd.'

LOVE'S CONSOLATION

'When in disgrace with fortune and men's eyes,
I all alone beweep my out-cast state,
And trouble deaf heaven with my bootless cries,
And look upon myself, and curse my fate,
Wishing me like to one more rich in hope,
Featur'd like him, like him with friends possess'd,
Desiring this man's art, and that man's scope,
With what I most enjoy contented least:
Yet in these thoughts myself almost despising,
Haply I think on thee,—and then my state
(Like to the lark at break of day arising
From sullen earth) sings hymns at heaven's gate;
　　For thy sweet love remember'd, such wealth brings,
　　That then I scorn to change my state with kings.'

NOVELTY

'My love is strengthen'd, though more weak in seeming
I love not less, though less the show appear:
That love is merchandis'd, whose rich esteeming
The owner's tongue doth publish everywhere.

Our love was new, and then but in the spring,
When I was wont to greet it with my lays:
As Philomel in summer's front doth sing,
And stops his pipe in growth of riper days:
Not that the summer is less pleasant now
Than when her mournful hymns did hush the night,
But that wild music burdens every bough,
And sweets grown common lose their dear delight.
  Therefore, like her, I sometime hold my tongue,
  Because I would not dull you with my song.'

LIFE'S DECAY

' That time ot year thou may'st in me behold
When yellow leaves, or none, or few do hang
Upon those boughs which shake against the cold,
Bare ruin'd choirs, where late the sweet birds sang.
In me thou seest the twilight of such day,
As after sun-set fadeth in the west,
Which by and by black night doth take away,
Death's second self, that seals up all in rest.
In me thou seest the glowing of such fire,
That on the ashes of his youth doth lie,
As the death-bed whereon it must expire,
Consum'd with that which it was nourish'd by.
  This thou perceiv'st, which makes thy love more strong,
  To love that well which thou must leave ere long.'

In all these, as well as in many others, there is a mild tone of sentiment, deep, mellow, and sustained, very different from the crudeness
of his earlier poems.

THE END.

INDEX OF SHAKESPEARIAN CHARACTERS DESCRIBED

INDEX OF SHAKESPEARIAN CHARACTERS

GENERAL INDEX

385

GENERAL INDEX

Molière, 81, 130, 314
Montaigne, 7
Montfort, Mrs. (actress), 157 f.n.
More, Hannah, 66
Mori, Miss (cantatrice), 64

Nelson, 97

O'Neill, Miss Eliza (actress), 156
Oxberry, William (actor), 59

Petrarch, 45
Plato, 135
Plutarch, quoted, 218–20
Pope, 25, 26, 39, 71, 79, 324
Poussin, Nicholas, 163
Priestley, Joseph, 49
Prior, 80

Quakers, 49, 50, 130

Rabelais, 43
Raphael, 70, 76, 78, 79, 86, 131, 145, 151
Rembrandt, 76, 121, 147, 151
Reynolds, Sir Joshua, 68, 85
Rousseau, 17, 67, 68, 116, 117
Rubens, 76, 78, 85, 146, 151

Schiller, 76
Schlegel, August, quoted, 239, 253, 270, 346, 353–6

Shaftesbury, Lord, 100
Shakspeare, 13, 105, 106, 164
Sheridan, 127, 257
Siddons, Mrs. (actress), 156, 189, 325
Spenser, 39, 110
Staël, Mme de, 88
Steele, 8, 9
Stephens, Catherine (actress), 62
Storace, Mme Anna Selina, 155
Suett, Richard (actor), 155
Swift, 43

Titian, 45, 76, 77, 78, 86, 151, 163
Turner, 76 f.n., 148

Vanbrugh, 13
Vandyke, 77, 146
Vanhuysum, 74 f.n.
Vansittart, 104
Vestris, Emma (Lucia Elizabeth Mathews), 86
Voltaire, 86, 89 f.n., 116

Walton, Isaac, 57
West, Benjamin (painter), 148
Wilkie, Sir David (painter), 148
Wordsworth, 45, 46 f.n., 92, 250 (quoted), 319
Wycherley, 13

Zanga, 209